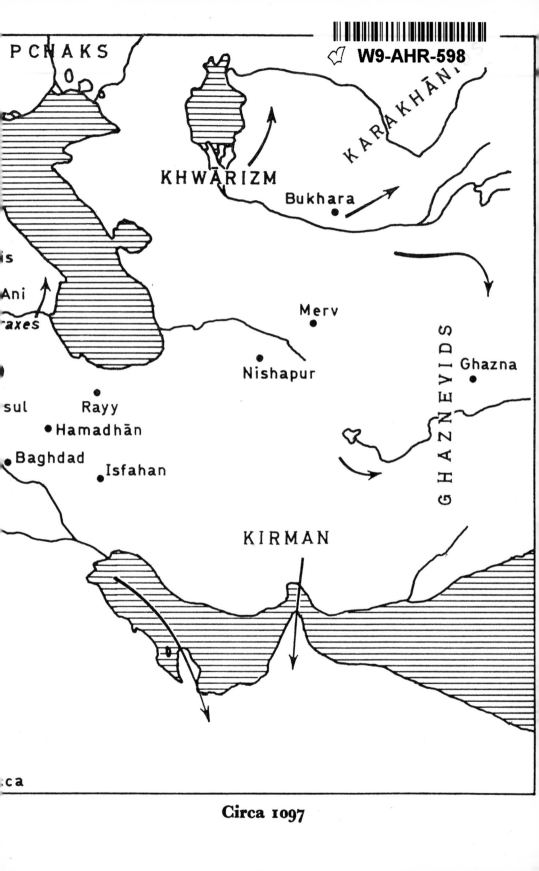

PCHAKS

KHWĀRIZM

KARAKHĀN

Bukhara

Ani

raxes

Merv

GHAZNEVIDS

Ghazna

Nishapur

sul

Rayy

Hamadhān

Baghdad

Isfahan

KIRMAN

ca

Circa 1097

Pre-Ottoman Turkey

PRE-OTTOMAN
TURKEY

*A general survey of the material and
spiritual culture and history
c. 1071-1330*

by

CLAUDE CAHEN

*Professor of Islamic History
at the Sorbonne, Paris*

Translated from the French by
J. JONES-WILLIAMS

TAPLINGER PUBLISHING COMPANY

NEW YORK

First published in the United States in 1968 by

TAPLINGER PUBLISHING CO., INC.

29 East Tenth Street

New York, New York 10003

Copyright © 1968 Claude Cahen

Copyright in this translation © 1968 Sidgwick and Jackson Limited

Library of Congress Catalog Card Number 68-24744

Printed in the Republic of Ireland

To
My Wife and Children

Acknowledgements

I feel it impossible to quote here the names of all those who in Turkey and in the West, in different moments stretching over more than thirty years, helped me to the researches which result in the present book. Let only those who are still living allow me to do special mention of the recently deceased master of Turkish medieval history, Professor M. Fuad Köprülü, to whom I was indebted, when I started studying Near-Eastern Medieval History, of the first consciousness I got of the Turkish interest it involved.

It is now a pleasant duty for me to give special thanks to the friends and colleagues who helped me in gathering the plates reproduced herein. First of all I must acknowledge my debt to the aged master of Turkish medieval archaeology Professor Albert Gabriel. My main thanks must now be given to Mme Janine Sourdel (Ecole des Hautes Etudes, Paris) not forgetting her former student R. A. Unal (now University, Erzurum), and to Mme Nicole Thierry, who generously opened for me the treasury of her unpublished photographs; special mention should also be made of Professor Faruk Sümer, Ankara, and of Professor Mehmed Önder, Cultural High Counsellor, Ankara, for sending remarkable photographs from Kubādabād. A precious photograph too I owe to Mme Irène Mélikoff, CNRS Paris. And, not to speak of scholars of other generations, may I end with a salute to another great, recently deceased one, Professor K. Erdmann.

CLAUDE CAHEN

Paris 1968

Contents

ix

PART THREE

SOCIETY AND INSTITUTIONS IN TURKEY BEFORE THE MONGOLS

PART FOUR

THE MONGOL PERIOD

ILLUSTRATIONS

MAPS

Preface

The Turks consist of a group of peoples who, in the course of roughly the last two thousand years, have swarmed across vast territories from their homeland in central eastern Asia, to reach the Indian Ocean, the Mediterranean and eastern and central Europe. There they created or dominated many states and, at the end of what we know as the Middle Ages, they established a multi-national State, the Ottoman Empire, which in the event proved to be one of the most enduring known to history. Today they still occupy large expanses of territory in eastern Europe and Asia, and, with the Turkish Republic established in Asia Minor and to some degree several of the Republics of the Soviet Union, they thus have their place in the general evolution of the modern world towards the organization of what are now national States. In this series of facts there is just as much to claim the attention of historians as in the history of other peoples.

However, this expectation has not altogether been fulfilled. It is true that, in the nineteenth century and sometimes even earlier, the role played by the Ottoman Empire, in European history particularly, inspired works which were of importance in their own time and which, in part, can be, and indeed are, still used today (Hammer-Purgstall, Mouradja d'Ohsson, Zinkeisen, Jorga 1909). Since their panegyrist Léon Cahun devoted his *Introduction à l'histoire de l'Asie* (1896) to them, the other Turks too have formed the subject of writings of some value. And here, of course, I am referring only to general surveys, without mentioning the very numerous monographs and detailed studies which little by little have built up an independent field of study, Turcology. The fact remains that these studies and general surveys on the whole fall far short of the corresponding works relating to the history of Europe and even to certain branches of orientalism. It is worth noting briefly the reasons for this, in order to help as far as possible to remedy this backward state of affairs.

A primary reason is common to all non-European peoples. Through varying circumstances it so happens that no people outside Europe established or preserved before the modern period a general body of documentation such as is available for European history, either because they had not attained the requisite level of civilization, or because, though civilized, an interest in their own past was foreign to them, or, finally, because the preservation of their documents had suffered either as a result of their social organization or from historical catastrophes. Whatever progress may be achieved in the future in the study of these peoples, clearly it will always be impossible to fill in all the gaps in our knowledge.

Moreover, recent history has given Europe a considerable lead over some peoples who, at times in the past, had been further advanced on the path of civilization. As a result, it was generally by Europeans alone that the study of these peoples' past was initiated, following the methods of modern scholarship. This means, in the first place, that the work could only be performed by scholars who had previously undergone a sometimes long and arduous linguistic apprenticeship, with the consequence that the linguistic point of view gradually took precedence over the historical; furthermore, that in research the emphasis was often placed on what, for a variety of cultural or political reasons, was of interest to Europeans, rather than on what constituted the main issues in the life of these peoples, as they would have appeared if considered on their own merits and from the inside. I do not wish to exaggerate this last defect, since one cannot in fairness deny that European culture in particular has made an effort towards understanding others which still remains unparalleled elsewhere. But it is fortunate that an increasingly large number of peoples are now acquiring the ability to study their own past scientifically, not only to supplement the inadequate number of linguistically qualified Europeans, but also to assess that past in the new light of different points of view, which can only prove to be mutually rewarding. This is as true of the Turks as of others.

In respect of the Turks, the documentary position before the modern period is difficult. In Mongolia and Chinese Turkestan writings that derive from the Turks have been found; to these we shall return later. But in this same region and *a fortiori* for the whole area of the Eurasiatic steppes over which they spread, apparently without concerning themselves with writing, the essential part of the documentation is furnished by the more advanced peoples with whom they came in contact. This means that there are numerous gaps, for those zones and periods where such contacts were incomplete; and even when some information exists, the points of view are external and disconnected, and there are differences of language which at times make it difficult to reconcile exactly the information provided by Chinese, Arab, Byzantine and, later, Russian sources. It is not even always possible to determine if a specific people is or is not Turkish. For those of the Turks who later swarmed into western Asia, the situation is at the outset no better. At first, it is Arabs, Persians, Greeks, Armenians and others who tell us more about them than they do themselves, and, even when they in their turn begin to write, they often do so in languages other than their own, in Arabic and above all in Persian, thus presenting Turkish things in a somewhat alien garb. For the Ottoman Empire, particularly from the sixteenth century, the situation is potentially much better. Apart from its literature, the Ottoman Empire possessed archives fully comparable with those of the great European States; but too short a time has elapsed since their interest was first appreciated, too few specialists have concerned themselves with them, there are too few inventories and catalogues, there has been too little classification, to have allowed them to provide anything like what could legitimately be expected from them.

To these difficulties others can be added. At almost every stage of their history and in all the lands where their ventures took them, the Turks have been intermixed with so many established peoples, whose history has not ended with their arrival, that the distinction of what is and what is not Turkish is often difficult to make, and indeed devoid of any real significance. While it is true that the history of the Seljukid Empire cannot be omitted from that of the Turkish expansion, nonetheless it forms a phase of Iranian history. The conditions under which modern orientalist historiography has been established have often caused the Turkish factor to be underestimated; and the Turks themselves, as a result of being integrated in more comprehensive communities, did not in fact become fully aware of this factor until the advent of the modern and truly Turkish Republic. But obviously it is not enough to go to the opposite extreme in regard to this inadequacy and to insist in and out of season on the importance of the Turkish factor in order to give a truer picture of it. It has to be admitted that the scientific difficulty in this respect is increased by wholly extra-scientific considerations. Because the Ottoman Empire was at war with Christian Europe for longer periods than any other 'oriental' state, because, during the period of its decline, as contemporary national states were being established, it appeared in the eyes of Europe as the oppressor of brotherly Christian peoples, everything Turkish was often regarded as *a priori* retrograde, tyrannical and contemptible. The Turks naturally have reacted with vigour, but here too the opposite assertion, also *a priori*, could not scientifically establish the truth of the matter, even though it inspires the search for it. The historian must try objectively to establish facts, without considering whom they will please or displease. But the accumulation of accepted ideas makes the task difficult, and one cannot claim that even the most unprejudiced persons can today be sure of ridding themselves of them entirely.

*   *   *

The present book does not aim at giving the complete history of the Turks. Basically it will be concerned with the mediaeval Turkey of Asia Minor, the foundation of modern Turkey (that is to say of the only essentially Turkish state, if one leaves aside the Republics incorporated in the U.S.S.R. which, in themselves, are not of comparable importance). It is true that it will not be possible to embark immediately upon their history, and in an introductory section we shall have to trace, though more briefly, the history of the Turks who lived earlier or were neighbours of that country during the Middle Ages. But, when this is done, we shall in the main devote ourselves to Turkey in Asia Minor. It must be said that this will be virtually for the first time. Not that the historians of the Ottoman Empire have completely ignored this earlier Turkey – but they have treated it as a prelude to that Empire, in relation to which, however, as we shall see, it is difficult to portray it. A considerable number of monographs (some of them of importance) have been devoted to it. But hitherto there has been only one analytical and detailed account, which was premature and unsuccessful for reasons which we shall have to study. It is hoped that the present work will make it possible both to convey the character and intrinsic interest of early Turkey, as it was before the Ottomans, and also to guide future research by a clearer warning against what the author regards as certain misleading points of view.

It must, however, be stated frankly at the start that this work is a provisional synthesis, still incomplete in detail, of the research upon which I have for a long time been engaged. I hope soon to bring out a first volume, in French, giving the more detailed and exhaustive results of this research (*Histoire de la Première Turquie*, I, *Des origines à 1243*), but it will certainly be some time before the two succeeding volumes are ready. In these circumstances, perhaps no justification need be offered for the decision to provide the educated public – and what is more, in another language – with a work that is simpler to read, and at the same time to present to specialists some provisional facts and ideas: one never knows what may happen, particularly when one is no longer so young . . . Nevertheless, the fact remains that any constructive criticisms which may be expressed to me will be particularly welcome.

Much of the text will consist of what is now somewhat disparagingly called 'narrative' history. This is certainly not to say that the author's point of view is that of the narrator of anecdotes and episodes. But there are two reasons for this course, one connected with the state of the documentation, the other more general and a matter of principle. As far as the documentation is concerned we can only accept the situation, for it so happens that the sources at our disposal are almost exclusively of a narrative character. It is thus solely by means of narrative accounts that we can hope to penetrate more deeply into the structural facts which are now the historian's fundamental concern, and I feel that it would be unwise, and even slightly disingenuous, not to provide the reader with the essential part of the narrative material that we are using, but instead merely to present him with ready-made deductions. But there is a further reason which I would like to put forward, even though it lies outside the scope of one particular history. In a reaction against the period when our predecessors confined themselves to a narrative history 'of wars and kings', many modern historians are no longer willing to consider anything except the structural facts, and scorn simple events; and the young writers who are approaching history under their tutelage,

xvii

in both the East and the West, anxious to be modern, are carrying this contempt to dangerous extremes. Masters are masters, and moreover they have had the support of the solid framework provided by their predecessors who established 'narrative' history; pupils are not necessarily all masters, and they no longer always have the framework behind them. History is total, that is to say it combines together inextricably both 'events' and 'structures', and we have no theoretical right to separate them. History is evolutionary, and it is events which are the landmarks in this evolution. In a mere outline of structures this would run the risk of disappearing, or, with the latter omitted, the account given might appear to lack foundation. Events and structures react upon each other, in both directions, and I do not think it necessary to explain this characteristic to those who witnessed the two World Wars, or even one of them. On a lower scale, a document, even though not by its nature narrative, always has a place, a date, an occasion, in its way it is a small event among important ones: to study it without reference to that place, date or occasion is to run the risk of not understanding it. (Some illustrations of this point will be found later.) It is thus quite deliberately that, without attributing a fundamental importance to events, we have given them a large place.

In these circumstances, the ideal would obviously be to have constantly interconnected the two categories of facts in the text, as they are in reality. In practice this is impossible, and where important connections have to be strongly emphasized, the endless reference from one series to the other would make the book both immense and unreadable. We must therefore be satisfied with divisions which, though they may seem regrettably traditional, are nonetheless inevitable. The only point in question is with which series one should start. A Marxist would answer that economics conditions everything else, the infrastructure determining the superstructure, but only to add immediately 'in the last analysis', and that, at all stages, there are reciprocal effects, a fact which no historian would dispute. The reason for the choice made is thus not so much theoretical as practical. In practice, in all societies whose documentation is essentially narrative, it is more convenient to start with 'political' events, since they are the raw material of our work and since they furnish the places, dates, the identities of persons and various circumstances useful for the understanding of other documents. This is what we shall do here, even to the point of ultimately proving somewhat tedious, and we hope that there will be no misunderstanding of the reasoning which dictated this choice. It is quite obvious that when the detailed narrative fabric of mediaeval Turkish history has been completed, other writers will be able to refer to it without being obliged to reproduce it, except on special points. But unfortunately we are not yet at that stage, and it would be doing no service to evade the obligations of our generation.

The composite character of this work and the differing nature of its component parts explain the method that has been adopted with regard to references to sources and bibliography. For the introductory section, only a general bibliography is given, with no reference to sources. For the following parts, that is to say the main body of the work and everything relating to the Turks of Asia Minor, I shall give firstly an almost complete list of sources, arranged as methodically as possible according to periods and categories, and then a bibliography for each chapter or group of chapters, by means of which the specialists will have no difficulty in finding the information they need. In these circumstances it seems unnecessary to make use of foot-notes, which would be of value in exceptional cases only (where that is so, the necessary comments have been incorporated in the bibliography for the chapter in question). The sources of the narrative chapters are throughout and almost exclusively the chronicles indicated in the sources. For the other chapters, they are obviously more diverse, and for the most part are mentioned in the text. In any case, it is always easy to trace them from the bibliography and the comments included in it.

* * *

The transcription of ancient Turkish proper names cannot always be certain on account of dialectal variations, the inadaptability and diversity of the ancient authors' notations in the Arabic and other alphabets, and also the uncertain state of our historico-linguistic knowledge. In the text, the accepted forms have been given when they exist, and in other cases those which seemed most probable, expressed in the form most normally pronounceable for the English-speaking reader. This may lead to discrepancies with the transcriptions the reader will find in other publications, particularly the *Encyclopaedia of Islam* (and to a lesser extent the Turkish *Islam Ansiklopedisi*), in which the need to maintain a certain unity between the systems of transliteration used for the different Muslim languages has led the editors to admit forms which are at variance with the phonetic transcription. In some cases it may perhaps be thought that I have failed to keep in touch with some hypotheses expressed with regard to the pronunciation of certain names, for example Kutlumush, which I continue traditionally to give in this form, and not Kutalmïsh or the other forms suggested by some scholars. Without claiming any competence in the purely linguistic field on which suppositions of this sort are based, I think however that only too often purely etymological reconstitutions are doubtful and that they cannot in all cases be upheld when transcriptions are at variance with them. The Arabo-Persian alphabet denotes the vowels only poorly, but the Greek and Armenian denote them better, even if on the other hand certain consonantal sounds in these are imperfect for the notation of Turkish. One cannot discard their transcriptions solely because they fail to agree with our ideas about the etymology of the ancient Turkish dialects.

The eight Turkish vowels have been denoted thus: a, e, i, ï, o, ö, u, ü. Of the consonants, the only ones requiring explanation are kh (pronounced like the German hard *ch* or the *ch* in Scottish *loch*) and gh (pronounced almost like a simple lengthening of the preceding vowel).

Pre-Ottoman Turkey

Introduction

THE TURKS AND THEIR ISLAMIZATION
BEFORE THE SELJUKIDS

The Turks belong perhaps to a branch, known as Ural-Altaic (whose exact limits are in any event highly uncertain), of what are called the 'yellow' peoples (who probably also include all or part of the American 'Redskins'). Relatively more closely related to them than, for example, the Chinese are the Finno-Ugrians (Finns and Hungarians), the Samoyeds, the Tungus and, in particular, the Mongols. It is practically certain however that the earliest Turks known to history – although not called by that name – were the Huns. Known to us from the Chinese Annals as early as the third century B.C., the Huns were finally, after successive migrations, to establish Attila's Empire (fifth century A.D.) in the heart of Europe. Under the specific name of Turks (the meaning of which is uncertain), the Turks made their appearance, both in the Chinese sources in the East and in the Byzantine sources in the West, in the sixth century A.D. in the territory that is now Mongolia, but very soon also over a wide area, expanding towards the south and west. It is difficult to reconstruct their history in detail in the two or three centuries that follow, since the foreign sources that happen to mention them occasionally and even the few Turkish inscriptions, practically confined to Mongolia, which also appear from the eighth century, provide a succession of different names, in what consequently seems at first sight to be a list of distinct peoples, but which in reality is probably no more than an enumeration of the names of political groups and tribal federations within changing limits but including a part of the same peoples in different guises. Specialists are so hesitant over matters of detail that we can only refer to one or two landmarks. In the sixth century, a Turkish 'Empire' existed in the northern part of what in modern times has been called Russian 'Turkestan', from the Syr Darya/Jaxartes to the borders of Siberia, from the Altai to the Volga. The memory of this was long to survive among

I

the Turks, and even among other peoples in Central Asia. To the east and south of the Altai, in Mongolia, but also in what we now call Chinese Turkestan, the group of the Oghuz (later called the Ghuzz by Arabo-Persian writers) was dominant. They formed confederations or various states known, among other names, as the Dokuz-Oghuz (the Nine Oghuz) and Uyghurs (whose principal centre was near Kashgar). Before this expansion, the two 'Turkestans' had in ancient times been inhabited by the Indo-European peoples whom classical authors called Scythians, Sarmatians and so on, and whom modern discoveries have also made known under such names as Tokharians and Sogdians. No doubt the Turkish expansion exterminated or drove back some of them, but in other cases certainly there was a superimposition, or even an intermingling and an imperceptible evolution. There have been grounds for believing that the name of one of the Oghuz tribes, the Döger, recalls that of the Tokharians, and the description which contemporaries give us of one of the clans related to the Oghuz, the Kirghiz, who today are indisputably Turkish, would apply much better to Aryan nomads of the Scythian type. Finally, although none of the political groups mentioned above spread westwards across the Volga, the southern and central territory of modern Russia, as far as the lower Danube, is still occupied by descendants of the Huns who, having to a greater or lesser degree become intermixed with the 'indigenous' populations, whether Finnish or Slav, formed, among others, the 'Bulgar' peoples of the middle Volga (whose name recalls their own) and that of the Khazars who, in the seventh and eighth centuries, were to dominate the Black Sea coasts to the east of the Crimea and the steppes lying between it, the Caspian and the Caucasus. From the Bulgars, at the end of the seventh century, a branch was to break away and eventually to found what, when Slavized, became the modern Bulgaria.

It is evident that as they became dispersed over such vast territories, the various elements of the Turkish people lost in unity what they gained in area. Moreover, those nearest to China underwent Chinese influences, those nearest to Byzantium Byzantine influences, those nearest to Iran and its Sogdian and Khwārizmian borderlands Iranian influences, while, finally, those dwelling between the Aral Sea and Siberia, who were not in contact with any advanced culture, remained the most 'primitive'. In any case, most of them knew little or nothing of writing, with the result (we must repeat) that, apart from certain archaeological discoveries, we know them only from the haphazard and necessarily external accounts provided by foreign writers, Byzantine, Chinese and later Arabo-Persian. Nevertheless in the eighth and ninth centuries the Turks in Mongolia, using two successive alphabets, both phonetic (unlike the Chinese, which is ideographic) and perhaps derived from the Sogdian, set up near the banks of the Orkhon lengthy inscriptions which have been discovered and deciphered and which provide us with a more immediate knowledge of the environment within which they were created. In the period under consideration, the geographical conditions common to all the countries where the Turks lived and which explain their expansion also account for the similarity of their pastoral economy (based on the Asiatic camel which is inured to cold) and of their tribal society. However, the degree of nomadism must not be exaggerated. Particularly in those zones which were in contact with other cultures, but also at certain points of transit or at meeting-places on their routes of migration, there are traces of ancient settled populations, indeed of oases of semi-sedentarized Turkish populations; and, even with tents, there were places of assembly and, on the Orkhon for example, real capital cities of tent-dwellers. Moreover, not all animals follow the same nomadic habits, the seasonal migrations of sheep for pasturage differing from the distant journeyings of the camel. What is certain is that the nature of the country and the pattern of human life tend less towards the elaboration of ideas of ownership of land and frontiers than towards those of collective use by groups of men and ambitions of universal domination. Even in these 'empires', however, each tribe kept its autonomy, and it was almost wholly a matter of loose federations which might pass within a few days from a vast creation to utter disintegration or vice versa, one day following and the next disavowing a chieftain who, though sometimes of great renown, was no more than a leader of military operations: the name *khān* or *khāqān* given to him is probably of Tokharian origin. Various more static conceptions might emerge in those groups lying closer to organized states, for example among the Khazars as neighbours of

3

Byzantium. From the military point of view, the constant superiority of the ever mobilized nomad over more civilized sedentary neighbours is frequently attested; and the Turks inherited from the Scythians the practice of tactical movement and archery on horseback which for centuries made them redoubtable adversaries.

We have spoken of external influences: it was not only on the frontiers that these were exerted. From China or India, and in particular from Sogdiana, pilgrims and trade routes spread out, in Turkish times as earlier, not all frequented to the same degree but bringing men of religion and merchants into the centre of certain Turkish groups. The effects made themselves felt particularly in the spiritual field. The Turks were for the most part what are usually called 'shamanists', attached to various beliefs and practices in which they were guided by the shaman, a kind of soothsayer and wizard. In the main, it was a matter of rites and of somewhat earth-bound ideas, the loftier conceptions about Heaven and so on remaining vague in character and having little importance in daily life. Their funerary practices, however, at least for their chiefs, presuppose fairly clear ideas of the hereafter. But very soon Chinese and Hindu pilgrims, Nestorian Christian and Manichaean missionaries passing from Iraq across the forbidden land of Iran, and, lastly, to the West, Jewish merchants – all these caused many Turks to know and embrace their respective religions, to such a degree that, today, it is largely on the basis of Hindu, Sogdian, Syriac and other texts discovered on Turkish territory, out of the reach of persecutions by organized states, and later even on the basis of texts in Turkish, that modern scholars are able to supplement the inadequate documentation provided by the countries of origin of Manichaeism and the rest for the reconstruction of their history. Islam was later to follow the same paths and the same methods.

In the tenth century the pressure of new, and to a greater or lesser extent Mongol, populations compelled the Turks to evacuate the countries which had served as the base for their expansion and which were the scene of their greatest independent cultural development. 'Mongolia' became what its name implies, and (apart from Chinese Turkestan) almost no Turks remained except to the west of the Altai. But, by a chain reaction of a

4

familiar kind, the increase in the Turkish population of these regions compelled some of the Turks who had remained between the Altai and the Volga to undertake new migrations to the west or south. While the Karluks occupied the passes between the two 'Turkestans', the Oghuz settled to the north of the lower Syr Darya and the Aral Sea, driving back their Pecheneg cousins who, as early as the ninth century, had themselves driven their Finnish and slightly Turkicized neighbours, the Magyars or Hungarians, towards Europe. In the eleventh century the Pechenegs were to reach the lower Danube and to war against Byzantium, destroying on their way the Khazar State, which the Russo-Norsemen also attacked. On their heels followed a section of the Oghuz, whom the Byzantines called the Ouzoi, whilst other Oghuz, whom we shall come across later, pressed southwards against the Iranian frontiers, their place being occupied by the Kipchaks (known also, according to the region, as Cumans or Polovtsi), and so on. We must repeat that we are limiting ourselves to a few landmarks.

From the end of the seventh century the Turks of Central Asia had new neighbours to the south, the Muslim Arabs. As the populations whom the Arabs had overcome became progressively islamized, new men of religion and merchants, now Muslims, penetrated into Turkish territory along established routes, and even the military encounters and plundering raids, followed by exchanges of prisoners, helped to make the new religion and the neighbouring culture, or at least some aspects of them, known to the Turks. There can be no real doubt that Islam had made some slight penetration among the Khazars, though the aristocracy had in the main been won over to a kind of Judaism. In the ninth century there are records of Korans being found even among the Bulgars in the Balkans, although they were in process of adopting Christianity. But it was above all among the Bulgars on the Volga that the most celebrated and spectacular advance was made by Islam into what was in some measure Turkish territory. For reasons among which political and military needs played as important a part as propaganda and religious evolution, the prince of the Bulgars on the Volga sent a request in 920 to the 'Abbāsid Caliph of Baghdad, not only for an engineer for fortifications but also for a scholar capable of instructing him in the Islamic religion. Included in the mission that was sent to him by way of Central Asia (a better organized route than that via the Caucasus, and avoiding the Khazars) was a certain Ibn Fadlān who has left us his account of it, a document of the highest importance on the subject of the customs, which he observed excellently, of peoples about whom, but for him, we should know almost nothing. The town of Bulghar, vast ruins of which still survive, was probably already of some importance at the time. Nevertheless, the remoteness of this state from the Muslim world prevented it ever becoming a great centre of Islamic culture, or of playing a great part in the islamization of other Turks – and moreover of related branches speaking different dialects. The islamization of the Turks who today still inhabit Russian territory is a later occurrence due to the Mongol conquest in the thirteenth century, which, for our present purposes, we can leave aside.

Of greater importance for their consequences are the contacts made by Islam with the Turks in Central Asia, though one must be careful to distinguish between the various types and stages. At the time when the Arabs were carrying out their conquests in Central Asia and Afghanistan, certain Turkish communities had already settled there and were gradually to be integrated, together with the other 'indigenous' populations, into the Muslim States then being formed. In Fergana and the surrounding districts they had set up small principalities whose chiefs bore the titles *afshīn*, *ikhshīd*, etc. and were sedentarized, rather in the tradition of earlier principalities in the Iranian border areas. Good soldiers, they became just sufficiently islamized to be associated with the Muslim armies and, eventually, to be employed in that capacity even in other regions of the Islamic world. There was a famous Afshīn, well-known by this title which has, as it were, become his name, who crushed the revolt of the heretic Bābek in Azerbaijan in about 830, while a little more than a century later an Ik*h*shīd, similarly known under that name, was sent by the Caliph to be the autonomous governor of Egypt.

Nevertheless, this recruitment of Turks remained on a small scale, with little impact upon the mass of Turkish people remaining outside the frontiers of Islam. But the Caliph and the rulers of the successor states knew the value of these men as soldiers, their particular aptitudes (as mounted archers, for example) for which they had no equals among the subjects of the Empire, who possessed complementary but different traditions. Moreover the Caliphate, after removing from its army the Arabs (who were too deeply divided by their politico-religious rifts to be of absolute loyalty), had also become suspicious of the Khorasanians, Iranians from the north-west whom the ʿAbbāsids had substituted for the Arabs and upon whom they depended too exclusively; in any case, they were free men and therefore not wholly reliable. From the middle of the ninth century Turks were preferred to Khorasanians, or at least were taken on in addition to them, but they were slaves, acquired in non-Muslim Central Asia by capture in war, as tribute, or by purchase, and subsequently brought up as Muslims. Contrary to expectations, they caused even greater difficulties than their predecessors, but with these problems we are not really concerned. The point to be emphasized here is that the supplying of slaves of this kind – whose status in fact was naturally far superior to that of domestic slaves belonging to private individuals – never seems to have been difficult or to have been resented by the Turkish population themselves among whom it operated. Slavery did not arouse in everyone the sentiments it later evoked, and for simple-minded poor peoples, who were to some extent aware of the superior civilization and wealth of a neighbouring society, it provided a means of making some money and of finding a place for their children. However that may be, from the second half of the ninth century the majority of the military commands, and hence, soon afterwards, of the political offices too, were held by Turks of slave origin who had been rapidly promoted. During the last third of the century Egypt was governed as a practically independent state by one of them, Ahmad ibn Tūlūn, and by his son, from whom the Caliphate took it back, only to be compelled to hand it over to an Ikhshīd, as has been said. It is difficult to believe that the Turks among whom this recruitment operated did not keep some idea of the Turkish world; but, of course, those who were taken away while still young became strangers to it, and did not return to it or keep in touch. Having been acquired as young individuals to be brought up in another culture, they did not introduce any really Turkish spirit into the Muslim world, nor *a fortiori* anything of Islam to their own Turkish relatives. For our present purpose we can therefore leave them aside to some extent. Moreover, when, later, true Turks as such were to conquer Muslim lands, these other Turks were not the last to resist them. The question of 'national' feeling does not arise.

Certainly of far greater importance is the islamization that took place on the borders between Islam and the Turkish world proper, since this constituted a penetration by the new religion among the Turkish peoples themselves. The Islam that was introduced to them was of a particular kind. It was not the Islam of the great scholars, but that of the itinerant popular monks, of merchants of varying degrees of culture and of frontier soldiers, and was compounded as much of various practices, words and charms as of true dogma. It was not the Islam of the sectarian controversies (although the different sects may have sent representatives there) but, without the new adherents understanding these sectarian differences or knowing to whom they should attribute whatever belief they adopted, it was rather the universal, primitive Islam at war with its infidel neighbours. On the frontiers there had long been volunteers fighting for the Faith, *ghāzīs*, recruited both among the local people and in other regions, volunteers very different from the soldiers of the regular armies, who were becoming increasingly detached from the holy war. They made no conquests but only *ghazwa*s or razzias, by means of which their contempt for the infidels was fostered, while at the same time connections with them developed between the raids, either through negotiations for the exchange of prisoners and booty or simply because proximity and the necessary similarity of a way of life carried on under the same geographical conditions gave rise to a kind of mutual understanding. And among these *ghāzīs* there were Turks, in increasing numbers as conversions multiplied. This facilitated matters still further – so much so that, from both sides, the frontiers ceased to exist; Muslim territory could no longer be forbidden to Turks who had become Muslim, and the old Turkish land, over an increasing area, became an undefined Muslim march. It is in this period that the word Türkmen/Turcoman appears, obscure alike in origin and meaning, which designates the nomadic Muslim Turks, contrasting them on the one hand with the sedentarized Turks and on the other with those nomads who had remained unbelievers. The full significance of all this will appear later.

8

Even more than Christianity in respect of the European peoples originally outside the Roman tradition or than other religions in different countries, Islam was presented, wherever it was adopted, not only as a dogma, a form of worship, a way of private life, but also as a principle of superior political organization – a fact as true in modern, and even contemporary, times as in the Middle Ages. It must not be forgotten that, in addition to a religion in the restricted sense in which we habitually use this word, the Prophet Muhammad created also a community, and that the Law which governs relations between the members of this community is the same as that which is observed by the same members in their relations with their God. While it is true that Islam thus succeeded in penetrating in humble ways among the individual people, it is also certain that at a given moment it was adopted by the rulers, for reasons in which spiritual motives and political interests were inextricably, and to some extent consciously, combined, and that the rulers' conversion to a certain degree brought with it or accentuated that of their peoples, such opposition as they encountered being due as much to social grounds as to devotion to the traditional faith. There is no question that the conversions which we shall shortly observe among certain Turkish groups combine these various factors.

It is customary for Turkish scholars to consider that the first genuinely Turco-Muslim State was the Ghaznevid State, which was set up during the second half of the tenth century, straddling the two slopes of the high mountain ranges that link or separate eastern Iran (including Khorasan) and the basin of the Indus. This view calls for some brief discussion at this point. It is of course true that the founders of the military principality which was the origin of this State, and later its great princes Subugtegin and Mahmūd of Ghazna, were Turks, and that their army was Turkish – in the same sense, however, that Ahmad ibn Tūlūn and the Ikhshīd and half the troops of the ʿAbbāsid or Būyid army had also been Turkish. These men had been officers of the Sāmānid State before freeing themselves from it, but their status and upbringing were of the same nature as the status and upbringing of Ibn Tūlūn and Ibn Tughj the Ikhshīd. Indeed their relative proximity to the Turks' country of origin, the relations they were able to maintain with rulers who still belonged to those countries,

9

a beginning of penetration in some regions in their possession by islamized Turkish populations, all these perhaps gave a somewhat more 'Turkish' quality to their régime than to those of the Turkish leaders who, travelling far afield, had become rulers of Egypt or, to some extent and for a time, of Iraq. Nevertheless this 'Turkish aspect' must always be understood in the sense that the Arab writer al-Jāhiz, in the ninth century, celebrated the virtues of the Turks integrated within the service of the Muslim community, and not as the foreshadowing of a Turkish 'nation'. Subugtegin and his predecessors had been acquired as individuals and taken away from their peoples, as had Ibn Tūlūn, Afshīn and many others before them. The Ghaznevid régime was a régime under the command of rulers who happened to be Turkish, over peoples who were not, and followed traditions according to which the heritage of those peoples counted for far more than their own (so far as they could recollect them) and generally in continuity (except in India) with the earlier Sāmānid régime, in which the rulers were Iranians. The race of the princes was different – a matter which might indeed be of significance, but there was no transplantation of a Turkish people as such, bringing with it its own organization and traditions. In reality, those who today think that the Ghaznevids were the first rulers of a genuinely Turco-Muslim State are perhaps in part the victims of a kind of inverted illusion: it so happens that the principal theorist of the far more Turco-Muslim State of the Seljukids, the Khorasanian Nizām al-Mulk, whose masterly work has survived, was brought up within the Ghaznevid State, which he constantly puts forward as a model. It follows therefore that the model must already to some extent have been what the semi-copy was later to be. We shall see to what extent any real continuity existed, but such continuity as there was in no way detracts from the fundamental distinction which must be made between those states which were created under Turkish rulers but within the previously existing Muslim political framework and without a mass immigration of a Turkish population organized as such, and those states which were primarily based upon such a migration: examples that are intermediate or mixed – such as the Great Seljukids – could also of course exist. I do not say that study of the Ghaznevid régime does not offer a certain specific interest, from the Turkish point of view, for the reasons which we have just noted; but it must not be misinterpreted, and it seems that in general the Ghaznevid State was still merely following the tradition of earlier states with Turkish rulers, and the real break should be placed after it and not before. In any case, there is no justification for calling an institution *ipso facto* Turkish because it occurs under the Ghaznevids.

From our point of view, the first important genuinely Turco-Muslim political structure is that of the Karakhānids. The conversions of other groups are recorded in the second half of the tenth century, their possible connection with one another being obscure, but this one alone led to the establishment of a State. This State, which goes back to a semi-mythical Satuk Bughra Khān (middle of the tenth century), at first included the regions on both sides of the Altai, its two principal centres being Kashgar (Chinese Turkestan) and Balāsāghūn (basin of Lake Balkash), both of which are outside the former Muslim territory. But at the end of the tenth century, by conquest from the Sāmānids, at first with the support of the Ghaznevids but later holding these territories in opposition to them, there was added the whole of Māwarā'annahr (Transoxania), from the Syr Darya/Jaxartes to the Amu Darya/Oxus, that is to say a land profoundly islamized for several centuries, ethnically Sogdian-Iranian, where large numbers of the new Turkish people now settled. Here then we find a genuinely original creation, its elements being combined together in different proportions in different regions. The Karakhānid (sometimes called Ilek-khānid) ruler was a Muslim, and desired to be recognized as such by those of his subjects who had themselves long been Muslims, in keeping with their ideal of what a Muslim ruler should be; so that in their towns he founded hospitals, mosques, *madrasas* (orthodox colleges) and caravanserais, richly endowed by the Muslim institution of *waqf* (the inalienable pious foundation). He even allowed himself to be involved in theological disputes, at least if the supporters of a certain doctrine appeared to him to be rebelling against his authority or had been denounced to him on such grounds by those of the 'natives' on whom his power rested. Nevertheless he was a man whose title Tabghach-Khān (Sovereign of China) recalls Far Eastern ambitions and contacts, and was moreover a nomad, living in a tent and surrounded by the tents of all those accompanying him, who were known as the Ordu (the Horde), from the word which the Mongols were to make famous. He was a prince who, some thought, reigned according to the Muslim concept of a ruler, but over a society in which the Turkish element remained organized according to its tribal traditions, and whose entire material and military strength rested on that element (and not on an army of Turkish recruitment but formed of slaves and technically organized in the manner of the 'Abbāsid or even the Ghaznevid Turkish army). The structure of the dynasty is also very typical of conceptions foreign to Islam (although, in part, these are also found among the Daylamites, precisely because they were converts sprung from a very archaic society). Not only were the territories of the Empire divided among all the 'princes of the blood' under the suzerainty of the eldest of the family (in the widest sense of this last word), but indeed a whole hierarchy linked those sharing a title and a district with others, through deaths and births, according to the place they held there (and as it was often by their titles that they were named, the result is a 'Chinese puzzle' for modern scholars, since the same man could bear several names, and the same name could denote several men).

Moreover, although in Persian-speaking Muslim countries men continued to write in that language, and even occasionally in Arabic, the Karakhānids do not appear to have taken any particular interest in these writings. On the contrary, it was among them that Turco-Muslim literature was born (quite oblivious of the Turkish literature of the Orkhon, whose alphabet was far better adapted to Turkish phonemes than was the Arabo-Persian now adopted). Although later he wrote for the Caliph of Baghdad, it was from among them that Mahmūd al-Kashgharī came, whose *Dīwān lugat at-turk*, an encyclopaedic dictionary of Turkish, is a mine of incredibly abundant and profound information of all kinds. It was among them that the *Poem of Wisdom*, the *Kudatku Bilik*, was written, a work basically of little interest, but the first to succeed in expressing the ideas of the new religion in Turkish. And, at the very end of their domination, it was among them also that the truly mystical poet Ahmed Yesevī began to write. In this respect the Karakhānids are far in advance of the Great Seljukids, and even slightly in advance of the Seljukids of Asia Minor.

Politically, history has less to tell of them than of these others, since they remained enclosed within restricted regions, interfering little in the life of those countries which had a rich literature recounting the deeds and achievements of their princes, and because quite soon they fell beneath the control of the Seljukids, before being destroyed in the twelfth century by the semi-Mongol pagan Karakhitāy. Nevertheless, the significance of the Karakhānids still remains pre-eminent, when considered from the point of view of a comparative history of the Turkish peoples.

Alongside the Karakhānids, who relied on the Karluks in particular, the Oghuz also had created, further to the west a political structure in which the prince (*yabgu*) at first remained pagan but later, in about 1000 A.D., was converted to Islam. Their centre was the market town of Jand on the lower Syr Darya, whose extensive ruins have been discovered in recent Soviet excavations. It appears that, in the tenth century, there was some kind of vague alliance between the lords of Khwārizm (semi-autonomous vassals of the Sāmānids, in the vast delta of the Amu Darya on the Aral Sea, the turning-point for trade with the 'Russian' steppe), the Oghuz and the rest of the Khazars, against the Russo-Norsemen, the Bulgars and the Karluks. However, the rise of the Oghuz is linked not so much with this system, which was not to endure, as with the history of the particular group led by the Seljukids, to whom we must now turn.

ASPECTS OF THE MUSLIM EAST IN THE ELEVENTH CENTURY

In order to understand the events which were to follow, it is necessary to refer briefly to certain aspects of the Eastern Muslim world in the eleventh century. In theory, the 'Abbāsid Caliphate of Baghdad was still recognized throughout the greater part of Muslim Asia; in fact, this area was split up, both politically and in the matter of religion. We have seen how, in the East, the Sāmānids had just been overthrown by the Karakhānids and Ghaznevids. These dynasties both belonged to what is called the Sunnī branch of Islam, which, in the political sphere, recognized the legitimacy of the 'Abbāsid Caliphate, from which they sought the legitimation of their own authority. But central Iran and Iraq obeyed a dynasty which had sprung from the South Caspian people of the Daylamites, the Būyid dynasty (divided into several branches), which was Shīʿī, that is to say devoted in principle to the descendants of the Prophet Muhammad's cousin and son-in-law, ʿAlī, and his daughter Fātima. Under their protection they had preserved the ʿAbbāsid Caliphate, for the Shīʿīs of the group to which they belonged, the 'Twelvers', had at that time no recognized claimant of their own to support and because the Caliphate's prestige caused them to tolerate Sunnīs, who were in a majority in many regions. However, quarrels between the two communities were at their height, and although the first Būyids were military commanders and politicians capable of organizing a state, the last were puppets incapable even of maintaining order. Consequently there was some talk of a hoped-for ʿAbbāsid restoration, through the intervention of the Ghaznevids, who were then proving victorious both on the Indian front in the East and in central Iran and in the West.

Apart from these dynasties there was a multitude of others, various Shīʿī ones on the shores of the Caspian, Sunnī Kurdish ones in north-west Iran on the Armeno-Byzantine and Caucasian frontier, Arabo-Bedouin Twelver Shīʿī ones on the middle Tigris (ʿUqaylids of Mosul) and in Aleppo (Mirdāsids), and again a Sunnī Kurdish dynasty in Diyār Bakr (Marwānids). Central Syria, for its part, belonged to the Fātimids of Egypt, whose influence was predominant also in Arabia, in the Holy Cities and the Yemen. There were also Shīʿīs there, but of quite a different sort, whose doctrine, Ismāʿīlism, while recognizing the claims to the Caliphate of a line descended from ʿAlī and Fātima (hence their name), had woven around these claims doctrines entirely foreign both to Sunnism and to ordinary Shīʿism, and which – more significantly from the point of view we are considering at present – had organized in all countries a vast propaganda which was sapping the politico-social and religious foundations of the hostile régimes.

The end of the ninth and the tenth centuries had been periods of sometimes impassioned, though on the whole quite remarkably unrestricted, confrontations of doctrinal differences. The adherents of each hoped that its triumph would at the same time indicate the remedy for the defects that had been observed in the governments of Muslim society. The eleventh century shows a reaction against this mentality. The disappointments caused by the results of certain victories, the tediousness of the fruitless disputes, the resistance of different groups threatened by orthodox régimes – all these led to a decline of heterodox propaganda, a lack of interest in doctrinal controversies and a preference for semi-mystical forms of religion. The vigour of this movement varied according to the region, but it was especially intense in Khorasan. We shall see its effects.

Socially, the peoples were to an ever-increasing degree subjugated by military aristocracies, often foreign, from whose ranks the rulers came. We have already seen the part played by the Turks among these aristocracies. In proportion as local social systems felt themselves to be supported by these régimes, they upheld them, but in other cases they resisted them. In any event, the masses could feel nothing but indifference towards their princes personally and any changes of dynasty. Moreover, as they were armed only at exceptional times, their feelings could be expressed only in trivial ways. This fact is common to many medieval societies, but is particularly evident in Islam during that period.

With these facts clearly in mind, we must now turn to the history of the creation of the Seljukid Empire.

PART ONE

The Empire of the Great Seljukids

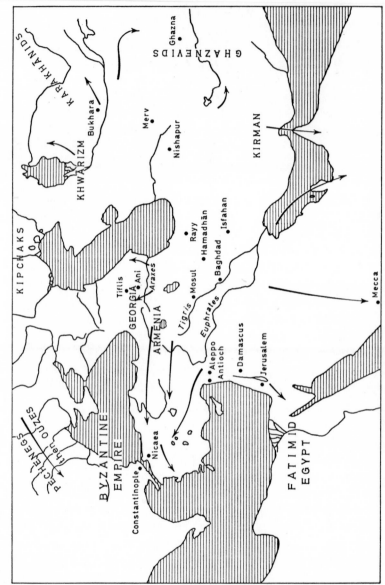

MAP I. The Seljukid Empire at the end of the Eleventh Century

I

THE RISE OF THE SELJUKID EMPIRE

We do not propose in the present work to give a detailed history of the Seljukid Empire, which belongs as much to Iranian as to Turkish history. Nevertheless, it is indispensable to consider it a little more closely than the earlier states or confederations, not only because it is an essential link in Turkish history, but also because a correct understanding of what Turkey in Asia Minor was to become depends largely on the ideas of it that we form at the start.

The Seljukid dynasty, which gave its name to the Empire, derives its name from Seljuk, probably the first of its members to have become Muslim, when already at an advanced age, towards the end of the tenth century. As always, the origins of the family, which was not yet well-known, are wrapped in obscurity. Towards the middle of the eleventh century, at the request of the future Sultan Alp Arslan (at that time still heir presumptive to his father), an anonymous author collected together everything that could be discovered, which even then amounted to no more than an incomplete mass of semi-legendary narratives. This work, the *Malik-nāma*, is lost, but several authors made considerable use of it, until the end of the Middle Ages, and we can therefore form a reasonably clear idea of it.

According to the *Malik-nāma*, Seljuk was the son of Dokak, an Oghuz notable attached to a 'Khazar' prince, meaning probably one of the western Oghuz dwelling more or less within the Khazar zone of influence between the Volga or the Ural river and the Aral Sea. His descendants claimed that, though pagan, he sided with the Muslims even then and hence came into conflict with his prince. This is perhaps no more than a pious legend, yet it may be interpreted in terms of the politico-religious groupings in Central Asia referred to above. However that may be, his son Seljuk, breaking away from the 'Khazar' chief, went to settle in the region of Jand, the market-town mentioned earlier, on the borders of the

Turkish steppe and islamized Central Asia. There he died at a great age (107, according to the legend), perhaps after being converted to Islam late in life, at the same time as his sons, shortly after the period when the Karakhānids were converted. Henceforward, in fighting against the pagan Turks of the steppe, he was himself following the traditions of the *ghāzīs* on the frontiers of the neighbouring Muslim peoples, and a gradual interpenetration between them and his Turks took place. However, his three sons, born before his conversion, bore names – Mīkhā'īl (Michael), Isrā'īl and Mūsā (Moses) – which, while not impossible in Islam, would suggest rather a biblical – Jewish or Nestorian – influence. Without exaggerating the significance of this fact, as has sometimes been done – for the names may have been assumed without retaining their original significance – nevertheless they apparently hint at a dissemination in Oghuz society of certain traditions, either Jewish (as among the Khazars) or Nestorian (as among their kinsmen in Central Asia, whom we considered earlier). But this is scarcely of importance for the sequence of events.

On the death of Seljuk, who was buried at Jand in a tomb his heirs were later to embellish, the members of the family were divided into two branches. Mīkhā'īl having been killed while still young and Mūsā being far from dynamic, the respective chiefs were Isrā'īl, known also by the Turkish name Arslan (Lion), and Mīkhā'īl's two sons, Chaghrï-Beg and Tughrïl-Beg. As a result of their conversion to Islam, their entry into the Muslim territory to the south of the Syr Darya was eventually facilitated at the very moment when first the Sāmānids, threatened by the Karakhānids, and then, after their fall, certain Karakhānids who were fighting against some others, felt an increasing need to seek whatever help could be found. It was for this reason that Arslan/Isrā'īl had been sent by his father to the aid of the Sāmānids, which perhaps had been the occasion of their conversion, and in the end he settled in the steppe near Bukhara. But his nephews, driven from Jand by the Yabgu of the Oghuz, had parted from Isrā'īl and for a time lived with a Karakhānid further to the north. In 1025, however, the first certain date, they all came together in the service of 'Alī-Tegin, the Karakhānid of Bukhara, at the time of his defeat by Mahmūd of Ghazna. As a result of that defeat, Arslan/Isrā'īl agreed to move with his men to Khorasan, where Mahmūd wished him to settle and where his services could be relied upon, out of the reach of ʿAlī-Tegin. Chaghrï and Tughrïl, for their part, took refuge for a time in Khwārizm, the vast estuary of the Amu Darya, south-east of the Aral Sea, protected by its chain of deserts and belonging to an autonomous vassal of Mahmūd. The history of the Seljukids is thus divided into that of two groups which have not always been differentiated correctly.

The Khorasanian group brought Mahmūd more trouble than help during his last years. It was in vain that he held as a hostage Isrāʾīl, who apparently died in a fortress on the borders of India: the Oghuz herdsmen were incapable of respecting the ban on entry into cultivated, well-governed provinces. In 1029 he had to drive them back. Evading him, they escaped across Iran to Azerbaijan where the local princes, to divert their ravages, were happy to employ them against their rivals and even for raids against the Armeno-Byzantine frontier: this is the first appearance of these warriors who were later to play so important a part there. At one time, disagreement between Mahmūd's sons allowed them to return to western Khorasan, whence they made minor plundering raids in all directions. Mahmūd's son Masʿūd emerged as victor from the contest and turned his attention against India and the Būyids, rather than against the Oghuz who, lacking as they did any single leader, appeared merely to be bandits, calling for routine local police action.

However, the other Seljukids, of Khwārizm, on being threatened by the Yabgu of the Oghuz, the master of Jand, sought leave to occupy the area of central Khorasan left vacant by the departure of the first body of Turcomans. When permission was not granted them, they took possession by force. This time, in the two brothers Chaghrï and Tughrïl, they had leaders who knew what they wanted. They procured for themselves recognition as 'clients of the Prince of the Faithful', and sent out raiding parties on all sides. But at the same time they set themselves up as perfectly orthodox, and cemented relations with orthodox circles in the large towns, with such success that the day finally came when the latter, weary of the devastations which the Ghaznevid government, however skilled in levying taxes, could not avert from their agricultural estates, decided to submit to the Seljukid leaders, so that at least their followers' warlike ardour might be directed elsewhere. In this way Merv and Nishapur submitted to Chaghrï and Tughrïl (1028–9). It was only when this happened that Mas'ūd became aware of the reality of the danger. Troops were despatched against the Turcomans. But they were heavy-armed troops, incapable of capturing the Turcomans in the desert and demoralized by thirst and by the lack of any prospect of booty. One day the Seljukids decided to risk a battle, in the plain of Dandānqān, north of Merv. It was a rout for Mas'ūd, who fled to India (1040). Khorasan and, beyond it, the whole Iranian plateau lay open to the Turks.

Leaving Mūsā, and later others, to harass the frontiers of the Ghaznevid State proper (corresponding to modern Afghanistan) by way of Seistan (eastern Iran), Chaghrï and Tughrïl shared out the conquests won and those still to be made, Chaghrï keeping their base, Khorasan and its surroundings, Tughrïl being left free to conquer all he could to the west. To Khorasan, Chaghrï added Khwārizm, while he compelled the Karakhānids and Ghaznevids to respect him. Whatever the latter may have expected at the time, they were to keep Ghazna, protected by its mountains that were so uninviting to the Turcomans. Chaghrï died in about 1058, and was replaced by the son who had long been the real ruler of the country, Alp Arslan. Another of his sons, Kavurt Kara-Arslan, had meanwhile carved out for himself an autonomous principality in Kerman (southern Iran) which was to survive, without any great distinction, until the end of the twelfth century.

It was to the south-west and west that, under Tughrïl, the most spectacular developments were accomplished. In view of the methodical way in which combined military and diplomatic operations were conducted from the outset, it is difficult to doubt that, at a very early stage, this Seljukid held clearly defined ambitions. His conquests had as their aim the occupation of the Iranian plateau or, to be more precise, of the routes across this plateau, which led in the one direction to Baghdad (and the Pilgrimage), in another and secondary direction to Azerbaijan, Armenia and Byzantine Asia Minor. The preliminary attacks were for the most part carried out by his half-brother Ibrāhīm Inal, the final annexation by himself. In this way, between 1040 and 1044, he occupied the Caspian areas of Khorasan, and then Rayy and Hamadhān, on the plateau, with suzerainty over

Isfahan. In this advance he encountered the first body of Tur-comans, who refused to recognize him as their ruler and moved down, through Kurdistan, into Upper Mesopotamia. There they were exterminated by Kurds and Bedouins, who joined forces against these rival herdsmen. Seljukid prestige suffered little from this; on the contrary, the local princes began to think that the best way of avoiding new devastations was to come to terms with Tughrïl-Beg.

Tughrïl, however, could not forget that the essential part of his strength still resided in his Turcomans. These raised a difficult problem for him, for he could not risk quarrelling with them, but on the other hand his aims were not theirs. If he wished to gain recognition as sovereign by an increasing number of Muslim provinces, it was essential for him to restrict their pillaging. In their view, however, pillaging was the sole aim of warfare. There was a solution: from northern Iran a traditional route led to Armenia and Asia Minor, which belonged to the Byzantine Empire, that is to Christians, against whom therefore a holy war could be waged, following the tradition that the Turks had learned from the *ghāzīs* of Central Asia, some memories of whom were perhaps revived for them by the Muslim frontier-dwellers of Azerbaijan and Mesopotamia. In itself this did not interest Tughrïl, but it could bring him prestige, it would be an advantage to send the Turcomans there between expeditions in Islamic countries, and, to avoid any over-independent initiatives, it would be better to provide a leader or to lead them himself. Such is the character of the two expeditions, led by Ibrāhīm Inal in 1049 and by Tughrïl himself in 1054, into Armenia. In addition, they also enabled the Seljukid to have his suzerainty effectively recognized by the Kurdish petty princes of north-western Iran and to inspire respect among the Georgians.

It was at this juncture, in 1055, that the decisive event in Tughrïl's career took place, his entry into Baghdad. There has been much discussion of the circumstances in which this entry was made. Of the fact that it was more or less peaceful there is no doubt. But was terror sufficient, or were there, even in Baghdad, some who were in favour of establishing the Seljukid power? On Tughrïl's side, there is no question that he negotiated this victory. Proclaiming himself the Caliph's faithful client, determined to restore to Baghdad the orthodoxy which the Būyid princes, the protectors of the Caliphate but Shī'īs, were compromising, and, still further, to fight as soon as possible against those particularly dangerous heretics, the Ismā'īlian Fātimid Caliphs of Cairo – in short, while assuming the programme which the Ghaznevids had been unable to execute, Tughrïl-Beg announced his further intention of putting an end to all plundering and all unduly harsh forms of occupation in Iraq; and, in proportion as his troops advanced into the difficult Kurdistan, his conduct seemed fully to confirm his words. In Baghdad, the last Būyids no longer succeeded in morally justifying their protectorate by showing the ability to maintain order, even among their own troops. Since disagreements between Caliphate and Sultanate were later to follow, some writers refuse to believe that Tughrïl's entry into Baghdad can have been desired among the Caliph's actual entourage. With regard to the vizier Ibn al-Muslima, however, the matter is hardly in doubt, and it is difficult to believe that he acted without his master's knowledge. From 1050, at the time of the final annexation of Isfahan by Tughrïl, this man was awarded certain *laqab*s (honorific titles) which placed him above all the princes. Finally the entry into Baghdad took place, with the two powers combining together, while the general in command of the Būyids' Turkish troops, al-Basāsīrī, took to flight. The Caliphate, which for over a century had endured the 'protectorate' of military leaders, could not expect to recover its former authority. But with this Turkish prince, who showed it a greater degree of respect and who was in any case Sunnī, it could cherish hopes, and indeed it enjoyed greater material comfort and a larger part in the administration (at least of Baghdad) – a genuine, if subordinate, sphere of government. Upon Tughrïl the Caliph conferred the title 'King of the East and West', which gave him the right and the mission to conquer all Muslim territories, and especially those which did not recognize the 'Abbāsid Caliphate. He also gave him the title of Sultan, a title which the people had long used but which now seems to have been conferred officially for the first time, and signifies the granting of the fullest power, with the guarantee of the Caliph's sanction. Finally, the Caliph married a niece of the Sultan.

It is true that, at one moment, everything seemed to be

imperilled. Under the aegis of Fātimid emissaries, a vast coalition was organized, including not only al-Basāsīrī's forces which had been driven out, but also the Arab princes of Iraq and Mesopotamia, who were nervous of Seljukid domination both because they were mostly Shī'īs and also because they feared its political ambitions and the competition which Turcoman herdsmen would offer to their own Bedouins, the basis of their strength. At the same time a certain discontent was appearing among the Turcomans, who were angered by their long stay in Iraq, without plunder, far from their families and herds, in a climate too hot for their camels, and with no prospect of any large-scale settlement. The princes of Tughrïl's entourage, formerly accustomed to regarding him merely as *primus inter pares*, were indignant to find him now assuming the style of an Irano-Muslim sovereign and insisting on being surrounded by Iranians and even Arabs, and they believed themselves inadequately paid for their services. As a result, a Turcoman revolt broke out in Upper Mesopotamia and Iran, linked with the Mesopotamian coalition and led by Ibrāhīm Inal and, more discreetly, by Kutlumush, a son of Arslan/Isrā'īl who had gone into his cousins' service. Tughrïl's firmness, the presence of mind of his vizier al-Kundurī, and Alp Arslan's assistance secured victory for the Sultan. Baghdad had been occupied by al-Basāsīrī, the Fātimid prayer had been recited there, Ibn al-Muslima had been put to death and the Caliph handed over to an Arab chief, when the Seljukid troops, victorious in Iran, reappeared, recaptured Baghdad, hunted down and killed al-Basāsīrī and freed the Caliph (1059). All the Arab princes then hastened to offer their submission and, as vassals, gained recognition of their territories, which in these circumstances Tughrïl did not wish to take from them. This was particularly the case with the most powerful of them, the prince of Mosul of the 'Uqaylid dynasty, Quraysh. The Kurds of the Marwānid tribe from the upper Tigris had for a long time done homage in this manner.

It is true that pride then impelled Tughrïl to take an over-ambitious step. Having saved the Caliph for the second time, he thought himself qualified to ask for one of his daughters in marriage. This was an entirely different matter, for, whatever the services he had rendered, in the eyes of the descendant of the

25

Prophet's uncle, Tughrïl was still no more than a barbarian and upstart; moreover, Tughrïl was about 70 years old and childless. The Caliph had to be compelled to understand that resistance was useless and the marriage took place, according to Turkish rites. But then Tughrïl died (1063), and it is impossible to tell how his relations with the Caliph would have developed. His successor Alp Arslan, either voluntarily or because he was occupied elsewhere, never set foot in Iraq, and, interfering less in the Caliph's affairs, maintained wholly correct relations with the ʿAbbāsid government.

The accession of Alp Arslan, the son of Chaghri and therefore Tughrïl's nephew, did not take place without difficulties, which are worth describing on account of the personalities involved. He had to fight against the son of one of Tughrïl's wives, a daughter of the Khwārizmshāh married at the time of their stay in Khwārizm (the son was not a Seljukid but yet had supporters, since Tughrïl had no son); against Qavurt of Kerman, who was defeated; and finally against Kutlumush, who relied both on the Turcomans and probably also on the heterodox inhabitants of northern Iran. Kutlumush was killed, but soon we shall come across his sons. The vizier al-Kundurī, who had hesitated between the parties, was now replaced by Alp Arslan's nominee, Nizām al-Mulk, but was put to death at the latter's suggestion, an unusual occurrence for which the reasons are not clear.

The reign of Alp Arslan, who in his person united the Khorasanian inheritance from his father and the Irano-Mesopotamian inheritance from his uncle, has been remembered by posterity primarily as that of a great military commander. So he proved himself on the frontiers of Central Asia, confronting the Karakhānids and Ghaznevids, but above all in the West. His policy has the same dual aspect as Tughrïl's, but it goes one step further. The Turcomans no longer having to be confined in Iraq or in central Iran, they now undertook a massive assault on Armenia and soon on central Asia Minor also, penetrating ever more deeply if only to plunder it. Some had their bases in Azerbaijan, others – fewer in number – in Upper Mesopotamia. All were helped by the nature of the Byzantine troops (see above), by disagreements between Armenian or Byzantine leaders, and by the withdrawals of frontier troops which sometimes resulted from them, when there was not a frank and open appeal to the Turks against a rival. Thus, in a few years, they plundered the entire region of the Araxes and the two upper branches of the Euphrates as far as their confluence and Malatya/Melitene. In 1059 one group even reached the important communications centre of Sivas/Sebastea, much further to the west. Other attacks, reaching as far as Edessa, were made against Greek strongholds on the south-eastern borders of Asia Minor, recent Byzantine acquisitions.

We must however distinguish between two groups of these Turcomans, although the dividing line between them is by no means clear. There were some, particularly among those taking the south-easterly route, who were probably sent by Alp Arslan for the express purpose of opening up the way for his later ventures. But there were others who were acting independently of any orders or authorization, or who were in fact rebels searching for refuge – even if temporary – outside the Muslim territory that was dependent upon him. This was the case, for example, in 1067–8, with a certain Afshīn, who reached Kayseri/Caesarea, Niksar/Neocaesarea and even Amorium, far out on the western Anatolian plateau; and also, in 1070, with an uncle of Alp Arslan, Erisgen (?), who, when pursued by Afshīn, who had now returned to favour, entered the service of the Byzantines, among whom we shall come across him later. In addition, bands of various origins sought to enter the service of different Syrian and other princes, such as a certain Ibn Khān who forced himself on the Mirdāsids of Aleppo, after previously serving the Marwānids and even the Byzantines, and similarly a subordinate of Erisgen who, with a troop of Yavuki, in 1070 entered the service of the Fātimids for the conquest of the Bedouins of Palestine and then, finding his reward insufficient, in 1071 took possession of Jerusalem for his own benefit.

To prevent the invasion of its territory, Byzantium had on various occasions attempted to negotiate with Tughrïl-Beg and later with Alp Arslan. The latter, whose great project was a campaign against Egypt by way of Syria, was not *a priori* opposed, although he was not reluctant to have his Byzantine flank covered by the Turcomans during this last advance, and although too it was in practice impossible for him to influence those of the

27

Turcomans who were not his subjects. In his reign two periods can be seen. In the first, with the help of the Turcoman incursions, he brought about, in 1064, the important annexation of Ani, the former capital of the Armenian kingdom recently annexed by the Byzantines. This was still not precisely a matter of traditional Byzantine territory, and there had been Muslim emirates in Armenia. Alp Arslan also wished to recapture from the Byzantines the fortified places, such as Edessa, that jutted out from Asia Minor into Muslim territory, each one a potential threat. But in 1068, when he was making a new expedition in the holy war, conceived originally to strengthen his domination over the undisciplined petty princes of extreme north-western Iran, it was against the Georgians that he turned his forces. In 1071, he went down into Syria and compelled the prince of Aleppo who, like his subjects, was a Shīʿī, to introduce the prayer in the name of the ʿAbbāsid Caliph and to acknowledge himself his vassal (whereas hitherto he had been a vassal of the Fātimids); and finally he made preparations to attack the Fātimids.

In Byzantium, however, the relative failure of the policy of negotiation had provoked a military revolution. Romanus Diogenes, the new Emperor, a general, had decided to react with armed force. But, either because he failed to distinguish between the different Turks or for whatever other reason, he began by attacking Aleppo and Ibn Khān, capturing Manbij (1068). In the following year he turned towards Armenia but, characteristically enough, was unable even then to prevent Turkish forces from carrying out operations in the unguarded rear areas, under cover of the concentration of armies on the frontier. In 1071, however, he planned a great coup. Alp Arslan apparently thought he was safeguarded by the negotiations which he had entered into earlier, since he started out for Egypt. It was then that he learnt that the Byzantine army was attacking the frontiers of his own states, by way of Armenia.

There may have been an impression that there was general confusion among the Turks, but the mobility of their troops made such an impression compatible with a re-concentration of forces in a predetermined region. As for the Byzantine army, it was unwieldy. It was certainly far more numerous than the Sultan's, but it was demoralized by the devastation of the regions through which it had travelled, and it was composed of mercenaries of all races who had often rebelled against each other or against the Emperors and were devoid of patriotism. Indeed, they suspected one another of treason, Armenians suspecting Greeks or Turks and vice versa, not to mention Russians and Franco-Normans. The encounter took place in August 1071, near the Byzantine – but formerly Muslim – frontier-fortress of Manzikert/Manāzgird, on the upper reaches of the southern branch of the Euphrates. Even allowing for a certain amount of exaggeration or imagination among the later Muslim chroniclers, it must be admitted that this direct confrontation of the two Emperors made a deep impression, that people were aware of the great issues at stake and that not everything was false in the exhortations which, according to the chroniclers, were showered upon the Turkish forces by the official preachers of the Caliphate. However that may be, Alp Arslan laid a trap in the traditional Turkish style and, by means of a feigned flight, disorganized the Byzantine army. Its demoralization did the rest. By the evening, for the first time in Muslim history, a Basileus was a prisoner of the Muslims.

The measure of his success, against a Byzantine Empire incapable of repeating a similar effort, was such that Alp Arslan would apparently have been able to occupy the greater part of Asia Minor without much difficulty. In view of this, it is all the more remarkable to observe the extraordinary moderation of his policy. He set Romanus Diogenes free in return for a ransom, a promise of alliance, and the restitution of the frontier-strongholds acquired by the Byzantines from the Muslims in the preceding half-century. He was not interested in the conquest of a country which had nothing Muslim about it, if indeed the idea even occurred to him: 'Rome' was an eternal entity, like Islam. Moreover, the Turcomans would merely have been able to increase their power and independence there, and the difficulties he would have encountered from that quarter would have jeopardized his great project, the campaign against Egypt, and the necessary defence of his other frontiers. The real historical significance of Manzikert lies in the fact that, from that time, the Turcomans were able to enter 'Rūm' without difficulty, but this was not the Seljukids' intention. We cannot tell what Alp Arslan would have done if he had been given time to formulate a policy when the

Byzantines refused to receive back Romanus Diogenes, whom
Michael VII Ducas had replaced. There are no grounds for
thinking that there would have been any substantial modification
of his line of action. In fact, he had been compelled at that
moment to undertake an expedition in Central Asia, against the
Karakhānids. It was there that the man who had captured a
Byzantine Emperor, who was at the head of the greatest Islamic
Empire to have been seen for generations, and upon whom
Manzikert had just conferred immortal prestige, died obscurely,
killed during a quarrel by a prisoner of undistinguished origin, a
fitting story for the moralists.

The succession fell to his son Malik-Shāh, still a minor and
under the guardianship of the vizier Nizām al-Mulk, who retained
the substance of power. Unlike his father and Tughrïl, Malik-Shāh
himself was not a Turk of the steppes by birth, and even the name
by which he is known, combining the Arabic title *malik*/king and
its Persian equivalent *shāh*, in place of his predecessors' Turkish
names, signified a programme of unification of Islam within its
ancient territories. By his youth and upbringing, Malik-Shāh was
thus something wholly different from his two predecessors, both of
whom were military commanders. And although Nizām al-Mulk
on occasion led troops, he was of course primarily an admini-
strator and diplomatist. Under their government, however, the
Seljukid Empire made further substantial progress, due in part to
diplomacy, in part to the activities of subordinate commanders,
and finally and most important to the universal desire to resume
an ordered, peaceful life under the protection of the strongest
authority.

We shall return later to the subject of the ensuing events in
Asia Minor, which, as will be seen, hardly touch upon Malik-Shāh
and the Seljukid State. For the rest, apart from some extensions of
the frontier in Syria and Arabia, the strengthening of the Empire
consisted mainly in the direct annexation of principalities which
remained vassals. In Central Asia, Malik-Shāh maintained an
effective protectorate over the Karakhānids, who were divided
among themselves, and made peace with the Ghaznevids. In
Arabia, thanks to Artuk, he reduced the Qarmatian retreat,
Bahrain, and at times succeeded in gaining recognition of his
suzerainty, linked with that of the ʿAbbāsid Caliphate, over the

Holy Cities (which in general however inclined towards Egypt, not through any Fātimid leanings but on account of their need for supplies of food). It was in Mesopotamia and Syria in particular that progress was made. The main achievements, very briefly, were as follows. To begin with, the Caliph's vizier Ibn Jahīr obtained permission from Malik-Shāh to reduce the Marwānid principality of Diyār Bakr, although it had always remained faithful. Meanwhile a series of complicated events had taken place in Syria. Atsïz, in conflict with the Fātimids, had come to terms with Malik-Shāh and become master of Damascus and the whole of central Syria (apart from the coast), in addition to Palestine, but, when threatened by an Egyptian offensive, he renewed his appeals to the Sultan. Moreover in Aleppo, the Arabs also, finding fault with the Turks and losing confidence in their dynasty which was incapable of protecting them, sought to obtain a better guarantee from Malik-Shāh. Now Malik-Shāh had established an autonomous march in Central Asia for one of his brothers, Tökösh, and was anxious to do the same in Syria for his other brother Tutush. Under the pretext of going to aid Atsïz, Tutush entered Damascus and put his predecessor to death (1079). On the way he had attacked Aleppo, but his maladroitness had led the inhabitants to adopt an intermediate solution, submission to the ʿUqaylid prince of Mosul, Muslim ibn Quraysh, who was a vassal of Malik-Shāh and his brother-in-law. Malik-Shāh thought it politic, for the time being, to recognize the *fait accompli* and thus to allow a principality to be set up which included the provinces of Mosul and Aleppo, together with the routes connecting them, just as the Hamdānids had done in the tenth century and as the Zengids were to do once again in the twelfth. To the north-west, this state was flanked by a principality created by an Armenian subordinate of Romanus Diogenes, Philaretes. On the Syrian coast, the ports in the south remained Egyptian, while on the Lebanese coast an autonomous Shīʿī principality was formed under the control of the *cadi*s of Tripoli, the Banū ʿAmmār. Finally, we shall see how the Byzantine province of Antioch fell to Sulaymān, a son of that same Kutlumush of the Seljukid branch of Arslan/Isrā ʾīl who had earlier met his death when disputing the throne with Alp Arslan. War broke out between him and Muslim, who was killed. The people of Aleppo appealed to Malik-Shāh and, pending his arrival, to their neighbour Tutush. Sulaymān was killed. Malik-Shāh merely had to come and reap the rewards that lay waiting. The 'Uqaylid territories were annexed, as was the province of Antioch itself, and the Sultan, leading his horse to 'drink the water' of the Mediterranean, gave thanks to Allah, who had allowed him to extend his dominions from the Eastern Sea to the Western Sea. Tutush stayed on, but now of course on the condition that his apanage should be under closer surveillance and better integrated within the Empire (1086). Beyond Syria, Malik-Shāh had probably not abandoned his father's projected campaign against the Fātimids who, for their part, had not failed to intrigue against him, but he was to die without realizing this project, which was never again to be revived, at least by a Seljukid. Nevertheless, in about 1090 we are at the apogee of the Empire which, stretching almost to the ends of Arabia and the borders of India, embraced nearly all the Muslim territories of Asia.

2

THE SELJUKID EMPIRE AND THE TURKS

The time has now come to consider the Empire itself at that period. We must repeat that to make a complete study of it would come just as much, or even more, within the realm of the history of the Arabs and the Iranians as within that of the history of the Turks, and there can therefore be no question of it in the present work. Nevertheless, we have to consider in some detail two types of questions: on the one hand, what does it contain that is specifically Turkish? and, on the other, what is there in its organization which must be understood at the outset in order to understand that of the later 'Turkey' in Asia Minor?

To start with, we are for the first time dealing not with an introduction of young Turks, as individuals and soon denationalized, but with a migration of a people as such, men, women and children, not to mention their animals, with their own social structure and customs. In the matter of population, however, we must neither exaggerate nor generalize for all regions alike. Any idea of calculating the number of the immigrants is clearly fruitless. Several tens of thousands, certainly; but that they numbered several hundreds of thousands is doubtful. And even if it were possible to give an estimate of the original figure, it would quickly lose its significance since new conditions may, according to circumstances, either stimulate or retard the birth-rate. In particular, the important question is not so much the absolute number as the relative number compared with the indigenous population, a thing which it is not easy to evaluate. And here, too, the relationship may change quickly if a relatively large number of indigenous young women are taken as wives by the new-comers, either forcibly during raids or in a friendly way when the populations wish to protect themselves from misfortunes. All this being granted, and with Asia Minor left aside for the moment, there was probably no large region with a new Turkish immigration apart from Azerbaijan, where the Azerī dialect, one of the branches of the Oghuz languages, still survives today, more important than the ancient Iranian substratum. To Azerbaijan was added part of Diyār Bakr, the extension beyond the mountains of northern Kurdistan. In the rest of the Seljukid Empire the climate was normally too hot and dry to suit the Turcomans and their flocks, and there were only certain isolated settlements in Khuzistan, in Fars, and in some parts of the Kurdish mountains. The few who settled in Syria were to be driven back by the Crusaders, and therefore are of little account historically. Apart from these groups there were, of course, garrisons in all the towns. Here, however, we are no longer considering the Turkish population but, rather, an extension of that old institution, the professional army, and as time passed there was even a difference of origin between the Turcoman people and the army, which was recruited from among slave elements obtained directly in Central Asia or in the Russian steppes.

One would like to be able to give an account of the economico-social condition of the immigrant Turcoman people. The modern Turks suffer from a kind of inferiority complex at the thought that their ancestors may have been nomads, and they are inclined to lay stress upon the sedentarized elements which they may have

33

included. We have already made this point in regard to Central Asia, and, even with the nomads themselves, it is possible that some of them became settled quite quickly. We shall come across the same problem in Asia Minor. It is, however, difficult to deny that, at the time of their immigration, we are in general dealing with nomads. Furthermore, a distinction has to be made between those nomads who travelled long distances, the owners of the two-humped camels adapted to withstand cold winters, and those owning sheep or other livestock requiring only local movements for pasturage, or those who to some extent combined both types. It would be interesting to know if the demarcation between the types corresponds to divisions between the tribes. For the moment, this last problem can only be stated. The one point that must be emphasized is that rivalry with the indigenous herdsmen and the conditions of settlement amongst them differed according to the category. The wide-ranging nomads were to offer little competition to the mountain-dwelling Kurds, who were primarily local migrants. Politically, their wide range of movement, among other factors, later made them better suited to more unified organisms than to the much-divided Kurdish groupings. As with the Arabs, some of whom owned camels while others had none, the distinction rests rather on the line of demarcation between the Central Asian camel and the dromedary of the hot deserts.

Whatever the value of these general observations, and at the present time it is difficult to go beyond them, the reader must reflect, as he would in the case of the Arab conquest and expansion some centuries earlier, that the accepted custom of regarding the nomadic herdsmen as a destructive, uncivilized and always negative element can be just as much mistaken as it may be correct. When, for whatever reason, it is a question of nomads attacking cultivated land, the result is obviously negative. But it is not necessarily so. The nomadic economy is adapted to certain territories which could not be exploited for agricultural purposes, and thus it can, in a positive sense, bestow value on regions which previously possessed none. In that event it contributes to the agricultural economy, instead of impairing it. It is clear that such is the case in Asia Minor, the Fertile Crescent and the Iranian plateau. In the Fertile Crescent, the arrangement had been more or less worked out with the Arabs long before. This was less true in Asia Minor, where there was much stock-breeding, mostly however in the hands of semi-sedentary shepherds, and in Iran, away from the mountains of Kurdistan, Luristan and Baluchistan. The arrival of new-comers could thus give rise to tacit agreements between neighbours, such as had long existed in the Near East or in Central Asia, sedentary dwellers and nomads exchanging their respective products, not to mention the distribution of the manure from their animals on the land for cultivation. For the moment, these are little more than unsupported observations, but as attention becomes more clearly focused on them it will perhaps become possible to detect some historical illustrations of a kind that all geographers are familiar with in contemporary societies.

We referred to the Turcoman, Oghuz, tribes. The legend fixing their number at 24 was already fairly well known, to judge from the material scattered through Mahmūd al-Kāshgharī's dictionary. Nevertheless, one cannot fail to be struck by the contrast between the almost complete silence of the texts that are close to the Turkish expansion and the minute details of the semi-legendary accounts at the end of the Middle Ages. Before the Mongol invasion in the thirteenth century, which was to drive back or bring in new elements, the only ones of the 24 tribes which can be identified, in the Seljukid realm, are the Kïnïk, the Döger, the Yaghma, the Salghur and the Avshar, a little later the Iva, and then, once again, the first-named, but solely with reference to the fact that they are the Seljukids' own tribe (the Döger are the tribe of the Artukids). Everything suggests that the emphasis placed on the tribal aspect and on the traditions of the different tribes was bound up with the rise of the Turcoman States in the fifteenth century. At the time of the Seljukid conquest, apparently less was said about them, although we cannot tell from non-Turkish literary sources exactly what the Turks were thinking. At all events, it seems that the tribal structure did not possess all the implications that it had for certain Arab circles, and that in any case conquest and migration were carried out by disjointed, intermingled groups.

The Seljukid Empire, which had owed its original strength to the Turcomans, was however an Empire in which they very soon assumed the aspect of a body that was, if not foreign, at least distinctive. The lands they had conquered for their masters were old Muslim countries, possessing a traditional administrative and military organization which imposed itself on the new masters, inasmuch as they themselves were lacking in any equivalent traditions, or as their own traditions could not be applied to their new subjects. On the whole, the new state thus consists of a pre-existing society within a Turkish framework.

This Turkish framework was at first of course represented by the reigning dynasty, which preserved certain individual character-istics. That Tughrïl-Beg and Alp Arslan should still have followed an essentially Old-Turkish way of life, that the former should have been completely ignorant of Arabic and should have hardly known Persian, is to be expected. Even Malik-Shāh and his successors were to continue to speak mainly Turkish, and the last representatives of the family in Khorasan, Sanjar, in the twelfth century, probably continued to dress and to wear his hair in the Turkish style, although his kinsmen in western Iran perhaps no longer did so. Semi-traditional details reveal the persistence of certain practices: it was an ancient custom of the Oghuz, as indeed of many peoples in Central Asia, to regard the bow and arrow as a symbol of authority, and a message received its guarantee of authenticity if accompanied by the characteristic arrow of the chieftain who was sending it. Now we also find records of this practice under Malik-Shāh and, for the Artukids, even as late as about 1120–5.

One particular and well-known institution, that of the *tughrā*, is in its origin connected with this practice. Many people will have had an opportunity to see, on Ottoman diplomas, the intricate symbol in stylized, interlaced letters, the whole thing in the shape of a butterfly's wing, which authenticates the text. Under the Ottomans, this was no longer anything more than a stereotyped design, the significance of which was lost. But, in reality, it goes back to the Seljukids. Under the name *tughrā*, which is of uncertain etymology but equivalent in meaning to what other Turkish or Mongolian tribes called by the more widely used name *tamgha*, they meant a mark which, when affixed to livestock owned by the chieftain or to writings emanating from him, indicated his authority. Now it is certain that the *tughrā* of the first Seljukids usually consisted of variants of the design of a bow and one or more arrows, an emblem also used in various ceremonies, which

36

marked their sovereignty. After being affixed to diplomas drafted according to the traditions of the old Irano-Muslim official departments, the design gradually lost its importance, in view of the names and titles that were added, and the successive states of the Seljukids, the Zengids, the Ayyūbids, the Mamluks and also the Seljukids of Rūm altered the original *tughrā* from which the Ottoman form ultimately derived. But originally it was distinct even from the traditional formulae for the authentication of diplomas, and was appended by a special official, personally representing the Sultan.

In the organization of their family we also find certain earlier Turkish institutions, though these were still evolving. It is uncertain what was the original function of the *atabek* and, although various societies have had certain equivalents, the other Turks and even the ancient Oghuz have not as yet revealed any precedent. From the time of Alp Arslan at least, the *atabek* is a military chief in the ruler's entourage, to whom the ruler entrusts the education and care of his son, ultimately marrying him to the pupil's mother. We shall see later what developments took place in certain cases in the office of *atabek*, which in this way was to pass to various of the dynasties immediately succeeding the Seljukids and even, at least as a title, to the Georgians.

On becoming a Muslim Sultan, the Seljukid prince acquired some notion of the conception of the unity of sovereign power held by the Caliphate and, earlier, by several princely dynasties (but not that of the Būyids, who had sprung from a more traditionalist people, the Daylamites of northern Iran). However, the idea had never been renounced that all members of the family had a certain right to a share of the inheritance, pre-eminence being given to the eldest of the family in the wide sense: hence the partitions and conflicts, some of which have already been noted, while others were to be repeated in the twelfth century; hence also – although there are other reasons as well – the granting of apanages, such as those of Töküsh and Tutush.

The name Malik-Shāh and the essentially Arabic names of most of his successors signify a relative de-nationalization of their cultural and political outlook. However, besides their Islamic name they often retained a Turkish one, by which they may happen to be better known, such as Sanjar, whom we shall come

37

across later, in the twelfth century. And at the end of the dynasty, as though to endow a declining authority with the prestige of its great ancestors, the last two Seljukids of Iran were called Arslan and Tughrïl. Unlike those of the Seljukids of Rūm, their names did not draw upon the legendary mythology of Persia. In their full list of titles, however, Arabic, Persian and old Turkish titles were mingled together.

The strength of the régime rested essentially on the army. Originally it consisted only of Turcomans. But from the time of Malik-Shāh onwards the vital part of the army was a professional army half recruited from slaves, even though the Turcoman chiefs, detached from their background, like Artuk, still figured in it. To bring up the young Turcoman notables at court for a military career was one way of securing their loyalty. But in the twelfth century the Seljukid army once more became what the army of its Arabo-Iranian predecessors had been, save for some free companies. Even ethnically it was not exclusively Turkish when it became customary for Kurds to enrol in it.

What distinguishes Malik-Shāh's army from that of the Būyids, which also was mostly Turkish, is above all its numerical strength. Owing to the extent of the Empire, the facilities for and the political usefulness of partial recruitment among the Turcomans, it seems to have included about 70,000 cavalry, and Nizām al-Mulk opposed plans to cut it down for the sake of economy. It had to be paid and maintained, and this brings us to the question of iqṭāʿ, upon which we must dwell a little on account of the misconceptions to which it has given rise.

In the early days of Islam the name qaṭīʿa, parcel of land, was given to the allocations of land in limited ownership made from the State domains to the notables, with the duty of keeping it under cultivation. The limited ownership of the qaṭīʿa brought certain rights (of gift, sale, inheritance, etc.) but also involved certain duties (payment of the tithe on harvests) and limitations (no administrative or 'seignorial' rights). So long as the army had been purely Arab this system, combined with the ordinary army pay, had sufficed for its upkeep. When, during the ninth century, it was transformed into a more professional and technically heavier army mainly recruited abroad, it was no longer sufficient. Precisely because the qaṭīʿa was hereditary, it was impossible to repeat such allocations indefinitely. Another system was therefore introduced. With the exception of the land belonging to the State, at the time of the Arab conquest the remainder of the land had been left in the hands of the former landowners in return for the payment of a fairly heavy rent, *kharāj*, corresponding to the land tax of earlier governments. These estates could not be taken away from their lawful owners, but it was possible to grant to notables the rights to the taxes from them that were vested in the State. This meant, in effect, that they were sent to take their army pay direct from the source. For a certain time the revenue thus acquired was regarded as ordinary revenue and hence subject to the tithe, the balance formed by the excess of the *kharāj* levied over the tithe due representing the individual's pay. This system had the advantage of maintaining the State's control over the district. But the military leaders, the beneficiaries by this new type of concession, did not pay what they should. Under the Būyids, it was decided to calculate their concession by including in it the tithe that they should have paid, and making no further claim against them. Henceforward the officer was the sole representative of the administration in the district which had been granted to him as his pay, and for whose expenses he took responsibility out of the income yielded. It is this new concession which, from then onwards, was called *iqtā'*, from the same root as *qatī'a*, but which literally means, in the abstract, the act of allocation.

The *iqtā'* of this kind however did not constitute a seigniory, and care was taken that it should not become one. It was determined by its fiscal value, and an attempt was made to keep a strict idea of this. Moreover, since what was due to the officer was his pay, and not the district, it might happen that the district would be withdrawn from him in order that he might simply be paid in cash or in kind, or it might happen equally often that he himself would ask for the district to be changed, if he thought its value inadequate, or that the State might change it to prevent him from becoming firmly established in it and, by the acquisition of dependents and actual property, from gaining a dangerous independence. This had the disadvantage that it prevented any interest being taken by the officers in the rational development of their districts, but it seemed to safeguard the sovereign's rights more completely.

From al-Maqrīzī onwards, the Egyptian historian of the fifteenth century, writers have repeated that Nizām al-Mulk put an end to this system and replaced it by what, in European terminology, is known as the 'feudal' system. The testimony of the period, including that of Nizām al-Mulk himself, formally denies the validity of this assertion. The conception of *iqtāʿ* held by the Great Seljukids was exactly the same as that of the Būyids, with greater authority to secure its observance. The later developments which are to be seen in the twelfth century and which led to the establishment of hereditary domains were the result of the decline of the Seljukid régime, not of its power, and of the new conceptions of the régime that arose precisely from its dismemberment.

Is there then nothing to be placed to the credit of the Seljukids in this respect? Modern Turkish historians appear to attach a certain national pride to the idea that there was a specifically Turkish feudal conception. I confess I find it difficult to see, if that were true, in what respect there would be an occasion to feel either pride or regret, and indeed I also fail to see (what is more important) how this idea can be justified. Our certain knowledge consists of the two following points: on the one hand, the importance of the Seljukid army and the extent of the Empire caused *iqtāʿ* to be introduced into regions where it was hardly known and led to an increase in its importance; on the other hand, the immigration of nomadic groups led to the establishment, on their behalf, of certain forms of concessions of more or less collective application – but of a kind already in use among certain Kurds and Bedouins. Perhaps, on this last point, these were customs acquired by the Turks in their contact with the Muslims of Central Asia. But I do not see that more than that can be conceded and, what is more, I cannot find in this any cause for offence to our Turkish friends. Historical evolution is in no way concerned with value judgments of this kind.

On the other hand, one innovation of the Seljukid Government was the institution of the *shihna*, which was particularly favoured by the development of the army. The earlier Muslim capital cities had a police force, the *shurta*, but in practice most of the towns depended for their policing upon various more or less official types of militia, recruited locally. For this reason such militias, besides being ineffective when needed for military purposes, were a danger to the authority of the foreign and often unpopular princes. The Seljukids automatically replaced them by a garrison, *shihna*, of the regular Turkish army, this name (a Persian word) in reality serving to denote the leader who commanded it.

For the rest, the Seljukid administration consisted of what they had come to know in Ghaznevid Khorasan, where they had first gained experience and which provided them with almost the entire body of their original personnel, starting with the two viziers al-Kundurī and Nizām al-Mulk. The ideas of the latter are known to us, since he expounded them in a Persian work, the *Siyāsat-nāma*, which survives. In it he takes account, it is true, of the specific elements in the new régime he was serving, but his enduring interest is the Ghaznevid régime and his general ideas are derived from Irano-Islamic experience. People sometimes like to regard him as the spokesman for specific Seljukido-Turkish conceptions: this too seems to me to be erroneous and a mis-interpretation.

The administration of pre-Seljukid Khorasan was not funda-mentally different from that of the more central Islamic States. However, it possessed certain individual features, particularly of terminology, which it is both interesting and natural to find wide-spread later throughout the whole Seljukid area. The heads of departments at court had purely Persian names, even when the official language remained Arabic. The senior civil officials formed a special category, the ʿamīd, plur. ʿumadāʾ, from whom the governors of the provinces were selected, as well as the man most closely connected with them, the head of the postal service or *barīd*. The controller of the accountancy department, elsewhere called the head of the *zimām*, was here known as *mustawfī*. Finally, special emphasis was placed on the general control of justice, both of the corps of *cadi*s and the special jurisdiction for the redressing of wrongs, *mazālim*, which was entrusted to an *amīr-i dād*, signi-fying in Persian 'chief of justice'. As elsewhere, at the head was a vizier. The Sultans, being foreign and for the most part devoting themselves to military affairs, were compelled to rely upon a power-ful subordinate; and this fact, together with his own experience of government, enabled Nizām al-Mulk to remain for 29 years in the vizierate which, under Malik-Shāh, was almost tantamount to full control, and which was long to be regarded as a model.

Whatever may have been the precise circumstances of the establishment of the Seljukid protectorate in Baghdad in 1055, various problems of mutual adjustment obviously derived from it. The difficulties were in fact mostly resolved because the Caliph was served by the two Ibn Jahīrs, father and son, as his viziers, almost without a break. Both succeeded in winning the confidence of Nizām al-Mulk and his masters by family alliances, while at the same time being careful not to offend the Caliph's susceptibilities. There is no doubt however that at the end of the sultanate of Malik-Shāh, relations were deteriorating. Malik-Shāh and his all-powerful vizier regarded the sultanate as an institution deriving its legitimacy from itself. In any case, no one doubted that it had the right to deal with all matters including religious ones. In Baghdad in particular, the situation might lead to clashes. Alp Arslan had avoided them, but this was not the case with Malik-Shāh, who enjoyed staying in the 'Abbāsid capital. Towards the end of his reign there was a question of exiling the Caliph. The circumstances under which Malik-Shāh died suggested to some the idea of an intervention by Allah at the hands of the Caliph, but this remains unproven.

In religion, the characteristic feature of the Seljukid period consists in the organization of a strongly orthodox Sunnī movement. It is true that propaganda of all kinds had succeeded in reaching the Turks, most of whom were incidentally not sufficiently advanced to care about disputes between theologians. But the Great Seljukids, whether through conviction or policy, posed as champions of orthodoxy against the laxity and wranglings of preceding generations, and we have already suggested that their conquest had been facilitated by the support they received on this account from the Khorasanian, and later from other, orthodox notables. Many of the features of their conduct in this respect must therefore be attributed less to their own individual merits than to the force of the general movement of orthodox reaction which is characteristic of Islam from the eleventh century, in comparison with earlier generations.

The Seljukids were great builders of mosques and other public centres. But their principal innovation was the *madrasa*. Certain precedents had existed in Khorasan, and across the sectarian barriers, among the Ismā'ilians, similar interests had made their appearance. But the Seljukids were the first to give them any real importance and to cause them to be put into practice on a large scale. The *madrasa* is an establishment for instruction which, unlike earlier instruction, is specially organized for the teaching of the religio-juridical sciences from the orthodox point of view. It acquired great wealth, in the form of pious foundations (*waqfs*) which were allocated to it, and it was from among the students taught by its masters that the officials of the régime were to be recruited. There was no persecution, in the strict sense, of the heterodox, so long as they did not constitute a political danger. But by the simple fact that, for both masters and students, all means were placed at the disposal of orthodoxy and that almost all the best positions in the fields of administration and justice were consequently reserved for them, the heterodox were obviously placed at a disadvantage. Within the field of orthodoxy, the Turks themselves had for the most part been won over by the Hanafite school, one of the four accepted juridical schools with the largest following in Khorasan. It does not seem, however, that the attitude of the Great Seljukids included any desire to favour Hanafism in particular, since Nizām al-Mulk was and always remained a member of another school which was fairly widely disseminated throughout the whole of Muslim Asia, the Shāfiʿite. It was Nizām al-Mulk himself who founded, in Baghdad, the most famous of all *madrasas*, the Nizāmiyya, to which he summoned the greatest scholars of the time, including al-Ghazālī. In theology, he was personally an adherent of the still much disputed teachings of al-Ashʿarī; but the Nizāmiyya was not as exclusively restricted to these doctrines as has sometimes been thought, and the Sultan's government made particular efforts to avoid disputes, provided naturally that people remained within the bounds of what it considered to be compatible with orthodoxy.

What is more, orthodoxy was broadening. It was adopting, for example, certain forms of Sufism, that is to say mysticism. Hitherto, Islam had shown itself suspicious of men who claimed too easily to enter into communion with God and to have no need of the usual methods of devotion. But the mystics of the eleventh century were becoming more anxious to affirm their orthodoxy. They were beginning to organize themselves in groups which, little by little, were to become true congregations. On the

43

other hand a general movement, with al-Ghazālī as its most famous spokesman, was seeking to combine the religious attitude which, for the theologians, was fundamentally intellectual or ratiocinative, with regeneration through the heart. Perhaps, in its way, the social influence of the Turks accentuated this movement because these new converts, as yet unacquainted with the scholarly discussions of earlier Islam, were more immediately receptive to the religious demonstrations of the Sufis. In any case, from the end of the eleventh century it became one of their forms of piety to establish or patronize the *khānqāhs*, the 'convents' of Sufis, or, as they were called in an Irano-Turkish environment, dervishes. Here too, through material competition, their preference could be of use to certain 'orders' at the expense of others.

There is one point which must be emphasized, on account of the misunderstandings to which, since the Crusades, the religious policy of the Seljukids has given rise in Europe: in relation to non-Muslims and particularly to Christians, it in no way changed the toleration which was the general rule in Islam. It is true that the conversions, which had cut down the numbers of the formerly influential Nestorians in Iraq, reduced their need to exercise such toleration, but it still remained, and there was no alteration in the condition of private individuals. The Turcoman invasions did of course inflict sufferings on several Christian communities; but they inflicted them also on many Muslims, and in any case we must make a distinction between the territory of the holy war, in Asia Minor, and the territory within Islam (which came to include Asia Minor as it became integrated into Islam). In Asia Minor, the Byzantine Church suffered more particularly, as is natural. But the new masters often succeeded in utilizing the animosity of other Christians against it. Sometimes, through a confusion of the dates, the pilgrimage of 1064 has been cited as an illustration of the insecurity and intolerance which, from then onwards, hampered western pilgrimages to Jerusalem. The massacres in Jerusalem in 1075 have also been cited. The reality was quite different: when the great pilgrimage of 1064 was attacked, it was by Bedouins, for whom neither the Fātimids in Egypt, their masters in theory, nor still less the Turks, who were not yet there, were responsible; and even certain writers of the time show clearly that the Bedouins' cupidity had been inflamed by an excessive display of wealth. In

Asia Minor, pilgrims could no longer pass, which was an incon-
venience. But in Palestine they continued to be welcomed, as in
the past. And, far from it being necessary to say, in view of the
occurrences of 1064, that they were compelled to band themselves
together for greater strength, on the contrary they continued to
come by sea, in a less conspicuous manner. As for the massacre of
Jerusalem, this followed a pro-Fātimid revolt and was directed
solely against Muslims suspected of Ismā'īlian sympathies, while
the Christians and Jews, who shortly before had been gathered
together in autonomous quarters of the town, were spared. The
Copts of this period give more praise to the government of Atsïz
and, afterwards, of Artuk, the lieutenant of Tutush, than they
were later to give to the government of the Crusaders. And elsewhere the name of Malik-Shāh, the restorer of order but also a
man generous to all, is greeted by a chorus of praise from the
Armenian writers and, in a more restrained way, from the
Monophysites. There had been only one real persecution in
Islam, by the half-mad Fātimid al-Hākim, at the beginning of
the eleventh century. In the West, everything was confused
together, al-Hākim with the Turks, Asia Minor devastated by the
war with the normal Muslim régimes. Nine centuries later, however, this historical injustice can certainly be redressed.

Meanwhile, of course, there still remained some heterodox
subjects who did not accept the Seljukids. These were found in
particular among the adherents whom the Ismā'īlian missionaries
had recruited in Iran. But it so happened that during the reign of
Malik-Shāh the Ismā'īlians were split by a schism over the
question of the person of the legitimate Caliph, and, while one
pretender was successful in Egypt, the Ismā'īlians of Persia
remained faithful to another, Nizār. Their sect thus became
autonomous. Moreover the Seljukid power, which allowed them
little opportunity for normal development, made them incline
towards terrorist action. Without warning they seized certain
mountain fortresses difficult to recapture, like Alamūt, which for
nearly two centuries was to remain the residence of their Grand
Master. The man who organized them was Hasan al-Sabbāh,
whom legend presents as a former school-fellow of Nizām al-Mulk
and the mathematician Omar Khayyām. As he used to give his
disciples a foretaste of the joys of Paradise by making them take

hashish, popular language often gave them the name *hashīshīn*, and as they became famous from their systematic murders, the Crusaders, who soon became acquainted with their regional branch in Syria, carried back to Europe the terrible name 'Assassins', with the meaning that the word has retained. For these murders, a form of holy war offering the reward of martyrdom, they secured from their devotees a blind obedience and a remarkable self-command. The first victim of note was Nizām al-Mulk himself (1092), though his enemies, and even Malik-Shāh (who by then tolerated his vizier's authority only with some impatience), were accused of plotting the assassination – or even the Caliph. We cannot tell how Malik-Shāh would have governed without Nizām al-Mulk, since he followed him to the grave after only a few months, while still young.

The death of Malik-Shāh marks the beginning of a decline which might have been foretold and which lasted for a century. But it must not be generalized. The political dismemberment in no way threatened the religious orientation which we have described. It did not even affect the extent of the Turkish penetration, which became more marked through the progressive replacement of the remaining Arab, Kurdish or Persian lords by Turks.

Among the various causes of the decline – the indiscipline of the Turcomans, the ending of rich conquests, the threat from the Assassins – the principal one, at the start, was the absence of any precise rule of succession. The struggles which set Malik-Shāh's sons and uncles against each other were brought to an end with an agreement in favour of one of his sons, Muhammad, who in appearance restored the unity of the Empire, but he had been obliged to turn the whole of Khorasan into an autonomous apanage held by another, Sanjar. Syria was practically autonomous and was moreover split up, quite apart from the territory that the Crusaders, taking advantage of the prevailing state of affairs, were then overrunning. The province of Mosul was becoming an undisciplined military command, and beyond, in Diyār Bakr, the Artukids were carving out a group of domains for themselves, while at Akhlāt on Lake Van a former officer had installed himself with the high-sounding title Shāh-i Arman, Persian for 'King of the Armenians'. Naturally in these circumstances the Sultan's resources were dwindling, Muhammad was powerless to reduce the Assassins, and in the interplay of local rivalries some princes were relying on them. The movement gathered momentum under Muhammad's successor Mahmūd with, for example, the lawless acts of the Bedouin chief Dubays at the very gates of Baghdad, and particularly during the time of Mahmūd's brother Mas'ūd, against whom Sanjar, who as the eldest of the family had secured some recognition as suzerain, supported various other nephews. The most dramatic episode was the siege of Baghdad, in 1133–4. In the struggle between the pretenders, legitimation by the Caliph was clearly of importance, and hence the Caliph was able to use it for bargaining purposes, while the Sultans, being short of money, tended rather to increase their material demands. The Caliph Mustarshid had sided against Mas'ūd, who besieged him. Certain Turks, undecided in which master's service their future would best be guaranteed, provided him with the rudiments of an army; however, he was defeated and, with his friend Dubays, 'assassinated'. So too was his successor Rāshid. But the trend of events which, by weakening the Sultan, emancipated the Caliph, could not be reversed, and their successor, without having to fight, achieved in practice the regional independence for which the other two had died. Indeed at the end of Mas'ūd's reign, although he was the sole Sultan in title, he was in fact the puppet of a number of powerful officers, whose loyalty he had to reward with immense concessions and whose power was limited only by the rivalries between them. The *atabek*s of the various child-princes acquired for themselves in practice the authority that had in theory been granted to their wards. It was by these means that the Zengids held Mosul and Aleppo, and Ildegiz and his descendants Azerbaijan. The Seljukid principality of Kerman preserved some degree of independence, while the tribal chiefs in their turn carved out principalities for themselves, for instance the Salghurids in Fars. It was only through the tolerance of these princes, who hoped thereby to gain recognition for themselves against the rest, that the last Seljukids retained a little authority on the Iranian plateau. When the last of them, Tughrïl, attempted for a time to resume a somewhat more active career, the Caliph caused him to be attacked from the rear by the Khwārizmshāh (of whom more will be said shortly). In this way, in 1192, the dynasty ended in obscurity.

In Khorasan, where the dynasty had at one time appeared to be more illustrious, its dissolution on the whole came about more rapidly. Sanjar had established his effective suzerainty over the Karakhānids of Transoxania and the Ghaznevids. But in Central Asia there was beginning once again a movement of peoples which was to overthrow the existing Empires. The Khitāy, probably a Mongol people, who in the vocabulary of Marco Polo and the West were to give their name to China (Cathay), were then creating for themselves an Empire that straddled western and eastern Turkestan, and crushing the Karakhānids. Called in to help the victims, Sanjar in his turn was defeated (1141), and the Khitāy conquered the whole of Transoxania, as far as the Amu Darya. Their rule was very lax and brought no great changes in the life of the country. In the field of religion, however, it was of considerable significance, since they were not Muslims. Their sovereign was the Gūr-Khān; and there were among them some Nestorian Christians. The story then spread through the eastern Christian communities of a Priest-King who was to crush Islam from the rear. When brought to the West, this was the origin of the legend of Prester John which, after various transformations dictated by political events, at the end of the Middle Ages ultimately became attached to the Negus of Ethiopia.

Sanjar retained his own domains, but the Khitāy advance had once again set in motion the Oghuz who still remained in Central Asia. They became more and more difficult to control and keep in order. Finally, in 1153, they defeated and captured Sanjar and, while continuing to show him respect, overran his territories, pillaging and killing. The flight of the Sultan, whose age gave him genuine prestige, in no way changed the situation. When he died in 1156, nothing remained of the Seljukid Empire of Khorasan. And, unlike the Oghuz who had followed the Seljukids, these showed themselves to be incapable both of choosing a single ruler and of organizing any lasting political structure. While one of them, Malik Dīnār, went to take possession of Kerman, putting an end to the local Seljukid dynasty, the others divided Khorasan between themselves, as ransom. Only one peaceful sanctuary remained, Khwārizm, behind its ring of deserts. The Khwārizm-shāhs had been turbulent vassals for Sanjar. Now they appeared to be his only possible heirs. By massive purchases of Turkish

'Kipchak' slaves in Central Asia, made possible by their country's continued prosperity, they established a powerful army, though it was half-barbarian and in the long run proved ruinous. This 'Khwārizmian' army conquered Khorasan for its masters, and through it they gained a footing in Iranian politics. It has already been related how the Caliph al-Nāsir called them in against the last Iranian Seljukid. But they then plotted to secure the Sultanate for themselves. Only the Mongol conquest, in 1217, was finally to free the Caliphate from their threats, before destroying the Caliphate itself in 1258.

It was under this same Caliph al-Nāsir that the emancipation of the Caliphate was fully achieved, no longer it is true as a political power dominating the whole Islamic world, but at least as a regional power, and moreover one endowed with a certain superior prestige. This Caliph (who had, incidentally, a Turkish mother) was a curious character, who scandalized the traditionalist spirits of his time because, in his desire to bring about, under his aegis, at least a moral reunification of the various spiritual families of Islam, he was led to adopt attitudes which, to the orthodox, appeared to be heterodox. One of his successes consisted in bringing back the Assassins of Alamūt more or less into the fold of Islam. But his most famous achievement and, without perhaps his having foreseen it, the most rewarding in the future, was his reorganization of the *futuwwa*.

This was the name given to a movement of non-professional semi-initiatory corporations which included many popular elements, linked together by a spirit of solidarity and comradeship, in most of the towns of Iran and Iraq. At times when the central authority had lost control, the adherents of the *futuwwa*, the *fityān* or *'ayyāruūn*, exercised a real reign of terror in the towns, even in Baghdad, over the 'rich' and the governments. When authority was strong they withdrew into the background, as they did when the Seljukids installed the military garrisons of the *shihna* in Baghdad and elsewhere, except when there was a united opposition to the rulers. But with the decline of the Seljukids, they reappeared in the thirteenth century, and men of ambition supported the *futuwwa* in order to benefit from its strength. Rather than fight against it, al-Nāsir himself also gave it his support and indeed became its Grand Master. From the moral principles

49

which it recognized he endeavoured to formulate more precise regulations, to transform it into an instrument of social solidarity. For the same reason he brought the notables into the movement and, since by an accident of documentation this happened to be the aspect of the institution which first came to the knowledge of nineteenth-century historians, it was wrongly thought that it was a kind of order of chivalry. At the same time he made use of propaganda to influence Muslim sovereigns throughout Asia to organize a similar *futuwwa* in their countries, under his personal aegis. For political reasons, many agreed to do so. The success was much wider socially in Turkish Asia Minor, where we shall come across it again, and constitutes the reason why these brief remarks have been devoted to the *futuwwa* here.

3

ART AND LETTERS IN THE SELJUKID PERIOD

Contrary to what might have been supposed, the Seljukid period is characterized in the cultural field by a new advance of the neo-Persian language. In Central Asia, among the Karakhānids, who were barely touched by Iranian influences, a new Muslim Turkish literature was born, and it had adopted the Arabic alphabet; however limited they were, the new works nevertheless betrayed a forward-looking orientation. Among the Great Seljukids established in Iran, there was no comparable movement. But, whether or not by intention, it seemed as though exception were taken to the language of the ancient ruling aristocracy, Arabic; and for that reason, and because the Turkish aristocracy had some knowledge of Persian but almost never of Arabic, the learning of Arabic was discouraged. There were, it is true, some scholars who knew Arabic, and certain branches of instruction were necessarily conducted in Arabic. In Khwārizm in particular, the life of al-Zamakhsharī, the great scholar in many fields, fell within the Seljukid period. But there can be no doubt that Persian rapidly took the place of Arabic among the mass of educated people; literary works, properly speaking, were written almost exclusively in Persian, the administration (but not justice, which is a matter of Koranic Law) now expressed itself almost exclusively in Persian, the ancient Arabic works which maintained their prestige were translated into Persian, and so on. The Irano-Turkish symbiosis led simultaneously to a de-arabization, which had in fact started in the East alone, and to a new iranization, or rather, if the word be preferred in view of the influence of that region, a new 'khorasanization'.

The history of art might also inspire somewhat similar reflections. It is a highly controversial matter to decide whether a specifically Turkish art exists, or, to put it more intelligently, to determine the measure of the purely Turkish contribution to the art which flourished in the countries which they governed and dominated politically. Leaving aside for the moment Asia Minor, which has its own particular problems, it is certain that, so far as the state of preservation of the remains allows us to form a picture of it, almost everything that was achieved in the Seljukid period had its antecedents in earlier Islamo-Iranian art. However, it is no longer permissible to doubt that, even though the condition of the archaeological discoveries may falsify certain questions of degree, the fullest achievements and the clear and precise affirmation of certain innovations date from the Seljukid period. The purely Turkish technical contributions are somewhat meagre (representations of living beings?), for the Turks of Central Asia had lacked opportunities as builders except in some limited fields (mausolea?). But in this field as in others they may have carried the practices of Transoxania or Khorasan further afield, and on the other hand, the religious policy of the Sultans and their followers, requiring the enlargement of mosques, the creation or multiplication of *madrasa*s and the like provided indigenous artists with opportunities and possibilities of action such as they had not previously, save in exceptional instances, enjoyed. And, at the start, the simple power and 'magnificence' of the new sovereigns took the same direction. There is no need here to enter into any of the technical problems, some of which will be described in relation to Asia Minor, but this general characterization had to be considered. Even when they were not creators, the Turks very often gave others the means of developing what they themselves had as yet been unable to develop.

PART TWO

Turkey in Asia Minor from the End of the Eleventh Century until 1243

I

THE SOURCES

Before the reader embarks upon the history of the Turks in Asia
Minor, it is indispensable that he should be given some indication
of the various sources, with the help of which an attempt can be
made to reconstruct it. For this purpose, the period considered in
the present work has to be divided into five sections, corresponding
broadly to the five centuries covered.

For the eleventh century (or, more exactly, the second half of
that century, which alone is relevant here), if we leave aside the
memories transmitted very much later through legend in the
Dānishmendnāme (of which more will be said later), there exists no
documentary material that derives from the Turkish milieu itself.
In so far as the Turks' penetration of and settlement in Asia
Minor are connected with the expansion of the Great Seljukids,
they find a place in the general histories devoted to them (particularly that of Sibt ibn al-Jawzī/Ghars al-Niʿma Muhammad).
But the account which follows will make it clear that, in reality,
the policy of the Great Seljukids and the Turkish expansion in
Asia Minor constitute two almost wholly independent series of
facts. Moreover, as, in Asia Minor, there was not, among the
invading Turkish peoples, any department for official correspondence, nor among the indigenous population any Muslim
element accustomed to this kind of correspondence with the
Islamic capitals, it is easy to understand that the chroniclers who
based their writings on such documents were in fact ignorant of
most of the events that occurred in the country. The indigenous
Christian population, on the other hand, was accustomed to such
correspondence or the recording of certain facts, and some recollections of them have consequently been preserved which, later,
were available either to the Armenian, the Jacobite (Syriac) and
to a lesser extent the Georgian monastic writers, or, more remotely,
to the Byzantine historians of Constantinople. Naturally, what
interested these authors was the account of the Turkish invasion,

in so far as it affected their own peoples, not a continuous history of the Turks for their own sake. Moreover, the very disorder engendered by the invasion disorganized correspondence and the preservation of the archives, with the result that, even when allowances are made for their particular points of view, there are gaps in the accounts which these authors were obliged to leave. The light cast by the historians of the First Crusade, which crossed Asia Minor, is in the same way useful but incomplete, and covers only a very short space of time.

This being said, it is necessarily with the help of these authors that we have to try to reconstruct the history of the period. Leaving aside the occasional sources which will be found listed in the Bibliography, the essential and general sources are:

For the Greeks: Cedrenus, revised and continued by Scylitzes; Michael Attaliates; Nicephorus Bryennius; and, at the beginning of the twenfth century, Anna Comnena.

For the Armenians: Matthew of Edessa, who wrote shortly before 1140.

For the (Jacobite) Syrians: Michael the Syrian, who wrote in about 1190.

For the Latins: besides the Norman Anonymous author and Raymond of Aiguilhe, who wrote only of the Crusade itself, Albert of Aix and Fulcher of Chartres, who go down to 1113 and 1118 respectively.

For the twelfth century the situation is not fundamentally different. Although a number of (Arabic) inscriptions and coins were made for the new masters, they still had no historical literature. The chronicler Ibn Bībī was later to state categorically that it was impossible to discover anything of their history before the very end of the sixth/twelfth century. In these circumstances the essential sources, after Anna Comnena, remain the Byzantine Cinnamus and Nicetas Choniates; Matthew of Edessa; and then Gregory the Priest, who continued his account; and Michael the Syrian, who was still writing. The complete break which, as we shall see, exists between Asia Minor and the Great Seljukids' successors explains why Mesopotamian literature, with the partial exception of the Universal History (the *Kāmil*) of Ibn al-Athīr (written in about 1225), contains nothing on the subject of the Seljukids of Rūm. The only Muslim authors who concerned themselves with them were the Syrians – Ibn al-Qalānisī of Damascus, in the middle of the century; his contemporary in Aleppo al-ʿAzīmī; and the great writers of Aleppo of later date, Ibn Abī Tayyī and Ibn al-ʿAdīm – and, in the extreme North of Mesopotamia, Ibn al-Azraq al-Fāriqī, in so far as Seljukid policy impinged upon the territories where they lived. There are some Greek inscriptions in the churches of Cappadocia.

From the very end of the twelfth and for the whole of the thirteenth and the early fourteenth centuries, things are somewhat better. With Ibn Bībī, an Iranian immigrant to Anatolia, we have at last an author who wrote in Persian in the actual country and who, as a member of the class of senior officials of the now organized Anatolian State, presents their point of view. In addition to his *Seljūknāme*, which stops at 1282, there were also, particularly for the second half of the century, the work with the same title by an anonymous citizen of Konya and, of especial importance down to 1292, but reaching the beginning of the fourteenth century, the chronicle of Karīm al-Dīn Aqsarāyī (a brief record only before 1243), both works again in Persian. Moreover there still survive a certain number of documents from archives, deeds for the foundation of *waqf*s, correspondence such as that of Jalāl al-Dīn Rūmī, documents of a religious nature like the *Manāqib al-ʿĀrifīn* (collected biographies of famous mystics) of Aflākī (who wrote in the fourteenth century), collections of copies of chancellery papers or models for the use of scribes – a whole group of documents which today enable us to see from within the history of some at least of the various circles composing the society of the Seljukid State of Asia Minor. The two principal dangers which have to be constantly borne in mind are, firstly, that they may lead us to take a limited view, instead of one embracing the whole group of classes in the State, and, secondly, that as for the most part they derive from the period of the Mongol Protectorate, they offer a picture of the period of Seljukid independence which may be invalidated by the new view of that period. Moreover it is important to lay stress upon the manner in which the *Seljūknāme* of Ibn Bībī should be utilized. For a long time this work was accessible only in a slightly abridged edition actually made in the author's lifetime; the complete text, which is now available, shows that omissions of substance were rare. However, to a slight extent

on account of the distrust attaching to the abridgement of Ibn
Bībī, but above all mainly because the Turkish language was
more familiar to Turcologists than was Persian, instead of the
Persian text of Ibn Bībī use was often made of the Turkish adaptation which had been produced in the fifteenth century by the
Ottoman Yazïjï-oghlu. This writer introduced into his adaptation,
which he incorporated in a more general history, some additions
and interpretations which are of interest in certain respects but
which are not found in the original text, and so must be rejected
or treated with the necessary critical reserve. This has not always
been done.

In comparison with this now considerable Muslim literature of
Asia Minor, the other sources clearly lose a little of their relative
value; they remain nonetheless important and, in terms of
absolute value, their content is even enhanced, because the
development of the Seljukid State gave it a new place on the
international scene, and its incorporation in the Mongol Empire
brought it once again into the field of vision of oriental historians
who hitherto had ignored questions concerning Asia Minor. We
cannot here enumerate all the Syrian or syro-Egyptian historians
(Syria and Egypt being politically reunited) who may occasionally
touch upon the history of Asia Minor. We shall call attention only
to the principal ones, since they have not always received adequate
emphasis, and not all of their writings have even been published:
Ibn Wāsil (in course of publication) down to 660/1262, with a
very rich fund of information on the history of Syria and its
neighbours; the biographies of Sultan Baybars by Ibn ʿAbd al-
Zāhir, the complete text of which was discovered only a few years
ago and which is still unpublished; and Ibn Shaddād, only half
of which has been discovered and made available in a Turkish
translation; and the historian of about the year 700/1300,
Baybars Mansūrī, who gives a wealth of information (derived
from a Christian secretary) concerning events in Asia Minor in
the middle of the thirteenth century. In addition to these however
there were also ʿIbn Natīf, Abd al-Latīf (in Dhahabī), Yūnīnī,
and others.

Occasional items of information continue to be found in the
Armenian chronicles, both in Azerbaijan and, above all, in
Cilicia, such as the chronicle by the so-called Royal Historian

(perhaps Sempad the Constable), as well as in the Jacobite Syriac Bar Hebraeus, who both supplemented the early parts and also continued the chronicle of Michael the Syrian as far as the end of the thirteenth century. The Georgian chronicle has some important passages, and Byzantine literature, of almost no interest for the first two-thirds of the century, becomes increasingly valuable with the Turcoman expansion towards the west in the last third of this and in the following century. Diplomatic and commercial relations with the Italians and Cypriots have left documents, to be referred to later, and Western travellers, like the missionaries Simon of Saint-Quentin and William of Rubruck or the merchant Marco Polo, and the Hispano-Arab geographer and traveller Ibn Sa'īd, have important things to tell about the country of Rūm. Finally, monumental inscriptions and coins were multiplying. It is thus a century that was relatively favoured, permitting exhaustive study.

What at first sight seems strange, the documentary situation becomes extremely bad in the fourteenth century, apart from the early years. The dismemberment of the Mongol Empire removed almost all its interest for Persian historiography, which was itself for the moment in decline, and the political division of Asia Minor caused the more general chronicles to disappear. What has so far been discovered is, in a Turkish adaptation of the fifteenth century, a chronicle covering some years of the history of the emirate of Aydïn (on the Aegean coast) in the middle of the century; another and very detailed chronicle of the reign of Burhān al-Dīn in the province of Sivas and its surroundings at the end of the century; and, though semi-legendary and not chrono-logical, an account by Shikārī of the reigns of the Karamanids (western Taurus) down to the fifteenth century, the value of which has not yet been fully established. Ottoman historiography proper, which for us does not start until the fifteenth century, touches only incidentally on the other principalities which the Ottoman Empire incorporated provisionally, and does so with obvious partiality and, what is more serious, with obvious periods of silence. The accounts of Timur's invasion give a useful picture, though a fleeting one. In these conditions, short abridged chron-ologies assume a relative interest – like the Short Chronicles of Byzantine history. And exactly the same thing is true of Armenian

6

historiography, which has no major work except an account of Timur's campaigns, but consists of brief chronological tables and colophons still almost unused. There are almost no Syriac or Georgian ones, but there is interesting Greek documentary material from Trebizond (Panaretos and others). The potentialities of the various non-historiographic works of the Muslim circles of Asia Minor have not yet been sufficiently explored, although some individual investigations reveal their possible interest. Various inscriptions and coins, deeds of *waqfs*, official letters and other material are again available, but their authenticity must be submitted to rigorous critical appraisal, some at least having obviously been forged or modified later for the greater glory of the Ottoman or occasionally some other dynasty, or in the interest of a charitable foundation or some other institution. The Italian and Venetian archives for Crete ought to be explored more thoroughly than has as yet been done, though without any too great hopes being raised; similarly those of the Hospitallers and those relating to Cyprus. In the middle of this somewhat discouraging situation there appears a twofold ray of light, which unfortunately illumines only a few years, between 1330 and 1340 – the fascinating account of the travels (through the whole country, or almost all of it) of the Hispano-Arab Ibn Baṭṭūta, and, secondly, the description of the country of Rūm inserted in the Encyclopaedia of the Egyptian official Shihāb al-Dīn Faḍl Allāh al-ʿUmarī, who was indebted for his information to an itinerant Muslim mystic and, typically enough, to an influential Genoese merchant who had become a prisoner and slave of the Mamluks in Cairo.

The situation remains more or less the same for the fifteenth century, but without anything to equal these two authors. For historiography, it was the period when each dynasty tried to give itself the chief place. Shikārī has already been mentioned. There are valuable works on the Ak-koyunlu in eastern Asia Minor. But, above all, there is the Ottoman historiography. This is at once valuable and hazardous for, even if it now reveals many facts, it presents them in its own way and plays down the history of the other principalities, except to describe their submission and annexation. However, for Asia Minor, historiography in other languages loses its importance. Some accounts by Western travellers provide useful supplementary material or summaries, from Schiltberger to the Burgundian Bertrandon de la Broquière.

For the moment, therefore, it is particularly difficult, in spite of the special interest that it would present, to write the history of the period of transition from the Seljukido-Mongol State to the Ottoman State in Asia Minor. This can only be done by bringing together, from fields far removed from one another, unrelated items whose interest often can only be seen through some interconnection which is made still more toilsome by differences of language. This is certainly not to say that one must despair, but rather that it is essential to guard against premature conclusions and that the task will be a long one. In the circumstances, the last pages of the present volume will be no more than a deliberately brief and even somewhat tentative survey, indicative more of the research still to be undertaken than of the results already achieved.

2

GEOGRAPHY OF ASIA MINOR

There is clearly no need here to give the reader a detailed geographical description of Asia Minor: nevertheless it will perhaps be helpful to make a few observations that may lead to a clearer understanding of the conditions underlying the historical facts, to which we shall then turn.

Asia Minor as we understand it here, and which broadly speaking corresponds to the territory of the present Turkish Republic without Thrace or the upper Tigris basin, can be regarded roughly as a rectangle, about 750 miles long and 300–375 wide. Its geography is dominated by the contrast between the high interior plateau, often of steppe-like character, and mountain ranges more or less parallel with the coasts, coming closer together in the east where they merge into the Armenian massif, but further apart in the west where the plateau drops down by valleys that open out to the Aegean and Mediterranean – a conformation that results in climatic differences and makes communications difficult between the sea-coast and the continental plateau, except in the west. The northern (Pontic) ranges, narrower and high in the east, become broader and lower in the west, and are separated by long valleys linked together by the rivers which, changing direction abruptly, flow through transverse gorges. The southern ranges, which are more rugged and follow a more varied pattern, for the most part of arid calcareous formations, in the west enclose a number of valleys which run down from north to south to the Mediterranean, while in the centre and east they form a lofty range, the Taurus, which increases in height in a S.W.-N.E. direction towards Armenia, separating the narrow interior plateau from the middle Euphrates basin and the Syro-Mesopotamian Fertile Crescent. In the east, western Armenia for the most part consists of two elevated longitudinal valleys, those of the two Euphrates, to the north the Kara Su, continued by the Araxes (which flows towards Iran), to the south the Murad Su, continued by Lake Van, valleys separated by lofty mountain ranges, partly volcanic, culminating in the famous Ararat (nearly 17,000 ft. in altitude). Eastern Armenia, sloping towards Azerbaijan, is of no concern here. To the west the plateau, here wider, comprises Anatolia properly speaking: it is cut off from the eastern plateaux by the high volcanic massif of Erciyas/Argaeus, to the north of the middle Taurus, to which it is joined.

The mountains in the south-east and, in particular, the Pontic range along the Black Sea coast have a high rainfall which is favourable for forests. At the eastern end of the Black Sea these are in fact luxuriant. At a higher altitude are pasturages of an alpine type. In the drier interior, where temperatures present a violent contrast between summer and winter, the landscape is mostly steppe-like and consequently well-suited for a nomadic pastoral economy. Agriculture is possible in the river-valleys which can be irrigated, and over most of the western valleys. The social conditions, upon which depends closely the upkeep of works of development and plantations, in certain periods and regions could bring about large-scale transformations, as a study of the economy of the Seljukid State will show.

In view of this geographical structure, the main natural and historic routes are orientated east-west, in particular the one from the Araxes by the northern Euphrates, which then follows the inner edge of the Pontic ranges along the upper course of the Kïzïl Irmak and finally reaches the Straits. To the south, it has its counterpart in the more mountainous route which runs from Lake Van along the southern Euphrates and the northern edge of the Taurus, to reach the Anatolian plateau. But there this route alters course to join another, not explained by regional geography but required for communication between the Straits and Syria – the route which runs N.W.-S.E. across the Anatolian plateau, partly through steppe, then crosses the Taurus to Cilicia, climbing again over the small parallel range of the Amanus and dropping down once more to Syria. At certain periods, some transverse routes were added to these or driven across them, linking some port on the Mediterranean or the Black Sea with the interior, in spite of the difficulties of the mountainous terrain – Erzurum to Trebizond at the eastern end of the Black Sea, or Sivas to Samsun or Sinope further to the west, or Konya and the Anatolian plateau to Antalya on the Mediterranean, to the north-west of Cyprus.

The reconstruction of the history and historical topography of a land such as Asia Minor encounters very considerable difficulties from the fact that most of the place-names have changed in the course of time, with the language of the dominant peoples. It even happens that certain authors, contemporaries of one another but writing in different languages and representing different traditions, use different names for the same place. We cannot here embark upon exhaustive discussions of the specific and particular problems raised by this situation, but it must be made clear that it does exist. We give some particulars in the bibliography for those who wish to study the question. In the text of the narrative we shall give, wherever it seems necessary, both the Byzantine form which usually goes back to the classical period, and the Turkish form which is to be found on modern maps.

ASIA MINOR ON THE EVE OF THE ARRIVAL OF THE TURKS

The conquest of Asia Minor by the Turks and its transformation into the country of 'Turkey' has always appeared to Europeans to constitute without question something at once incomprehensible, inadmissible and slightly outrageous. This is no more so than the establishment of Hungary in Pannonia, or of the Slav states in Illyria. We begin with the assumption that Asia Minor in the middle of the eleventh century must still have been, apart from some points of detail, the highly urbanized, cultivated and Hellenized Asia Minor of Roman times. Even for Antiquity, this idea is an over-simplification. Geographical conditions have never permitted the same degree of development of this kind in central and eastern Anatolia as in the provinces facing the Aegean. But, whatever the exact position may have been, the subsequent wars against the Persians and Arabs had profoundly changed the face of the country. For generations, vast areas, particularly on both sides of the Taurus and Cappadocia, had suffered from retaliatory raids, plundering and devastation. On both sides, the existence of a no man's land had at times been regarded as the best defence against the enemy, not to speak of massacres, such as that of the Paulician heretics by the Byzantines in the ninth century in the region of Divriği/Tephrike. When, on the other hand, an attempt was made to repopulate certain zones, it was necessarily by means of imported populations which, in the case of the Byzantines and depending on their reconquest, were often Slav or Bulgar, and were, of course, of a military character. These frontier-dwellers – Byzantine *akritai* and Muslim *ghāzīs* – though fighting against each other, were alike in their physical and spiritual isolation from the governments, which took almost no part in their activities, and as a result they sometimes almost fraternized. Evidence of this is provided in the chivalrous romances or poems which recount the exploits of both sides, and it will suffice here to cite the romance of Sayyid Battāl Ghāzī, on account of its subsequent interest for Turkish history. When, little by little, the encroachments of the great land-owners had destroyed the small peasant-military properties of these frontier-dwellers, they lost interest in the defence of the country, and some even went over into the service of the other side. In any case, so far as Byzantium was concerned, in the eleventh century they were nothing more than private troops enrolled by the great land-owners, with the result that the State, being suspicious of the latter, preferred to engage mercenary troops wholly foreign to the country. In the north-east of Asia Minor, Byzantium had always kept a foothold in Armenia, and the Armenians had played a considerable part in the Byzantine Empire. At the end of the tenth century and the beginning of the eleventh, Byzantium had progressively annexed the principalities of Armenia as far as the borders of Azerbaijan, and eliminated the small Muslim emirates which had been established among them without subjugating them. As far as the geographical situation allowed, Armenia was populated and, despite internal quarrels, a kind of patriotism flourished there. As annexations were made, the Byzantine Government preferred to replace the Armenian frontier troops by a regular Byzantine army, and to install important Armenian families, with their dependents, in regions in the interior to repopulate them. In this way Armenians can be seen populating Cappadocia, Cilicia, various provinces of northern Syria and the Mesopotamian border territories, such as Edessa. The advantage gained was clear in some respects, but apart from the fact that these Armenians were divided among themselves, as they had been in their own country, they introduced an additional element of disunion wherever they were in contact with other and longer-established populations. Moreover the different Christian Churches in the East had never succeeded in becoming reconciled with one another, and those possessing adherents in Muslim countries had been entirely freed from the Byzantine tutelage of the early Middle Ages. When Byzantium re-annexed territories occupied by Armenians, Jacobites and others, the Orthodox Church resorted to harassing tactics against the rest, even going so far, for instance, as to intern ecclesiastical leaders, as a result of which disaffection increased.

65

Finally, in the Byzantine army of mercenaries, which included Scandinavians, Turks and Normans, christianized and civilized in varying degrees but in any event strangers to the country, there was again no lack of internal dissensions. All this shows clearly, without it being necessary to go into detail, that with the exception of the maritime provinces and some other isolated districts (especially in Cappadocia), Asia Minor was no longer what it had been and was incapable of offering a solid or united front to resist a foreign danger.

The technique of warfare added to these weaknesses. It is true that the Byzantine army had powerful equipment, but, for that very reason, it lacked the mobility to be able to dart forward instantly to check or pursue enemy razzias. It held fortresses at what were said to be the strategic points, but it maintained insufficient watch between these points, nor were there adequate reserves outside Constantinople in the event of an invasion succeeding in penetrating in depth. In some respects therefore the Byzantine army was powerless to act against the type of adversary whose strength essentially lay in his extreme mobility, and who passed unconcerned between the fortified places. It is true that the Byzantine army had to some extent come across this feature among the Muslim *ghāzīs*, but in Asia it had had no experience of any invaders who possessed it to such a degree as the Turks. And equally, in battle tactics, the effects of the calculated crushing blow aimed at by the Byzantine army lost all efficacy in the face of troops who were perpetually in movement, making use of ambushes, feigned flights and a rain of arrows falling from all sides.

4

THE FIRST INCURSIONS BEFORE 1071

The Turkish penetration of Asia Minor falls into two clearly distinct periods. Until Manzikert (1071) and leaving aside the frontier strongholds held by the Seljukid Sultans themselves, it was a matter of razzias of ever increasing depth, followed however by the raiders' return to bases in the east without any attempt to establish themselves, apart from some exceptional cases of enrolment in the Byzantine army itself. After Manzikert, not on account of any change of policy by the Sultans, but simply because the whole strength of the Byzantine resistance crumbled away, the former raiding-parties stayed on, as yet with no idea beyond living on the country, but by the mere fact of their presence they progressively altered its character.

The *ghāzīs* of the early period, it will be remembered, were not so much contingents sent by the Sultans (unless it was a matter involving only the frontier zones) as Turcomans, either virtually independent or even outlawed by the Seljukid authorities. More-over, Seljukid troops were sometimes sent in pursuit of them to bring them to heel. For these *ghāzīs*, some of whom were fugitives, Asia Minor, an integral part of the 'Roman' Empire, the country of Rūm, was indeed a country where there were livestock and captives to be taken, where men could enjoy the occasional satis-faction of killing infidels, and later graze their herds and hold the peasants to ransom. Nonetheless it was also an undisputed place of refuge, and although there was generally no question of sub-mitting to any kind of Byzantine authority, even so they knew that they were in Rūm, the territory or, rather, entity which possessed a kind of eternity just as real as that of the Empire of Islam, now its enemy. And there was no question of bringing to an end either its existence in principle, or even the administrative organization, strictly speaking, inasmuch as it applied to others besides the Turcomans. The idea of replacing it by some other new state was absolutely foreign to them.

The principal episodes of the Turkish penetration in the period before Manzikert have already been described briefly in the general history of the Great Seljukids. The first warning, which preceded these, came on the Armeno-Byzantine frontiers in 1029, and the Armenian historians on that occasion describe the invaders' long hair and tactics of fighting with mounted archers, hitherto unknown to them. This appearance has often been put at an earlier date, and linked with the cession to Byzantium of his kingdom by the king of Vaspouragan. But the earlier date seems to be impossible, and if it is realized that the Armenian authors explained this humiliating cession by the motive which in fact later led to the cession of other principalities, and when allowance is made for the aggressiveness of the Kurdish princes of north-western Iran, this cession is explained clearly enough by the pressure exerted by the Byzantine Emperor Basil II, who had planned it long beforehand. The first Turcoman threat to occur after 1029 came in 1043, this time from the south, from the region of the sources of the Tigris, and was brought about by the same Turcomans who were now fleeing before the Seljukid advance, and were finally decimated. One group of them however forced the Byzantine frontier, and defeated and captured the Byzantine governor Likhoudes.

It was only a few years later that the real Seljukid pressure on the Byzantine frontiers started – or rather pressure from Turcomans more or less commanded by the Seljukids. At that moment Byzantium had just annexed the Armenian kingdom of Ani, partly on account of the threat posed by the Kurdish Shaddādid prince of Ganja and Dvin, Abu'l-Aswar, whose aggressiveness may perhaps have been increased by the enrolment of some Turcomans. A razzia led by a relative of the Sultan, this time starting from Azerbaijan but striking southwards, was destroyed by the Byzantine generals Aron and Katakalon in 1045 or early in 1046. But, in 1048, a larger force was led by Tughrïl-Beg's foster-brother Ibrāhīm Inal, this time straight to the west, following the classic invasion route along the Araxes and the upper northern Euphrates (Kara Su). Fanning out to plunder from the southern Euphrates (Murad Su) to the hinterland of Trebizond, the Turks reached Erzurum, which underwent an appalling sack. Some of the Byzantine troops had been recalled to check a revolt. The others, with the governors of Iberia (Georgian borders), Vaspouragan and 'Mesopotamia' (between the Murad Su and the Kara Su) and the 'Iberian' prince Liparit, tried to surprise the Turks on their return; but they managed to break through, and took Liparit prisoner. The chroniclers date the start of the Turkish incursions from this year, and contemporaries, in particular the Armenian Arisdagues of Lasdivert, can find no words to describe the full extent of the catastrophe. The reprisals organized, probably soon afterwards, by the Byzantines against Abu'l-Aswar, who had by then complied with Seljukid policy, naturally left the principal danger untouched. At the same time the Byzantine Government was trying to negotiate with the Sultan, but we have already described the degree of illusion which such approaches necessarily implied.

In 1054 it was Tughrïl-Beg himself who attacked Byzantine Armenia. No doubt for him it was a question of bringing the petty princes of north-western Iran under his effective suzerainty, and at the same time maintaining his hold over the Turcomans who had remained on the Armeno-Georgian borders, with his cousin Kutlumush and other chiefs. Nevertheless, his aim was apparently different from the Turcomans', namely to reconquer for Islam the ancient frontier fortresses annexed by Byzantium a little earlier. While his light troops went off to plunder almost the identical regions visited six years earlier by Ibrāhīm Inal's men, he himself captured Arjīsh and Bergri on Lake Van, and then laid siege to the important strategic fortress of Manzikert on the Murad Su route. But he was not in a position to sustain operations for a long time; negotiations were re-opened, eventually concluding in a truce as fragile as the preceding one. His prestige had not suffered, and it was in the following year that he entered Baghdad.

Many Turcomans however remained on the Byzantine borders. The details of each year's incidents on the frontiers are not always easy to ascertain, and it may be that some of them are not known. A later allusion, for example, makes us attribute some activities on the approaches to Georgian territory to a certain Tughtegin, about whom however we have no direct knowledge. It can hardly be doubted that a state of war, though on a minor scale, continued almost without interruption, but we hear only of its most spectacular manifestations. Those who had participated in the first phase were joined by others, who had come from the east at the time of Inal's revolt or were drawn by the lure of plunder and adventure, such as Yākūtī, known as the Salār of Khorasan, son of Chagrï-Beg and brother of Alp Arslan. And if perhaps an event such as Inal's revolt could momentarily relax the Turcoman pressure, revolts in Byzantium, for example the almost contemporaneous revolt of Isaac Comnenus, equally reduced defensive vigilance on the Armenian frontier; not to speak of disagreements between the Armenians themselves, between contingents of different nationalities, and others. In this way we are told of a destructive raid by a certain Samoukht (?), around the Araxes-Murad Su route, with the complicity of the Franco-Norman Hervé (1055 or 1066). Then Ivane, Liparit's son, fighting against Katakalon, who had taken the side of Isaac Comnenus, called in the Turks to plunder in the mountains of Trebizond and Khanzit (at the confluence of the two Euphrates, the Murad Su and the Kara Su), in 1057. Some months later, possibly the same bands plundered Shebin Karahisār/Kughūniya (Colonia) and Kamakh on the northern route, while, in the South, a certain Dinar reached Malatya/Melitene which in turn underwent a terrible sack. It is true that, on the return journey, the Armenian chief of the Sassūn, Thornig, surprised and killed Dinar and his men, but this mishap was something far too exceptional to discourage their successors. The whole of Armenia was subsequently pillaged, and since it was found to be advantageous to go still farther in search of booty, Samoukht and others, taking the northern route, succeeded in attacking Sivas (1059 or 1060). In 1062, taking a new direction, Yākūtī raided the edge of the Byzantine territories between the sources of the Tigris and Euphrates below Malatya, and went to sell his prisoners in the Marwānid town of Āmid (Diyār Bakr). This town was punished by the Greeks, and on the return Hervé destroyed a group led by a certain Yūsuf, but the greatest number of the Turcomans once again escaped (1063).

On becoming Sultan, Alp Arslan in his turn proceeded to a show of strength in Armenia, for the same reasons as Tughrïl before him. It was the Araxes valley and the intermediate regions between Armenia and Georgia which seem to have interested him most. He undertook the conquest of various fortresses, then laid siege to the great Armenian capital Ani, which stood in isolation amidst its ravaged surroundings. The resistance was vigorous, but finally, perhaps with the help of an earthquake, the town fell, and was then sacked and given to a Shaddādid. The king of Georgia gave one of his daughters to the Sultan, various lords made their submission, and Kars, which had already been attacked several times and which its prince had just given to Byzantium, now in its turn, in obscure circumstances, fell into Seljukid hands (1064). From that time, the frontier was re-adjusted, to constitute a solid base for the Turcomans' attacks and to hinder any Byzantine counter-attacks in depth. The campaign conducted by Alp Arslan three or four years later against Georgia was not to modify this state of affairs, nor is it of concern here.

That Alp Arslan made no further attacks on Byzantium is perhaps because Byzantium had once again negotiated with him – though again in vain in regard to the Turcomans who intensified their earlier attacks. Those of them who were operating in some measure of agreement with the Sultan confined themselves to storming the frontier fortresses recently acquired by the Greeks to the South of the middle Euphrates or eastern Taurus. This was done by Yākūtī who, aided by quarrels between the Greeks of Antioch and Edessa, reached the latter town in 1065, before meeting his death on the return journey in the Marwānid capital of Mayāfāriqīn, where the prince had treacherously invited him. It was also done by the *hājib* (chamberlain) Gümüshtegin in 1067. They thus marked out the way for Alp Arslan's Syrian campaign in 1070–71. But other chiefs acted without the Sultan's consent, and, while attacking the country of Rūm to force an entry and find a source of livelihood, they also sought a place of refuge as remote as possible. This was true of Afshin, a subordinate of Gümüshtegin, who, after killing him in a private quarrel, went away to sack Kayseri/Caesarea, spent a short time in Cilicia and Byzantine Syria and, while a Byzantine army was attacking the province of Aleppo, made his way across its rear to Asia Minor. There he went northwards to attack Niksar/Neocaesarea and even Amorium, incredibly far to the west, in western Anatolia; after which, returning to the East, he obtained pardon from his master the Sultan in view of these exploits (1067–8). Others took up the struggle, and while Philaretes, the Armeno-Byzantine leader and governor of Malatya, was unable to stop them, they once more penetrated into Anatolia behind the Greek army, which was then occupied with overcoming the Franco-Norman Crispin in Armenia. They sacked Konya/Iconium and returned through Cilicia, while the Duke of Antioch failed to destroy them (1069). Finally, in 1070, as has been said, Alp Arslan's brother-in-law Erisgen, when fleeing from his wrath, repulsed the Greek general Manuel Comnenus near Sivas. It is true that he then entered the service of the Byzantines, but Afshin, who had been sent in pursuit of him on account of the knowledge of the country he had acquired, being unable to have the rebel handed over to him, devastated the whole region as he passed, reached Chonaï, and left his contemporaries with the impression that he had been 'as far as the sea of Constantinople'. He succeeded in returning to the east without hindrance, early in 1071. It was at that moment that the Basileus Romanus Diogenes, the same who had led the army into the province of Aleppo, anxious to strike a powerful direct blow at Azerbaijan through Armenia, started out on the campaign which was to end in the conclusive disaster of Manzikert.

However deep and destructive the raids made up to this point may have been, it must be repeated that, except in the case of fugitives, the raiders had no purpose other than to collect plunder and seek out warlike adventures. There was no question of remaining in the country, and each time, their plundering accomplished, they returned to their northern Iranian bases from ever increasing distances. Manzikert was to change the whole situation. Henceforward, there would no longer be any need to return, they could remain without danger, and indeed, since the Byzantine factions relied on these newcomers, even with profit. As was said earlier, Alp Arslan did not envisage the fall of Rūm. This was in fact brought about gradually, almost by force of circumstances.

5

FROM MANZIKERT TO THE FIRST CRUSADE
(1071–97)

It is impossible to reconstruct the situation in Asia Minor in the years following Manzikert and the death of Romanus Diogenes. Contingents that to some extent were officially Byzantine still remained, even as far afield as Armenia, but, in the absence of any control or liaison, in practice they operated in their own interests or those of their leaders; and among them, even in the centre of the country, were bands of Turks, equally uncontrolled and operating as they pleased. The two sides, Byzantines and Turks, alternated between warfare and negotiation, and, no doubt by chance, the memory of certain episodes has survived while others remain unknown. There is no reason to suppose that Alp Arslan, who had gone to the east, or, after his sudden death, his young son Malik-Shāh and Nizām al-Mulk, the latter's tutor and vizier, modified the policy of non-annexation defined earlier. Since Michael VII, the new Emperor in Constantinople, had seized power from Romanus, the treaty between Alp Arslan and Romanus had probably lapsed and it was necessary, on the Seljukid side, to give a free hand or even occasionally to show encouragement to those bands of Turks who were able to enter Anatolia on the pretext of seeking revenge. On the other side Michael VII reopened negotiations with Malik-Shāh, since this formed an essential part of his policy, and the Sultan could not allow complete freedom to these bands which, being in foreign territory, were in a position to renounce his authority. No doubt it is in the light of these interdependent considerations that we have to interpret the story of the quarrels between the leader of the Frankish mercenaries, Roussel, various Turks, and Michael VII, or rather his generals. Roussel's 'treason' led to the capture of Isaac Comnenus by the Turks, to the west of Ankara. In opposition to Michael, Roussel put forward the latter's uncle who had been sent against him, with the result that Michael, to meet this threat, summoned to the outskirts of Nicomedia, near the Bosphorus, a Turkish leader who was later to play a prominent part in Upper Mesopotamia and Syria, Artuk, who here makes his first appearance in history. As he afterwards appeared under the command of Malik-Shāh, it is possible – though it cannot be stated categorically – that he was then in Asia Minor with the Sultan's approval, for the purpose of hunting down or rounding up other Turks. But on this occasion it was Artuk who set Roussel free. The Byzantine general Alexis Comnenus bribed a new Turkish leader who is less clearly identified and with whose help he succeeded in having Roussel handed over to himself, near Amasya; nevertheless Alexis had the greatest difficulty in escaping from other Turks near Kastamonu. And, at the same time, still other Turks were in the suburbs of Trebizond and even in Miletus on the Aegean (1073–4).

It is very shortly after this that we hear for the first time of the four sons of Kutlumush, one of whom was later to found the

Seljukid dynasty of Rūm. Paradoxically, this was due to an intervention on behalf of the Fātimids against Atsïz in Syria, which serves to remind us of the position of this branch of the family. which was possibly heterodox and certainly indifferent to orthodoxy. We are told that they came from Rūm and, when defeated, that it was to Rūm that they returned. In order to explain the Fātimid appeal, however, it may be surmised that they lived on the southern borders, somewhere in the region of the middle Taurus or even further to the south, a circumstance which perhaps confers a certain reality upon the legendary accounts transmitted by later works in which they are represented, after their father's death, as having been deported by Alp Arslan to the Syro-Euphrates borders. The later authors, influenced by the official version promulgated under the Seljukids of Rūm in the thirteenth century, would have us believe that, at the time of his accession, Malik-Shāh officially accorded the country of Rūm to his cousins, the sons of Kutlumush. It is true that Malik-Shāh seems in general to have favoured the establishment of frontier apanages for the most important of his relatives. But in this case there is no evidence of any such policy, and the pro-Fātimid episode just referred to, as well as others to be noted later, makes this version improbable. It is likely that the sons of Kutlumush managed to escape from surveillance at the time of Alp Arslan's death, and they took refuge beyond the frontier, among the Turcomans who remembered their father.

Having proved victorious, Atsïz sent two of the sons of Kutlumush whom he had captured, to Malik-Shāh, with whom he was anxious to establish closer relations. Shortly afterwards, in 1079, Malik-Shāh despatched his brother Tutush to Syria to supplant Atsïz. During the interval, apparently, according to the sole source Bar Hebraeus, he had also sent Bursuq, an old officer of his and a former military governor of Baghdad, to Asia Minor against the two remaining Seljukids, Mansūr and Sulaymān. He succeeded in killing Mansūr, but not in killing Sulaymān or destroying his forces. And perhaps the unification of the command in favour of Sulaymān helped to strengthen his position.

The first Turks mentioned, those led by Artuk and others, seem to have penetrated westwards particularly by the northern routes, and the Seljukids by the southern ones. But just as the Turks in the north did not represent the only force there, so the Seljukids did not hold the whole southern side of the Taurus, particularly in the region where the Armenian Philaretes, the former general of Romanus Diogenes, was to establish his principality. The events of 1078 had perhaps freed him temporarily from their threat. In Asia Minor, Nicephorus Botaniates, a former comrade in arms of Romanus Diogenes and Philaretes, had led a revolt against Michael VII, and he left Philaretes a free hand from the Cilician Taurus to Edessa and Malatya/Melitene by way of Marʿash, Antioch, and elsewhere. Nicephorus must certainly have had more troops, and there were others, hostile to him, in Malatya, under Nicephorus Melissenes. In Constantinople Erisgen/Chrysosculos, now a Byzantine, supported Botaniates. Against him, Michael VII appealed to the sons of Kutlumush, but Erisgen – whose adherence to Byzantium thus did not damn him irreparably in their eyes – won them back to the side of Botaniates, to whom they paid homage (thereby in a sense making themselves also Byzantines). Thus they established themselves near the Straits, making the Asiatic side inaccessible. Nor did they withdraw, since Botaniates needed their help in Europe against a rival, Nicephorus Bryennius, though this does not seem to have prevented them from supporting Melissenes who had revolted in Asia and who, in his turn, approached the Bosphorus. They were still only in the country areas but he threw open the towns to them, Nicaea in particular, which at that time they would never have been able to occupy by themselves. Melissenes failed, it is true, and Alexis Comnenus, the most recent to revolt, overthrew Botaniates with the help of some Turks, among others, and set out to liberate the region of the Straits; but he was attacked in Europe by the Normans, and so compelled to make peace with the Seljukids in order to obtain assistance. Even beyond the Straits, the whole Aegean coast was in its turn overrun.

In the same period, the Byzantine texts begin to employ the term 'Sultan' to designate Sulaymān. He had not of course received this title either from Malik-Shāh, who regarded himself as the sole Sultan, or from the Caliph, the only source of legitimate titles, who was 'protected' by Malik-Shāh. But there is nothing to prevent us thinking that, as happened in many other instances,

75

Sulaymān's men started to call him by this name, without either his wanting it or even asking his Byzantine allies to give him the title, or indeed reviving it in order to recall the former rivalry between his father and the other Seljukid branch, as his son Kïlïj Arslan was to do after him. At all events it can be accepted that Sulaymān was regarded by a certain number of Turcoman groups in Asia Minor as their chief, though without it being possible to specify which ones or within which territorial limits, in so far as this expression had any meaning for them.

In any case, it is now clear that it was the Byzantines themselves who encouraged the Turks to advance further than they would have done at once of their own accord, and provided their leaders with the basis of solid power by throwing open to them towns which would have held out within their walls, at least for a time: thenceforward Nicaea was Sulaymān's capital. Internal quarrels among the Byzantines were the cause, but there is also a question of mentality which will have to be borne in mind on various occasions, and which perhaps should be taken into account. It does not appear that the Byzantines regarded the Turks as enemies in the full sense, as they did the Arabs. They had known them for a long time and used them in their army, and had assimilated them into their population. Those in Asia Minor were Muslims, but their Islam might still seem to be of no importance, as something new and primitive, without mosques, scholars or the Arabic language. In time they would be absorbed, in the way that Byzantium had absorbed many peoples. And the temporary loss of central Asia Minor, costly as it was, mattered little so long as the ports which were a source of profit held out.

Again, it was partly through Byzantine policy that Sulaymān was able to establish, if not an actual kingdom, at least a certain domination over the approaches from the Bosphorus to northern Syria. Alexis Comnenus could not look favourably on the maintenance of the sovereignty of Philaretes, the former ally of Botaniates; and in Antioch the clans were divided between supporters and opponents of the Armeno-Greek general. Although the texts say nothing explicitly as to the cause, it is not impossible that the new Basileus concluded an agreement with Sulaymān which in practice abandoned central and eastern Asia Minor to him, the territories of Philaretes and other adversaries. Apart from ridding himself to good purpose of enemies held to be even more dangerous, Alexis, in a more Machiavellian way, could perhaps have been counting on the advantage of diverting the Turks' attention from the Bosphorus; and perhaps he found it preferable to give Sulaymān an extensive command, thus enabling him to keep control over the Turcomans, rather than to endure the eroding effects of marauding bands, plundering at their will. The introduction of the title of Sultan may thus be not unconnected with these considerations. Taken in isolation, all this is hypothetical, but it would fit in well enough with the sequence of events, either those that followed immediately or with their aftermath as far as the twelfth century – not to anticipate, three centuries in advance, subsequent Byzantine policy towards the first Ottomans and their rivals.

However that may be, Sulaymān, leaving his subordinate and relative Abu'l-Qāsim in Nicaea and going beyond Konya, which he was later to possess, in 1084 occupied Cilicia, for which he sought a *cadi* from the Prince-cadi of Tripoli 'Ibn Ammār. This latter, a member of the non-Ismā'īlī Shī'ī branch of Islam, took a neutral part in the politico-religious interplay between Baghdad and Cairo, and the merchants of his port, which at that time was very active, no doubt had much traffic with the Cilician ports. It was at this point, when he had just occupied Cilicia, that Sulaymān received from Antioch an appeal from one of the native factions that was hostile to Philaretes. Without striking a blow he was able to enter the Christian metropolis of Syria, just as he had entered Nicaea a little earlier, and with some measure of Byzantine authorization. Nonetheless, the conquest acquired a certain celebrity in the Muslim world with the news that St Peter's cathedral had been converted into a mosque, and perhaps even some popularity among non-Orthodox Christians, who were given two churches earlier refused them by the Greek Church, to which Philaretes belonged. It is possible that Sulaymān took advantage of the event to attempt a rapprochement with Malik-Shāh, as one or two authors claim, but the matter is very doubtful, and in any case the course of events was to spare Malik-Shāh the difficulty of having to decide what policy to follow. To Muslim ibn Quraysh, the Arab prince of Aleppo who was more or less the vassal of Malik-Shāh, and who had demanded from him (Sulaymān), on

77

the grounds that he was a Byzantine governor, the continuation
of the tribute that Byzantium had paid, Sulaymān replied not
only by refusing it as being a Muslim and a vassal of the Sultan,
but also by himself claiming, as governor of the province as defined
in Byzantine terms, some fortresses which had formed part of it
and which the people of Aleppo had recently taken. In the war
that followed, Muslim was killed and Sulaymān laid siege to
Aleppo. As we have seen, the inhabitants called in Malik-Shāh
and, pending his arrival, his brother Tutush who was nearer at
hand in Damascus. The last-named had just been joined by a
familiar figure, Artuk, who meanwhile had been warring in the
Persian Gulf and Mesopotamia, both in the cause of Malik-Shāh
and in his own interests. In the battle between Sulaymān and the
army of Tutush, in which Artuk took the lead, Sulaymān was
killed (1086). At the request of Christians and Muslims of all
kinds, all of whom now longed above all for the restoration of
order, Malik-Shāh was able, as was described earlier, to acquire
without any difficulty the combined inheritance of Sulaymān, in
Syria, and of Muslim and Philaretes (apart from Marʿash, and
while retaining Christian governors in Malatya and Edessa). It is
not clear why Sulaymān's vizier in Antioch preferred to submit
to Malik-Shāh, handing over to him his late master's young son,
Kïlïj Arslan, as a hostage, rather than withdraw to Nicaea or
elsewhere: did he think he could not win acceptance by Abu'l-
Qāsim or others?

It is at about this period that we first hear of certain leaders to
whom Sulaymān's death possibly brought increased importance.
One of them, in southern Cappadocia, was a certain Buldaji,
brother of Abu'l-Qāsim, and perhaps identical with one Hasan,
who is heard of in the same region a little later and who indeed
appears to have given his name to the mountain still known as
Hasan Dagh. The sparseness and vagueness of the documents
and the conflict between statements by reliable historians and
legendary details collected together in the *Dānishmendnāme* (see
p. 82) make it difficult to give a more exact account. As for
northern Asia Minor, it is *a fortiori* impossible to tell if Dānishmend, who was very soon to be in that region, was in fact already
there.

However that may be, it seems possible nevertheless to discern some at least of the main features of the policy of Alexis Comnenus on the one side and of Malik-Shāh on the other, towards the Turks of Asia Minor. Malik-Shāh had no greater wish than his father to annex the 'country of Rūm'; but, regarding himself as head of all the Turks; he wished to intervene everywhere, and particularly in those places where Turkish groups or leaders were likely to set themselves up as independent powers in rivalry with him. For Asia Minor, where it was clearly in the interests of the Byzantines also to restrict the Turcomans, Malik-Shāh tried to simplify the task by an agreement with Alexis Comnenus. The latter's ideas seem to have been more vague or more tortuous. The alliance with Malik-Shāh appeared to him perhaps to conceal dangers, if not impossible demands (when marriages were mentioned). Perhaps, as well, he was not fully aware of the divisions among the Turks themselves, and therefore did not believe in the possibility of disrupting them, or, on the contrary, he may have thought that he could make use of various assimilated Turks against Malik-Shāh, whom he considered to be dangerous. And so, while not refusing to take advantage of the Sultan's interventions, he put off concluding the proposed treaty until eventually the Sultan died.

Within this general framework, the principal known facts are as follows. For Malik-Shāh, the essential point lay in the consolidation of his authority in Azerbaijan and Arrān, where his Kurdish vassal in Ganja had revolted. The country was divided into military 'fiefs' under the command of his old officer Sarhang Savtegin and, after his death, of Būzān. The importance of the position was twofold: on the one hand, it faced the Georgians, whose aggressiveness was shown particularly by a temporary occupation of Kars; on the other hand, as Azerbaijan remained the ethnic base of the Turks of Asia Minor, any influence over them presupposed a firm hold over that country. Since Būzān was governor of Edessa and intervened in Asia Minor, as will be seen, it is fair to assume that Malik-Shāh had entrusted Būzān with a general command over the north-western frontiers and affairs in Asia Minor, in the same way that Malik-Shāh's son Barkyārūk was later to appoint Ismā'īl, son of Yākūtī.

For Alexis, the main problem was now presented by Abu'l-Qāsim. Anticipating by two hundred years the emirs of the fourteenth century, and possibly helped by certain natives who by tradition were devoted to a maritime life, Abu'l-Qāsim had established himself firmly on the shores of the Aegean, where he had built up a fleet. Alexis succeeded in holding him in check, with the help of a Byzantinized Turk Tatikios (who will reappear), and aided by the fact that, immediately after the capture of Antioch, Malik-Shāh simultaneously despatched against him Bursuk who already knew the country. At the same time, Malik-Shāh asked Alexis for an alliance, by the terms of which he would, so far as he could, have withdrawn the Turks from western and maritime Asia Minor. Alexis took advantage of the embassy to secure the restitution of Sinope which had fallen into the hands of a certain Kategin, at what date we do not know. Alexis thought it a clever move to bribe the ambassador by making him a Byzantine duke and, regarding Bursuk as more dangerous than Abu'l-Qāsim, to accede to the latter's request for reconciliation. Abu'l-Qāsim was received in Constantinople and then in Nicaea, which had been reinforced against Bursuk. The latter had to retreat, probably not without the tribute to which another source refers, although not mentioning the occasion (1087?).

Malik-Shāh however did not give up. In 1092, it was Būzān who was entrusted with a campaign against Abu'l-Qāsim, and also with an offer to Alexis of a formal alliance: a daughter of Alexis was to marry a son of Malik-Shāh; the whole Anatolian territory from Nicaea to Antioch, that is to say the whole territory formerly held by Sulaymān, was to be restored to Byzantium; and, in order to procure the subjection of the Turcomans, the Sultan was to place at the disposal of the Basileus whatever forces he should need. Būzān was unable to reduce Nicaea, but occupied enough of Abu'l-Qāsim's territories to make him think it prudent to go to Malik-Shāh and seek his pardon: the Sultan sent him to come to terms with Būzān, who had him strangled. Alexis, for his part, though unable as a Christian to accept the idea of the marriage, this time did respond to the approach. Unfortunately his ambassador, while on his way, heard of Malik-Shāh's death. He returned, Būzān retired to Edessa, and Abu'l-Qāsim's brother Buldaji, coming in haste from Cappadocia, succeeded him in Nicaea without difficulty (1092–3).

Just as, on the death of Alp Arslan, the sons of Kutlumush had made their appearance in Asia Minor, so on the death of Malik-Shāh, Sulaymān's son, Kïlïj Arslan, in his turn succeeded in escaping. He was somehow able to get himself acknowledged by most of his father's former officers, and to establish himself in Nicaea. The disintegration of the Seljukid Empire which followed Malik-Shāh's death, put a stop to any attempt to intervene in Asia Minor (in this respect Ismāʿīl's command was deprived of all real significance, with the possible exception of Armenia). The Turks who were there, were thus able to carry on their activities quite independently of their cousins in the East. It is unnecessary to lay stress once again upon the part taken by the Byzantine Government in the situation.

This remained largely unchanged from the coming of Kïlïj Arslan until the arrival of the Crusaders. The harassing of Byzantium by land and sea was continued, if not by the new sultan in person, at least by his subordinates. Alexis had to make two campaigns to dislodge one of them, Il-Khān the Beglerbeg, from Apollonia ad Rhyndacum and Cyzicus. Another, Chaka, whose exploits were to leave a lasting memory since they were later alluded to in the *Dānishmendnāme*, settled on the coast of the Aegean at Clazomenae, Phocaea and Smyrna, proceeded on his own account to build up a fleet with native sailors, landed on the islands of Chios, Mitylene and Samos, and closed the Dardanelles by Abydos, among other achievements. Most serious of all was that Constantinople was threatened at that moment, from the European side, by kinsmen of the Turks sweeping down from the Russian steppe and the lower Danube, the Pechenegs, and Chaka started negotiations with them to unite their efforts. Although he was Kïlïj Arslan's father-in-law, he did not perhaps enjoy the approval of that ruler who, if later impressions of him were in fact true, was more interested in strengthening his eastern connections. In any case, Alexis succeeded in estranging Kïlïj Arslan from Chaka, whom he caused to be assassinated: but this obviously did not provide a lasting solution, and others, who are less well-known, took Chaka's place. Kïlïj Arslan for his part, with the co-operation of a certain Alp-Ilek ibn Kutlumush who had settled on this coast and was probably his uncle, attempted to dislodge the Armeno-Greek Gabriel, a former lieutenant of Philaretes, from Malatya, where Malik-Shāh had established him.

81

Malatya is the principal centre of communications between the Anatolian plateau and Mesopotamia, and lies on the more southerly of the two routes leading to Iran. It will be seen later how important it was for Kïlïj Arslan to hold it rather than possibly to let it pass to other Turks. But we may recall at this point that Malatya probably formed part of the territory ceded by Alexis to Sulaymān, and that Gabriel was one of his former adversaries.

It was around Malatya that contacts were developed between the rising power of Kïlïj Arslan and the other Turks in north-eastern Anatolia. The principal character in this connection is a chief now known to history by the Persian name Dānishmend (learned man), whose origins are as obscure as his role, and later that of his descendants, was important. A great deal has been written on this subject since he is the hero of an epic romance, the *Dānishmendnāme*, which survives in a fourteenth-century adaptation of the thirteenth-century original, the contents of which, an intricate blend of genuine memories and legendary versions, have unfortunately been accepted as authentic by Ottoman historiographers and, following them, even by modern authors. The principal interest of the story is clearly that it bears witness to the great impression created by this man, who must therefore have been of importance. In it are related his exploits and those of his associates, against the various sorts of Christians in Asia Minor, especially in the region of Amasya, Tokat and Niksar, which was to preserve his name. But the Turks, who in Khorasan had become familiar with the popular Iranian hero Abū Muslim and in Asia Minor with the popular Arab hero Battāl Ghāzī (known to history from his part in the early wars against the Byzantines), were anxious to link Dānishmend with their traditions and to claim that Malatya, Battāl's town, was his birthplace. Some Armenian authors indeed wished to regard him as a Persarmenian, or even as a descendant of the Arsacids. These traditions are of great interest in revealing later ethno-cultural interpenetration, but they are entirely useless for the purpose of establishing historical truth. There is no justification for making Malatya the birthplace of Dānishmend, who in that event would be a converted native, as he would be if he came from any other region of Armenia. It seems unlikely that the Turcomans, if only on account of the barrier of language and customs, would have chosen as their leader and, still more, as the hero who personified them one who was foreign to their stock. Taylu, which is perhaps the true name of this personage, has a Turkish appearance; and the name *Dānishmend*, found among the *ghāzīs*, recalls the prestige of a 'wise man', the islamization of the ancient *baba* or shaman of their Central Asian ancestors.

Moreover, various later authors have tried to establish a relationship or connection, at least through the female line, between Dānishmend and Sulaymān or Kïlïj Arslan, and to represent him, in the Turcoman tradition, as head of the Sultan's army, even appearing at the battle of Manzikert. It will be readily understood that many important families were anxious to have had an ancestor at Manzikert, just as there were those in Europe who fabricated Crusader ancestors. It will also be understood that authors brought up in the Seljukid tradition would have found it difficult to admit that any leaders other than the Seljukids could have been of importance; the same phenomenon was to reappear later in regard to the Ottomans. It is not absolutely impossible that Dānishmend may be concealed under the name of one of the leaders, only vaguely known, occurring in the texts before 1095, but it has to be admitted that no definite mention of him before that date exists. At the most, in view of the part he was soon to play in the operations against the Crusaders, it may be thought that his rise to fame began earlier. Even so, despite the sparseness of the documentation for this region, the absence of any reference to him makes it difficult to imagine that it can have been much earlier. We are forced to reach a conclusion by a weighing of negative evidence, and there is little chance of the question ever being decided more positively. Moreover, there appear to be many historical parallels of great families, or even of great men, whose beginnings are obscure. Even the founder of the dynasty of the Great Seljukids, Tughrïl-Beg, did not know his own age.

Amidst so much uncertainty, however, one thing is clear. While the Seljukid prince controlled the southern route from the Taurus and Syria to the Straits, Dānishmend, by holding Ankara, Kayseri and Sivas, on the eve of the Crusade controlled the northerly route, and in particular central Asia Minor and Cappadocia. It is obvious that the important factor was not, strictly speaking, a matter of territories, but of routes of penetration which everyone tried to extend, and of fortified places which controlled them. There is no means of telling if the rivalries which later divided the two powers already existed, although this appears to be possible.

6

ASIA MINOR AFTER THE FIRST CRUSADE
(1097–1110)

It would perhaps have been in western Asia Minor, thus anticipating Ottoman history by two centuries, that the Turks would have achieved their principal development, if the external factor of the First Crusade had not intervened. It has already been made clear in what respects their presence in the country explained or did not explain this Crusade. For themselves it was to have considerable consequences, but these must not be overestimated or misunderstood. The popular traditions briefly related in the later histories of the Seljukids ignore the Crusades, and even though there may be traces of them in certain episodes of the *Dānishmendnāme*, they are so inextricably interwoven with accounts of the wars against Christians of every kind in Asia Minor as a whole that it must certainly be felt that the coming of the Crusade had not left any very precise memory. The Crusaders crossed Asia Minor but did not stay there, and the Turks in that country were indifferent as to what they would do in Syria or Palestine, regions foreign to them. The Crusaders caused confusion among the Turks, and killed a certain number, but not more than they lost themselves; and, over the greater part of the country, their passage did not prevent the Turks, by their nature still semi-nomadic and accustomed to a war of movement, from returning without any difficulty when they left.

If nevertheless the Crusade is a landmark in Turkish history, it is so for the reason that it drove the Turks back from the coast and enclosed them on the plateau. This did not of course occur in a direct fashion. As positive gains, the Crusaders could count only the capture of Nicaea (with Kïlïj Arslan's wife and children), which was restored to Alexis Comnenus, and, to a lesser extent, the victory of Dorylaion, which compelled Kïlïj Arslan to retreat eastwards. The fruits had been slowly gathered by the Byzantines behind them. The Crusade had compelled Alexis to break with the Sultan who, until then, had rather been his ally; but it prevented him from assisting the chiefs who were established on the Aegean coast, even if he had wished to do so. It was thus possible to conquer the piratical strongholds of Chaka's successors (in Smyrna), and of a certain Tengribirmish (gift of God) in Ephesus, to reoccupy the Meander valley and even, on the southern coast where the Turks do not seem to have gained a firm footing, to link up with Cilicia and Syria where the Franks were in occupation. The north coast being also held or recovered as far as Trebizond, the Turks thus found themselves thrown back onto the high plateaux and mountains of Asia Minor in the interior, from which, for geographical reasons, it was difficult to make any attack towards the sea except to the west; nevertheless the climate and vegetation there were very reminiscent of the conditions of life that they and their flocks had known in Central Asia and northern Iran. It was therefore to a continental way of life that they turned, like the modern Turkish Republic, rather than to a maritime one, like the Ottoman Empire, whether or not this was by their own desire or with their full consciousness.

A second result of the Crusade added weight to the first. The Turks had come to Asia Minor by way of Iran. All that they had learnt of Islamic civilization they had learnt at the hands of the Iranians. In so far as they maintained relations with their kinsmen who remained behind, it was with the Turcomans of northwestern Iran. This Iranian pre-eminence might have been diminished if links with Syria and Egypt had been established by sea, and with Syria by land, as it was closer than Iran. But it was precisely the fact that the Crusaders established themselves in Syria and even on the north-western borders of Mesopotamia for half a century, so helping Armenian colonization a little further to the north, that made such links difficult to create. It was almost outside the Arab world that the Islamo-Turkish society of Asia Minor was to take shape, and the indications and consequences of this fact are to be seen on many occasions.

Moreover the Crusade temporarily affected relations between the Seljukids and Dānishmendids. Dānishmend had agreed to support Kĭlĭj Arslan against the Crusaders. But, after they had left, the causes of antagonism still remained, and while the Sultan was slightly weakened by his losses in the west and cut off by the Franco-Armenians of the central Taurus from his normal connections with the Malatya route, Dānishmend for his part had suffered no losses and there was nothing to stop him, if he so desired, from taking control of the region himself, irrespective of Kĭlĭj Arslan's wishes. In 1100–1 his strength was revealed by the capture of the Frankish prince of Antioch, Bohemond, who had been called in by Gabriel to aid Malatya, and afterwards by the disasters he inflicted on the last wave of the Crusade in Cappadocia, where this Crusade had thought it could venture in order to free Bohemond and extend the work of reconquest. And in 1102, in spite of Baldwin of Edessa, he was to take Malatya.

In these circumstances the rivalry between the two powers emerges clearly, together with Kĭlĭj Arslan's consequent desire to resume with Alexis Comnenus the good relations which had been momentarily interrupted but which were necessary for the consolidation of his power at home and for the maintenance of his eastern connections. Several allusions in texts close to the facts bear witness to this situation, the most familiar episode being concerned with Bohemond. Moreover, hostilities between Dānishmend and Kĭlĭj Arslan took place near Marʿash, that is to say in the region which, though held by Armenian lords who were Philaretes' heirs and at times connected with the Franks, was needed by the Seljukid in order to approach the eastern Taurus and Malatya. After complex bargaining Dānishmend, now master of the town, set Bohemond free, precisely because he knew him to be an enemy of Alexis. On the other hand, Kĭlĭj Arslan and Alexis were reconciled against Bohemond, whom they regarded as their common and most dangerous enemy. When Bohemond, who had returned to Europe, in 1106 raised an expedition there which attacked Byzantium through Epirus, Kĭlĭj Arslan sent Alexis reinforcements which played some part in his success. Meanwhile Dānishmend had died, and the temporary difficulties that ensued allowed the Seljukid in his turn to take possession of Malatya (1104).

To all appearances he stayed on there. His relative proximity gave the emirs of Mosul and Harrān (Upper Mesopotamia), enemies of Sultan Muhammad (of the branch of the Seljukids ruling in Iraq and Iran), the idea of calling him in to help them against their master. Kïlïj Arslan for his part had perhaps established relations with them, and in any case he cannot have forgotten either the eastern origins of his family or the hereditary enmity between the two branches, from which he himself had to suffer. He hastened to intervene, succeeded in taking Mosul and Mayāfāriqīn, the capital of Diyār Bakr, and came face to face with Muhammad's army on the Khābūr, a tributary of the middle Euphrates on the left bank. Nevertheless, he was weakened by having sent reinforcements to Alexis, and quite as many of the emirs were disturbed by his intervention as were hostile to Muhammad. The battle proved disastrous both for his army and for himself, and he perished in it (June 1107).

Following the death of Kïlïj Arslan certain events took place which might give the impression – though momentary and exceptional – of a reversal of the situation through the intervention of the eastern Seljukids in Anatolia. It is necessary to dwell a little on these events, however unimportant in themselves, since their significance throws a retrospective light on the state of affairs towards the end of Kïlïj Arslan's reign.

The death of Kïlïj Arslan certainly seems to have led in practice to a division of the Seljukid possessions in Asia Minor. On the one hand there remained Kïlïj Arslan's wife (or one of his wives), the mother of his young son Tughrïl Arslan, who had stayed in Malatya during her husband's Mesopotamian campaign. To retain power, in the course of a few years she married in succession three Turkish chiefs, whose names tells us nothing and upon whom she conferred the title of *atabek* to the young prince. Finally, in 1118, she married Balak, giving him the same title. This Balak, about whom a good deal is known, was one of the descendants of Artuk, referred to earlier, who at times supported, at other times opposed the policy of the Irano-Iraqi Seljukids, and were in process of carving out principalities for themselves in the upper basin of the Tigris and its borders with the Euphrates. Balak, for his part, was establishing himself in Khanzit (chief centre Khartpert/ Hisn Ziyād, near the present Elaziz) in the loop of the Euphrates east of Malatya, which made it possible for him to intervene in the affairs of Malatya. Moreover, she had thought it necessary to improve relations with Sultan Muhammad, firstly by encouraging Turcoman raids against the Franco-Armenians in the Middle Taurus while Muhammad was sending armies to fight them to the south of the Euphrates and in Syria; secondly, by going so far as to hand over her second husband to him, on the grounds, true or false, that he was intriguing with the enemy.

On the western side, around Konya, Kïlïj Arslan's principal place of residence, his second son Shāhānshāh, by then an adult, was regarded as his heir, since the elder son had died. But Shāhānshāh had been taken prisoner in the disaster of Khābūr, and the cousin Hasan of Cappadocia, who acted as regent in his name was preoccupied with maintaining good relations with Muhammad, and does not seem to have raised the question of Malatya. Perhaps, as elsewhere, the division of a minor's inheritance or the granting of apanages from it was regarded as normal practice. He secured the release of Shāhānshāh by Sultan Muhammad, who had no doubt induced his prisoner to acknowledge some kind of suzerainty. Kïlïj Arslan's death had been followed by a resumption of aggression by the Turcomans on the Byzantine frontiers, either because the regent had been unable to restrain them or because he had thought it preferable politically to give them a free hand, if not indeed to encourage them. While isolated bands had to be fought at Lampe (south of the Hellespont), Smyrna, Pergamon and Kelbian (but that implied that the Aegean provinces remained in fact accessible), Hasan of Cappadocia, whether or not he was regent, attacked Philadelphia. On his return, Shāhānshāh put his cousin to death, for what reason we are not told. But he resumed the attacks to the west, on Philadelphia again and Kelbian, and a contingent sent by Sultan Muhammad – he also sent others against the Franks – gave assistance. For once the Turcoman *ghazwa* coincided with the Sultan's holy war, which brought together the Franks of Syria and the Byzantines as common enemies. On Muhammad's part, however, it was an episode with no sequel, the last intervention of an eastern contingent in Anatolia. It was paradoxical that Alexis Comnenus and Muhammad, both enemies of the Franks, against whom Alexis was fighting in Cilicia and Syria, should themselves have been enemies. In 1110 Alexis sent an ambassador to Muhammad to give him encouragement in the war against the Franks. In 1112 negotiations took place in Asia Minor between representatives of the two sovereigns, who, leaving Shāhānshāh aside, finally concluded a peace, the terms of which are unknown, and which incidentally had no practical consequences, although its significance is clear.

Thus, in two theatres of war it is evident that the weakening, not the growth, of the prince's power encouraged the Turcomans' activities on the frontiers of the rising Seljukid State of Rūm. Although slightly inferior in comparison with that state at the time when it reached as far as Nicaea, but now on equal terms with it, the Dānishmendids' State, further to the north, was, in its origins, probably even more exclusively of Turcoman inspiration, since Dānishmend was purely a Turcoman chief. The contrast must not be exaggerated, for Kïlïj Arslan and his immediate successors, whatever their outlook may have been, had no source of strength other than Turcoman. Moreover, the *ghāzī* spirit common to all Turcomans does not necessarily mean the combining of operations by all of them or the attainment of a unity that excluded rivalries between groups. Broadly speaking, however, it is probable on the whole that the dynastic rivalries between Seljukids and Dānishmendids were accompanied by a hostility between the Turcoman spirit and a state-controlled, organizing spirit which, in itself, implied an attempt to secure a certain relaxation of tension on the Byzantine front. Kïlïj Arslan had been the opponent of his eastern kinsmen, but he was quite incapable of visualizing the power that he sought to exercise in Asia Minor as being established otherwise than, in part at least, on the model of theirs, the only power he had known.

For the Dānishmendids, *ghazwa* activities could be pursued in three separate directions – occasionally to the south, helped by the indefiniteness of the frontiers with the Seljukids in the Taurus region; to the north, against the Byzantines who were entrenched along the Black Sea coast, from the Bosphorus to Trebizond; and, lastly, to the west, where their domination extended as far as Gangra and Ankara. But, except in the south, almost nothing is known about these. Moreover, it is difficult to tell how far eastwards the authority of Dānishmend and his son Gümüshtegin

Ghāzī extended. We do not know the date of the death of
Theodore Gavras, who once saved Trebizond from the Turks but
was afterwards captured and put to death at Erzurum. In 1098
Bayburt and in 1105 Shebin Karahisār/Colonia were still dependencies of Trebizond, where Gregory Taronites, perhaps the son of
Theodore Gavras, attempted to come to terms with the Dānishmendids, making himself independent of Byzantium. It was
perhaps a Dānishmendid who attacked Bayburt in 1098, but by
1103 at the latest Erzurum, where Sultan Muhammad had for a
time taken refuge, belonged to a new ruler, 'Alī ibn Saltuk, from
whom the Saltukids are descended. In 1118 Erzinjān and Divriği
belonged to yet another leader, Mangujak, also the founder of a
dynasty, although nothing is known of the original relations
between these families and those of Dānishmend or the Irano-
Iraqi sultanate. In spite of the distance apart, it is not impossible
that 'Alī of Erzurum was the 'Sultan of Armenia' whom the
Armenian lord of Mar'ash, to the south of the Middle Taurus,
captured near Adiyaman/Hisn Mansūr in 1108. If this was so, he
obtained his release. He died in about 1123 (?).

The events described in this section mark the end of a period.
Driven back from the sea by the Crusade or its aftermath, precluded from any return to the east by the disaster of Khābūr, the
Turks of Anatolia were however from then onwards also free from
any intervention by the eastern Sultans. What is more, they were
secure from any new Turcoman immigration since the Turkish
immigration in Iran itself had become stabilized, while, in addition, the Turks established in Asia Minor no longer permitted
any others to come among them and divide their spoils. Henceforward, then, they were to evolve in a state of isolation, at least
relatively speaking. And it will be noted that, although it was
clearly from their contact with Iran that they came to know
Islam, nevertheless, for the Turks of Asia Minor, the period of
contact had been hardly more than a generation, unlike the case
of their kinsmen who had remained in Iran.

The foregoing episodes have been dwelt on at considerable
length because they are somewhat difficult to place, in view of the
documentary situation, but nevertheless are indispensable to an
understanding of the main outlines of later history. Henceforward,
for more than a century, the fundamental features of Anatolian

history were not to undergo any substantial modification, and there was merely to be an internal evolution in the relations between the forces involved. Politically, the Seljukids were finally to be the victors, but only after some twenty years during which, on the contrary, the leading place was held by the Dānishmendids.

7

RISE OF THE DĀNISHMENDIDS AND THE BYZANTINE RECOVERY 1110–41

The situation of the Turcomans being as described, it will be readily seen that, even on the western side, the separate peace with Sultan Muhammad could not result in an effective cessation of hostilities. Indeed, for a time Shāhānshāh himself sent against the Byzantines his official *beglerbeg*s, whose names (including a certain Monolykes), in the Greek rendering of Anna Comnena, provide no specific information. In 1113 they are found attacking Lopadion, Abydos and other places south of the Dardanelles, Adramyttion on the Aegean, and capturing the governor of Nicaea. However, Alexis took them by surprise on their way back to Kütahya and defeated them. Alongside the Turks of Asia Minor were 'Muslims who had come from Karmeh', whose identity cannot be established with any certainty, but whose presence perhaps indicates that various *ghāzī*s were called in. The reverse in 1113 did not prevent this same 'archisatrap' (*beglerbeg* ?) Monolykes from reappearing before Nicaea and Poïmamenon in 1116, and Shāhānshāh himself from preparing a large expedition. In these circumstances, it seems that Alexis Comnenus may have modified his policy. Until then he had regarded the Franks of Antioch as the principal enemy and, looking on the Turks either as vassals or as lesser enemies, had skirted their territories in order to keep to the coasts and from there to reach Syria. Now, while preparing for a reconciliation with prince Roger of Antioch, he decided to strike a powerful blow at the Turks. By way of Dorylaion, Polybotos and Philomelion, he invaded the land they occupied. In their usual way the Turks retreated, ravaging the country. Unable to expect a lasting re-annexation, Alexis repatriated the Christian population, while the enemy harassed their return march.

The Byzantine expedition had however disposed Shāhānshāh and his principal counsellors once again to make a direct attempt to secure an agreement with Alexis, such as had proved of advantage to his grandfather and father. The facts, as related by the daughter of the Basileus, Anna Comnena, are difficult to reconstruct in detail, but their general significance is nevertheless instructive and clear. According to her, Shāhānshāh came with Monolykes and others to pay some kind of homage to Alexis, which we can accept, and he is said to have promised to leave the 'Roman' Empire its frontiers as in the time of Romanus Diogenes, to withdraw his Turks from it, and not to molest the Byzantine frontiers again. The withdrawal was obviously impossible to carry out and hardly conceiveable, and there can scarcely have been anything beyond a recognition in principle of Byzantine sovereignty over the land held by Shāhānshāh, who became his vassal, and an assurance of peace on the western borders. But even that was far more than many Turcomans and others could endure. A plot against Shāhānshāh was hatched, under the leadership of Poucheas, governor of Philomelion and son of the regent whom Shāhānshāh had put to death shortly before. There can be little doubt that they had the support of the Dānishmendid Gümüsh-tegin. It was in vain that Alexis, when informed of the plot, warned Shāhānshāh: the latter was captured, blinded and strangled, and the plotters brought his brother Masʿūd to power (1118). Shortly afterwards Alexis himself and, in Iraq, Sultan Muhammad also died.

Understandably, Shāhānshāh's overthrow was accompanied by a continuation of hostilities on the frontiers. At the time of Alexis' death, the Turks had infiltrated into the entire upper valley of the Meander, were in control of Denizli/Laodicaea and Uluborlu/Sozopolis and had cut the route from Antalya, and consequently communications with Cilicia and Syria. John Comnenus, son and successor of Alexis, had to drive them from these positions which were then fortified to consolidate their recovery. There is no record of any reaction from Masʿūd, who avoided encounters of this kind, although that did not seriously hinder the Turcomans' razzias.

In the east, the picture was the same. The Franks having taken advantage of the crisis brought about by Shāhānshāh's death to recover the Djahān, Tughril Arslan of Malatya, co-ordinating his action with Balak's campaign on the Euphrates, regained it from them, this time permanently, in spite of reprisal raids against Malatya. Another Seljukid, Daulab, met his death on the Syrian borders fighting against a Frank, William of Azaz, while co-operating with the head of the Artukids, Ilghāzī, who was then in course of establishing himself in Aleppo.

The Dānishmendids, for their part, now directed their activities principally towards the east. In the years 1118–20, there were hostilities between Tughril Arslan and Balak on the one side, and Mangujak on the other. Remarkably enough, the latter went to the Greek duke of Trebizond, Constantine Gavras, to seek reinforcements. Then Balak called in Gümüshtegin, who crushed and captured the two allies: the first, Mangujak, his son-in-law, was liberated, as also was the second, Gavras, but in return for a ransom of 30,000 dinars. A little later Balak's uncle Ilghāzī, together with ʿAlī of Erzurum, was involved in a defeat by the Georgians, though it had no consequences for either.

After Balak's death (in Syria) in 1124, a quarrel over the succession broke out between Tughril Arslan and two of Balak's cousins in turn, Sulaymān and, on his death, Timurtash, both sons of Ilghāzī and masters of Mayāfāriqīn. Gümüshtegin, strengthened by the support of Masʿūd, to whom Malatya was no longer of concern, took the opportunity to attack Tughril, who eventually succumbed, after appealing in vain to the Franks, who were then occupied with besieging Aleppo: at the end of 1124 Malatya once again formed part of the Dānishmendid domain, and was to remain so for a long time. On the other hand, Khanzit finally fell to another Artukid, Dāʾūd, a cousin of Timurtash and Balak, who harried the dependencies of Malatya, though without any marked results.

As we have seen, the Turks did not scruple to rely on Christians, any more than the Byzantines did to rely on Turks. And the practice spread to the principal Seljukid domain. His brother ʿArab revolted against Masʿūd, who was accused of betraying their family. Mas'ūd fled to John Comnenus, and it was with an army recruited with his help, and in alliance with Gümüshtegin, that he recovered his position. 'Arab fled in his turn and took refuge with the Armenian prince of Upper Cilicia, Thoros, returning with Armenian and Turkish contingents to conduct operations against Gümüshtegin, at first with success. In the end, 'Arab was defeated (1128), and died among the Byzantines. Gümüshtegin was in control of the situation in Asia Minor.

The advantages gained by the Byzantines from these dissensions were in danger of being offset by counter-appeals made by Greek rebels to the Turks. In 1129 or 1130, when Gümüshtegin made some raids in the direction of the Black Sea, perhaps in reprisal for assistance given to 'Arab, a Greek governor Cassianos surrendered to him without any real resistance. Shortly afterwards, when a plot failed, it was Isaac, the brother of John Comnenus, who took refuge with Gümüshtegin; from there he went on to Trebizond, then returned to Gümüshtegin, and proceeded to join Thoros, who gave him his daughter in marriage, with Misis/Mopsouestia and Adana as her dowry. He travelled to Jerusalem, quarrelled with his father-in-law, and fled to Mas'ūd; and it was only in 1140 that he made peace with the Basileus, after inciting all his enemies, Christian and Turkish alike, against him. A little later Isaac's son, in his turn, joined Mas'ūd, was converted to Islam, and married a daughter of the Seljukid. However, it was not a question of revolts in the Byzantine Empire, and ventures of this kind did not endanger the position of John Comnenus.

Gümüshtegin had also wished to take revenge on Thoros. Having gone into Cilicia, he there happened to encounter the Frankish prince of Antioch Bohemond II, who was also an enemy of Thoros and whom he defeated and killed, sending his head to the Caliph (1130). In 1131 he compelled Thoros's brother and successor, Leo, to pay tribute, then attacked the County of Edessa through the provinces of Mar'ash and Tzamandos. He was frequently accompanied by Mas'ūd, his son-in-law and pupil, who perhaps conferred a measure of legality upon his activities.

Finally, in the winter of 1134-5, though not knowing that he was dying, the Caliph and Sultan of Iraq-Iran sent him the insignia of 'king', *malik*, investing him formally with the 'northern land'. It was his son Muhammad who was to take these, without consulting anyone. It is difficult to think that a Seljukid of Rūm, either Mas'ūd or a predecessor, had not at some time received some grant of title at least equivalent to this, but we have no knowledge of it, and such a grant would perhaps have been at variance with Byzantine investitures. Neither epigraphy nor numismatics can throw any light. However that may be, the Dānishmendid was henceforward officially a Muslim sovereign, a matter of greater significance for this former leader of marauding bands in a foreign country than for the military commanders who had been officially invested, in the old Muslim countries, with the conquests that they had made.

This investiture had possibly been sought by Gümüshtegin as a reply to the attacks of John Comnenus, who, after being diverted from Asian affairs by threats in Europe for so long, now decided to combat the new power. In 1132, setting out from a base on the Rhyndakos which he had fortified, the Basileus invaded Paphlagonia, entered Kastamonu and even crossed the Halys, and obtained some sort of submission by the chiefs. His historian enumerates these with satisfaction, but the only names to tell anything are those of Amasya, a certain Inal, who is possibly identical with the Dānishmendid of that name known to us from a coin, and a certain Alp Arslan of Chankïrï, whose existence perhaps explains the later traditions which would see in them the descendants of the illustrious Alp Arslan. This advance was indeed revealing; but by the winter of the same year Gümüshtegin had recovered Kastamonu.

Muhammad's accession gave rise, as always, to difficulties. He had had one brother executed, but another, 'Ayn al-Dawla, revolted in the Djahān: he was driven out after two years, and could not be prevented from taking refuge in the county of Edessa. John Comnenus thought this an opportune moment to renew his campaign, and re-occupied Kastamonu and Chankïrï, where some Turks entered his service. At one point he even won over Mas'ūd, whose followers however abandoned him. In spite of this he considered his control of communications in Asia Minor sufficiently secure to undertake the memorable expedition which was to take him in 1136-7 as far as Antioch in Syria and even beyond. But Muhammad, who had preferred to direct his activities against the Count of Edessa, then became reconciled with Mas'ūd. They began to harass John's lines of communication and, taking advantage of his absence, recaptured Chankīrï and harried the 'country of Cassianos' and also that of the Sangarios: this was one of the reasons for the hasty return of John Comnenus. That fact made it possible for Gümüshtegin's Turks in their turn to renew attacks on the Armenians in Cilicia and the County of Edessa, through both the Djahān and Malatya. Then John Comnenus, who incidentally had re-established his direct domination over Trebizond, made an attack along the Pontic coast against Niksar/ Neocaesarea, which had been fortified by Muhammad, but it proved inconclusive, owing to the desertion of Isaac's sons (winter of 1139–40). In 1141 he embarked on new operations which were once again to free Sozopolis and the Antalya route (along Lake Karalis/Beyshehir Gölü). At that moment (in 1141?) Muhammad died and John Comnenus, who possibly as a result had set out once again for Cilicia, himself died there at the beginning of 1143.

8

DISRUPTION OF THE DĀNISHMENDID KINGDOM; THE SELJUKIDS BETWEEN BYZANTIUM AND NŪR AL-DĪN; THE RESULTS OF MYRIOKEPHALON (1141–86)

Muhammad's death ended the co-operation between Dānish-mendids and Seljukids, since the unity of the Dānishmendid kingdom did not survive him. A revolt against his son Dhu'l-Nūn was made by Muhammad's two brothers, Yaghī-basan, the governor of Sivas, and 'Ayn al-Dawla, who had returned from the Franks and held Malatya. It was now Mas'ūd's turn to appear as protector of a Dānishmendid, and at first he showed favour to Dhu'l-Nūn. Later, however, he turned to Yaghī-basan, the eldest and probably best fitted to be head of the family, and supported some kind of partition which apparently allotted Sivas and Kayseri/Caesarea to Dhu'l-Nūn (1143–4). It was possibly at this time that he annexed Ankara and Chankïrï, that is to say the western provinces of the Dānishmendid territory, facing the Byzantines, and the Djahān, facing the Armeno-Franks. Henceforward he was the most powerful figure in Asia Minor.

These quarrels naturally interfered with Turco-Byzantine relations. When Manuel Comnenus led back the Byzantine army from Cilicia, after his father's death, he was obliged to disperse a number of Turks who had again ventured onto his route, as well as in the Sangarios and Meander regions and even to the southeast of Nicaea. Since these Turks were to some extent Mas'ūd's subjects, Manuel's relations with Yaghï-basan became closer. In 1146 he set out on an expedition directed against Konya. In the fighting Mas'ūd lost a member of the Gavras family who had long been in his service, and who was captured by the Greeks. The outskirts of Konya were pillaged. However, Mas'ūd became reconciled with Yaghï-basan, and Manuel was able to destroy the opposing army. He disregarded the peace overtures conveyed to him by the Turkish wife of his cousin John Comnenus (who had himself also gone over to the Turks). What would have happened if he had persisted? But at that moment came the news of the arrival of the Second Crusade. He therefore accepted the offer of peace, and withdrew.

As we know, relations between the Byzantines and the Crusaders were bad. Faced by the Graeco-Turkish reconciliation, which continued after they had crossed the country, the Crusaders convinced the people of the West that there had been a betrayal of the Christian cause, and modern historians have perhaps not always dissociated themselves from this over-simplified view of affairs. The reality was different. The political situation in Europe was such that Manuel Comnenus was bound to feel some disquiet in welcoming the Crusade, and its leaders had not accepted the conditions he had laid down during the preliminary negotiations. It was quite understandable that he should feel the need to have a free hand. Moreover, the Turks of Asia Minor had no interest in Jerusalem, and it was in no way essential for the Crusaders to pass through the Seljukid States, or even their border territories. The over-simplified idea held by the Crusaders that all Muslims were united was a mistake, the responsibility for which rests neither with the Byzantines nor with the Turks. And equally, of course, in all the Christian consciences of the time there was no idea of a single cause of Christianity, transcending all divisions.

From the Turkish point of view, the Second Crusade was much less important than the First, which itself has in some respects been exaggerated. Seljukid territory was now almost restricted to the Anatolian plateau, and Conrad II, who was intending to cross it without more ado, was compelled to turn back. Louis VII, who did no more than follow its borders, was attacked in the unsettled frontier zone. The Greeks, whom the Crusaders treated without consideration, sometimes helped the Turks. For the latter, the essential point was to re-establish peace with Constantinople.

Once again, the principal consequence was to direct Seljukid policy again towards the south-east, henceforward particularly against the Franks. Having become master of the Djahān, Masʿūd was neighbour of what remained of the County of Edessa between the Taurus and the Euphrates since Zengi, the Muslim ruler of Mosul and Aleppo, had secured the fall of Edessa in 1144 (this being the cause of the Second Crusade). Zengi had died in 1146, but his son, Nūr al-Dīn, in Aleppo continued his policy against Joscelin II of Edessa, who had taken refuge in Tell-Bāshir, and against Raymond of Antioch. Masʿūd may have felt aggrieved with the Franks of Edessa for having sheltered rebels or rivals on several occasions, as has been seen. But, in a wider sense, he may have wished to re-absorb the Franco-Armenian possessions to form a 'glacis', an extension of his possessions to the south-east, and to embark on a policy of penetration, by way of northern Syria, into the affairs of the Turco-Arab States of the old Muslim territory (whether or not he recalled the fact that his grandfather had held Antioch, and saw a way of securing, by different means, what his father, Kĭlĭj Arslan, had failed to achieve some forty years earlier).

Nūr al-Dīn, the champion of the anti-Frankish struggle, in a sense could only congratulate himself that his enemies should have been attacked from the rear while he was attacking them in the south: caught in a vice, as it were, they were bound to collapse. On the other hand, he had no desire to see a sovereign whose power might limit his own, gain a footing in Syria. Consequently there followed between them a strange game of alternating alliances and withdrawals. Despite some earlier skirmishes, the real starting-point was the disaster inflicted by Nūr al-Dīn on the Franks of Antioch in 1149, in which Raymond was killed. Then the action flared up. In 1149, Mas'ūd occupied Mar'ash. The principal question thus became Tell-Bāshir, its conquest and assignment. Nūr al-Dīn had changed sides, and even favoured a truce between Joscelin and Mas'ūd, when it so happened that the Frankish prince was captured by Turcomans from Syria (1150). It was then agreed that they should both join in laying siege to the fortress which would pass to Nūr al-Dīn as the dowry of a daughter of Mas'ūd, whom he would marry. In practice, Mas'ūd then found pretexts for contenting himself with the annexation of Kaysūn, Behesni, Raban, 'Ayntāb in 1151, and other places, that is to say the northern dependencies of Tell-Bāshir out of which, thus making clear its importance, he created a march for his son and heir presumptive, Kïlïj Arslan. As for Tell-Bāshir, the Franks, hoping for some effective help, or simply to save face, ceded it to Manuel Comnenus, whose small garrison was unable to defend it against Nūr al-Dīn.

Other ventures also revealed and extended this same policy during Mas'ūd's last years. In Malatya, after the death of 'Ayn al-Dawla, Mas'ūd demanded formal homage from his young son Dhu'l-Qarnayn, with the outright threat of expulsion (1152). In Cilicia, where Thoros II was establishing a principality, mostly at the expense of the Greeks, he intervened, no doubt to his own advantage but also with benefit to Manuel Comnenus; and in 1154, in any case, his intervention was at the request or at least with the agreement of Manuel Comnenus. In 1153 he had allowed himself to be persuaded into a truce with Thoros, while some more or less independent Turcomans in the western Taurus were beginning to penetrate into a very promising field, the hinterland of Selefke/Seleucia. In 1145, with Kïlïj Arslan, he returned, and although Thoros's brother Sdephane, helped by the Templars from Amanus and by the mosquitoes, got the better of him, nevertheless for the first time he crossed the whole Cilician plain as far as the outskirts of Alexandretta.

Yaghï-basan for his part was attacking the Greeks, but as he no longer had any easy way of expansion westwards, it was to the north that he turned, where the direct dependencies of the

Empire and those of Trebizond met, towards Ünye/Oenoe, Bafra/ Paurae, and Samsun. It was of course to be a long time before any annexation of coastal districts took place, but the orientation is significant.

Mas'ūd died in about April 1155, after a reign of 39 years. In spite of the usual difficulties at the start, the reign of his son Kĭlĭj Arslan, which was to last almost as long, does not reveal any change in comparison with the closing period of his father's life.

Kĭlĭj Arslan's difficulties over the succession were reduced by differences among the Dānishmendids and the policy of Manuel Comnenus, which had the result that no one was able or willing to take real advantage of them. Kĭlĭj Arslan rid himself of one of his brothers and the notables who supported him, but was unable to prevent the revolt of another of them, Shāhānshāh, in his apanage of the new possessions of Ankara and Chankĭrĭ. Meanwhile Yaghĭ-basan and Nūr al-Dīn had become allies and, with the help of the Armenians who were discontented with their new masters, were attacking the territories recently won by the Seljukids on the northern Syrian borders. However, intervention by the religious authorities allowed Kĭlĭj Arslan to be reconciled once again with Yaghĭ-basan, while he secured the neutrality of Manuel Comnenus without difficulty by handing back a number of fortresses in Isauria. In 1157 he re-established his authority over the province of Kaysūn, taking steps to conciliate the Christians, and proposed to the Christian princes of Cilicia, Antioch, and Jerusalem a coalition against Nūr al-Dīn.

It was the policy followed by Manuel Comnenus that prevented this project from succeeding. In 1159 he re-adopted his father's great plan and, skirting Seljukid territory without penetrating into it, went on into Cilicia and thence to Antioch, where he promised the Franks that he would fight against Nūr al-Dīn, in order to justify the protectorate he was imposing upon them. In reality, his aim was not so much to destroy Nūr al-Dīn, a thing which would have freed the Franks from any need for his assistance that they might feel, as to make use of him against Kĭlĭj Arslan, towards whom he now sought an opportunity to pursue a more active policy. Circumstances were favourable, since the dissensions between Kĭlĭj Arslan, Dhu'l-Nūn's protector, and Yaghĭ-basan, Shāhānshāh's protector, flared up ceaselessly. In 1160 these became more intense over the question of the succession in Malatya, where Dhu'l-Qarnayn had died. Finally, when a brother of Nūr al-Dīn, after quarrelling with him, took refuge with Kïlïj Arslan, Nūr al-Dīn himself recovered possession of the disputed Syrian border territories.

On his way back from Syria to Constantinople, Manuel Comnenus had suffered quite severely from the harassing tactics of bands which, in varying degrees, were dependents of Kïlïj Arslan. In the winter of 1159–60 he organized reprisals, which were followed by counter-reprisals. It was quite evident that the matter could not be cleared up by local operations of this kind, and Manuel thought it necessary to strike a powerful blow against the Seljukid Sultan himself. For this purpose he entered into closer relations with Yaghi-basan and Shāhānshāh, and sent for the Franco-Syrian and Armeno-Cilician contingents that had been promised him in 1159. Then the Seljukid Sultan once again decided, even at some cost to himself, to try to obtain peace with Manuel and also his allies. He recognized Nūr al-Dīn's conquests, the Dānishmendid's occupation of the Djahān, and Shāhānshāh's possessions. To Manuel he offered to return the prisoners, to accept and compel respect for the Byzantine frontiers, to hand back the towns that had been captured, to fight against the enemies of the Empire, and, in return for subsidies, to provide him with contingents whenever required. Finally, to prevent any counter-intrigues, he committed himself to a spectacular move by sending his Christian Chancellor, Christopher, to ask Manuel for a meeting in Constantinople. This meeting was arranged with the ceremonial so dear to Byzantium. The triumph of imperial policy had to be made abundantly clear to all, and at the same time the barbarian had to be crushed beneath the weight of festivities and gifts. The treaty negotiated earlier was supplemented by the guarantee given by a number of Turkish chiefs. At the price of having to supply reinforcements (for example in 1167, against the Hungarians), and above all of satisfying the demands of prestige and principle, Kïlïj Arslan had in fact assured himself of freedom of action in Asia Minor against his other adversaries (1162).

Chance helped him in respect of the Dānishmendids. Yaghï-basan, who had tried to extend this power at the expense of the Artukid of Khartpert and the Mangujakids, died in 1164. Revolts broke out against his successor Ismāʿīl, and Kïlïj Arslan took advantage of them to re-occupy the Djahān. Then, breaking with Dhuʾl-Nūn who was wavering and of no further help, he deprived him of all his possessions (1168). In the following year, it was the turn of Shāhānshāh, who was forced into exile. Apart from Ismāʿīl, there now only remained against Kïlïj Arslan the young prince of Malatya, Afrīdūn, with the traditional support of the Artukid of Hisn Kayfā and Khanzit.

Unable to count on Byzantium, the dispossessed princes turned to Nūr al-Dīn, who, being fully occupied with the conquest of Egypt by his lieutenants Shīrkūh and Salāh al-Dīn (Saladin), had handed back to Kïlïj Arslan the disputed Syrian border territories to avoid any complications in the north (c. 1167). But in 1171, with Saladin firmly established in Egypt, he was free to turn again to the north, where the Seljukid's increased power must have displeased him. Shāhānshāh, Dhuʾl-Nūn, and Afrīdūn of Malatya were with the Syrian prince, now renowned as a result of his victories over the Franks and Egyptians. A vast coalition was formed, combining Nūr al-Dīn's own troops with contingents from his nephew in Mosul, from the Artukids of Hisn Kayfā and Mardin, and from the Armenian Mleh of Cilicia, all of which gathered together under Ismāʿīl; a famine caused by their presence in Sivas led to a rising, Ismāʿīl was assassinated, while another rising in Amasya, against his widow, gave Kïlïj Arslan the opportunity to seize that town, in the heart of the Dānish-mendid territory. Dhuʾl-Nun, who had inherited Sivas, was threatened in his turn. Thereupon Nūr al-Dīn set out in person on a campaign, after persuading the Caliph by some kind of argument to invest him with the northern territories. Then, as always, Kïlïj Arslan opened negotiations, and Nūr al-Dīn, being unwilling to risk his acquisitions by remaining too long away from his homeland, in unfamiliar and difficult country, responded. It was agreed that Kïlïj Arslan should leave Sivas to Dhuʾl-Nun with a garrison from Nūr al-Dīn, perhaps that he should restore Ankara to Shāhānshāh, in any case that, having failed in his obligations in respect of the holy war, of which Nūr al-Dīn posed as champion, he should resume them against the Byzantines (1173).

For some ten years correct relations had been maintained with the Byzantines. It is true that there had been frontier incidents, but the bands responsible for them were not loyal Seljukid subjects and, when the Byzantines took reprisals, Kïlïj Arslan did not defend them. Manuel Comnenus was able to construct fortifications, under the protection of which peasants once more settled, and he gradually succeeded in establishing a defensive area in what had long been merely a no man's land. The cost to Kïlïj Arslan was small in comparison with what peace on this sector had brought him on other frontiers, and the malicious even said that, as Manuel kept his goodwill by gifts, the more harm the Turcomans inflicted on the Greeks, the more presents Kïlïj Arslan received.

In 1173, however, there had been a crisis. The treaty with Nūr al-Dīn and his allies had given Manuel the impression of a reversal of alliances. When an explanation was sought, Kïlïj Arslan replied with an allusion to the reproaches being levelled against him by the Muslims regarding the holy war and to the Caliph's intervention on behalf of Nūr al-Dīn. However, after a Byzantine show of strength, he confirmed the treaty. Then in 1174 Nūr al-Dīn died. The garrison of Sivas at once fled, Dhu'l-Nun and Shāhāmshāh went to Constantinople, and Kïlïj Arslan, without striking a blow, set about occupying their possessions. There was, however, a clause in the Seljukid-Byzantine treaty which cannot be specified in detail, and which in any case had hitherto remained a dead letter, but which Manuel now demanded should be put into operation: Kïlïj Arslan's conquests from the enemies of Byzantium, or at least some of them, were to be handed over to the Greeks. In order to carry out his promise (as he put it), Kïlïj Arslan asked for Greek contingents, against whom he stirred up the populace, thereby facilitating his own occupation of towns that remained obdurate through loyalty to their old reigning family, particularly Amasya. This time Manuel neither wished nor was able to allow himself to be trifled with. He had had bases in the country re-fortified, Dorylaion in particular, and was making ample preparations, thinking they would all be of use for a series of operations undertaken jointly with the Franks in Syria (at that time his allies) against Islam, which was then looked upon as a single undivided enemy. It was in vain that, in the winter of 1175-6, Kïlïj Arslan sent to Manuel one of the Gavras family who had gone over into his service: in 1176 the attack began.

While a Greek contingent tried, by way of Paphlagonia, to reconquer Niksar for Dhu'l-Nun, though without success, Manuel himself thrust into the heart of the Seljukid country. To new overtures from Kïlïj Arslan he replied that peace would be dictated in Konya. However, the Sultan also had had time to make preparations. The large Greek army had to pass through the defile of Myriokephalon. Of necessity, it was stretched out over a great distance. Kïlïj Arslan had posted his troops in an ambush behind the high ground. The Greek army, impeded by the baggage and the bodies of the slain, was cut into two sections, one of which was massacred, the other encircled. Greeks and Turks waited for the dawn to bring a resumption of the battle, but Kïlïj Arslan, ever prudent and mindful of the future, made an offer of peace which Manuel was now only too glad to accept. He was compelled to pay a certain tribute and to destroy the fortresses of Dorylaion and Sublaion.

It was the disaster itself, rather than these trifling clauses, which proved a serious matter for him. A repetition of Manzikert, just a century later, it signified that, although the Turkish occupation had been regarded in Byzantium as something temporary, superficial, and capable of being gradually absorbed, it was necessary on the contrary to make the best of it and to dispel that illusion. A new state had actually come into existence, a force to be reckoned with, and there was no longer anything that could be done in Asia Minor apart from trying to preserve what remained of Greek dominion. In the longer view, Myriokephalon signified the collapse of the great Franco-Byzantine project. Kïlïj Arslan's moderation after Myriokephalon was all the more remarkable, like Alp Arslan's after Manzikert. In the years that followed it is true that Turcomans were implicitly encouraged to make more incursions into Byzantine territory, but it so happened that the raiders were wiped out, and Kïlïj Arslan gave them no direct help. The war with Byzantium had been imposed on him, it did not correspond with his own wishes. The annexation of western territories, some of which were devastated, others populated with inhabitants who, unlike those of central Asia Minor, were firmly Hellenized and attached to Constantinople, cannot have seemed inviting. The essential thing for him was to unite Asia Minor and the Turks who were there, in support of himself, and then be able, as head of a state that was gradually becoming better organized, to play a part in politics alongside the Muslim states bordering on Syria and Mesopotamia – all matters whose success would have been compromised by too many warlike operations in the west.

This was in fact the project to which he devoted himself after Myriokephalon, henceforward without resistance. One of the princes who for some time had been quarrelling over Malatya, with his support finally handed it over to Kïlïj Arslan (1177). In Syria and Upper Mesopotamia the rising power was now Saladin, who dispossessed Nūr al-Dīn's descendants in turn. Kïlïj Arslan intervened against him to help the prince of Aleppo by taking Raban which had been ceded to Saladin, and also by attacking the Artukid of Hisn Kayfā and Khanzit, Saladin's ally in Upper Mesopotamia. He did not achieve any great success, but he was present in a territory from which he had hitherto been absent, and it was that that counted.

If, finally, in Manuel's lifetime, the effects of Myriokephalon had appeared to be limited, his death (1180) and the troubles that followed it revealed, though now with no danger to Kïlïj Arslan, the growing pressure of the Turcoman thrust, thereafter to be irresistible. The different stages are difficult to follow, since it was not a matter of combined operations, but the fact and the general direction can be seen, as can the help again given to this thrust by strife between factions and rivalries among the Byzantines themselves. Before the Third Crusade (1190), less by means of sieges than through exhaustion or treachery, the Turks had secured the fall of Kütahaya, Uluborlu/Sozopolis, and various places on the Antalya route. Laodicaea remained Greek, but in a country infested with Turcomans, who penetrated as far as the Lycian coast, opposite Rhodes. And although a town such as Philadelphia, in the centre of the territories, remained Greek, it was in the hands of a rebel, relying on Turkish troops.

Kïlïj Arslan no longer had any reason for not claiming these conquests as his own. They had to be organized gradually, and the one that gave him his first outlet to the sea was of particular interest to him. An echo of it reached the Andalusian traveller Ibn Jubayr, thanks to the ostentatious pilgrimage to Mecca made at that time by the wife of Kara Arslan of Āmid, Kïlïj Arslan's daughter. And the Sultan issued victory-communiqués, which he sent as personal letters to various eminent figures in his world. Remarkably enough, among the addressees appears the Jacobite patriarch Michael the Syrian, who usually lived in the monastery of Mar Bar-Sauma, south of Malatya. His evident willingness to insert this letter in his Syriac chronicle, which was clearly not intended for the Sultan's eyes, suggests that he himself, though one of the most 'oecumenical' minds of the time, did not regard the Seljukid conquests as a particular defeat for Christianity.

9

EASTERN ASIA MINOR IN THE TWELFTH CENTURY

Very little is known of the history in the twelfth century of the principalities of Erzinjān and Erzurum, between which eastern Asia Minor was divided. By collecting together and completing the various references to them that have occurred, it is possible to give the following account, starting with Erzurum.

The genealogies that the Saltukids gave themselves in their inscriptions name as one of their ancestors a certain Abu 'l-Qāsim, although it is impossible to be certain that he ever existed under that name – one of the Prophet's – or held any such authority. The first known Saltukid is 'Alī, of whom it is recorded that he was ruler of Erzurum in 496/1103, when he came to enter the service of Sultan Muhammad, Malikshāh's son, who had taken refuge in Akhlāt after a defeat. It was possibly to him that a reference had been made some years earlier by the Armenian chronicler Mkhitar of Aïrivank, in a passage whose chronology is confused, but in any case he was known to the Latin chronicler Ordericus Vitalis in 1123 as an ally of the Artukid Balak, to whom he sent some Frankish prisoners. However, two years earlier, when the other Artukid Ilghāzī, in alliance with various princes against the Georgians, came to Erzurum, the historians of the expedition did not give his name: had he gone away, or was he regarded merely as a vassal of Sultan Tughrïl of Arrān (north-western borders of Azerbaijan)? It is impossible to decide.

On the other hand, it was principally when there was fighting with the Georgians that mention was made of his son and successor Saltuk, who must have succeeded him shortly after 1123. He had a daughter or sister, who, soon after 1130, married the Shāh-i Armin of Akhlāt, Sukmān II. In 1153 or 1154, and again in 1156, disturbances in Ani, the old Armenian capital now in the hands of the Shaddādids, induced Saltuk to intervene on behalf of that Muslim dynasty, who were in danger of being expelled by a combination of native Christians and Georgians. He was taken prisoner, but ransomed by the princess of Akhlāt. In 1164 the Seljukid of Rūm, Kïlïj Arslan, wishing to be allied with him against the Dānishmendid Yaghï-basan, asked for the hand of one of his daughters, but she was seized while on her way by Yaghï-basan and forced by him to marry his nephew Dhu'l-Nūn. According to his contemporary Ibn al-Azraq, Saltuk died in Rajab in 563/May 1168. From the surviving coins issued by himself and by his son Muhammad (other aspects of these coins will be discussed later), it appears that these princes continued to give nominal allegiance, not to the Seljukid of Rūm but to the representatives of the Seljukid dynasty of Iran, even after its decline. This is not the only time that Erzurum appeared to be more closely connected with the Iranian than with the 'Roman' world.

All that is known of Saltuk's son Muhammad is of his relations with the Georgians at the end of his reign. His son al-Muzaffar Malik-Shāh, like several other neighbours, had the idea of marrying the young queen of Georgia, Thamar, even though this meant renouncing Islam. After being suitably received by her and then rejected, by way of consolation he was given an illegitimate princess 'of the blood'. This episode did not permanently improve relations between the two neighbours: David, the husband chosen by Thamar, attacked and sacked Erzurum. The rejected suitor succeeded his father after 585/1189, but reigned only a short time, since by 593/1197 at the latest he in turn had been replaced by his son 'Alā' al-Dīn Abū Mansūr, the last of the dynasty before the events to be described below. Muhammad had founded the Great Mosque of Erzurum; Abū Mansūr embellished it. In the inscription commemorating the event, as was customary, he gave himself such purely Muslim high-sounding titles as 'Tamer of the Heretics', 'Ornament of the Pilgrimage', and 'King of the Greeks and Armenians, of Diyār Bakr and Diyār Rabī'a'.

*　　*　　*　　*

Little more is known of the history of the Mangujakid dynasty. The earliest mentions of the family's eponym, Mangujak, goes back not to the battle of Manzikert, as uncritical later genealogists imagined, but only to 1118 when, from Kamakh, he threatened Malatya. Faced with retaliation by the Seljukid of Malatya and his tutor the Artukid Balak of Khartpert, he went to seek help from Gavras, duke of Trebizond, as was recorded earlier. Though defeated with the Artukid by Gavras, who had been joined by the Dānishmendid Gümüshtegin, he was however set free without penalty because he was Gümüshtegin's son-in-law. But this initial episode is followed by such complete silence, in chronicles from all sources, that it has to be accepted that the principality was not the scene of any very striking events. It included Erzinjān, Shebin Karahisār/Kughūniya and Divriği as the main centres, and Kamakh and other important fortresses. The genealogies of later princes give Mangujak a son and successor named Ishāq, who divided his territories between Sulaymān (Divriği) and Dā'ūd (Erzinjān and the whole northern part). With one exception, only the Divriği branch left any epigraphic record, and in any case it appears to have been more active than the others in the matter of building.

The first reappearance of the Mangujakids at a known date occurred in 1163, when Dā'ūd was killed in a conflict. At the time, he was in alliance with a descendant of Balak against Yaghī-basan. After the next generation there is slightly fuller information. Shāhānshāh of Divriği is known from inscriptions of 576 and 592. His cousin Bahrāmshāh of Erzinjān, probably his suzerain, does not appear to have been a builder, but some of his coins survive. On one of them he dignifies himself with the title of *ghāsī*, which, if not purely a formality, may be a reference to campaigns against Trebizond. In a later chapter he will be considered as a patron of both Persian and Arab writers. During his reign of sixty years, he devoted his energies, as will be seen, to preserving a relationship of dutiful vassalage with the increasingly powerful Seljukids, who were to await his death before putting an end to his branch of the dynasty. Thanks to its insignificance, the Divriği branch was to survive longer, though entirely under the Sultan's influence. A third branch, at Kughūniya, whose origin is unknown, disappeared at the same time as that of Erzinjān.

The territory of modern Turkey includes the essential part of what, in the Middle Ages, constituted Diyār Bakr and the province of Akhlāt, on Lake Van. The reader may therefore perhaps be surprised to find no account of their history in this work, particularly since, even in the Middle Ages, the Turkish population of Diyār Bakr already had almost the same boundaries with Syria and Iraq as it possesses today. However, there are valid reasons for the omission. Despite the originally Turcoman character (as in the case of the Saltukids and Mangujakids) of the dynasties which became established in Diyār Bakr at the end of the eleventh century and the dynasty of the Artukids which gradually supplanted them in the twelfth, the general history of the region – a region partly arabized and islamized since the Arab conquests – remains fundamentally connected with Mesototamia as a whole. The Turkish princes themselves who were in the region, based their activities essentially upon what was happening in Mosul or, still more remotely, under the Caliphs and Sultans of Baghdad and Iran, in whose service the earliest of them had begun their careers. On the other hand, Akhlāt, where Persian was spoken, was more in touch with Iran, or at least with Azerbaijan, although its princes were also involved in Syro-Mesopotamian affairs. But these princes were by origin ordinary Mamluks of the Irano-Iraqi Seljukids and, with due allowance made for the gaps in documentation, their proximity to the principalities of eastern Asia Minor, strictly speaking, played a relatively secondary role in their history. It is true that the state of Akhlāt was established largely at the expense of the Byzantine Empire, unlike the lordships of Diyār Bakr, but nevertheless in territories which Byzantium had acquired recently and into which Islam had penetrated. On the same meridian, the principality of Erzurum was very different in every respect. It was, incidentally, to be integrated into the Seljukid State of Rūm from the beginning of the thirteenth century, whereas with Akhlāt this took place only very much later, and momentarily, and with Diyār Bakr in its western part only, and again for a short time. Any limit is somewhat arbitrary, but the line must be drawn somewhere, and the one adopted here can be defended.

10

THE CRISIS IN EXPANSION (1186–1205)

At the very moment when the Seljukid State had just achieved its most spectacular successes of the century, it was nevertheless shaken by a crisis which, while essentially a crisis resulting from its expansion, at the same time brought to light dangerous and revealing symptoms which were in fact partly due to that very expansion.

The immediate cause of the crisis lay outside the Seljukid State, and indeed outside Asia Minor, strictly speaking, since it occurred in Upper Mesopotamia. At the start it was a matter of quarrels between Kurdish and Turcoman shepherds, such as no doubt occurred frequently. Why then did these disputes assume a wider importance and give rise to a vast Turcoman movement? Contrary to the impression to be gained from the silence of the texts, was it a fact that the Turcoman disorders in Khorasan and the Khwārizmian reaction which then followed had repercussions as far as Azerbaijan, Armenia and Mesopotamia? And did this movement, which is now to be described, have a religious aspect, like others to be encountered later? These are questions to which we can give no answer.

What is certain is that, after fighting had taken place in Diyār Bakr and Diyār Rabī'a (1185), the Turcomans, led by a certain Rustem (an Iranian name famous in epic), started to massacre the Kurds. Then, without regard for the inhabitants' religion, they extended their ravages from the borders of Georgia to Cappadocia. In the winter of 1186–7 they moved down towards Cilicia and northern Muslim and Frankish Syria. There they were in part destroyed by the Armenian prince Leo and the Frankish prince of

Antioch Bohemond III. Rustem was killed in the battle against Leo, while the news of the Frankish victory was on the way to Constantinople. An Armenian reprisal raid was made into Seljukid territory. But these incidents do not appear to have in fact destroyed the power of the Turcomans who, it seems, even continued to designate themselves by the name 'Rustem'.

It was at about this point that Kïlïj Arslan, now over seventy years of age, decided to divide his dominions among his sons. There were ten of them, and in addition a brother of the Sultan and a son of that brother were to be included. However, one of the ten sons must have disappeared, since the sources are agreed in mentioning only eleven shares: Tokat (to Rukn al-Dïn Sulaymānshāh), Niksar (to Nāsir al-Dïn Barkyārūkshāh), Albistan (to Mughīth al-Dïn Tughrïlshāh), Kayseri (to Nūr al-Dïn Mahmūd Sultānshāh), Sivas and Akseray (to Qutb al-Dïn-Malikshāh), Malatya (to Muʿizz al-Dïn Qaysarshāh), Nigde (to Arslanshāh), Ankara (to Muhyī al-Dïn Masʿudshāh), Uluborlu/Sozopolis (to Ghiyāth al-Dïn Khusraw), and lastly Heraclea in the Taurus and Amasya, given respectively to Sanjarshāh and Nizām al-Dïn Arghūnshāh, Kïlïj Arslan's brother and nephew. Their appointments were officially noted in Kïlïj Arslan's Dïwān, and each of them was obliged to lead his troops to join his father once a year. At the start, Kïlïj Arslan seems to have intended to keep only the capital, Konya.

Did Kïlïj Arslan hope to allay his sons' impatience, or to ensure that, on his death, none of them should be dispossessed of what he was entitled to have, according to the old family conception? Or had he in mind some more effective action, such as was everywhere becoming more necessary on account of the Turcoman disturbances, among others? Whatever the explanation, jealousy soon sprang up among the brothers, and even impaired their relations with their father, whenever he appeared to be supporting any one of them against the claims of his rivals. Conflicts started, providing an irresistible opportunity to exploit the Turcomans' warlike ardour, while directing it elsewhere. As a result, the family dissensions extended the field of activities of the Turcomans into new territories.

The eldest son was Qutb al-Dïn Malikshāh. Whether or not designated as the heir and his brothers' suzerain with the right to

Konya, he intended in any case to make certain of this inheritance without delay by taking control of the town and his father's territory. In the first half of 1189, aided by the Turcomans, he fought an unsuccessful battle against him. But he did succeed in stirring up mistrust between his father and the latter's old counsellor, Iktiyār al-Dīn Hasan ibn Gavras, who asked leave to retire to the home of the Mangujakid Bahrāmshāh of Erzinjān, in whose territories, as a member of the old Trebizond family of the Gavras, he apparently possessed estates. On the way Hasan was murdered by Turcomans, possibly with the complicity of Bahrāmshāh, for whom his presence would have raised delicate problems and who inherited his possessions (Sept. 1189). Then, in the winter of 1189–90, in obscure circumstances but still with the aid of his Turcomans, Qutb al-Dīn succeeded in forcing his father to allow him to share his authority and in taking control of Konya.

This was the situation which Frederick Barbarossa's Crusade encountered. Even before 1178, on account of the opposition of Manuel Comnenus to his Italian policy, the German Emperor had established relations with the Turkish Sultan. In 1188, remembering these earlier contacts, in order to prepare for his troops' passage across Asia Minor as well as across the Byzantine Empire, he sent a German nobleman, Gottfried von Wiesenbach, to the Sultan. A first reply reached him while he was still in Germany, at Nuremberg; a more formal embassy, headed by a certain Tokili (?), accompanied by Gottfried, was intended to meet him while on his march, but owing to the extreme tension between Barbarossa and the Greeks it was detained in Constantinople for several weeks and robbed of the gifts it was carrying. Liberated on the conclusion of the agreement between Isaac Angelus and Barbarossa, who was then at Adrianople, it reached him on 14th February, 1190, with a promise of the Sultan's co-operation for the journey through his dominions, and was to remain with him until the start of the campaign. Some days later another embassy arrived, sent by Qutb al-Dīn to overtake the one his father had despatched before being obliged to submit to him (Qutb al-Dīn). This embassy made the same promises, but its purpose, quite certainly, was to prevent Barbarossa from becoming involved in any Anatolian policy inimical to Qutb al-Dīn.

In fact, although there are no grounds for thinking that Kïlïj Arslan did not sincerely wish to arrange for the peaceable passage of the new Crusaders, this attitude, once again, could not have been shared by all the Turks. He himself must have taken Saladin's growing influence into account. He sent congratulations to him by Hasan ibn Gavras at the end of 1187 on the capture of Jerusalem, and betrothed his son Qutb al-Dīn to one of his daughters, and naturally Saladin encouraged the Seljukids to resist the Crusade. Moreover, it is self-evident that the Turcomans, apart from their natural indiscipline, had a natural tendency to try to attack the Christian army; and we have seen that Qutb al-Dīn had connections with them.

Here then is the explanation of the equivocal behaviour on the Turkish side which, to the poorly informed Germans, could give the impression of duplicity. In April, the Crusade left Philadelphia and Laodicaea, the last Greek strongholds, already surrounded by Turcomans. In any case, for these frontier-dwellers any kind of safe-conduct from the Sultan was unknown. Kaykhusraw of Uluborlu/Sozopolis had just lent his services to the rebel Manguphas, and in league with him they had ravaged Caria and Phrygia, while the Basileus had paid Kaykhusraw to hand over the rebel. That they should have refused to provide supplies for the German army, and that they harassed and tried to take it by surprise, was only to be expected, as Kïlïj Arslan's envoys explained to Barbarossa, even pretending to show pleasure at the defeats he had inflicted on rebels against the Sultan's authority. It seems clear, however, that soon afterwards Qutb al-Dīn himself also intervened, with other Turcomans who, according to the author of the *Gesta Frederici*, were commanded by a certain Rostagnus. It seems that this name also must be taken to mean Rustem who, if not himself alive, had left his name as an appellation among the Turcomans he had led. In these circumstances, official Seljukid leaders such as the prince of Ankara Muhyī and al-Dīn and the emirs of Chankïrï and Philomelion were induced to engage in hostilities with the Crusaders, and the ambassadors of Kïlïj Arslan himself, anxious about their own fate, were persuaded to leave Barbarossa, on the pretext (they said) of going to settle matters, though they did not return. The result of all this was a series of engagements in which the Turkish forces were dispersed, and the Germans arrived at the walls of Konya, no longer well-disposed but now resolved to punish by force their adversary's perfidy. Kīlīj Arslan tried in vain to negotiate, but could only take refuge in his citadel. Qutb al-Dīn was defeated when trying to free the capital, and the Germans started to plunder the town, with the result that the young prince's influence declined. He had already been criticized by his brother Muhyī al-Dīn, and was now content to leave it to his father to settle matters. The latter, placing the blame on his son, concluded with the German Emperor, who was anxious to reach Syria, an agreement which only differed from the one in February in that he now had to give hostages. The attacks which the Germans suffered from other frontier-dwellers, from Laranda in the Taurus, though in this matter the Sultan was guiltless, induced them to take with them the hostages who should have been returned when they entered Cilicia. A few days later Barbarossa was drowned in a Cilician river (June 1190).

The situation of Qutb al-Dīn, already shaken by these events, suffered even more in the following year. In Malatya, Mu'izz al-Dīn, whom he wished to supplant, had turned for help to Saladin, who had arranged his marriage to a daughter of his brother al-'Ādil, then engaged in conquering Diyār Bakr. Henceforward he felt himself to be secure. Qutb al-Dīn then resolved to seize the share of the inheritance held by Nur al-Dīn Sultānshāh, and took Kīlīj Arslan towards Kayseri, but the latter seized the opportunity to escape. For a time the old father lived a wandering life which struck the imagination of the chroniclers. He travelled from one son to another, endeavouring to restore agreement and obtain help against Qutb al-Dīn, who remained master of Konya and Akseray and of the Treasury. In the end he reached an understanding with Kaykhusraw, the son, born of a Byzantine mother, whom he had, possibly for that reason, established on the Western borders and who could probably rely on the assistance of certain Christians and in particular of the Turcoman frontier-dwellers in the region, even against other Turcomans in the east. It was in fact with their help that Kaykhusraw set out to re-establish his father in Konya and to attack Akseray. At this juncture Kīlīj Arslan died, aged 77, after reigning for 38 years, and after recognizing Kaykhusraw as his heir (1192).

Discord then became even more intense. Kaykhusraw was

powerless to compel his brothers to recognize him. Each of them behaved as an autonomous prince, even striking his own coinage, and some tried to aggrandize themselves at the expense of the rest. Qutb al-Dīn remained master of Sivas and Akseray, and in the winter of 1193–4 took Kayseri, where he had Nur al-Dīn and his minister Hasan executed. Then he attacked Albistan, and its prince Mughīth al-Dīn escaped defeat only by becoming a vassal of the Armenian prince Leo and obtaining his assistance in the winter of 1194–5. But Qutb al-Dīn died. The reconstruction he had started was taken over by his brother Rukn al-Dīn, who added the whole of his inheritance to his own share, Tokat. In 1197 he seized Konya from Kaykhusraw, then Niksar and Amasya from their respective masters, and finally, in 1201, Malatya from Muʿizz al-Dīn who took refuge with al-ʿĀdil. Soon afterwards he captured Erzurum from the Saltukids and installed his brother Mughīth at-Dīn there, in exchange for Albistan which he ceded to him. Lastly, in 1204, he occupied Ankara and there put to death his brother Masʿūd, who was accused of being in league with the Byzantines. The latter were unable to help him, since the Latins of the Fourth Crusade were then installing themselves in Constantinople. Kaykhusraw himself was compelled to flee from Uluborlu to Constantinople, and Seljukid unity was thus re-established.

It is true that, a few days after the capture of Ankara, Rukn al-Dīn died. Paradoxically, the final heir proved to be Kaykhusraw. The frontier-dwelling Turcomans in the west and certain notables in the Anatolian State itself, in particular three Dānishmendids, hatched a plot against Rukn al-Dīn's young son Kïlïj Arslan III, and recalled Kaykhusraw, who had taken refuge with Maurozomes, a Byzantine governor, now independent as a result of the events in Constantinople. After some resistance from 'orthodox' elements Kaykhusraw took possession of Konya in 1205.

There is probably no need to repeat that this crisis in the Seljukid State was not accompanied, indeed very much the reverse, by any slowing down of the Turcomans' activities or of the disintegration of the Byzantine frontier. A rising against Isaac Angelus was made by a pseudo-Alexis who, before Kïlïj Arslan was ousted by Qutb al-Dīn, had obtained from him a body of

Turcomans, with whose help he devastated the Meander region and the town of Chonas. It was during this same period that occurred the exploits of Manguphas, mentioned earlier, when he was expelled from Philadelphia but pillaged Caria, Laodicaea and Chonas with his bands of Turcomans, before being handed over by Kaykhusraw. This was a reversal for Manguphas, no doubt. But there are no grounds for thinking that the Turcomans abandoned the districts into which they had been introduced in this way, and P. Wittek, the eminent historian of mediaeval Turkey, has established on the contrary that it was at about this time that Laodicaea ceased to be Greek, although a true Seljukid administration was perhaps not organized there until the Maurozomes episode described below. Early in 1197, a dispute having broken out between the Basileus Alexis III and Kaykhusraw over the question of merchants from Konya who had taken some Egyptian horses to Constantinople as a gift, Kaykhusraw made a swift campaign along the Meander, roughly as far as Antioch, and though the town itself did not fall, further devastations in the same region are also recorded during the succeeding years. The friendly welcome accorded to Kaykhusraw a little later might therefore seem surprising, were it not for the fact that relations between Byzantium and Rukn al-Dīn were strained, as will be seen. The last episode in these struggles for the time being occurred during the second sultanate of Kaykhusraw. It will be remembered that, in 1204, he had taken refuge with a lord named Maurozomes, who had even given him his daughter in marriage. But Maurozomes was not on good terms with the new master of the Greeks in Asia Minor, Theodore Lascaris of Nicaea, with the result that Kaykhusraw took Maurozomes to Konya when he returned there. In order to be allowed to pass freely through Greek territories, Kay-khusraw had promised Lascaris that he would restore Chonas and Laodicaea, but his sons whom he had surrendered as hostages escaped, thus releasing him from his commitments. To fight against the Latins, Lascaris needed peace on the Turkish side, and he therefore accepted a compromise: Chonas and Laodicaea were given to Maurozomes as a vassal of the Turks, and when this latter, who is possibly the man called Comnenus in the Seljukid texts, disappeared (c. 1230), the two towns remained finally incorporated within the Seljukid domains.

Farther to the north, Eski-Shehir/Dorylaion had also succumbed, perhaps before the death of Kïlïj Arslan, though without
being at once incorporated into the Seljukid domains proper. On
this sector, the Turks were further aided by disagreements among
the Byzantines. In 1196 a second pseudo-Alexis, who had at first
taken refuge in Cilicia, led a revolt on the borders of the Empire,
helped by Mas'ūdshāh of Ankara. Thanks to him he took possession of the frontier strongholds of Devrek/Dadybra, Gerede/
Krateia and Bolu/Claudiopolis. He was soon overcome, but the
territory was not recovered. The Byzantine historian Nicetas
Choniates, writing some years later, himself reveals the turkifica-
tion of the country by employing the Turkish name Baba-Dagh
for the small chain of mountains dominating Devrek. Alexis III
however, needing assistance against the Wallachians (Vlachs),
renounced his claim to the region, and reached agreement with
Mas'ūd, to whom in return he had to give help against Rukn
al-Dīn (see p. 115).

On the Pontic coast the Turcomans in the Tokat region, who
had long disturbed the coastal districts of Ünye/Oenoe and Bafra,
remote from both Constantinople and Trebizond, in about 1194
had occupied Samsun, so winning for the Seljukid State, for the
first time, a good outlet to the Black Sea. In about 1200 Alexis III
attacked the merchants of Samsun, Seljukid subjects. Possibly
this town had played some part in his rupture with Rukn al-Dīn,
since a common hostility to Kaykhusraw must have linked them
together at the time. In this case, however, the Turkish occupation
was not permanent. In about 1204 or 1205 David Comnenus of
Trebizond, perhaps taking advantage of the minority of Kïlïj
Arslan III, marching westwards to fight Theodore Lascaris,
'closed the sea', in the words of the Muslim historian Ibn al-Athīr.
Samsun probably had not been given any real organization or a
strong garrison. On becoming Sultan, Kaykhusraw tried in vain
to gain access to the coast. It was only under his successor, this
time by the conquest of Sinope, that a secure outlet to the
northern coastline was finally assured to the Seljukid State.

It was particularly to the eastern and northern frontiers of the
Seljukid State that Rukn al-Dīn, unlike Kaykhusraw, turned his
attention. One reason for this was probably the geographical
situation of his original domains and the interests of his own

Turcomans. Perhaps also, despite his attacks on the Pontic coast, he thought it preferable not to make any frontal assault on Byzantium. Perhaps, like his forbears, he gave precedence to the need to unify Muslim Asia Minor, and the Rustem movement had shown the benefits of eastward expansion. However that may be, between 1201 and 1203, at the head of Turcoman contingents and reinforcements led by his brother Mughīth al-Dīn Tughrïlshāh of Albistan, Bahrāmshāh of Erzinjān and perhaps the Artukid of Khartpert, he attacked the Saltukid prince of Erzurum who was probably refusing to participate in the anti-Georgian and anti-Trebizond policy that he wished to promote, in order to attract to Samsun the caravans that hitherto had unloaded at Trebizond. Though the details are obscure, he seized Erzurum and installed Mughīth al-Dīn there, as described p. 115.

Finally, in face of the Ayyūbid al-ʿĀdil whose friendship Muʿizz al-Dīn of Malatya was cultivating, as has been said, Rukn al-Dīn resumed the traditional policy of guarding the Euphrates, while re-establishing a Seljukid protectorate over Khartpert, taking as his vassal al-Afdal, a son of Saladin, exiled by al-ʿĀdil to Samosata, and helping another of Saladin's sons, al-Zāhir of Aleppo, and his ally prince Bohemond of Antioch to drive Leo (who had now become Leo I and was trying to take Antioch) from Cilicia. It was in his interest to arrest the growth of the Armenian principality which, aided by the disintegration of the Byzantine Empire, had seized the Isaurian outlets from the western Taurus inhabited by the Turcomans. On all these points Kaykhusraw found it advantageous to follow the policy of Rukn al-Dīn. Mughīth al-Dīn himself made no difficulty over recognizing the new Sultan, in a vain attempt to oppose the ambitions of al-ʿĀdil regarding Akhlāt.

At the beginning of the thirteenth century the Seljukid State had thus not only surmounted the crisis but had even achieved new progress. The first forty years of the century were indeed its apogee.

THE APOGEE OF THE SELJUKID STATE
(1205–43)

The course of the narrative has already taken the reader some way into the history of the reign of Kaykhusraw. Although brought up in the western territories, Kaykhusraw, it will be remembered, had concluded an agreement with Theodore Lascaris in order to be able to assume the throne, while on the other hand he had in his turn revived the eastern policy of his predecessors, including Rukn al-Dīn.

Now that the Seljukid State was becoming more powerful and better organized, one great problem was the acquisition of an outlet to each of the two seas that bordered it. The Turcomans' wanderings in zones without any large port could continue no longer, and even Samsun had proved to be too difficult to defend. However, the temporary occupation of Samsun made it clear that the regions into which expansion was normally possible were those over which the disintegrated Byzantine Empire no longer exercised any real authority, on account of their remoteness, and which also lay outside the authority of the other local Christian powers, Trebizond in the north-east or the Franco-Armenians of Cilicia, Syria and Cyprus in the south. Not only was the attack made easier in military terms, it also had the advantage politically that it could sometimes be accomplished without any direct clash with those States with which they were anxious to avoid any complications.

It is these considerations that explain what was to be Kaykhusraw's great success, in default of a recovery of Samsun – the acquisition, on the other sea-coast, of Antalya, the great southern port of Asia Minor. Just before his accession the Turcomans had occupied Isparta, to the north of the route leading to Antalya. Since the fall of the Byzantine Empire in Constantinople, Antalya itself had come into the hands of a Tuscan adventurer formerly in the service of the Byzantines, Aldobrandini. Kaykhusraw had received complaints from Egyptian merchants who claimed to have been maltreated by the Franks in Antalya. The Sultan decided to attack the town. The inhabitants appealed to the regent of Cyprus, Gautier de Montbéliard, who occupied the town but was unable to prevent the Turks from devastating the surrounding country where the Antalya notables had their estates. Disagreements then seem to have arisen between the Franks and the Greeks, who felt inclined to submit to the Sultan. In March 1207 the town was taken by storm. Kaykhusraw established it, with its province, under a new government headed by Mubāriz al-Dīn Ertöküsh ibn ʿAbd Allāh.

The end of Kaykhusraw's reign was, however, marked by a new rupture with the Greeks in the west – the last recorded in Seljukid history. The reasons appear to be numerous: intrigues against Lascaris by the old Alexis III, who came to ask Kaykhusraw for help, in return for the help he had himself once provided by giving him refuge; intrigues also by the Latin Emperor of Constantinople, Henry, and by the Venetians who, shortly after the capture of Antalya by the Turks, obtained important privileges there; the persistence of problems raised by the Turcomans' indiscipline on the Seljukid-Nicaean borders; and lastly, according to one source, the indignation of one Greek faction at the loss of Antalya. Kaykhusraw attacked Antioch on the Meander, and a battle with Lascaris was fought nearby. The Sultan was the victor but he was killed in the pursuit, in obscure circumstances (1211). The frontier remained stabilized beyond Antioch, from which the Turks fell back.

* * *

The succession to Kaykhusraw, who had three sons, gave rise to some further difficulties, but without any crisis comparable to that over the succession to Kīlij Arslan. The late Sultan had established his eldest son, ʿIzz al-Dīn Kay-kāūs, in Malatya, and another, ʿAlā al-Dīn Kay-kubādh, in Tokat, while a third, Kay-ferīdūn Ibrāhīm, was in Antalya at the time of his father's death. The question of the succession having arisen unexpectedly, it appears that the choice in fact rested with the great emirs. The majority were agreed on Kay-kāūs, who came to Kayseri, but Kay-kubādh had the support of Mughīth al-Dīn of Erzurum,

Leo I of Armenia and the Dānishmendid Zahīr al-Dīn Ilī the *pervāne*. Agreement between the allies did not last, however, and Leo and Zahīr were won over by Kay-kāūs, who entered Konya. He then started to attack his brother, who, having taken refuge in Ankara, was backed by the Turcomans of Kastamonu. At the same time Kay-kāūs was negotiating a peace with Lascaris, who set free the leader of the Turkish troops taken prisoner at the battle of Antioch. Kay-kubādh was defeated and sent to honourable confinement in an eastern fortress. With Kay-ferīdūn, matters were more serious, since he had stirred up Antalya with the aid of Cypriot Franks anxious to recapture the town; but he too was overcome, and was confined in a small apanage where he soon died, abandoned by everyone.

The peace negotiated between Lascaris and Kay-kāūs was perhaps not regarded by the participants as of greater importance than many others concluded earlier: it stipulated only that both sides should respect the frontiers. In actual fact, it marked the beginning of a peace which was to last for half a century, and even longer if a distinction is made between the official policies of states and the independent activities of frontier-dwellers. Henceforward it was solely on the eastern fronts, which were Christian in the case of Trebizond and Cilicia, and Muslim in the trans-Euphrates region and in Syria, that the Sultans conducted their operations. To explain this attitude is a matter of conjecture. As we know, this was not the first time that the Seljukids had thought it desirable to maintain or resume pacific relations with the Byzantine Empire. But, at the moment, they were faced only by the small residual 'Empire' of Nicaea, which moreover was under attack from the Franks. As they were at the apogee of their strength, it may well be thought that they would have had no great difficulty in destroying it or reducing it still further. Perhaps, while maintaining cordial relations with the Latins of Constantinople and the Venetians, they thought it preferable to maintain the Greek buffer state of Nicaea between the Latin and the Seljukid territory. Perhaps the annexation of Christian territories was of little interest to them, since they did not possess sufficient Muslim administrators to organize them. Lastly, as the disturbances which befell the Muslim world in the east became intensified (Turcoman movements, Khwārizmian and then Mongol invasions, the rise of the Ayyūbid power, among others), perhaps they considered it necessary to devote their entire attention to that sector. The Nicaean Greeks, for their part, were obviously bound to want peace to be maintained on the Turkish side so that they would be better able to contend with their Latin rivals, among others. Furthermore, the fact that they were now massed together in this place of refuge clearly led them to pay more attention to its defence than they had done earlier when, in Constantinople, they had looked upon it simply as a difficult frontier. When they later returned to Constantinople the frontier would once again be breached. However that may be, the political orientation of the Seljukid Sultanate is absolutely clear, and the line of action taken by Kay-kāūs, in perfect continuity with that of his father, aimed at developing the outlets to the sea and extending Seljukid influence in matters concerning Cilicia, Syria and Upper Mesopotamia.

In the south, once Antalya had been taken, Kay-kāūs set about helping the port to resume its activities by reaching a *modus vivendi* with the Cypriots, whose interests in the matter were now bound to coincide with his own. The difficulty was that, in the Syro-Cilician political manoeuvres, Seljukids and Cypriots supported opposing sides. However, correspondence exchanged from 1213 to 1216 in increasingly specific terms made it possible to separate the problems and to ensure favourable conditions for trade between the two countries, while leaving each of them free to support or resist Leo I or his enemy Bohemond IV of Antioch, helped by the Ayyūbids of Aleppo.

In the north, the great success of Kay-kāūs's reign was the now permanent acquisition of an outlet to the Black Sea, this time Sinope. The urgent need for this acquisition was all the greater since Lascaris had just defeated the Greeks of Trebizond and was extending his rule eastwards with such success that, unless some break with him came, there was a risk that it would soon become impossible to gain a footing on the Pontic coast. On the other hand, by carrying through the desired annexation quickly, it was accomplished at the expense of a remote outpost of Trebizond, without any direct affront to Lascaris, who in future was separated from his rival by this tongue of Seljukid territory. Hostilities had already occurred between the Turks and Trebizond, when the

Turcomans of the frontier region were fortunate enough to capture the Emperor of Trebizond, Alexis Comnenus. He was released in exchange for the return of Sinope and the conclusion of an agreement making him a vassal of Kay-kāūs, and he was compelled to pay tribute and on occasion to provide a military contingent. The ramparts were restored at the expense of fifteen emirs and inscriptions still record their respective contributions, a Turkish garrison was installed, and the leading church was converted into a mosque. But the command was given to an Armenian, Hethoum, possibly a convert to Islam, but in any case better qualified than a Turk to deal with the predominantly Christian merchants who frequented the port.

The interventions made by Kay-kāūs on his south-eastern frontiers were less consistently successful. He could not forgive Leo I of Cilicia for his intrusions into Seljukid affairs; moreover, Leo had been called in against him by Bohemond IV, from whom he had just taken Antioch, and by the latter's ally al-Zāhir of Aleppo. Hostilities took place in 1216–18, the Armenian Constantine the Constable was captured, and various fortified places in the Taurus were acquired, among them being Lu'lu', on the route from Sis to Kayseri, which the Seljukids later made one of their strongest bases. In Aleppo, al-Zāhir had died, after securing recognition of his young son al-'Azīz by al-'Ādil. In opposition to him, Kay-kāūs supported his Ayyūbid vassal in Samosata, al-Afdal, and, relying mainly on the troops of the lord of Mar'ash, Nusrat al-Dīn Hasan ibn Ibrāhīm, he seized the territories in northern Syria which had already been occupied several times by his forbears. The prince's mother, the regent of Aleppo, then appealed to a son of al-'Ādil, al-Ashraf, who at the time was in Syria and who crushed the Seljukid army (1218).

Kay-kāūs sought to take his revenge in Upper Mesopotamia, where al-Ashraf was his father's representative in the Ayyūbid possessions. By marriage, the Seljukid Sultan had strengthened his relations with his neighbour and to some extent vassal, Bahrāmshāh of Erzinjān. He had nothing to fear from Mughīth al-Dīn, the opponent of Ayyūbid ambitions, and he had ingratiated himself with the Caliph by accepting the *futuwwa*, which will be described later. Now al-Ashraf and his ally Lu'lu', the powerful minister of Mosul, were opposed in Upper Mesopotamia

123

by a relative of the young Zengid prince whom Lu'lu' was trying to supplant, and the Artukid of Āmid and Hisn Kayfa. They appealed to Kay-kāūs for help. Kay-kāūs was preparing for a campaign when he died (end of 1220), and the coalition broke up. It was reserved for his successors to win, in this sector, the victories that fate had denied him.

'Alā' al-Dīn Kay-kubādh, who succeeded his brother Kay-kāūs without any great difficulty, was to leave posterity so enduring a memory as the most illustrious prince of the dynasty that, in later times, many Turkish leaders tried to trace back their ancestors' titles of nobility to his sponsorship. This glorious reputation he probably owed in part to the fact that he was the last of the Seljukids to die in independence, but also to the indisputable successes of his policy and to his outstanding personality. Ibn Bībī, who also knew many of his contemporaries, says that he was versed in all branches of knowledge, athletic, generous, and anxious to seek inspiration from the examples of the great masters of politics. Some found him haughty; in any case, what is unquestioned is the constant attention by means of which he succeeded in keeping the greatest of his emirs within bounds.

On all his frontiers, Kay-kubādh's policy was even bolder – and more successful – than his predecessors'. The earliest conquests were gained either from the Armeno-Cilicians or from Graeco-Armenian lords, formerly dependents of Byzantium who were now no doubt in varying degrees under the dominance of the Armenian kings of Cilicia. First, in 1221, came the conquest of Kalon-oros, on the eastern coast of the Gulf of Antalya. Its Greek lord finally surrendered in exchange for the command of Akshehir/Philomelion, in Seljukid territory. Renamed 'Alā'iyya (now Alanya) in honour of the Sultan, the fortress became one of the Seljukid sovereigns' principal strongholds, as well as their winter residence. The occupation of the coast towards the east was completed between 1221 and 1225, as far as the approaches to Selefke/Seleucia, which the Hospitallers held under Armenian suzerainty. At the same time, infiltrations were being made into the Tauro-Isaurian hinterland, and were facilitated by the political situation. Leo I had for a time been succeeded by a son of Bohemond IV, now once again master of Antioch, but Constantine the Constable having overthrown the young prince and set up his own son Hethoum in his place, the old Franco-Seljukid alliance was renewed. Operations were partly conducted for Kay-kubādh by the emir Comnenus (= Maurozomes, a descendant of Isaac Comnenus) and finally led to the establishment of a frontier march, in the Ermenek and Mūt regions, which was granted to a certain Qamar al-Dīn, whose name became attached to it. At the same time the Turcomans were attracted there and soon became a powerful force, as will be seen. During Frederick II's Crusade there may possibly have been a Cypriot plot to regain Kalon-oros/ʿAlāʾiyya, but it was forestalled, and occupation of the territory was finally established without disturbance.

It was on the opposite coast, on the Black Sea, that Seljukid policy seems to have been most enterprising, since it no longer restricted itself to attacks on Trebizond along its frontiers but, even as far away as the Crimea, challenged at sea the politico-commercial pre-eminence acquired by Trebizond since the fall of the Empire in Constantinople. The details of events are sometimes difficult to piece together, but the essence is clear. Relations were established between the inhabitants of the northern shores of the Black Sea and the subjects of the Seljukid Sultan. At the time of the first Mongol invasion of southern Russia, merchants from the large Crimean port of Sughdaq had taken refuge in Asia Minor. According to the Muslim historian Ibn al-Athīr, one of their ships had been wrecked off Sinope, and according to custom the Seljukid authorities had plundered the cargo; according to the sources in Trebizond, on the other hand, this vessel was carrying tribute from Cherson to Trebizond and is said to have been deliberately attacked by Hethoum. Whatever the truth of the matter, hostilities broke out between Sinope and Trebizond, and ended with an exchange of conquests (1223). It was in connection with these events that the writers in Trebizond mentioned the disaster suffered at the gates of Trebizond by an assailant whom they call merely 'Melik', and who was probably Mughīth al-Dīn Tughrīlshāh of Erzurum. This latter, who had perhaps felt some disquiet in regard to Kay-kubādh since abandoning him in 1212, acknowledged himself as a vassal (?) of Trebizond. Events in the succeeding years do in fact show him to have been on good terms with Trebizond. Clearly their economic interests coincided, against those of the Seljukid trading centre of Sivas and its maritime outlet at Sinope.

Meanwhile the memorable Crimean campaign had taken place. This time the Mongols had not halted, and Russian influence was now prevalent in Sughdaq where the merchants, who were Seljukid subjects, claimed to have grievances. Kay-kubādh entrusted command of a naval operation against Sughdaq to his former associate from Ankara days, Husām al-Dīn Chupan, ruler of the province of Kastamonu where he had large Turcoman forces at his disposal. The inhabitants appealed to the Kipchaks for help, but without success, and as the Russians were anxious to negotiate, the port capitulated. In addition to indemnifying the plaintiffs, it was compelled to accept the establishment of a Seljukid protectorate, marked by the building of a mosque and the installation of a Turkish garrison (1225). There exists no information from which to tell how far this protectorate remained effective when the final Mongol conquest took place in 1239.

In the east, Kay-kubādh's policy led to the unification of Asia Minor and the extension of his influence in Upper Mesopotamia and northern Syria. He had now become reconciled with al-Ashraf, who was opposed in Syria by his brother al-Muʿazzam and in Diyār Bakr by the Artukid of Hisn Kayfa and Āmid. At the request of his Ayyūbid ally, Kay-kubādh had the Artukid stripped of all his possessions west of the Euphrates, that is to say both Chimishkesek and also the fortresses on the southern slopes of the eastern Taurus (1227). The successes he thus achieved disturbed even al-Ashraf, and helped to incline him towards a *rapprochement* with his Ayyūbid relations. A series of missions sent by Kay-kubādh to the various Ayyūbids proves that he wanted to play a part in their negotiations, but what in fact came of it is not known.

It was in connection with these events that Kay-kubādh annexed the principality of Erzinjān and intervened in that of Erzurum. In Erzinjān, the aged Bahrāmshāh had died in 1225. In opposition to his son Dā'ūdshāh, some emirs had intrigued with the Seljukid Sultan. Dā'ūdshāh had managed to reach agreement with him, but must have felt that a rupture was imminent, since he started negotiations with the prince of Erzurum, with al-Ashraf, even with the head of the Assassins of Alamūt, who some time earlier had resumed his allegiance to the Caliph, and finally with the Khwārizmshāh Jalāl al-Dīn Manguberṭī, on his approach. To all of them he offered his fortress of Kamakh. Kay-kubādh did not wait for a coalition to be formed. A Seljukid army attacked Erzinjān, and Dā'ūdshāh had to agree to abandon his principality, in return for a considerable fief for his lifetime, in the centre of Anatolia. Another Mangujakid, the holder of Shebin Karahisār/Kughūniya (Colonia), also had to accept a similar arrangement. The Mangujakid principality had never worried the Seljukids, and it is clear that the intrigues of Dā'ūdshāh's opponents had merely served as a pretext for the Sultan. The real cause was apparently the imminence of a decisive reckoning with Erzurum and the Ayyūbids, behind whom could be discerned the Khwārizmian threat, of which more will be said shortly, and which made the Sultan realize the need for a direct and firmly based occupation of eastern Asia Minor. It was only in Divriği which, situated further back, did not present the same danger, that he allowed a Mangujakid to remain. To judge from inscriptions and a waqf-deed, the latter lived there at least until 1252. Control of Erzinjān was given to the same Ertöküsh who had been commander of Antalya and who was now promoted to be atabek to Kaykhusraw, one of Kay-kubādh's sons, but not the one chosen as first in succession. The principality was probably intended to constitute his apanage.

In Erzurum, it will be remembered, Mughīth al-Dīn Tughrīl-shāh had for a long time pursued a policy parallel to that of the other Seljukids, particularly when, taking advantage of the extinction of the dynasty of the Shāh-i Armin of Akhlāt he had, though without success, disputed the possession of this town by the Ayyūbid sons of al-ʿĀdil. His subsequent rebuffs by Trebizond have been described, and also his rapprochement with it. Moreover, he had to keep a watch on the increasing power of the Georgians, who for the most part directed their attacks against Azerbaijan but who, at the beginning of the century, had also occupied Kars. In about 1223 he accepted the proposal put forward by the queen of Georgia, Russudan, that she should marry a son of Tughrīlshāh, if he became Christian. He died in 1225, at about the same time as Bahrāmshāh.

It was with his successor, Rukn al-Dīn Jahānshāh, that Dā'ūdshāh of Erzinjān had negotiated. As soon as the attack on

Erzinjān began, Kay-kubādh also organized one on Erzurum, which was interrupted by a diversion by Trebizond. The short-lived alliance between Kay-kubādh and al-Ashraf had been dissolved, as we have seen, while on the contrary the Ayyūbid and the Seljukid of Erzurum were drawn together by the imminence of the Khwārizmian danger which formed a direct threat to both.

In 1226 a Khwārizmian detachment had pillaged the country round Erzurum and then attacked Akhlāt. Jahānshāh came to the help of al-Ashraf, who reciprocated in 1228, sending him large reinforcements commanded by his lieutenant in the east, Husām al-Dīn ibn Abī ʿAlī.

In the last few pages there have been several references to Jalāl al-Dīn Manguberti and his Khwārizmians. It was in fact at this point that this extraordinary adventurer began to make an impression as a political factor in the Near East. He was the son of the Khwārizmshāh Muhammad, who had been expelled from his dominions in Central Asia in 1217 by the Mongols, dying soon afterwards in poverty on an island in the Caspian. He had succeeded in regrouping, under his leadership, bands of 'Khwārizmian' cavalrymen, in reality Kipchaks, the basis of the strength of the Khwārizmshāhs in recent times. Fleeing before the Mongols, forced to make conquests in order to live, and taking advantage of the decay of Iranian power, he was carving out for himself by the sword an Empire with north-western Iran as its centre. His destiny, constantly poised between power and death, until the obscure end that overtook him immediately after his greatest successes, and the terror inspired by his followers – these won him a considerable reputation among his contemporaries, in which admiration and fear were mingled. An echo of it is preserved by his secretary and biographer al-Nasawī. Among the Turks of Asia Minor, who, though threatened on his account, still recognized him as one of themselves, it is certain that he was regarded with both fear and respect.

For some years his influence in the Mesopotamian rivalries between Ayyūbids, Artukids and Luʾluʾ of Mosul was appreciable. However, while his aggression had revealed itself at the expense of the Georgians, and indeed of al-Ashraf and Jahānshāh, the long-term danger that the Seljukid State might face from the

Khwārizmian conquest of strategic strongholds such as Akhlāt, guarding one of the traditional invasion routes, was compensated in the short term by the resultant weakening of troublesome neighbours, and as the Khwārizmshāh for his part was not anxious to provoke any intervention by the Seljukid power in support of his immediate enemies, relations between them had at the start been correct. Even if Jalāl al-Dīn asked for financial aid at least against the pagan Mongols, the common foe of all Islam, when he undertook the siege of Akhlāt in 1227 he offered an alliance against al-Ashraf, confirmed by the marriage of Kay-khusraw to one of his daughters.

However, in 1229 events took another turn. After a fearful siege, Jalāl al-Dīn had just captured Akhlāt, aided by the absence of al-Ashraf, who had been detained in Syria by Frederick II's Crusade. In this emergency the Artukids gave him the homage that earlier they had pledged to Kay-kubādh. More serious were developments concerning Jahānshāh of Erzurum, who had at first aligned himself against Jalāl al-Dīn, as described above, but who now thought it safer to seek his help against Kay-kubādh. Whether or not Jalāl al-Dīn had earlier hoped to conquer Asia Minor, it was to Jahānshāh's side that he resolved to turn. Kay-kubādh's ambassador Kāmyār could only hasten away to inform his master.

Kay-kubādh reacted without delay. Despatching a holding force to Erzinjān, he sent Kāmyār to explain to al-Kāmil, the head of the Ayyūbids in Egypt who was then across the Euphrates, and to his brother Al-Ashraf that an anti-Khwārizmian coalition was essential for both of them. Al-Ashraf was of course already convinced of this, and al-Kāmil was easily persuaded, although the presence of Frederick II prevented him from joining the expedition in person. In addition to his five thousand picked men chosen from troops from Aleppo and Diyār Bakr and the Seljukid army proper, and apart from the Turcomans, there was also a Franco-Armenian contingent which, since his defeat, the Armenian king of Cilicia was under obligation to furnish in case of emergency. The Ayyūbid contingent was led by al-Ashraf himself, and the rallying-place for the troops was Sivas, with Jahānshāh powerless to intervene. Jalāl al-Dīn, who was laying siege to Manazgird/Manzikert, decided to invade Asia Minor immediately. The encounter took place in the grassy valley of Yassï-

chimen, to the west of Erzinjān, on 25 Ramadān 628/29 July
1231. The battle lasted three days, and the Syrian troops seem to
have played a decisive role. Jahāl al-Dīn, defeated for the first time
by forces other than Mongols, fled to Azerbaijan, abandoning
Manzikert and Akhlāt as well as his treasure. The Khwārizmians
were massacred or taken prisoner in a body. The moral effect was
considerable, and Christians and Muslims alike gave a triumphant
welcome to Kay-kubādh, the conqueror of a sovereign hitherto
considered invincible.

Materially, the principal benefit for him was the annexation of
the kingdom of Erzurum, whose prince had been captured during
the disastrous defeat of his protector. Like the Mangujakids, he
was given a fief for his lifetime in the centre of the Seljukid
dominions. Erzurum itself was not formed into an apanage but was
annexed directly. In this way the Seljukid State was extended
eastwards, in face of the Mongol threat, just as the Byzantine
Empire had earlier been extended in face of the Turkish threat –
and, as the future was to demonstrate, with the same lack of
success.

However, al-Ashraf, aided by a Seljukid force, recaptured
Akhlāt. It was then that news came of the ʿAlāʾiyya plot, mentioned above, which compelled Kay-kubādh to depart with all
speed. Taking advantage of the dispersal of Muslim forces in Asia
Minor and of the crushing of the Khwārizmians, a Mongol force
which had meanwhile penetrated into Azerbaijan made a raid as
far as the outskirts of Sivas and Malatya. When the Seljukid army
under Kāmyār arrived, the raiders had already disappeared. It
was decided to take revenge on the Georgians, who had assisted
the invaders, possibly under compulsion, but nevertheless by an
action quite in keeping with their traditional enmity (for Russudan
had broken with her Turkish husband), and to recompense themselves at their expense for the losses suffered by the devastated
provinces. A great number of frontier strongholds fell within a
few days. Russudan had no wish to impose upon her country,
which had already been devastated successively by Khwārizmians
and Mongols, the further hardship of war with the now victorious
Seljukids. With her new neighbour she therefore revived the
policy of alliance earlier maintained with his predecessors, and a
marriage was arranged between Kay-kubādh's son Kaykhusraw

and the daughter whom Russudan herself had borne to Jahānshāh's brother.

Moreover, as al-Ashraf appeared to be losing interest in his most easterly provinces, now ruined, and confining himself to Syria, Kay-kubādh, who no longer needed him as an ally and considered his attitude to be in fact prejudicial to the defence of his own territories against the approaching Mongol danger, gave orders to Kāmyār to occupy Akhlāt. The measures adopted for its re-organization prove that it was really a complete annexation, and a military commander, Sinān al-Dīn Kaymaz, was appointed as head of the whole eastern defensive area.

Finally, to perform these new tasks, more troops were needed. Jalāl al-Dīn had died, when fleeing from the Mongols, at the hand of a Kurdish peasant from Diyār Bakr. There were still many of his former men who, being left stranded, were ready to hire themselves to the first bidder in return for some modicum of security. Some of them, led by Kīrkhān, had been welcomed by the Ayyūbids of Akhlāt and Mayāfāriquīn, and now, through Kaymaz, they entered the service of Kay-kubādh, who distributed the province of Erzurum among them as *iqtā's*. It is true that, in this form, the solution proved to be illusory. Taken by surprise by a Mongol raid, the demoralized Khwārizmians fled and asked for lands that were less exposed. Kīrkhān was given Erzinjān, his colleague Bereke received Amasya, others had Laranda, Nigde and other places. It was hoped by this means that, providing that they were no longer on the borders, it would be possible to rely on their forces against foreseeable attacks and to ward off any future enemies.

Now, just as Yassï-chimen had led to the unification of eastern Asia Minor, it had also led to that of Diyār Bakr in the hands of the Ayyūbids. Their leader, al-Kāmil, had captured Hisn Kayfa and Āmid, and all that remained of the Artukid dynasty was the most southerly branch in Mārdīn, narrowly hemmed in and reduced to vassalage. The whole had been given by al-Kāmil as an apanage to his young son al-Sālih Ayyūb. Henceforward, Ayyūbid and Seljukid ambitions came into direct conflict with each other, and the capture of Akhlāt by Kaykhusraw could not leave al-Kāmil unmoved. The impression gained by the Syrians as they watched the anti-Khwārizmian campaign was that a conquest of the Seljukid State would not be very difficult. Al-Kāmil gathered together an army, which even included contingents from Aleppo as well as the sons of Al-Afdal of Samosata (who had recently died), though their reason for joining is not known. Preparations on such a scale could not pass unnoticed, and Kay-kubādh had sent Kāmyār to guard the defiles of the northern Syrian Taurus. Failing to force these, the Ayyūbid army turned away eastwards, putting Hisn Mansūr to fire and the sword, and crossing the Euphrates towards Sevaverak/Suwaïda with the intention of resuming the invasion from there, through Khartpert, where the Artukid ruler, having revolted against Kay-kubādh, was an ally. But the powerful relieving force sent forward by al-Kāmil to Khartpert was driven back by the Seljukid army, including Khwārizmians, into the fortress which itself was compelled to surrender. Kay-kubādh set free the Syrians without ransom: he knew that al-Kāmil's vassals and allies had no common purpose to inspire them, and that they suspected him of wanting to give them what they felt to be highly unattractive territories in Anatolia, in return for their Syrian territories which he would appropriate. Possibly some of them had even intrigued with Kay-kubādh. Al-Kāmil was compelled to withdraw to Egypt, with no hope of returning (1233). Kay-kubādh was even able to have the whole of Diyār Mudār occupied immediately, with Harrān and Edessa, and part of its population was deported. This region was in fact too vital for the Ayyūbids, who could not reach their possessions in Syria and Upper Mesopotamia without crossing it, and too remote for the Seljukids to be able to defend it well. Al-Kāmil re-occupied it. Kay-kubādh prepared to turn against Āmid, the strategic centre for the whole of Diyār Bakr, which he attacked in alliance with the Artukid of Mārdīn and various contingents, among whom were Frankish and Georgian vassals. The Caliph caused the siege to be raised temporarily, but Kay-kubādh prepared to resume it with the aid of the coalition that was being formed among the Ayyūbids themselves against the dictatorial al-Kāmil. It was only by his successor, however, that this ambition was to be realized.

Despite these minor setbacks, Kay-kubādh was at the peak of his glory, and one of the great powers in the Orient. The undisputed master of the whole of Asia Minor, from the coast opposite Rhodes to the sources of the Tigris and from Dorylaion to Mount Ararat, he had moreover reduced to some kind of vassal status or brought back into his alliance the small neighbouring Christian States, Armeno-Cilician, Georgian and probably also that of Trebizond, and, through the first-named, he received Frankish reinforcements. Indeed, various coins testify to these facts, for example one which combines the names of the 'takavor' (Armenian 'king') Hethoum and Sultan Kay-kubādh.

In the background, however, the Mongol threat was beginning to take shape. It was this that had helped to turn Jalāl al-Dīn against Asia Minor and, by taking him from the rear, had transformed the defeat inflicted on him there into a conclusive disaster. Reference has already been made to the raids on Sivas and Malatya, and later raids against the Khwārizmians of Erzurum. That Seljukid territory was not penetrated even more fully was because the Mongols were only concerned with covering their position, and their objective at that time was Georgia. In 1236 an embassy arrived from the Great Khan, demanding the annual despatch of an envoy with tribute. In fact, nothing came of this for several years, on account of questions of succession to the Great Khan then confronting the Mongols. But this was merely a postponement. Kay-kubādh had prepared a courteous reply, but it was his son who sent it, for he died on 4 Shawwāl 634/31 May 1237.

Kay-kubādh had three sons, 'Izz al-Dīn, Rukn al-Dīn and Kaykhusraw. The first two were the sons of his Ayyūbid wife, and it was to 'Izz al-Dīn that Kay-kubādh had caused an oath of allegiance to be sworn. But Kaykhusraw was the eldest, and it was to him that the great emirs rallied, since he was the most powerful. Thus initiated, the reign opened with bloody conflicts, which however did not interfere with foreign policy.

At the start, Kaykhusraw's policy was inspired by Köpek, formerly controller of hunting and buildings, an ambitious man who wished to rid himself of any emirs who might overshadow him. The chief of the Khwārizmians apparently being undecided which of the sons of Kay-kubādh to support, Köpek had him arrested. The result was that the Khwārizmians, thrusting aside the Seljukid armies, retreated across the Euphrates into Diyār Mudār, where they went to offer their services for the future to the Ayyūbids. Köpek accused certain emirs of inciting them to do this, and had the *atabek* Altunbeh executed, although a consistently loyal supporter of Kaykhusraw. Meanwhile, as Kaykhusraw's own line was assured by the birth of sons, his young brothers and their mother were strangled. The last victim was Kāmyār himself, the most eminent of Kay-kubādh's servants.

Köpek was of course eager to strengthen his position further by successes abroad. Circumstances helped him. Al-Ashraf, and later al-Kāmil, both died within a few months. Against al-Kāmil, Kaykhusraw entered into closer relations with al-Nāsir, the young prince of Aleppo, and his mother the regent, in return for some kind of vassalage, as various coins testify. Then, when al-Kāmil too had died, a coalition of all the princes of Upper Mesopotamia and Syria was formed against his son al-Sālih Ayyūb, the holder of the Ayyūbid territories beyond the Euphrates. The coalition was joined by Kaykhusraw, who, as his share of the spoils, was promised Samosata and Āmid. Köpek actually occupied Samosata, which al-Afdal's sons did not try to defend. But the coalition's successes went no further because al-Sālih obtained the support of the Khwārizmians in return for the grant of Diyār Mudār as an *iqtā'*. Whether for that reason or from natural apprehension, Kaykhusraw laid an ambush for Köpek, who was assassinated (1240).

Influence then passed to three men, Jalāl al-Dīn Karatay, Shams al-Dīn al-Isfahānī, *nā'ib* to the Sultan, and Muhadhdhab al-Dīn, the vizier, of whom more will be heard. They arranged for the conclusion of the marriage, previously planned, with the Georgian princess. She was accompanied by her cousin David, of whom Russudan was anxious to rid herself, so that she had him imprisoned by Kaykhusraw on a charge of intriguing with the queen. The Georgian alliance might prove beneficial in future dealings with the Mongols, who were again presenting a threat, and Russudan was their vassal. Moreover, Kaykhusraw tried to call back the Khwārizmians but, having no success, he joined the coalition that was again being formed against al-Sālih, then involved in dramatic Syrian complications, and his troops took part in the victory that was gained over the Khwārizmians (November 1240). While Harrān, the capital of Diyār Mudār, was restored to Aleppo, the Seljukid troops started once more to besiege Āmid, which finally surrendered early in 1241. Two years later, after the crushing of the Turcoman revolt, to be described later, an attack was launched even against Mayāfāriqīn, the capital of the Ayyūbid Diyār Bakr, where al-Ghāzī, a surviving brother of al-Kāmil, was trying to revive al-Sālih's policy for his own purposes. Perhaps it might have proved successful, if the news that the Mongols were approaching had not come at that moment.

It has already been stated that, from the time of the accession of Kay-kāūs, generally speaking, peace had prevailed between the Greeks of Nicaea and the Turks, and indeed no reference to any hostilities between them since that time has been made. However, the Syrian chronicler Ibn Natīf, an exact contemporary of Kay-kubādh, refers in about 1230 to two battles between that Sultan and 'Laskari' (John Vatatzes, son of Theodore Lascaris), the first of which was successful but not the second. It is difficult to think that these battles, which are not mentioned either by the chron-iclers of Seljukid Asia Minor or by those of the Empire of Nicaea, can have been anything more than frontier clashes of no signifi-cance. Nevertheless, we know that, at the end of his reign, Kay-kubādh sent an embassy to Pope Gregory IX, and that Kaykhusraw who was receiving the Latin missionaries with favour, in about 1242 was negotiating with Baldwin II of Con-stantinople for a marriage. Baldwin revealed this to Blanche of Castile, the queen of France, justifying it by their common hostility to Vatatzes. The arrival of the Mongols was to change everything since, in face of this new enemy, Kaykhusraw and his successors preferred the immediate assistance of Nicaea, which was nearby, to the distant alliance of the Franks. But there is little doubt that there was a state of tension and that, but for the Mongol invasion, its results might have become important.

Taken as a whole, Kaykhusraw's power was apparently fully equal to his father's. According to Brother Simon of Saint-Quentin, who is referred to later and who, though possibly guilty of exaggerations or misunderstandings, did not invent, the king of Armenia had to provide him with 1,400 lances for four months, the king of Nicaea with 400, with no limit of place or time, Trebisond with 200, and Aleppo with 1,000 (perhaps paid for by him). According to this account, the first two even came to Kayseri to reach an understanding with him. Perhaps this is a reference to the exceptional circumstances of the campaign against the Mongols, but even so it would not have been possible if Kaykhusraw's power had not been well-known.

Nevertheless, it was during his reign that an event occurred which helps us to grasp one of the causes of weakness in the Seljukid State, and which is certainly a matter of real importance, to judge by subsequent facts, despite the inadequacy of the surviving information on the subject. As in the time of Rustem, it concerned the Turcomans, but this time their revolt was undeniably of a religious, as well as of a social, character. To this first aspect we shall return later, but the external facts must be described here for their part in political life.

In the Kafarsūd region, that is to say on the Syrian-Euphrates-Taurus borders, there was then a *baba*, a popular Turcoman preacher, Ishāq, who called himself the *Rasūl* (Prophet) of Allah. By various means he succeeded in attracting a group of fervent and warlike adherents. He then extended his propaganda to the region of Amasya, much further to the north. Soon the whole area, from the Syrian borders to Malatya, from which place they even tried to win over the Khwārizmians, and then the regions of Amasya, Tokat and the intervening ones of Sivas and Kayseri were penetrated and overrun by them. It was in vain that various troops were sent against them from Malatya, and later from Amasya and elsewhere. It is true that they succeeded in capturing Baba Ishāq himself, and that he was then put to death; but this fact in no way restricted his followers' ardour, indeed the contrary. The best Seljukid troops had to be brought in to put an end to them finally in the Kïrshehir region. Among these contingents the Franks are mentioned specifically, and Brother Simon states that it was almost solely to them that the victory over 'Paperoissole' was due. Themselves guilty of so much pillaging and massacre, the insurgents were in turn exterminated with even greater savagery. However, their descendants were to appear in due course.

These events, which occurred in about 1240 and lasted for two or three years, are difficult to interpret. We do not know what Baba Ishāq preached or claimed. It is not clear in what way the events in the East, the flights and conquests of the Khwārizmians or the Mongol thrust could have had repercussions on the conditions of life of the Turcomans in central Asia Minor, or if any repercussions had resulted from the extension of the Seljukid authority or the settlement of the Khwārizmians. We can only state that one of the fundamental elements of the population found itself in violent opposition to the Seljukid government, and that it was necessary to call in against it forces which could have been of use elsewhere. It is certain that the acquisition of new territories did not constitute merely an increase in strength, and that it raised new problems. It is true that the Mongols had defeated other powers; even so, without these weaknesses the Seljukid State would perhaps have been better able to resist them. It was in fact at this moment that the Mongols came. Held up for a time by difficulties over the succession to the Great Khan Ogodaï, they returned under the nominal command of Jurmāghūn, a sick man, and under the distant supervision of Bātū in Russia, with Bayjū at their head as their effective leader. In the winter of 1242–3, while other Mongols penetrated into Upper Mesopotamia, Bayjū attacked Erzurum. As usual, in addition to the massive scale and ferocity of the Mongol attack, treachery played a part, and the 'Tartars' took the town without having to proceed to a siege which, at that season and that altitude (over 3,000 ft.) would have been arduous. They thus held the key to Asia Minor, which they invaded in the spring. At the news of the danger, the imminence of which he does not seem to have foreseen, Kaykhusraw not only recalled his distant troops but also sent requests, accompanied by large sums of money and gifts, for the maximum possible reinforcements, to his vassals, his allies, even to his former enemies, now reconciled by the common danger facing them – Ghāzī of Mayāfāriqīn (a town the Mongols had just taken, only to evacuate it), Aleppo, Trebizond, Nicaea (?), Armenians, Franks and others. The rallying point was to be Sivas, where the Sultan went. Around him, people alternated between the usual panic seen wherever the Mongols approached, and impatience to go out to halt them, rather than wait until they had occupied or devastated half the realm. With a powerful but ill-assorted army, and without waiting for those who were delaying (the Armenians, who were already humouring the Mongols), Kaykhusraw moved off to take up his position in the defile of Köse Dagh, in the province of Erzinjān. For Bayjū, it was a difficult position from which there was no escape, but he succeeded in disorganizing his enemies by the old expedient of a feigned retreat followed by a sudden advance. On the evening of 6 Muharram 641/26 June 1243, the Seljukid army no longer existed. The Sultan collected his treasure in Tokat and escaped to Ankara, while his mother went to Cilicia. The Mongols occupied Sivas and, meeting with a brief resistance from Kayseri, took their revenge by sacking it ruthlessly. That they advanced no farther for the moment was perhaps because they were unwilling to extend beyond their other fronts, and because Kaykhusraw's vizier intended eventually to negotiate. But the defeat of Köse Dagh was not of the kind that can be redeemed. In one day, the course of the history of Asia Minor had been altered beyond recall.

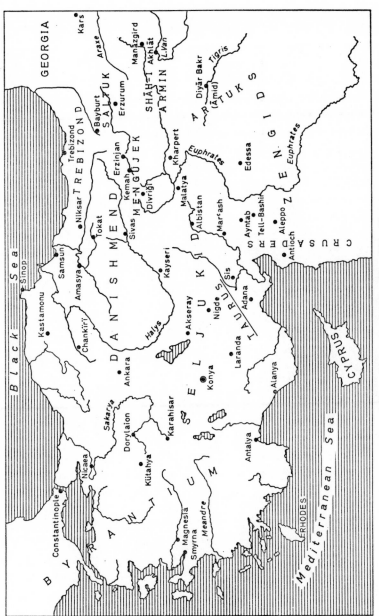

MAP II. Anatolia in the Twelfth Century

11

PART THREE

Society and Institutions Before the Mongols

I

THE BIRTH OF TURKEY

As was said earlier, the 'turkization' of Asia Minor, even though incomplete, has often appeared to be a source of astonishment, a fact that is itself astonishing. In the course of their history many other countries have changed their ethnic character, and we merely have to try to understand in each case how this took place and, if possible, in what degree and proportion.

It is obviously impossible to give any figures for the Turkish immigration into Asia Minor. Generally speaking, it is difficult to believe that movements of peoples at that period can have involved more than a few tens of thousands of individuals in any one operation, at the most two or three hundred thousand, even though the texts give the impression of enormous masses (it should be remembered that regular armies in battle contained at the most a few thousand men). However, various factors come into play which, either in general or in Asia Minor in particular, increase, if not the actual scale of the numbers involved, at least its relative effect. On the one hand, as has been noted, Asia Minor, taken as a whole and with some regional exceptions, was thinly populated at the time of the Turkish penetration; and the flights, massacres and enslavements during the phase of conquest reduced the population still further. In the second place, its component elements were so disparate that, even though their total numbers were obviously far greater than those of the new immigrants, the distinction between both was already less clear, and in any case the disproportion is slighter, if the immigrants as a whole, are compared with each of those component elements, if the powers of penetration of the one side are set against the other side's powers of resistance. In any case it was the Turks alone, or certain of them, who were present in all parts, while there were Greek regions, Armenian regions, and so on. Thirdly, it is certain that the great majority of the Turks who set out from Central Asia settled in Azerbaijan and Asia Minor, most of them finally reaching the latter country. There they found living conditions sufficiently close to their own traditions to reduce the need for any adaptation, such as they had not found in the Arab countries or in central and southern Iran. Lastly, and perhaps this is the essential point, as has been explained, the ethnic effects of an invasion cannot be thought of in an instantaneous, static form. What counts is not merely the number of immigrants, but the economic and social position that they held, and also the way in which relations between the two peoples became organized, particularly marriages and births. Enslavement, or even discouragement, may have reduced the fecundity of the subject people, whereas the opening of wider possibilities in the existence of groups which tended to envisage riches and power in terms of the number of children, might on the contrary increase their birth-rate. Moreover, it is certain that, either by abduction or, more commonly, because the heads of native families hoped in return to be left in peace by the conquerors, many of the young native women must by right or by force have been taken into the victors' beds, and consequently, their children being brought up as Turks, it was the Turks who benefited by their progeny, at the expense of native society. We are of course unable to give figures or define these matters exactly, and perhaps they should if possible be modified or even called into question in certain cases. But the basic ideas, the general orientation of their evolution, in themselves appear to be distinctly probable. Naturally, a mingling of races of this kind resulted in a partial alteration of the Turkish type, but that did not prevent the children from regarding themselves or being regarded as Turks at heart. In certain cases the conquerors' racial superiority may quickly have been endangered by their monopoly of warfare, in which they suffered losses. To a slight extent, this is possibly what happened later, with the Mongols, just as it had with the Vandals in North Africa. But war never seems to have been sufficiently permanent or costly in lives to bring about any such consequences for the Turks of Asia Minor, either temporarily or locally, and other factors would have restored the balance.

However that may be, it is certain that, if Muslim authors continued to apply the name Rūm/Rome (which no longer bore its precise political significance) to Asia Minor, and then to the state created there by the Seljukids, on the other hand western writers, from the time of Barbarossa's Crusade at the latest, when they had to give a name to the country, spoke of it as Turchia, Turkey, a word they did not apply to any of the other countries under Turkish domination. It is thus clear that, in whatever way the Turkish character of Asia Minor is assessed, and however ill-defined the frontiers of Turchia, its Turkish aspect was felt by contemporaries to impart a specific identity to the whole. It is true, as will be shown in another context, that this Turkish aspect did not really make itself felt among the whole Turco-Muslim population of Asia Minor itself before the Mongol period; but that is no justification for dismissing the general impression held by foreigners, merely on the grounds that, from within, those concerned were more alive to the differences between their own component elements than to their unity as against others.

This being said, it is now necessary to enter into somewhat greater detail, and to try to identify certain more precise features of this phenomenon of 'turkization'.

Firstly, from the geographical point of view, it is probable that the turkization was not everywhere of equal intensity. As seen through the chronicles, which mostly relate the incidents on the frontiers, the turkization appears to have been considerable all along the borders of the politically Turkish domain, facing the Greeks in the west and north and the Armenians in the south (the Georgians, for their part, were more worried by their somewhat exposed frontier with Azerbaijan than by the difficult mountains separating them from Asia Minor). There is no doubt, and there are various episodes to remind those who are uncertain, that there were also some Turkish settlements in inland regions. The fact remains nevertheless that the truly Turcoman elements had been massed mainly on the frontiers, either spontaneously or by organized movement of population, according to the individual case. It sometimes happens that place-names are given by Byzantine authors in their Turkish form, suggesting that no one was left who remembered the native form.

The distinction made here shows at once that the problem is at least as much social as ethnic. When western writers speak of Turchia, it is certain that they have in mind, above all, the open country held by the Turcomans, who would have to be encountered in battle and whom, generalizing a term properly applied to nomadic Arabs, they sometimes also call Bedouins. For the towns, the problem is a different one, which will be considered shortly.

The turkization of the open country is thus essentially the work of the Turcomans. Varying naturally with the region, an indigenous rural population still remained, usually forming a large majority. Not all its members had fled or been killed and, whether free or subdued, many remained in Cappadocia, Armenia, on the borders of the Anatolian plateau and elsewhere. In the western frontier zones the Byzantines often brought them back after their victories, creating a sort of no man's land (and thereby increasing the Turcomans' importance), but sometimes the Seljukids also took them back and installed them, under conditions that guaranteed their stability. The principal question, and a difficult one to answer, is to know how to picture these Turcomans of the Seljukid period. Were they exclusively nomads, or were they no longer so? It has already been remarked that, for contemporary Turkish scholars, this question is a crucial one, perhaps excessively so, and that even in Central Asia there were modifications of nomadism (but perhaps fewer of the sedentarized elements emigrated than of the others). Moreover, a distinction has to be made between long-range nomads with camels, who were not to be in the majority in Asia Minor, and seasonal migrants with flocks of sheep, sometimes attached to villages according to the season, who surely were more numerous. Were there also sedentarized elements who became cultivators of land? Travellers describe the Turks exclusively as nomadic shepherds, but no doubt they only gave that name specifically to those who were nomadic, without including those who had ceased to be so. And from all the accounts of battles, which give the impression of a populace always ready to move, any conclusions must be subject to the same reserve. In any case, we know that there were Turcoman foresters and wood-cutters, occupations which, if not agriculture, are also not stock-breeding: this applied to many Turcomans in the Taurus, which was still covered with vast forests, and perhaps to certain ones, called the *Agach-eris*, whom we shall see again shortly. Pure nomadism was a rarity: there was almost always a symbiosis of nomadic herdsmen and sedentary cultivators. That the latter were in general indigenous is certain, but it cannot be ruled out that there were already many Turks among them in certain regions.

Waqf-deeds and other documents which we possess for the thirteenth century, and the more numerous ones dating from the fourteenth century (too few of which have as yet been published), can shed some light on the ethnic mingling of the peoples, and perhaps in certain favourable cases it would be possible, thanks to them, to follow the chronological rhythm of islamization or turkization. It is necessary only to be careful to differentiate between the regions and, more particularly, to note that in most cases the villages and plots of land whose owners or occupiers are named are in the neighbourhood of a town, where the process of islamization or occupation by Muslims was likely to be more rapid than in the remote countryside. This being said, it should be noted that, in the *waqf* which he founded with property situated on the outskirts of Konya in 598/1201, Altun-Aba explicitly refers to the abundance of 'infidels'. However, the villages and domains to which he refers have mixed names, and the conclusions to be drawn from them remain uncertain, since a village with a native name may have Turkish inhabitants, either still remaining there or brought back, the name being merely that of a proprietor or of one of the racial groups. Taken together, however, the combination is significant. Similar impressions are to be gained from reading the *waqf*s made by Karatay, to the south of Kayseri, from the middle of the century. More definite indications are provided in those instances where it is not a village or whole domain that is named, but an individual plot of land: on the whole, what emerges, always of course in an urban district, is that there are Muslims alongside Christians. But, on the whole, there is no reason to doubt the accuracy of the travellers' impressions that, in the open country, the great majority of real countrymen were Christians. These will be considered shortly.

In an earlier reference to mixed unions, it was remarked that in their usual form they did not really involve any loss of Turkish character by the Turkish element. It would be interesting to know how far there were any instances of a true mingling of populations. It is possible that this happened with certain Kurds, and perhaps the Germiyan, of whom more will be said, are an example. Possibly too there were others in the Taurus mountains, with the

Bulgar, or even Mardaite (?) colonies found by the Turks, which can hardly have disappeared completely. Here, too, we can only state the problem. It should merely be noted that, in the literature written to the glory of the Turcoman dynasties, far from any hostility being shown towards other rural Muslim elements, and especially towards Kurds, it seems to have been customary to serve beside them as fellow-soldiers, under Turcoman leadership. On the whole, in the possible examples of racial intermixture, turkization gained a definite advantage. There is nothing to show, and the fact of Turkish domination explains this sufficiently, that the Turks were absorbed by native groups; but there may have been a progressive turkization of some groups in which the ascendancy, even among males, was held by natives. And, in the towns, there were the *ikdīsh*, of whom more will be said.

It would be possible to go more closely into the history of the Turcomans of Rūm if we were certain, on the one hand, of the interpretation to be given to certain names of Turcoman groups, and on the other of the system of land tenure in Seljukid Asia Minor. The second question must be deferred until later. The first raises the subject of tribal organization and the identification of groups, and this is a point on which it is essential, as a principle of method, to regard Yazïjï-oghlu with suspicion. This writer, when making his adaptation of the *Seljūknāme* of Ibn Bībī in the fifteenth century, introduced into it the names of the tribes which, in the climate of opinion of the Turcoman states of the time, were considered to be the most important and which were evidently anxious to discover ancestors during the origins of Turkish Asia Minor. But none of these names appears in Ibn Bībī, and consequently it is impossible to believe that they possessed, in his time, the importance they had acquired by that of Yazïjï-oghlu. In these circumstances it is quite indispensable to confine ourselves to contemporary sources, or in any case to relatively ancient ones.

On the question of the Turkish migration that accompanied the formation of the Empire of the Great Seljukids, reference has already been made to the difficulty of following the traces of the different tribes, whose existence is, however, largely authenticated for that period. For Asia Minor, the question is complicated by the fact that, if the names of tribes there are exceptional (and they occur solely as epithets of individuals in the thirteenth century), there were on the other hand fairly frequent references, from the beginnings of the penetration in the middle of the twelfth century, to a group of men, of uncertain orthography, $(y)a(r)uki$, $(y)a(v)uki$ or other variants, a word for which no convincing interpretation has as yet been suggested. The Muslim authors, from the eleventh century, often give the frontier Turks the name $\bar{u}ch$ which means precisely 'frontier-men', and is thus merely an equivalent of the Byzantine *akritai* or, with a different etymological meaning, of the Arabic *ghāzi*. But it is difficult to discover through what linguistic modification $\bar{u}ch$ could be changed to $(y)a(r)uk$. Attempts have been made to link these people either with followers of Yabgu (see p. 20), something rather anachronistic, or with the *ivāi*, a tribe known in Azerbaijan in the twelfth and thirteenth centuries, or with the *nāvaki*, throwers of darts (in Persian *nāvak*), a body whose existence is attested, though not among the Seljukids, or, finally, with the *yürüks*, the name for Turkish nomads in Asia Minor which has survived until our own time, though not attested before the Ottomans. The last hypothesis, which is attractive historically but weak linguistically, ultimately proves as inadequate as the rest. The problem remains unsolved. The only thing that is almost certain is that it is not a matter of a tribal name. This means that, like the entire Seljukid invasion, the penetration into Asia Minor was undertaken, not in large tribal groupings but in parties made up of mixed elements. Moreover, there is no proof that the tribal spirit was as strong among the Turks as it had been among the Arabs.

The only other name occurring in the ancient texts as an unquestionably collective name is that of the *Agach-eris* (literally 'men of the trees'), which is not much clearer than the previous one. It is not the name of a traditional Oghuz tribe, nor, as at one time was thought on the strength of a fortuitous phonetic resemblance, is it an ancient people from Russia transplanted into Asia Minor (although it cannot be proved that these Agach-eris were exclusively Turkish). They are only recorded in the thirteenth century, and for the most part in the central and eastern Taurus region, as far as the gates of Malatya, essentially as unruly elements with whom the established authorities contended. It was probably the same people who, crossing the frontier in the wake of the Mongol invasion, were then recorded to the north of

Antioch and Aleppo as 'Turcomans from Syria', not to speak of the partial dissemination that can be found in later periods. In Syria, a contemporary described them as 'a primitive people without towns or castles, and who always dwell in tents of felt and have livestock in great abundance, such as sheep and some goats and even oxen and cattle, and live like shepherds, and undertake no gainful employment . . .' (Continuation to William of Tyre).

It is true that the place-names of modern Asia Minor include many names of localities and villages which are connected with those of most of the traditional Oghuz tribes. The important thing, for historical purposes, is to distinguish between the various periods, and to accept as pre-Mongol only the rare place-names which were recorded before the middle of the thirteenth century. The Mongols, either by driving back the Turcomans or by sweeping some of them aside, brought about a new influx of them, and also to some extent a redistribution of those already there; and the new arrivals cannot have been, tribally and socially, entirely identical with the earlier ones. Without maintaining that the groups whose existence is attested by later nomenclature cannot have existed previously, it is prudent to refrain from asserting that they did exist. The determination of the date of appearance of a place-name, where possible, may suggest the date of sedentarization of the group whose name is thus preserved. Perhaps, conversely also, the fact that the name given is that of a tribal group known in a certain period may, when supported by confirmation from some other source, justify a conjecture as to the period of establishment of the village and so of the sedentarization of the group of people who settled there. The period of sedentarization may be quite different, varying with the regions and the different categories of Turcomans. Among the names which can be noted are some which are the names of tribes recorded during the Seljukid migration generally, either directly as groups or indirectly as descriptions of individuals. But that is not enough to prove that either their establishment or their sedentarization in Asia Minor was prior to the Mongol conquest.

The Turks of Asia Minor officially were Muslim, while the native inhabitants were not. However, turkization and islamization must not be absolutely identified. At the time of the conquest or later, in order to save their lands or to establish a career, to

contract a profitable marriage or for some other reason, some
Armenian or Georgian notables in the first place, and then later
some Greek ones, became converted to Islam, in a manner that
ultimately must have led to the cultural and semi-ethnic turkization of their descendants, but which does not necessarily imply
that they were really turkicized themselves, or even that they had
any knowledge of Turkish, any more than they had of Arabic or
Persian. The slaves, who for the most part were soon enfranchized,
had been brought back from frontier raids (or, at first, from the
actual invasion of the whole country). They represent a further
islamized element (individuals of this category can often be
recognized from the fact that their father's name is given simply
as ''Abd Allāh'). And there were Iranian immigrants, who will
be discussed later and under whose increasing influence in particular the new Muslims were to be won over to Islam under its
least Turkish aspects. For the present, these allusions, which are
matters for ethnological study, must suffice. These questions will
recur again later when the cultural and social aspects are
considered.

All that has just been said applies essentially to the open
countryside, when it existed. Asia Minor, however, had previously
been, and after a certain time once again became, under the
Turks, a land of towns, or at least a land where there were towns,
which played an essential part. Naturally, at the start, the devastation of the countryside, which jeopardised the towns' supplies and
ruined the land-owners, and later the occupation of those towns
led to emigrations, particularly by those with the means to
undertake them; and the Turcoman chiefs did not settle in the
towns, which they regarded as nests of infidels, and hence did
not favour the townsmen. This situation continued to be perpetuated or repeated for a long period in particular regions on
the frontiers, where the surrender of the fortified urban settlements had generally been achieved after the countryside had been
laid waste. But it was not perpetuated in regions of true stabilized
occupation.

It is a known fact that, in the East in general, nomadic chiefs
settled down more readily as townsmen than as peasants (even if
their followers were inclined rather to become peasants), apart
from leaving the towns for occasional expeditions into the desert

or steppes. Whether nomads or not, the Turkish chiefs soon established themselves in the towns. From their own past the Seljukids were familiar with town life, and it will be remembered that Sulaymān was careful to provide one of the first towns to be conquered with its own regular *cadi*; moreover, at times when they would have delayed settling in a town, the Byzantines themselves installed them in it, as has been seen. Although more directly Turcoman, the Dānishmendids' behaviour does not seem to have been very different. Within a reduced perimeter they restored the fortifications of towns, and readily settled in them themselves, or established the governors of provinces or holders of apanages and their garrisons in them. In proportion as states were constituted, whatever may have been the proportion of Byzantine and Islamo-Iranian influences, the town was (apart from regional or native exceptions), as in all Muslim countries, at once the political, economic and cultural centre. It is true that in Asia Minor there was no town remotely comparable with Constantinople or Cairo as they were at that time, or even with Damascus or Baghdad; and indeed there was probably not a single town that could be put on the same footing as the four or five huge metropolitan towns of Iran. But there was a considerable number of fairly large townships and some cities which, nevertheless, were large and genuinely urban centres.

The point of concern for the moment is the population of these towns. It is certain that, at the start, the ordinary inhabitants, alongside the Turkish garrison with its slaves and freedmen, consisted of natives who had remained there or been brought back, the proportions varying, and with a more or less clearly defined hiatus between the earlier occupation and the new one. Gradually, however, certain people of mixed race were also added, the *ikdīsh*, whose part will later be examined. Later, Iranian elements, mainly from the north-west but also Khorasanians, as has been said, were also introduced and in the thirteenth century became of importance, perhaps numerically and certainly from the social point of view. It is true that there were elements of the Iranian civil or religious aristocracy, driven out by the Khwārizmians or Mongols, before being sent by the latter to represent them; but there were also more humble men of religion, officials, merchants or artisans. It is therefore certain that the population of the towns was not identical with that of the open countryside. Without question, the Turkish element was important, but it was not exclusive, and in the organization of the new régime in all its aspects, the other immigrants had a considerable influence which acted upon the Turks themselves. This subject will be referred to again, in connection with cultural life, but in the present context also it should be noted that these Iranians exercised an iranizing, and so in a sense anti-Turkish, influence on the Turks. At the end of the thirteenth century the citizen of Konya who was to write the *Seljūknāme*, and who although he wrote in Persian was certainly Turkish, to judge from some of his pronunciations, restricts the name 'Turks' to the Turcomans, with a hint of disdain, the townspeople being simply 'Muslims'. If this language is perhaps not that of all his contemporaries, it is nonetheless symptomatic. While in Egypt in the same period the Mamluks, confronted with the native population, considered and described themselves as 'Turkish', in Asia Minor, confronted with the Turcomans, even the citizens of Turkish stock were no longer really conscious of the fact, they thought of themselves as 'Muslims' and stated this in Persian as often as in Turkish. The conclusive, though still incomplete, turkization was to take place under the Mongols and after them.

It is no less certain that Asia Minor, even in its Turkish elements, gave foreigners, and particularly foreign Muslims, the impression of being a truly foreign country, of 'Turkey', in fact, as distinct from the Arab world in particular. In the twelfth century hardly any travellers went there, and an envoy of Nūr al-Dīn, al-Balkhī, on his return spoke of the country he had seen somewhat as a modern traveller might speak of an expedition into the heart of the most isolated parts of Asia or Africa. Even in the thirteenth century the impressions formed during his travels by the Caliph's ambassador Ibn al-Jawzī should be noted. Costume naturally differed from that of the Arabs and, in the country, the Iranians. But it was above all the women who impressed the Europeans as much as the Muslims, by reason of their life of freedom (the Turcomans at least were not veiled) and their robustness (Ricoldo di Monte Croce claims that they gave birth without halting the caravan).

When all this has been said of the Turkish and Muslim element, it is quite certain that, in Asia Minor, there remained some 'natives', whose total number probably greatly exceeded that of the Turks – by ten to one, William of Rubruck said in the thirteenth century. To determine the continuity of a population, it is not altogether enough to establish that some of it has remained even to the present century, since different circumstances may have encouraged people to return and recolonize zones which had been in part abandoned. It is possible that such may have been the case under the Mongol Protectorate, and it was certainly so during the last two centuries of the Ottoman Empire. Nevertheless, until the contrary is proved, the existence of a certain native group in modern times is presumptive evidence of its existence throughout its history. This of course does not release us from the need to search in the ancient sources for direct proof of, and more especially for details concerning, this existence. Further reference will be made later to these 'natives' in connection with the organization of inter-confessional relations and the system of taxation and land tenure. One or two words will suffice here.

Western Armenia remained a largely Armenian country. This is broadly true of Erzurum, although detailed information is lacking. The position is still more certain in respect of Erzinjān, which perhaps even at that time, and in any case under the Mongols and at the end of the Middle Ages, was to have greater importance than Erzurum and, despite its Turco-Muslim colony, remained predominantly a great Armenian city. The south of Armenia had however even then been more widely infiltrated by Kurdish populations. Further to the west, it will be remembered, Byzantine policy had partly armenized Cappadocia: the Turkish conquest caused some, but not all, of the Armenians in Cappadocia to move down into Cilicia, where an Armenian principality gradually took shape, and many of them remained there, particularly in the central Taurus and its southern slopes, straddling the frontier between Asia Minor and Syria or Mesopotamia. It would be difficult to explain the fact that the Monophysites had maintained the principal residence of their Patriarch in the monastery of Mar Bar-Sauma, in the mountains to the south of Malatya, if the large communities of them which existed in Upper Mesopotamia had not extended further in this direction. As for the Greeks or the Hellenized populations, they continued to be represented along the whole coastal and mountainous periphery of Anatolia proper, from Trebizond and its hinterlands as far as Isauria, passing through the Dānishmendid country, the provinces of Kastamonu and even Ankara, the upper valleys of the rivers flowing into the Sea of Marmora or the Aegean, and the region of Antalya. They still remained in considerable numbers, it must be repeated, in the very heart of Cappadocia and in the agricultural and urban parts of the Anatolian plateau itself.

The conclusion then will be a double one, and apparently contradictory. On the one hand, it is certain that the majority of the population was not Turkish, it was not even Muslim, and it was not unified. And yet it is equally certain that a country, Turkey, was in the process of creation because, as in the Russo-Asiatic steppe, and unlike the other countries politically subjugated by the Turks, there was here a Turkish people who were settling down in their own home, and whose dominating presence everywhere, when compared with the divisions of the natives, imparted a particular character to the whole of Anatolia. The 'Turkish' quality, as has been seen, was not characteristic of all the Muslims, nor even of all the Turks; but the orientation in this direction characterized Asia Minor, in contrast to the other Muslim countries.

2

ECONOMIC LIFE

If the chronicles of the First Crusade convey an impression of devastation in the interior of Asia Minor, the fact remains that, on the contrary, travellers who saw it in the thirteenth century brought back a recollection of prosperity, by the standards of their time. In large measure it was clearly a prosperity that had been restored: however, the first Turcoman invasion must not be given the credit for the results which possibly it did not produce. It is true that the Turcomans killed, drove out or enslaved a fair number of people, in relation to what population there was, and

155

this could not fail to lead, among other things, to the abandonment of much cultivated land and neglect in the upkeep of irrigation system. But, from that time, it must be repeated on the one hand that the economy of the interior of Asia Minor having previously been an economy of sparsely populated latifundia, the contrast was by no means extreme; on the other hand, the Turcomans did not act in the same way everywhere (they had no reason for instance to destroy plantations of trees, some of which were probably able to survive); and, once they were installed, however harsh they may have been, they had no more to gain than any other nomads from the destruction of the oases of sedentary agriculture. It is true that these are unfounded general observations, since we possess practically no evidence about the beginnings of their occupation, but they have some probability. In any event, after the passing of a few generations, the picture entirely changes. And it must be clearly understood that, quite apart from any merit or demerit in the conduct of those in possession, there was inherent in the establishment of the principalities and later of the Turkish State of Asia Minor a positive element, in that the Byzantine Asia Minor of the latter days, apart from the western fringe, had to a large extent been the foreign possession of powerful absentee landowners who were interested only in its exploitation in so far as it might provide them with revenues which they spent elsewhere, whereas the new centres established or restored by the Turks created, on whatever scale, a profitable local demand.

From the middle of the twelfth century there are indications of the development of the new state of affairs. The frontier zones were clearly the most harshly treated and, where possible, when they found peasants still there, the Byzantines repatriated them, to repopulate their own possessions further in the interior or territories not completely reconquered. But the converse also held good, and the Sultans established in their agricultural territories frontier populations which had been taken prisoner or brought there. It is probable that some of these peoples preferred a government still with little taxation, or the conditions granted for their establishment, to their memories of the Byzantine tax-collectors and owners of latifundia. It is probable too that some of them placed greater confidence in agreements with the Turks, even if

there were sometimes disputes, than in Byzantine military protection which proved to be illusory or in any event insufficiently
far-reaching. There is no reason why the example recorded of the
settlement of Greek peasants round Lake Karalis should have been
an entirely isolated one. And, *a fortiori*, the Sultans must have
fostered the exploitation of their territories in the interior. The
towns, we repeat, must have been centres for agricultural re-
development over a fairly wide radius. It is not our concern here
to discuss once more the part which some Turcomans themselves
may have taken in re-colonization, to some extent in frontier zones
where, though sometimes established by the Sultans themselves
for partly military reasons, their presence nevertheless had an
economic significance. In any case, even when they remained
nomadic, we know from the scandalized and uncomprehending
assertions of the Crusaders, especially in the Second Crusade, that
an economy based on normal exchange was becoming organized
between the Greek peasants and the Turcoman herdsmen, accompanied by a growth of good feeling.

When it is possible to begin to reconstruct a picture of the
economy of Asia Minor, particularly in the first half of the
thirteenth century, it is seen to be genuinely prosperous alike in
agriculture, industry and commerce, each supporting the others.

Brother Simon of Saint-Quentin, who spent some years in Asia
Minor just before and just after the disaster of Köse Dagh, clearly
was somewhat gullible and to a slight extent may be misleading;
but nevertheless he saw the country, and one part of his account
gives a picture of the wealth and power of the Seljukid State, in
both towns and countryside. He provides a few details regarding
agriculture, but places rather more emphasis on stock-breeding.
He appreciated the value of the flocks of sheep and the wool
produced, and also, a special feature, the breeding of goats, the
hair from which was also used. For this sort of question there is no
reason not to make use also of somewhat later descriptions. Ibn
Sa'īd, who wrote in Syria or Mesopotamia in the early days of the
Mongol domination and who derived his information from
travellers who must necessarily have seen the country somewhat
earlier, emphasizes, for the region that they knew well, stretching
from Kayseri to Sivas or to Akseray and Konya, the wealth of
cultivated land stretching almost continuously along the roads,

and the pasturages also, but more especially the gardens, irrigation systems and orchards of apricots, plums, pears, lemons, peaches, almonds and other trees. In the neighbourhood of Konya one particularly esteemed fruit was the so-called plum of Qamar al-Dīn, from the name of the emir who had created a garden in Konya that was already known to ʿAlī of Herat before 1200, and possibly identical with the man who governed the Isaurian Taurus under Kay-kubādh and gave his name to the region. Later, Mustawfī was to see, or imagine he saw, vines everywhere; and Ibn Battūta, near Antalya, mentioned apricots which were dried and exported to Egypt. According to this author, there was also cultivated land along the road from Erzinjān to Erzurum. Abu 'l-Fidā, who, also in the fourteenth century, repeated information given by Ibn Saʿīd, made too few changes for his account to possess any value as distinct and original evidence. However, he also mentioned the fruit-trees of the Malatya region and was surprised that, unlike ordinary Muslim countries, they did not belong to individual owners (in classical Muslim law, the peasant who planted fruit-trees on the property of a landowner was entitled to a share of the produce). Regions today deserted, such as that of the monastery of Bar-Sauma, were well cultivated in the time of Michael the Syrian. Ibn Battūta also mentioned timber from the southern mountains that was exported to Egypt from Antalya and the Gulf of Makrī, and Ibn Saʿīd refers to timber from the province of Kastamonu that was used for the arsenals at Sinope.

On agriculture and stock-rearing, al-ʿUmarī gives information which there is no reason not to regard as valid as early as the thirteenth century. Naturally, being particularly responsive to the country's special features, he too was impressed primarily by the fruit – lemons, oranges, dates (?) and bananas, especially on the Mediterranean coast. The stock reared included cattle and horses, but more important were sheep and goats, the latter of a breed with silky hair, large quantities of which were exported to neighbouring Muslim countries. The honey was exquisite, and there was also sugar. All these were at prices lower than in the rest of the world (but that, if true, is not necessarily a mark of prosperity). In addition to these general features, for each region he describes al-ʿUmarī also repeats similar impressions, with reference to cereals, wheat and barley, to those throughout the Mediterranean region. Horses, mules and sheep also appear among the tribute due to the Mongols. And *waqf*-deeds, in the neighbourhood of towns, testify to the great number of villages of agricultural workers.

It is difficult to feel sufficient confidence in the numbers of villages that al-'Umarī gives for several principalities in the fourteenth century to make it worth while repeating them, let alone adding them up to give a total figure. Nevertheless the impression, particularly for western Anatolia, is one of populated rural areas. Ibn Sa'īd, in his time, believed that the Seljukid realm contained 400,000 villages, 36,000 of which were in ruins. No doubt it would be going too far either to accept these figures at their face value or, since after all he cannot simply have invented them, to fail to see some pointer in them. The proportion of ruined villages, if reliable, is on reflection a low one if it takes into account on the one hand the devastations at the start, and on the other the fact that, in the regions and climates generally found in the Near East, it was often necessary, given the technical standard of the time, to abandon a site in order to move to another one nearby: in Syria and Turkey alike, toponymy recalls instances of 'ruins' which merely indicated removal and which sometimes were later re-occupied or re-exploited.

Whatever the complete list of all the varieties of produce and their relative importance, it would be desirable to know if the plants cultivated and the livestock reared, in whatever proportions, were exactly the same as in Byzantine times. In the gardens or estates of Anatolia, for example, did they acclimatize or propagate Iranian fruits that had not hitherto been introduced? The sheep, clearly, are in part descended from the ones that the Turcomans had driven before them at the time of the invasion; but in part only, and even so of what breed? And the special goats? Muslims from neighbouring countries were surprised to see that transport, which among themselves was carried out by camels without the use of any vehicles, was here effected by means of ox-carts, a tradition evidently linked with the country and not with the Turks. As for the relative abundance of horses, is this a heritage from Byzantium which used to breed large numbers of them there, or from Central Asia, which also bred them, or from both? It is perhaps impossible to answer these questions which nevertheless must be posed; and to solve them would indeed have a great bearing on the solution of the wider problem of the continuity or lack of continuity in the rural history of Asia Minor.

*   *   *

Similar problems arise in regard to industry and the exploitation of mineral resources. Brother Simon of Saint-Quentin knew of the existence of lapis lazuli quarries, salt-mines, alum quarries near Akseray (?) and Sivas, iron-ore mines and three silver mines. The alum and the metals in particular call for a few remarks. The question of alum does not strictly speaking relate only to Anatolia. This substance which was very widely used in mediaeval industry for dyeing, apart from certain secondary uses, had been known since antiquity, when deposits in Asia Minor, among other places, had been exploited. It is possible that some exploitation may have continued in Byzantine times although, to be accurate, we have no knowledge of it, and in any case there does not seem to have been any trade in it. In fact, somewhat paradoxically, the demand for alum came mainly from the textile industry of western Europe, since the East already possessed dye-stuffs which did not call for its use, and tastes and fashions there differed from those among the Franks. It is well known that, from the end of the thirteenth century to the middle of the fifteenth, almost all the alum used in Europe came from quarries situated in Asia Minor, and trade in it was practically monopolized by the Genoese. What is less well known is that, in the twelfth century, it was from Egypt that the West tried to obtain alum. In any case, the basis of the intensive exploitation of alum was not native industry, which made little use of it, but purchases by the Franks. This is very clear in regard to Egypt and seems to be no less so for Asia Minor, where, as we shall see, trade in alum in 1255 was handled by two Italians. It is difficult to know when and how its exploitation began. When in 1236 the commune of Marseilles obtained a commercial concession from the King of Cyprus, alum from Rūm is mentioned among the produce that passed in transit through Cyprus. It is possible that, some years earlier, this had been concealed under the name of alum from Aleppo mentioned in certain other documents, as the existence of alum near Aleppo was very unlikely (Aleppo would thus have been merely the market for the alum 'of Sivas'). However that may be, in the twelfth century there was none, while in the thirteenth its exploitation was in progress. The deposits not having changed, it has to be admitted that Sivas alum in reality came from Shebin Karahisār/Kughūniya (Colonia), and Akseray alum probably already came from Kütahya. We cannot say if, before 1243, the Franks were already directly concerned. Egyptian alum had not disappeared, but that from Asia Minor was equally good and, as the Egyptian alum was a source of profit for the treasury, perhaps slightly better terms could be obtained from the Seljukid State.

We do not know which are the iron mines referred to by Simon. A later text records one in the Isaurian Taurus, but there must have been many other shallow mines of modest size. Silver was more important for the state, which used it for coinage. As al-'Umarī quite correctly later recorded three mines, at Gümüsh Saraÿ, Lu'lu'a (taken from the Armenians by Kay-kubādh) and Bāburt (Gümüsh-khāne ?), it can be admitted that exactly the same ones were there in Simon's time. We are not told of the copper mines which, in the time of Marco Polo and Ibn Battūta, were to supply a famous industry in Erzinjān. We know in a general way that, as at present, there were important copper mines at Ergani/Erqanīn, north-west of Amid in Diyār Bakr; there is no reason why their working should have ceased when the country passed into the hands of the Seljukids. Various places bear the names containing ma'den (mine), but it is not possible to determine the date of exploitation. Among the witnesses to waqf-deeds are Muslim metalworkers and also goldsmiths.

It is mainly for the Mongol period that information is available about the textile industries of Rūm. However, something must be said about them here, bringing up the question of continuity again. There was of course a Byzantine textile industry, supplied with sheep's wool from Asia Minor, among other products; and the Turcomans, in their own way, naturally used the wool from their animals. Simon states that the red caps, such as they wore themselves, were sold even in France and England. Moreover, luxurious fabrics, by no means all imported, from then onwards appear among the Sultans' treasures, and 'Sivas carpets' were sought after at the beginning of the thirteenth century by a rich

Baghdad merchant, according to an author of the time, while in the middle of the century, according to the contemporary Ibn Saʿīd, Akseray also was famous for its carpets, and the Turcoman frontier-dwellers wove carpets for export. The word 'carpet' covers different things, and one has to make a distinction between the luxurious embroidered woven fabrics, the technique for which had been inherited by Byzantium as well as by the Muslim States from an earlier age, and knotted pile carpets, the invention of which appears to have taken place in Central Asia roughly during the first centuries of the Christian era, and which are properly speaking what are now called 'Oriental carpets'. It is not possible here to enter into technical details. We know that in the fourteenth century in Denizli the Greeks and, from the end of the thirteenth at the latest in Erzinjan, the Armenians both produced remarkable figured fabrics which apparently perpetuated or revived some of their peoples' ancient traditions. In the case of the Armenians, whose later carpets incidentally are famous, some texts give the impression that these carpets may have existed one or two centuries before the arrival of the Turks. However, the earliest carpets outside Central Asia that survive (leaving aside the products of a related technique in Spain) derive from the region of Konya in the thirteenth century. Thus we cannot avoid the impression, which is heightened by the texts previously mentioned, that the new technique may have been introduced by the Turks at the time of their immigration. On a wider scale, it is clear that the Turcomans did not get the natives to weave the material for their tents or their mats. From *waqf*-deeds we know of dyers with Muslim names. However, in the fourteenth century Pegolotti recommended merchants who wished to offer fabrics from the West at the market at Antalya to bring them in finished condition, due to the absence of croppers and finishers for work of that kind.

There is no country in the Near East that does not possess pottery of great antiquity. But decorative ceramics, used for instance as an ornamental wall surfacing, were particularly highly developed in Iran. Without question, the ceramics of Asia Minor were connected with those of Iran, but there is no doubt that, in the thirteenth century, they were produced locally by craftsmen, the names of three of whom survive, one Iranian, the second from Mosul, the third possibly Greek, giving proof of their diversity.

Woodcarving is also connected with a body of traditions wide-spread throughout the Near East. It is no surprise to find the names of two sculptors, one Georgian, the other from the Taurus, connected with forested regions.

*   *   *

Byzantine Asia Minor was crossed by several caravan routes which in the one direction converged on Constantinople, in the other fanned out towards the Syrian frontier (Antioch and Aleppo), Upper Mesopotamia (through Malatya/Melitene), and sometimes to Armenia, Azerbaijan and Iran. Coming from this last direction, however, caravans more often had to limit themselves to skirting eastern Asia Minor by way of Erzurum, and to ship their goods from Trebizond, proceeding onwards by sea. The importance of this trade in Byzantine Asia Minor must not be over-estimated. In so far as it passed through its territory, it crossed the country without being of real concern to it. At certain times, warfare restricted merchants' movements and, with more lasting effects, depopulation made any large market impossible. Perhaps a certain regional maritime trade, on the south coast, linked Antalya/Attalia with Egypt; but connections by sea were more frequently by the direct route from Syria or Egypt to Constantinople. As for the Black Sea, the trade from the whole coast-line was directed to Constantinople. The links which the Muslim world maintained with the people of the steppes and forests passed, to some slight extent, along the edge of the Caucasus and mostly through Central Asia.

Naturally the general disorganization that accompanied the warlike period of the Turkish conquest must temporarily have hindered whatever remnants of commerce there were, although there is no explicit confirmation of this. But if we turn to the beginning of the thirteenth century, particularly when the capture of Constantinople by the Latins had disorganized its markets, we observe that, on the contrary, the Turkish occupation aided trade, partly because of its integration, however incomplete, with the Muslim world, and also because the presence of a Court and centres important in themselves would henceforward attract merchants from markets out in the country, and not only those on the routes along which they travelled without halting.

It is extremely difficult to ascertain the rhythm by which this recovery took place or, in other words, to know if an appreciable trade already existed in Asia Minor in the twelfth century. If an anecdote from Abu Hāmid al-Gharnātī is to be believed, merchants are said to have come there from Russia even at the beginning of the century. The first caravanserais date back to the reign of Kïlïj Arslan II: they were to multiply in the following century, serving the Konya-Kayseri route. Built partly in the open country, they reveal the lack of sufficient urban stopping-places, as well as the attempts to revive trade and ensure the safety of merchants, especially when on their way to Court. Michael the Syrian records the loss, in snow, of a caravan of 400 Persian merchants, an indication both of reviving commercial enterprise and of its inadequate reorganization.

At the very end of the century there is increasing evidence of what was to be an active trade organized around new centres. In 1197, the Ayyubid al-ʿAzīz, who was sending some presents to Alexis Angelus, had them brought through Anatolia, and, when Kaykhusraw had them intercepted for political reasons, in retaliation all the merchants present in Constantinople who were Seljukid subjects were arrested. In 598/1201–2, a deed of a pious foundation, which incidentally refers to a new *sūq* (bazaar) in Konya, close to the old one, among the witnesses names not only a Turkish merchant from Konya but also two other merchants, from Tabriz in Azerbaijan. We have seen that in the same period Samsun, on the Black Sea, had for some years been a Seljukid possession: to recover a vessel wrecked at Giresun/Cerasonte, Alexis Angelus had pressure put on the Seljukid subjects who had come from there to Constantinople and who applied to Sultan Rukn al-Dīn for restitution. According to the contemporary Ibn al-Athir, even before 602/1205–6 Sivas was the meeting-place of traders who were natives of Syria and Mesopotamia, as well as Russians and Kipchaks (pagan Turks) from countries to the north of the Black Sea. It is certain that Sivas was then, and was long to remain, the great trading centre of Asia Minor, at the meeting-place of the routes crossing from east to west or leading from Syria, Mesopotamia and the Black Sea. It was there that there was a conflict of interests between Trebizond and the Seljukid States, the political consequences of which have already been noted. Trebizond, situated alongside the principality of Erzurum, naturally wanted to maintain exclusive control of the Iran-Erzurum-Trebizond route, at the same time attracting the Crimean and Russian merchants temporarily excluded from Constantinople by the fall of the Empire into the hands of the Latins. The crisis in Sivas caused by the loss of Samsun has been described. It was compensated for a little later by the more decisive conquest of Sinope.

The conquest of Antalya, on the south coast, during the same period, was unquestionably due to commercial causes, among others. Some Alexandrian merchants had complained of confiscations made by the Frankish lord of the town, the Tuscan Aldobrandini. And it is evident that many other Franks, particularly those who were now installing themselves in Cyprus, possessed an interest in the Anatolian port not wholly identical with that of the Muslims. Once the Turkish conquest had become irrevocable, they lent themselves for the same reasons to a policy of compromise. In 1213, an agreement was made for the reciprocal security of the subjects of the two states when trading in each other's territory. In 1216, a more formal treaty defined the mutual guarantees, particularly on the question of the dues to be paid and, a privilege that was usual but not automatic in the absence of treaties, respect for property in the event of shipwreck in 'territorial' waters. These texts obviously imply the existence of a fleet which, while apparently only the successor to the one that the people of Antalya had possessed in Byzantine times, was nonetheless from then onwards a Seljukid fleet.

The Venetians, the masters of the trade of the Latin Empire and the opponents of the Greeks, were of course extremely eager to try to cement direct and profitable commercial relations with the Seljukid State. This was done by way of the Black Sea, but, even earlier, by way of Antalya, since it is to this port alone that a concession must have applied, granted them by Kaykhusraw and renewed, with more favourable terms, by Kay-kāūs and later by Kay-kubādh. In the concession granted by the last-named, which has been preserved and dates from 1220, they were granted a reduction of customs duties (which must normally have been at least 10%) to 2% of the value of the merchandise, and even complete freedom for grain, precious metals even though worked, precious stones and pearls. They also of course obtained a guarantee of the security of their persons and goods even in case of shipwreck and, as in other Muslim ports at the same period, they were even granted legal autonomy for their internal affairs, together with a special advantage over other Latins since, in the event of a dispute with any of them, the arbitrators were to be nominated by the Venetians. The treaty was concluded for two years only, but there is no reason to suppose that it was not more or less tacitly renewed for a long time, and Venetian statutes of 1255 refer particularly to the link established by the Venetians between Alexandria and Antalya. As for the other Latins mentioned in the treaty, the only ones specified are the Pisans, but other texts prove that, in Antalya, there were also Provençal merchants (Cypriot concession of 1236) and Genoese (private deed of 1237).

In the Black Sea, the Venetians must have been almost the only Latins present, since it was impossible to penetrate from the Mediterranean without their good will. The documentation regarding their use of Turkish ports on that coast is meagre; one private deed mentions a Venetian visit to Samsun in 1212, when the port was in the hands of Trebizond, but it was clearly of no commercial interest except for its connections with the Seljukid hinterland. But above all it was the trade with Russia that interested them in the Black Sea.

Competition was between three parties – Venice (and occasionally also some other Latins), Trebizond and, since the occupation of Sinope, of which trade was the object, the Seljukid State. The political events alluded to earlier are here the only source of information but are sufficiently eloquent. For the Turks, trade with Russia was useful in supplying the furs, honey and slaves normally sought from there, and in addition in allowing them to compete with the people of Trebizond for the transit of goods to their destination in the more distant Muslim countries. In 1223, a Mongol army had just captured the great Crimean port of Sughdāq, the terminal point of this trade. Many merchants of that town and Russian merchants from elsewhere escaped to Asia Minor and were shipwrecked near the coast. A dispute ensued between the Seljukids and the people of Trebizond, since the former seized the goods that were salvaged, in keeping with the custom with regard to a place where there existed no concessions, while the latter maintained that the vessel was carrying tribute from 'Gothland' to Trebizond, its suzerain, and that the seizure thus constituted an act of overt political hostility. In fact, the allegiance of the Russian ports on the Black Sea to Trebizond irritated the Seljukids and, as the Mongols did not remain, it was certain to be re-established if no intervention were made. Pretexts were found. An Antalya merchant who had travelled from Syria to Cilicia, Antalya and Anatolia by land, and to the Black Sea, alleged that he had grounds for complaint against the Franks in Antalya, the Armenians in Cilicia and the Russians in the Crimea. In Sughdāq, the Seljukid subjects had been the victims of confiscations. We have seen how, in 1225, an expedition led by the commander of Kastamonu resulted in the establishment of a Seljukid protectorate over Sughdāq which was to last until the final conquest of southern Russia by the Mongols in 1239.

These events show that, even if foreigners visited 'Turkey', Seljukid subjects also, apparently of all faiths (since a mosque was built in Sughdāq), took part in the foreign trade of the country. But the foreigners did not restrict themselves to visiting the ports. As need hardly be said, many Iranians came there to trade, even reaching Sivas and Konya, one of them a spy for the Mongols. But there were also a number of Italians who had come from Syria or Cyprus, on their way to Damascus or Aleppo, and who met compatriots of other professions, as has been seen. Under the Mongols this feature was to increase, but it must be emphasized that it existed even before them, since not enough attention has been given to that fact.

It was therefore during the first decades of the thirteenth century that the great Sultans built the caravanserais whose ruins even today still mark the main trading routes of ancient times. There were caravanserais or *khāns* in all the Muslim countries, of course, and particularly in Iran. In Central Asia, where the merchants had to travel great distances under sometimes severe climatic conditions, the governments had built small halting-places as extensively as possible, near supplies of water when available. The *khāns* of Asia Minor no doubt sprang from the two traditions. It is emphasized that they were particularly useful in winter, when the caravans continued to travel in spite of snow, and the villages, lying far apart especially in mountainous districts, could not offer them sufficient shelter. The catastrophe that befell the Iranian merchants, referred to earlier, demonstrated this need, and as early as the twelfth century Kïlïj Arslan had a large *khān* built near Konya. Subsequently, Sultans and notables tried to outdo each other in this field. Before 1243 we know for certain of about thirty *khān*s, and probably about ten more, merely from existing ruins. Others were to be added under the Mongols. According to Ibn Sa'īd, on the road from Kayseri to Sivas alone, in the middle of the thirteenth century there were twenty. Some bridges, for example over the Kïzïl Irmak, had moreover been built or reconstructed. The roads appear to have remained as they were.

As in all towns, the retail trade was carried out in *sūqs*, of which we have no special knowledge. Mention has sometimes been made of fairs, but I know of no evidence of them, and in countries as much Muslim as Byzantine, true fairs are an unusual event (except during the Pilgrimage), of little importance in the economy owing to the stable permanent trade. Naturally there were times of year when foreign merchants arrived and, more locally, there were perhaps, as in other countries, periodical meetings in the suburbs of some of the leading provincial towns for exchanges between nomads and sedentary populations. For the moment, these are no more than hypothetical speculations.

To sum up, it is certain that, between the ordeals of the early and the later Middle Ages, Asia Minor experienced for about a century (including the beginnings of the Mongol régime) an exceptional economic development such as it had not had before and was not to have again for a long period.

Coinage and Prices

The coinage of the Turkish State of Asia Minor raises some difficult problems.

It is quite obvious that, throughout the period immediately following the Turkish settlement, there was no coinage in the country other than what the occupying peoples found there, which they must have amassed in quite considerable quantities either as tribute or from pillage, or which alternatively must have been hidden by the natives when possible. It is only under the Dānishmendid Gümüshtegin Ghāzī and, probably a little later under the Seljukid Mas'ūd, that the first minting of coins took place. At least until the middle of the century these were of copper only, that is to say intended solely for local trade. Silver was to make its appearance under Kĭlĭj Arslan II, gold only in the thirteenth century.

It will be no surprise that certain coins of Gümüshtegin, his successor Muhammad, the latter's brother Inal, and even Dhu 'l-Nun and Dhu'l-Qarnayn of Malatya bear Greek inscriptions, as does a seal of the last-named, for which there is no recorded equivalent for other princes. Nevertheless, there is no Greek inscription on any of the ancient Seljukid coins which were issued in regions at least as fully Hellenized. The Dānishmendid coins bear no mention of the place of minting, those of the first Seljukids mention only Konya. What is more remarkable is that the Dānishmendid coins bear representations that are either frankly Christian – the head and shoulders of the Redeemer, Christ laying His hand on the sovereign's head – or semi-Christian – St. George smiting the dragon – or else neutral as regards religious but of a Byzantine type – the sovereign's portrait or the representation of the lion. Only this last kind appears among the first Seljukids.

The first idea to come to mind to explain these features is that the coinage was the work of native craftsmen in the Byzantine tradition since there could have been no others, and the principal users were the native populations who would not have accepted or understood other coins. But the problem is a little more complicated than it seems, because the coins in question are not the only ones at this period to show these particular features, or at least to bear representations of the Byzantine type. There were some under the 'Frankish' Tancred of Antioch, there were perhaps some even in Syria, under the very ardent Muslim Nūr al-Dīn, and in any case there was an abundance of them under the Artukids of Diyār Bakr. Now here, in a country long islamized, trading more freely with the whole of Mesopotamia than with Byzantium or Asia Minor (incidentally copper was of no commercial importance), and for several centuries accustomed to Muslim Arab coinage, the arguments which apply to the Dānishmendids are no longer valid for the Artukïds, and consequently cast doubt even upon the validity of those which would otherwise be accepted for the

Dānishmendids. It will be pointed out in another context that the Turks did not feel the same reserve as the Arabs regarding the representation of figures, but those found in their works of art are not in the Byzantine tradition, and consequently this throws no light on the present problem. It can be accepted that the Artukids, like the Dānishmendids, when first established, gained possession of large quantities of Byzantine coins as the result of raids in Asia Minor (but these too were of gold and silver), and that some of their own coins were perhaps merely re-issues of earlier coins of this type, but it is difficult to accept that this situation should have prevailed for several generations. Clearly the influence of Byzantine tradition cannot be discounted, any more than the influence of war booty and payments of tribute (which were not in copper), but it still remains to explain why it was so strong and enduring. And I have to admit that, on this point, I have no suggestions to offer.

What is more, these reasons would apply equally well to the Seljukids, and their coins are more emphatically Muslim (except for the lion). It is possible that, at the start, they made use of the Byzantine coins then in circulation or in their possession, which would explain the fact that there is not a single specimen of a coin minted by them before the time when they were in a position to issue a Muslim coinage. Afterwards, their desire to have a Muslim coinage becomes clear. It may seem surprising that the Sultans, whose relatively pacific policy towards Byzantium has been emphasized, should appear to have been in this respect more intransigent than the Dānishmendids, representing the *ghāzī* spirit of the Turcomans. But it will also be seen that their political attitude in no way hindered (indeed the reverse) any attempt at islamization in the classical sense, while the Turcomans were as closely in touch with the natives in peace as in war, and had virtually no interest in the islamization of the coinage.

From the time of Kĭlĭj Arslan II silver coins survive. This fact probably signifies that the opening or re-working of the silver mines must date back to his reign. In the following century Simon of Saint-Quentin was to boast of the quantity of coins which, thanks to these mines, the Sultans were able to mint. This exclusive use of silver (as distinct from copper), for a certain period is easily explained and raises no problems, but even so it must be emphasized since it is a somewhat original feature. For quite a long time silver had been the main currency in Iran, but at the period in question it had almost disappeared in favour of gold, and in Byzantium also, despite its difficulties, gold was to remain the basic metal until the thirteenth century, certainly for large payments. Gold, in which the minting of coins started in Asia Minor in the thirteenth century, was not found within the country, and therefore it could only be acquired through trade (and from certain tribute). In its way it is thus a proof of the development of trade, which is all the more remarkable in that the time was approaching when the Muslim States of the Near East were beginning to find gold increasingly difficult to procure, as did Byzantium, and when the minting of coins was to emigrate to the Italian merchant towns.

It is perhaps impossible to decide if the early copper coins of low denominations were linked with their Byzantine equivalents in regard to their value. The silver dirhams and gold dinars of later periods were based upon the valuation which was accepted as statutory in the surrounding Muslim countries. There does not appear to have been any coinage of alloyed metal such as was minted in the same period under the Ayyūbids in Egypt (but in that case for reasons which, at least so far as silver was concerned, did not necessarily or solely derive from a scarcity of the metal).

In the fourteenth century, the impression conveyed by al-'Umarī on the subject of prices is that they were markedly lower than elsewhere, and especially so in the western principalities. The difference, thought slight in respect of agricultural produce, was very marked in regard to livestock (apart from the thorough-bred horses) and the produce from it. This characteristic is too natural for there to be any reason to doubt that it must already have been in existence during the period of independence. Low prices, incidentally, do not necessarily signify prosperity and, according to the circumstances, may indicate either wealth or poverty. There is too little definite information for it to be possible to reach a conclusion here as to the solution, which is to be sought in a comparative study of the circulation of money, the 'national' and 'average' income which no doubt will always remain impossible to calculate, and the standards of living. Perhaps it will be a little easier, from the partial disequilibrium of prices, to draw deductions relating to the history of international trade.

13

Weights and Measures

It is unlikely that the weights and measures described in the fourteenth century by al-'Umarī and Pegolotti, which with very few exceptions were different from their Irano-Mongol counterparts, had been radically altered in value as a result of the Mongol conquest. Thus, until there is proof to the contrary, they can be regarded as having been valid during the earlier period. There can be no question here of providing general tables of equivalents, but merely of deducing from a few examples certain principles which are of interest for their historical significance. The two basic units mentioned by al-'Umarī are the *mudd* (unit of capacity) and the *ratl* (unit of weight) – with the proviso that he may thus have translated some local names, *ratl* and *mudd* being fairly common generic terms. Whatever the truth of this last point, the unit to which he gives the name *ratl* is the equivalent, according to him, of 12 'Egyptian' (*misri*) *ratls*, or 1,680 dirhams by weight (sometimes only 8 and 1,180 respectively). However, according to Pegolotti, in Sivas the *ratl* was double the *ratl* of Acre, that is to say 1,440 dirhams. It is well known that no mediaeval country, even the most advanced, achieved a universally accepted system of weights and measures, and this diversity is therefore in no way surprising. What is striking, however, is the fact that in general the unit was so large, since for example the *ratl misri* was worth 140 dirhams ($=437 \cdot 5$ grammes), and what was called the *ratl rūmī*, the Roman pound (and not that 'of Rūm'), was worth $102\frac{6}{7}$ dirhams ($= 321 \cdot 43$ grammes). It was only in Iran that the name *ratl* was sometimes given to a large unit corresponding rather to the *mann* of the official Muslim system, equivalent to 2 *ratls*, the value of which tallies with that of the *ratl* of Asia Minor. Moreover al-'Umarī shows that the *ratl* in use among the Germiyān was of even greater weight, 3,120 dirhams, and similar units are also attested in eastern Asia Minor in the fifteenth and sixteenth centuries. But in the time of Ibn Bībī, a *mann* of 260 dirhams was also known, namely the 'legal' *mann* of Islam. It is difficult to draw any firm deductions from these data. The system does not appear to be related to the Byzantine tradition and it differs from the practice of the Arab countries, even if the word *ratl*, which is Arabic, was indeed used there.

However, the impression is different when other units are considered. It can hardly be doubted that, within the Arabic term *mudd*, of which al-'Umarī speaks, and which he says was sometimes pronounced *mūt*, the Byzantine *modios* was barely concealed, for instance in Syria. According to this source, and depending on the locality, it was worth from ¾ to 1½ *irdabb* of Egypt, that is, counting about 90 litres to the *irdabb*, from 72½ to 135 litres, which is in fact much the same as the Syro-Egyptian *modios* and would not correspond to any kind of *mudd*. Here then there is a possible relationship with Byzantine territory. Moreover, several texts refer, as a measure of superficial area, to the *faddān*, an Egyptian term (we are not told to what it corresponds); but, as has already been said, it is symptomatic that the Iranian unit *par excellence*, the *jarīb*, does not occur, even in the texts of authors writing in Persian. On the other hand, land was measured in terms of a unit of cultivated land varying in area, named a *chift*, a term borrowed from Persian but translating the Byzantine *zeugon/jugum* and conforming with a practice that existed in Byzantium but not in Iran.

In short, with the greatest diffidence, it may be suggested that there was a mixture of weights and measures of varied origins, and that perhaps there was a more marked continuity with Byzantium in respect of questions of land, and with the Iranian world in matters of commerce.

3

THE SYSTEM OF LAND TENURE AND TAXATION

Osman Turan was the first to realize that the system of land-tenure in mediaeval Turkey, when compared with the classical Islamic plan, revealed some wholly original and individual features. Naturally, this constitutes a question of the highest importance for the whole history of the country's society and institutions.

In the Byzantine Empire, as in the Muslim States, a clear distinction was observed between, on the one hand, private property (which was essentially individual), and, on the other, the property of the State. In both the Byzantine Empire and the Muslim States, on the eve of the Turkish conquest, the State domain had been reduced as a result of distributions made from it in the form of grants which were virtually equivalent to gifts of ownership, and, in the sphere of private property, large estates had developed at the expense of the smaller ones and of the free peasantry. Nevertheless, to avoid frequent misunderstandings, there are certain distinctions to be borne in mind, one of which was noted earlier in connection with the *iqtāʿ* under the Great Seljukids – on the one hand, between the agricultural properties which were almost always individually owned and the pastoral semi-desert lands or lands in collective use without individual ownership, and on the other hand between the actual properties of the State and the rights it possessed over private properties. To these last properties, although forming a special category, the sovereign's personal estates belonged. Finally it has to be repeated once more that, from the fiscal point of view, classical Muslim Law draws a distinction between lands subject to land-tax (*kharāj*) and those liable only to tithe. The former consisted of those which, at the time of the Arabo-Muslim conquest, belonged to native owners who had been left in possession; the latter were properties, henceforth Muslim, with which the *qatīʿas* or *iqtāʿs*, distributed to individual recipients from those parts of the public domain not retained by the State under its direct control, had in practice been assimilated.

The Turks in Central Asia and Iran had become acquainted with these various methods of land-tenure. Nevertheless, for all those who continued to live in accordance with tribal tradition, the idea of individual ownership of land, especially for agricultural use and clearly defined both territorially and administratively, remained a concept that was hardly understood or accepted, and they tended to consider all land as being of collective use, or at the most as distributed regionally among groups. It is difficult to imagine that, when they entered Asia Minor, they had been so influenced by jurists in the traditional Islamic sense as to lose this attitude. The only question is to know whether, as had been done on their behalf in the Central Asiatic States whose service they had entered earlier, collective territories had been assigned to them in non-appropriated zones of countries which retained their

classical administrative organization, or whether they had regarded themselves as masters of the whole land, even though
allowing the survival, in places where it suited them, of isolated
groups of subject land-workers which retained locally their original
structure. In view of the fact of conquest, the second solution will
more readily be adopted, while at the same time it must be noted
that, at the level of the organization and development of ideas
which they had then attained, the practical difference between
the two solutions was not perhaps apparent. On the other hand,
this difference could and must subsequently have been evident to
the officials who gradually established an organized state in the
conquered territory, and who had received some training in the
law and terminology of classical Islam. The example of what was
done at the time of the annexation of Akhlāt makes it probable
that, by the first third of the thirteenth century at the latest, a
general survey of the land of Rūm for taxation purposes had been
made. At that point, in accordance with a process for which many
other historical parallels exist (for instance in Hungary), the State
apparently regarded as the public domain everything that was not
the object of individual ownership, even while conceding to
certain nomadic or pastoral groups the collective use of some
territories, though for the future these were to be strictly limited.
It is difficult to doubt that, in this public domain, a large number
of cultivated areas were included, the cultivators of which were
not regarded as the owners. In an evolution of this kind it is
understandable that, unlike what took place after the Arab
conquest, there was no place for distinctions either between
Muslim property and native property (i.e. between lands subject
to tithe and lands subject to kharāj), or between the property of
the State and the State's rights over private properties (the
distinction of the two types of iqtā'). On the whole, and possibly
with some individual or regional exceptions, there existed only a
State domain, and it was within its framework alone that different
conditions could be established for individuals or groups. From
this domain, private properties could even then be re-established
by alienation. But in general they had not survived from before
the conquest, or, if by chance they proved to have done so, they
could be maintained only through the legal fiction of a new concession by the State, which was in theory the owner. Although

expressed in terms which are not those of Osman Turan, and although, as we shall see, on certain points I find it impossible to concur with him, all this agrees with his conception and in its general orientation seems difficult to dispute.

It is true that there is another aspect of the matter to which Osman Turan devoted less attention, on account of his primarily Turkish point of view, namely that of the possible continuity with the Byzantine system. I have placed so much emphasis on the fact that the Turks entered Rūm often almost as the Emperor's agents, and in any case without any conscious desire to destroy the established institutions of the Empire in so far as these did not affect them personally, that there is no need to raise the question of the possible continuity even in the system of land-tenure. But, in fact, there is no contradiction here with the impressions derived from the conditions of the Turkish conquest. On the one hand, we have to remember that almost none of the Greek peasant pro-prietors still remained (perhaps in the case of the Armenians the situation was less extreme) in the regions where the Turks were to become established, and as the great land-owners were absent or had fled, their tenant farmers automatically found themselves falling into the power of the conquerors with no one interposed between them, and usually with no chance of re-establishing small individual properties; on the other hand, in many regions, the evacuations, movements of population and the like created a hiatus between the Byzantine régime and the Turkish. Only an intensive study of the agrarian structures and methods of calcula-tion of taxes or rents – a study which, owing to the state of the documentation, could be made only by including several centuries – would enable us to decide to what extent in the various regions a certain continuity may have existed between the Byzantine and Seljukid periods. It is *a priori* admissible that there were instances of continuity and of discontinuity at the same time but for our present view it is enough that the way in which these things occurred does not appear to contradict our earlier conclusions.

Moreover, the importance in the Ottoman Empire of the State *mīrī* lands is one of its characteristic features, so clearly emphasized by the works of Ömer Lütfi Barkan that, *a priori*, there is no ground for surprise if we find this same feature existing already in the very origins of Turkey. Up to a certain point, this argument alone is insufficient, but it can be added to others. Nevertheless, the continuity is not as simple as it may appear, for, as Osman Turan has himself pointed out, although his interpretation does not seem to me to be always correct, the Mongol Protectorate altered the system of State lands established under the Seljukids, and moreover the Ottoman State was not confined to its Anatolian territories. The continuity is therefore probably less simple and direct than appears at first glance. It does not follow that there was none.

All this being granted, there was nevertheless some private property, both Muslim and native, before the Mongols. Confining themselves to documents prior to 1243, the authenticity and interpretation of which can scarcely be questioned, we have for example the deed of a *waqf* or pious foundation in Konya dating back to the year 598/1201. This kind of deed is interesting because a pious foundation of this type, being conceived as valid in principle for an indefinite period until the end of the world, cannot apply to revocable customary rights but, under classical Muslim law, only to full ownership or something comparable; and *waqf*-deeds are always drawn up in conformity with the stipulations and according to the terminology of classical Muslim law. In this particular deed the founder, the *amīr ispahsalār* Shams al-Dīn Altun-aba, specifies formally that the property which he constitutes a *waqf* is wholly owned by himself. It should be noted only that they are mostly urban properties and, when rural properties do occur, they seem to be situated in the Konya region. Another example can be taken from a passage in the chronicle of Ibn Bībī, who was too conversant with chancellery business to confuse technical terms, and who stated that Kay-kubādh gave some villages in full ownership (*mulk, tamlīk*), with a diploma confirming this, to the Greek governor of Alanya/Kalon-oros, Kīr (Kuros) Farid, on his submission; and he distinguished between this grant and that of an *iqtāʿ* which Kay-kubādh conferred on him elsewhere. It is probable that the private property thus constituted was created out of the public domain, a fact which enables us to witness the beginnings of a process which was to gain momentum under the new conditions of the Mongol Protectorate.

Moreover, it seems almost certain that the foregoing considerations, which apply to the open countryside, have to be distinguished from the case of property in and near the towns, in proportion as life in the towns revived. For the moment there is no need to stress this point and more will be said when the towns are discussed.

*Waqf*s have just been mentioned. These were an institution of classical Islam which almost certainly appeared in Asia Minor only after the spread of traditional Muslim culture. Although, in Muslim countries, *waqf*s can serve private as well as public purposes, at the period now under consideration they were to an increasing extent established for the benefit of a religious institution (or a social one, which amounts to the same thing) such as a mosque, *madrasa*, hospital, caravanserai and so on – and for Seljukid Asia Minor this is, I believe, the only type attested. The *waqf* consists in the 'immobilization' of a property for the benefit of the institution in question, or rather of the men who undertake its upkeep and activities. The concession is made for all time, and therefore without any possibility of alienation (although certain forms of tenancy are inevitable). From then onwards it was common throughout the whole Muslim world. In Asia Minor, we know of it from the end of the twelfth century, but I do not think that the practice became general before the Mongol period, when *waqf*s became more numerous in order to guarantee the security of family possessions, under the cloak of the management of a *waqf* property, or to guarantee the necessary funds for institutions which until then had been maintained by the ordinary State budget, now itself endangered. In the rest of Islam, *waqf*s were in practice made from private properties, though possibly at the end of the Middle Ages, under the Mamluks in Egypt, some were established from the State lands also. In Asia Minor, this latter type seems more common, precisely on account of the large size of the public domain. When, for example, in 613/1216 Ertöküsh established various properties as a *waqf* for the benefit of a mosque in Antalya, then recently conquered, and other institutions in the same province or the neighbouring one of Burghlu, to the north, he did so probably not in his capacity as an individual owner of these properties but, as we know that he was the semi-autonomous governor of the whole of southern Anatolia, because he had authority to dispose of the State lands situated there.

Properties constituted as *waqf*s retained all their earlier characteristics, that is to say the peasants living there, in the case of cultivated land, came under the new beneficiaries and their agents, just as they had previously been under the owner or the State. The result was that they owed these new beneficiaries the same dues that they had owed to the earlier ones. In classical Muslim countries a property thus granted as a *waqf*, which previously had been liable to pay *kharāj* or tithe to the State, in its new status continued to pay these taxes, except however in the event of the State renouncing them as became general at the end of the Middle Ages. Under the system in Rūm, this stipulation was pointless: since almost all the land was in principle the property of the State, there was necessarily a confusion between what was apparently a tax paid to the State as the organ of government, and the rent paid to a land-owner who also proved in fact to be the State itself. In these circumstances, an estate that was alienated, in whatever way, was alienated together with the rents that it carried, even if those rents were given a name belonging classically to taxes, it being understood that the State could also make partial concessions, in which it reserved for itself certain financial or other rights (a thing which derives rather from the conception of *iqtāʿ* which we are about to consider). In these circumstances I cannot entirely agree with Osman Turan when he appears to think that there are some kinds of ownership which relate to taxes and not to the land itself, the State remaining the basic owner of this land. In those grants, such as the one made to Kīr Farid, in which the total amount of the income anticipated, as determined in the official cadastral survey, is defined, it is a question merely of stipulating explicitly the value of the concession made. It is only in the case of *iqtāʿ*s that the land itself is not really alienated, a situation which is very explicitly distinguished in the texts from that of true ownership. It is similarly necessary to indicate the income from a *waqf*, but this does not imply that the income alone was granted.

The word *iqtāʿ* has occurred several times, and earlier in this work the term was discussed with reference to the Great Seljukids. According to Osman Turan, the system of land-tenure of Seljukid Asia Minor entailed the general use of *iqtāʿ*s as its method of operation, since the State could not undertake the direct administration of such vast territories. This brings us back at once to the idea, adopted though not originated by Osman Turan, according to which the *iqtā'* is regarded as a Seljukid and Turkish innovation and, since the word is readily translated as 'fief', as characteristic of a specifically Turkish 'feudalism'. We have explained why we cannot accept this theory. In any case, in Asia Minor the problem is presented in different terms from those relating to the Great Seljukids, who ruled over former Muslim territories and never had at their disposal a public domain comparable with that of their kinsmen in Rūm. For this reason, while bearing in mind the distinctions made above in our general examination of the question, it is now necessary to examine this point with particular care.

In the ideas to be met with on the question of the 'feudalism' of Seljukid Asia Minor, there is, as in so many other cases, a confusion between the various uses of the term *iqtā'*, and even between this term and its incorrect translations in European languages. An *iqtā'*, it will be remembered, in the countries of classical Islam may relate to the quasi-ownership of a part of the public domain, or simply to the right to the taxes from lands in private ownership. In the first case, it automatically confers the right of inheritance, like all ownership; but this is foreign to the original conception in the second case, and it was only in the twelfth century it spread, giving for the first time a semi-feudal character to this kind of *iqtā'*. Moreover, a distinction must be made between the small *iqtā'*s, normally consisting of one or two villages, given to army officers in lieu of pay, and the great provincial governments which, in the twelfth century, began to be commonly known also as *iqtā'*s, in proportion as they acquired autonomy and the right of inheritance, though they did not possess these automatically and may, as before, have been allotted only to senior officials who were subject to removal, and ultimately rewarded with an *iqtā'* within their own administrative area. In Asia Minor, as elsewhere, we have to distinguish between the small *iqtā'*s and the provincial governments. It will be shown later (in contrast to what has always been said) that it was only in exceptional cases that the provincial governments in Seljukid Asia Minor were of the nature of an *iqtā'*. In any case, the holder of a great administrative area, whatever the type of concession by which it was conferred upon him, found himself in relation to local ownership in the same situation as the State, and the important thing for us in this connection is to know if this ownership had been assigned basically and directly by concession as an *iqtā'* in the proper sense, just as it might be by gifts or sales of ownership, or by the establishment of *waqf*s.

If we attempt to draw a chronological dividing line between the independent Seljukid régime and that of the Mongol Protectorate, a thing we regard as fundamental, the reference to ordinary *iqtā'*s that still survive are few in number. This may be partly the result of the inadequacy of the documentary material and the lack of interest attaching to minor figures, and any statistical approach is impossible. However, looking forward to what we shall say about the army, we shall advance the opinion that, in Rūm, *iqtā'* was not of the same military importance as in the other neighbouring Muslim States. However that may be, the *iqtā'* in Rūm necessarily differs from the *iqtā'* in the other states by the fact that, owing to the great predominance of State lands, it applied to properties which formed part of those lands, and not to fiscal rights over private properties. Nevertheless, those who organized the Seljukid State were not unaware of the way that *iqtā'* had been used by their neighbours, that it did not confer ownership, and was regarded in terms of its revenues. Thus the *iqtā'*s of Rūm, though carved out of the public domain, like the ones in the early days of Islam in countries conquered by the Arabs, were not conceived of as conferring ownership but only the revenue, which was here of this vague nature, half rent, half taxes, as we have seen. Furthermore they were temporary, sometimes bound up with the exercise of an office (not necessarily military), or for life only, and not normally hereditary; and the State could retain, within their area, whatever administrative or financial rights it wished, and these were defined in the deed of grant. Even the great *iqtā'*s of Kïrshehir and Akshehir, created for the princes of Erzinjān and Erzurum as compensation for their dispossession, certainly seem to have been of this kind. The holder did not possess the right to modify the obligations of the population either in taxation or in any other respect. To some extent the case of the holder (*muqta'*) of an *iqtā'* in Asia Minor might be compared with one in Egypt, where it was similarly connected with particularly strong state control over land in general.

These restrictive considerations naturally do not mean that

certain high officers and officials, by means of the various incomes they derived regularly or otherwise from their offices, did not succeed in creating huge fortunes – for example, the possession of immense herds of livestock on uncultivated lands. We shall see that Kay-kubādh dealt severely with what he regarded as an intolerable abuse in this respect. But this was precisely a matter, not of independent *muqtaʿs*, but simply of men who at the most had *iqṭāʿs* under their control (and even that was often uncertain).

In the Ottoman period, the State was to reward its warriors with grants of land not carrying with them any real public authority, but destined only to meet their needs. These concessions were to bear the name of *tīmār*. It is more or less implicitly admitted that there was a relationship between the *iqṭāʿ* and the *tīmār*. But it is important here to be agreed upon the exact point under discussion, and to pay attention to certain details in the method of research. If one wishes to assert merely that there might be some continuity of system between certain lands established as *tīmār* in the Ottoman period and those previously known as *iqṭāʿs*, this is possible, although no concrete example has as yet, to my knowledge, been put forward. This however does not necessarily mean that the conception of *tīmār* arose from that of the *iqṭāʿ*, with the mere substitution of the one word for the other. If this idea has been upheld, it is because the word *tīmār* occurs in the *Seljūknāme* of Yazïjï-oghlu. But as we have already said, there is no justification for using, for the Seljukid period, a term from Yazïjï-oghlu, whose Turkish adaptation of the Persian *Seljūknāma* of Ibn Bībī was made during the Ottoman period, if that term does not occur in Ibn Bībī's own writings; and the scholars who, since the Turkish language was more familiar to them, have worked on the basis of Yazïjï-oghlu have been guilty of a grave methodological error. Indeed, research has to make an entirely fresh start on the question of the origin of the word *tīmār* and of the institution itself. The word is Persian, and broadly speaking signifies 'forethought, means of providing for one's needs, of attending to those needs'. That it is possible to pass from that sense to the technical meaning defined above is understandable (just as the Latin *beneficium*, 'grant', was used to denote the European fief). But, to my knowledge, the technical meaning is not attested in any pre-Ottoman Persian text, any more in the

Mongol period than under the Seljukids. It is possible that the Ottomans borrowed the usage directly from the Byzantines, by translating the Greek word *pronoia* (forethought), the meaning of which is exactly equivalent to that of *tīmār*. There is no occasion to discuss the question here, but only to state clearly that there is no justification for deducing *a priori* certain ideas regarding the Seljukid *iqtāʿ* from those held in regard to the Ottoman *tīmār*.

A better knowledge of the system of taxation might help us to a clearer understanding of the system of land-tenure. However, in order to be fully aware of the problems to whose solution the various items of information that can be brought together must contribute, we must once again describe the fiscal system of the classical Muslim countries and also that of the Byzantine Empire.

In the classical Muslim countries, at the time of the Arab conquest, lands which had not been incorporated in the State domain (the domains of earlier states or great estates of private owners who had disappeared) as a general rule had been left with their previous possessors, on condition of payment of a land-tax, here known as *kharāj*, which incidentally corresponded to what they had paid under the preceding régimes. At that time, *kharāj* could be considered as characteristic of the situation of the non-Muslim, since as yet the only Muslims were the conquering Arabs, but afterwards it was in fact levied even on land-holders who had become Muslim, on the grounds that the land did not change its nature. At that time, however, a distinction which had existed in some regions (though not in all) became general, between the tax on land and a poll-tax, *jizya*, which ceased to apply in the event of conversion (when it was replaced by the *zakāt* or voluntary contribution paid by the believer towards the needs of the community). The practical difficulty of recognizing those cases in which there was one general tax and others in which there was a distinction between the two taxes, resides in the fact that originally the two terms denoting them had not received their precise technical meaning in the Administration, and that in the usage even of very late periods we therefore often find both *jizya* and *kharāj* used indiscriminately for each other or for an undifferentiated combination of the two.

The land-tax could of course be levied only on the land-owners, with whom were assimilated those in actual possession who held their lands under conditions in practice almost equivalent to legal ownership. The non-landowning peasants were tenants (*muzāri'*) paying rent in kind to the land-owners, their rent being roughly equivalent to what the *kharāj* would have been, but this latter was recorded by the Administration in the name of the land-owner. Moreover, this kind of tenancy was often the system employed, not for 'lands subject to *kharāj*' but for 'lands subject to tithe (*'ushr*)'. The tithe was an old tradition, but in Muslim law it had been regarded as the putting into effect of *zakāt* in the case where the property liable to this tax was a holding of land, this land being 'subject to the tithe' and not 'subject to *kharāj*' since at the time of the conquest it was the property of a Muslim. In the strict sense, this was infrequent outside Arabia proper, but with these Muslim properties there had been assimilated the *qatī'a* lavishly distributed by the new State from its domain which was too extensive to be exploited directly. In this case there was an important difference, in favour of the owner or quasi-owner, between the rent paid by his tenant farmers and the tithe which he owed to the State, with the result that the granting of a *qatī'a* had become the accepted method of conferring material rewards upon notables. The only condition imposed was that they should ensure the exploitation of the land by installing agricultural workers if none were already there.

Naturally the Muslim States had already developed, under various names, many other taxes on commerce, industry and so on. But their fiscal role was not of the same importance as the basic taxes just described, and for present purposes they can be left aside.

In the Byzantine Empire, the land-tax was still the basic tax, as is usual in any country in which, whatever developments of trade may take place, the land remains the principal source of wealth. The problem of determining to what extent a poll-tax was differentiated from it, and what form it took, remains obscure and does not concern us here. But the majority of the peasants had become tenants of the great land-owners, and therefore paid rent to them rather than a tax to the State. The situation was possibly less clearly defined in Armenia and the western valleys than in central Anatolia.

In fact, of course, we possess no information regarding the

system which became established at the start of the Turkish occupation. The Byzantine system of taxation was disrupted, and it is possible that, in some localities, for a time the people paid nothing. But obviously the conqueror demanded payments which, apparently having no precise official definition, must nevertheless have been burdensome, in view of the devastation of the very regions where the conquerors' presence made their demands most severe and impossible to evade. Then, little by little, a *modus vivendi* must have been established which, as a result of the islamization of the ruling classes, must as in all other respects have turned increasingly towards the models of classical Islam. Of what took place then we have almost no direct evidence, but it can be deduced in part from information from the Mongol period, precisely because the texts sometimes make it clear whether the particulars they give correspond to the Seljukid tradition or, on the contrary, are an Ilkhānid innovation. Incidentally, the Ilkhānid system was never completely applied in Asia Minor, which, even when it was administered by the Mongols, in this respect retained part of its autonomy (finance is always the field which a conqueror can change least easily).

Aqsarāyī, in the Mongol period, wrote that one (or the) essential feature of the fiscal system (again in the time of the Mongol Protectorate) was the *jizya*, and derides the newly-arrived Ilkhānid officials who knew nothing about it. This ignorance might be taken in conjunction with the fact that, in the states under direct Mongol administration, the *jizya*, which classically denotes the poll-tax on non-Muslims, no longer existed, because the Mongols, before their conversion to Islam, had done away with something that was a sign of the inferiority of one faith as compared with others. But it is possible that they had dropped it in the eastern half of Asia Minor itself. However important a poll-tax may have been in a country where the non-Muslim population formed the majority, it will be difficult to believe that it took precedence over the land-tax. In the Ottoman Empire, as a result of the verbal confusion noted above, the term *jizya* was generally employed to signify the land-tax, or the land-tax/poll-tax complex paid by non-Muslims, the word *kharāj* being rarer, and paradoxically denoting the poll-tax in the strict sense. It is tempting to believe that this usage already represents that of the

Seljukid period and that the text in Aqsarāyī therefore refers either to the land-tax or to the total complex of taxes paid by non-Muslims, in the event that both elements were explicitly combined in it (which is by no means certain). The word *kharāj* occurs incidentally in Aqsarāyī, but in an even vaguer way applicable to any kind of tax. In practice, the payment of the tax was made in kind, one of the possible modes of payment of *kharāj*, the land-tax, which was often proportional, and not conceivable in the case of poll-tax, the value of which was fixed. But, on the other hand, the classical land-tax (*kharāj*) implies that the person paying it was the land-owner – that is to say, according to the Law, it could not be demanded from tenants. However, if one starts from the idea that few real native owners still remained and that a large proportion of the soil was the domain of the State, it is difficult to think that the word *jizya* was applied to Muslim owners, and it is equally difficult to apply this name, in its accepted sense, to the rent that could be exacted from cultivators on State lands. On the other hand, it was customary that such rent should be paid in kind, whether or not in proportion to the harvest. It seems difficult to avoid the idea that there was great confusion both verbally and administratively or, to be more precise, that a Muslim terminology was applied to a state of affairs different from the classical Muslim system: the Seljukid officials no longer knew if *jizya* was a tax on land-owners or a payment made by tenant-farmers, nor if the rights of the State were those of a land-owner or of the treasury. There is no ground for thinking that the tenant-farmers were regarded as free tax-payers, but the terminology of the Law regarding free tax-payers was applied to them. In Ibn Bībī, for the period of independence, the usual tax 'on Christians (i.e. Greeks) and Armenians', the State's principal source of revenue, is called *kharāj*. It was of course in no case a question of 'lands subject to tithe', since the *iqtāʿ* paid nothing.

The very little that we know of Seljukid taxation before 1243 thus corroborates the impressions gained from a study of the system of land-tenure. Other taxes did of course exist, particularly in the towns, perhaps corresponding to those to be found mentioned under the vague general name *ʿawāriz-i dīwānī*; but of them nothing is known. Moreover the systems of land-tenure and taxation applying to Anatolia were not necessarily extended to the annexations made in Upper Syria and Upper Mesopotamia, in regions which had been familiar with the normal Muslim practice. Care must be taken, in the texts, to distinguish between regions as well as periods and, for example, not to extend automatically to the whole of Asia Minor the distinction between tenant-farmers (*muzāriʿ*) and free land-owners (sometimes heads of villages – *dihqān* – incidentally a variable term), a distinction valid in Iran, the existence of which for the region of Akhlāt is attested by Ibn Bībī.

It still remains to try to examine a little more deeply the precise nature of the tax, however named. Some related passages from Aqsarāyī may be of interest in this connection, although they refer to a later period, because there is no indication that this is a matter of a Mongol innovation. From these accounts it emerges that the tax on cultivable soil was levied by *juft-i ʿawāmil*, a Persian expression in which, however, the Arable word *ʿawāmil* has a meaning which translators do not seem to have understood: it means 'yoke of beasts for ploughing'. It is true that the word *juft* (whence the Turkish *chift*) was known in Iran under the Ilkhānids, but it seems to have been employed there only in its strict sense, the agrarian unit still remaining the *jarīb*, as in the past. On the other hand, in the texts mentioned earlier in connection with Asia Minor, and also much later in the Ottoman Empire, the term is applied to the unit of land defined as the area that a yoke of oxen can plough (similar terminological and economic usages are to be found in many countries). Now it was certainly also by the 'yoke', Latin *jugum*, Greek *zeugarion*, that the Byzantine treasury taxed its farmers. It would seem therefore that there is here a clear instance of Byzantine-Turkish continuity, an impression perhaps confirmed – though a more detailed study would be necessary – by the resemblances revealed later between Ottoman Law and Byzantine Law in these matters, in respect both of Asia Minor (already Turkish even earlier), and of the provinces directly annexed by the Ottomans from Byzantium.

Whatever the facts of the matter, the 'yoke' can be imposed in different ways – in kind, as a proportion of the harvest (in which case the agrarian unit is no longer of great importance), in cash at a fixed sum, and lastly in kind but for a fixed amount. In the

14

Muslim countries generally, private tenants paid proportionately in kind: cultivators or owners more often paid tax at a fixed sum for the agrarian unit, but sometimes in cash and sometimes in kind calculated by value. There is no doubt that, in Asia Minor in the thirteenth century, the total sum from the taxes due from a district was stipulated in cash. This would be difficult to credit, were it not that this was also the case with the 'yoke', which one of the passages in Aqsarāyī says was taxed at 1 dinar, though others refer to a tax by *taghar*, a measure of volume for grain corresponding to a weight of 10 *manns*, the value of the quantity collected naturally having to be calculated at an official rate or at the market valuation. A tax based on the unit of area was generally the Byzantine system; it was common in Islam also. But it is self-evident that the same area of land brought in different returns, according to soil, climate and cultivation, and thus had to be taxed differently. In countries based on the 'yoke', this was often done by making the 'yoke' represent different areas according to circumstances, while in countries with a fixed unit of area it was the rate of tax that varied. But unfortunately we know nothing about the system in Rūm. It appears that the tenants of private properties most usually had to make proportional payments: a *waqf* set up by Karatay (some years after the battle of Köse Dagh) stipulated that the demands to which the tenants were subjected should not exceed a proportion of one-fifth. In classical Islam, this was the proportion for mediocre lands requiring irrigation or other difficult work. This particular *waqf* is in the region of Kayseri, and we cannot claim that the proportion was everywhere the same. In any event, contrary to earlier belief, one cannot draw any certain conclusions from it as regards taxation.

In certain cases, in place of the normally calculated tax a comprehensive agreement (*muqātaʿa*) was substituted. This was so with the monastery of Mar Bar-Sauma, to the south of Malatya, the residence of the Jacobite Patriarch; and doubtless it was so too with the Turcoman groups, particularly on the frontiers. It may be conjectured that they had to surrender some livestock, a thing which would in fact agree with the rule of classical Islam for pastoral nomads, but we have no knowledge of this. I make no mention of course of tribute from vassals.

The total budget of the Seljukid State, so far as it had been possible to make an exact estimate in the thirteenth century, according to the later writer Hamd Allāh Mustawfī, was, under the Seljukids, about 15 million dinars of his time; and, after a marked decline, it only amounted to 3·3 millions (Egypt, about 4), as we shall see later.

4

THE TOWNS

It has already been remarked that, from the twelfth century, urban life in Rūm revived, and in the thirteenth century it certainly attained a higher level than had been known during the last centuries under Byzantium. In the middle of the thirteenth century Simon of Saint-Quentin declared that the Seljukid State included 100 towns, and Ibn Sa'īd that it possessed 24 provincial towns, each provided officially with its governor and *cadi*, a mosque, baths and cloth merchants. The towns were not named, and perhaps neither writer could have named them all, but the impression is a definite one, and there is no difficulty in supplying almost the full number of names from chronicles and travellers.

In general, despite the undeniable hiatus in their history formed by the period of the Turkish conquest, the Seljukid towns more or less correspond to the ancient Christian towns, either because occupation had been uninterrupted or because the site had been re-occupied: in a country which had been highly urbanized, geographical conditions rarely permitted the choice of an entirely new location. This continuity was often marked by a similar continuity of name, and it must be remembered that, in certain cases where the modern name does not correspond to the ancient one, the latter was still in use in the time of the Seljukids, the modern name coming later. Thus Colonia (south of Trebizond) was still called Kughūniya, and not as today Shebin Karahisār, and even Ankara, which preserves the old name of Ancyra, was then known as Ankuriya, a name closer to the ancient form. As for Konya/Iconium, Sivas/Sebasteia, Qaysariyya (not yet with its modern name Kayseri), Malatya/Melitene and others, that is to say some of the largest towns, these have retained their ancient names almost unchanged until our own times. In certain cases there was a more pronounced distortion of the name or complete replacement by another, but this pre-dated the Turks and was due, for example, to the Armenians or Arabs, as in the case of Erzinjān/Keltzine and Erzurum, also called Theodosiopolis, near the ancient Qaliqāla. Finally, in western Asia Minor in particular, new Turkish names had been introduced, especially for small and medium-sized towns, although unfortunately the documentation does not always make it possible to determine in what circumstances the transformation was made. In some cases it was not accompanied by any interruption in occupation, in others there may have been some interruption (for instance between Archelaus and Akseray), in others again a nearby site may have replaced the ancient one (in place of Laodicaea, known as Lādīq, Denizli which was then called Tunguzlu grew up close by; and, strangely enough, Eskishehir, whose name means 'old town', 2 miles to the south of the ruined Dorylaion; similarly Beyshehir, in place of Karaleia). There do not appear to have been any really new foundations, that is to say in districts where none had existed, but there may have been some re-foundations in the manner of the Roman colonies, such as Akseray, and some official changes of name, such as ʿAlāʾiyya for Kalon-oros, in honour of ʿAlāʾ al-Dīn Kay-kubādh. And lastly of course the relative order of importance of the towns may not have remained as it was before.

The towns were inhabited by elements of the various populations of Asia Minor. In Antalya it is recorded that Greeks, Jews and Turks each occupied their own quarter. But the fact that this is recorded suggests that it was not so elsewhere, and indeed in Konya, although there is one reference to an Armenian tavern, there is certainly no suggestion of any such segregation. Such a thing was in fact rare at that time, though less so in Byzantium than in Islam. The perhaps special case of Antalya may be explained by its situation as an international port, and possibly by the conditions of its capitulation which occurred far later than the conquest of the rest of the country. The presence of Jews there seems moreover to have been exceptional, in comparison with

Asia Minor, although there were some Jews in Konya. It is not known what Jews there were in Sinope, which was also frequented internationally, nor is there any means of knowing if the different ethno-confessional groups lived separately. Naturally the members of each group tended to cling together, but without any systematic segregation. In a large Armenian town such as Erzinjān it was the Muslim group which appeared to be isolated.

Neither in the Byzantine Empire nor in the Muslim world did towns have the autonomy that they enjoyed in classical antiquity or that they were to recover in the mediaeval West. It does not follow from this that they were without either vitality or a certain kind of corporate spirit, and equally it does not follow that none of them concerned themselves with the needs of their municipal administrations and similar matters. All this, quite simply, is an integral part of the general structure of the State and, even when they exist, Muslim Law does not recognize corporate bodies, collective organizations intermediate between the individual and the State. It is unnecessary to dwell here on these generalities which have been discussed many times. It must merely be borne in mind that on the whole, in Anatolia as elsewhere, and even more for the Muslims than for the natives, the town was the centre of all administration and all culture. The Turcomans, who in point of fact were outside the towns, were indeed at that time also outside society and culture, or at all events constituted another society with another culture, broadly speaking.

It was therefore in the town that the governor resided, with his garrison. It was in the town that there was the mosque, and the *cadi* who meted out justice and who, when possible, was chosen from among the leading jurists. The *muhtasib* has been referred to elsewhere, but a few more comments on this officer and the organization of trades are required. Juridically, the *muhtasib* was a subordinate of the *cadi*, particularly responsible for public morality, the regulation of non-Muslims and, above all, for the general well-being of commerce. This was so throughout the whole Muslim world in the Seljukid period, and it is not surprising that the State of Rūm should have adopted the institution. Unfortunately we cannot tell if it possessed any specific characteristics in that country, as a result of the large numbers of native merchants who had their own traditions and were more numerous there than elsewhere. And so long as they did no positive harm to Islam, all their traditions were respected.

An account ascribed to Jalāl al-Dīn Rūmī will serve as an excellent introduction to our knowledge both of the landscape and of the social structure of a large Seljukid town. 'In Konya', he says, 'the leaders, dignitaries and notables have thousands of houses, castles and palaces; the houses of the merchants and *ikdīsh* are loftier than the artisans', the emirs' palaces are loftier than the merchants', the Sultans' domes and palaces are even loftier than all the others, but the size and loftiness of the heavens etc. . .' To this might be added various passages from the chronicle of Ibn Bībī in which the notables, *ikdīsh* and *akhis*, and sometimes also the men of religion, are enumerated.

At the top, though below the Sultan in the case of his town of residence, were the emirs, the governor and so on, all the representatives of authority and the ruling class. As in Italian towns, so in certain Muslim ones, the loftiness of the dwelling was in direct ratio to that of its occupant's social rank. There was no difficulty in recognizing what social category was concerned. For those that follow, things were somewhat different.

The word *ikdīsh*, which was Iranian and Turkish before being adopted into Arabic, properly signifies a gelding or cross-bred animal, particularly a mule. From this meaning it passed, especially in Irano-Turkish countries, to that of a human being of mixed race. In Asia Minor it thus appears to apply mainly to children resulting from unions between Turks and natives, probably native converts given Turkish wives. The question has been raised, though it is impossible either to prove or to disprove this, whether, under the name *ikdīsh*, there were not also native converts pure and simple or, as was to be the case with the Janissaries under the Ottomans, young lads of Christian origin forcibly taken from the population to be brought up as Muslim soldiers. But there was no mention of this in Christian literature.

Whatever their ethnic origin, it is remarkable to find these *ikdīsh* belonging finally to the aristocracy of the purely town-dwelling population. They constituted a special corps, commanded by an *ikdīshbashī* or *amīr-i akādish*, a Muslim (but often the son of a native convert), the names of some of whom are known. When the chronicles referred to them it was usually because they were

carrying out military operations of a local character, in co-operation with or in place of the army proper. It is this fact that has led
to the idea that they were a military corps. It seems however that
this was no more true of them than it would be of a police force
or a militia normally entrusted with the simple maintenance of
order in a town. Possibly they had this function, and on one
occasion it even happened that a defeated pretender was placed
in the temporary keeping of an *ikdīsh* (of Ankara). On the other
hand, a model diploma of investiture drafted towards the end of
the thirteenth century and a letter of Jalāl al-Dīn Rūmī reveal the
ikdīshbashī and *ikdīsh* in the role of tax-collectors, even as assessors
of urban taxes. They thus played quite an extensive part in urban
administration, and the number of towns for which they are
mentioned is sufficiently great to allow us to think that the
system was general. In short, the Sultans controlled the urban
population, among whose lower ranks non-Muslims predom-
inated, and eventually the Muslims themselves, by means of this
local aristocracy of mixed race.

Nevertheless, as time passed, this social category lost its distinctive character and its justification: after several generations
there could no longer be the same distinctions as at the start
between Muslims by origin and those descended from converts or
mixed unions. And from the fourteenth century the word *ikdīsh*,
in its social sense, was to disappear, while the *akhi*s alone were
left to deal with the local policing, as will be shown.

Before discussing the *akhi*s, however, it is first necessary to
consider the merchants and artisans mentioned earlier, with
whom they were connected. And, at the start, the question has to
be put on a wider basis.

The organization of crafts in Asia Minor raises a problem, the
significance of which may extend beyond the country itself. It is
impossible here to enter into a detailed discussion, but it must be
outlined in broad terms. Both in Byzantium and in the late
Roman Empire, which it had succeeded, there was some organization of occupation by the State in the sense that trades were
distinguished from one another, but that the regulation of them
belonged to the State, and those in control were nominated by the
State. In western Europe there was an entirely different system
which was starting to take shape in the period corresponding to

that of the Seljukids: there were trade guilds, that is to say collective but private organizations which, in the absence of action by the states of the time, themselves drew up their own rules, chose their leaders and, for these reasons, influenced the general lives of their members by mutual assistance, religious ceremonies and so on, in a way that the 'collegia' on the Roman model were unable to do. It has often been thought, on the strength of a very superficial examination in which different things, periods and countries were confused, that Islam too had known trade guilds. For the so-called classical periods of Islam it is, broadly speaking, the converse which is true. There were some administratively strong states which, like the Romano-Byzantine State, exercised control directly and did not admit any intermediate body. Occupations were distinguished administratively and topographically, but direction of them derived from the State, that is to say from the *muhtasib*. It is true that, under him and to assist him, there were certain leaders (*'arif, amin, ra'is*) of trades who, for technical and psychological reasons, were recruited from those trades, but these were the *muhtasib*'s subordinates and they were not elected by the trades. And there is almost no sign that any wider human role was taken by these trades in their members' lives: when they grouped themselves together, it was in extra-professional movements like that of the *fityān*, to be discussed shortly. In the twelfth and thirteenth centuries in Syria and Egypt, as also in Muslim Spain, manuals of *hisba* were drawn up (the *hisba* is the office of the *mustasib*), the precise aim of which was to define the *muhtasib*'s duties from a purely administrative point of view.

From the end of the Middle Ages, however, it must be admitted that to some extent a certain evolution took place. In modern times, when states were less strong, and even in the Ottoman Empire in Constantinople itself, as a result apparently of circumstances of differing origins, the trades had a semi-corporate organization effectively combining a certain measure of State control with a measure of private activity. It is possible that Iran and Central Asia, which probably did not have exactly the same traditions as the former Roman countries like Syria and Egypt, were more advanced in this evolution than the rest of the Muslim world. This is a hypothesis which I cannot elaborate here but which, while regarding it merely as such, I may be allowed to take into account. And thus it is important to see where Asia Minor fits into this general picture.

Without completely ruling out the possibility that traditions brought directly by the Turks from remote Central Asia may occasionally have had some influence, it seems reasonable to admit that the life of craftsmen in the towns of Seljukid Asia Minor originally derived primarily from the juxtaposition of, or contact between, Greek and Armenian craftsmen on the one side and Iranian immigrants on the other. And, having granted that the Irano-Muslims took the essential part in forming the administration, it can be admitted that at least the framework of professional life was conceived in accordance with their ideas and traditions, even though the particular customs of each trade still exercised by the natives preserved the character they had possessed before the Turks. When this is said, what in actual fact is known? From the strictly Seljukid period, practically nothing – not even whether, as is probable, each trade had its own alley or quarter. At the end of the Mongol period, Ibn Battūta supplies information which is important but also difficult to interpret. But before considering this, we must introduce the *akhi*s.

The organization of the towns was in fact bound up with the organization of the *akhi*s, which, for reasons that will be understood, was not clearly revealed in its full vigour until the Mongol régime and later, but which nevertheless was in existence before it. The institution is of great interest, but also raises many problems. The combination is worth consideration at some length.

The first section of the present work included a brief account of the *futuwwa* or, if it be preferred, the *fityān*, commonly known as *ʿayyārūn*, who claimed to be related. It consisted of corporate groupings, popular but non-professional, highly interdependent, activated by social rather than by religious considerations, opposing the authorities and the aristocracy with considerable violence, although some members of the aristocracy tried to make use of it, powerful during periods of weak government when it became a true militia, more retiring during periods of strong government, though not for that reason ceasing to exist. There is no town in Iraqo-Iranian territory, and consequently in the territory that the Great Seljukids had possessed and traversed, and whose influence the Turks of Rūm continued to feel, which did not have its *fityān* who at times were the real masters of local politics. If the towns of Byzantine Asia Minor had nothing really equivalent, it was nonetheless the normal procedure that, as soon as urban life became organized, with men of varied origin collaborating in it, a *futuwwa* also appeared.

Of its existence in the twelfth century nothing is known, and until the closing years of the century it was necessarily of small account. But the moment when it made its real appearance was also, as has been seen, the time when the Caliph al-Nāsir, in Baghdad, tried to institutionalize the *futuwwa* and to make it an organ of social cohesion by recruiting the powerful as well as the poor, under explicit and modified regulations, and by encouraging all the neighbouring princes to make similar efforts, under his aegis. It will be noted elsewhere that for this purpose he sent to Kay-kāūs a great Shaykh of Baghdad who had been one of his advisers on the question, Shihāb al-Dīn ʿUmar Suhrawardī, and who made a great impression on the Turks in Konya, or at least on governmental circles. This was also at the time when the Seljukid Sultanate was becoming organized as a Muslim State and was anxious to pose as the upholder of orthodoxy, in order to win the Caliph's favour. Kay-kāūs therefore remained faithful to the *futuwwa* as reshaped by al-Nāsir and, although it is impossible to determine by what means, it can be accepted that as a result the organization of the *futuwwa* in Anatolia was stimulated, on lines possibly conforming more nearly with the Caliph's wishes than they did in the ancient towns where too rigid a tradition was dominant.

In Asia Minor, however, and in some neighbouring regions to the east, the beginnings of the *futuwwa* raise another problem. Indeed, in that country as well as in north-western Iran, that is to say the part of Iran most deeply penetrated by Turkish elements, the name which usually denotes the *fityān*, or sometimes more specifically their directors, is *akhi*, for which the rest of the Muslim world had no equivalent. The equivalence of the two terms in the thirteenth century in the territories in question is not in doubt, but it is not possible to affirm that it was original, and even the derivation of the word is uncertain. Indeed it was unknown to the *akhis* of a later period, for which alone reliable documents are available. The authors who mentioned them sometimes tried to equate them with the Arabic term *akhī*, which means 'my brother', but the forms in which the word appears in Persian or Turkish, or even eventually in Arabic texts, virtually exclude the possibility that the word was consciously used in this sense. A distinguished modern Turcologist has proposed a Turkish etymology for the word that is linguistically admissible, but which the historian is obliged to challenge because the earliest known *akhi*s, during the eleventh century in north-western Iran, certainly seem to have been Iranians, from whom the Turks may have learnt the word. In any case, the earliest *akhi*s were pure mystics who do not appear to have had any particular connection with any sort of *futuwwa*, let alone with a *futuwwa* on the lines of the urban *fityān* described above. Whatever the original meaning of the word (a matter of little importance since it no longer appears to have been understood), there is consequently a problem concerning the encounter of *akhi* and *futuwwa* in Asia Minor that is distinct from the history of the *futuwwa* in other territories.

It is easy to see that this is not merely a verbal question. We know that, particularly from the eleventh century, when mysticism won over the cities in orthodox Islam and tended to become organized in confraternities, on the one hand some elements of the *fityān* welcomed certain forms of mystical mentality, on the other certain mystics adopted in their own way the conception of the corporate life implied by the *futuwwa*. Shaykh Suhrawardī, mentioned earlier, is one of the examples of these converging trends. The so-called *futuwwa* literature, of which more will be said, is in this respect interesting and surprising. As only the literate were writing, it is their point of view alone that is presented. In practice this is shown by the fact that, while the chronicles or other texts portray the *akhi*s acting in positive and indeed violent social forms, the *futuwwa* literature tells almost solely of initiation rites and theoretical moral-religious considerations, to such a point that, if there were nothing more, one would hesitate to believe that they could be dealing with the same things and the same men. This is particularly true of the *futuwwa* writings of al-Nāsir's circle, which were to have such a great influence on those of Anatolia. What is certain, in general terms (and Islam could provide other examples of this) is that there took place an interpenetration of a certain form of social action and a certain form of mystical life, a certain adoption of certain social organizations by certain 'mystical' congregations (with due allowance being made for the variety of possible meanings of the word 'mystical'). For the moment, this is all that we can say.

Besides *fityān* and *akhi*s, popular language used certain terms to denote the members of the *futuwwa* which varied according to places and periods, like all jargons. In the period we are concerned with, the word *'ayyārūn*, which people of earlier centuries had used, is still found, but the most usual term in the various Seljukid territories is certainly *rind*, Arabic plural *runūd*, Persian *rindān*, 'rogues'.

The great ancestor of the *akhi*s as a whole is a certain Akhi Faraj Zanjānī (from Zanjān, north-western Iran) who lived in the first two-thirds of the eleventh century. But the Turkish *akhi*s were said to have an ancestor with the name, if the reading is quite certain, of Akhi Türk of Urmiya (on the Azerbaijan-Armenian border), who must have lived in the twelfth century. To some extent the leadership of the community, *fityān* included, was to stay in his family until the thirteenth century, at least in Konya. The earliest *akhi*s known were found also in other towns, and it so happens that the first one recorded was at Antalya, only a few years after its conquest, which shows that the organization took root at the same time as the Muslim immigration and thus was already a truly integral part of every Muslim urban community.

Nevertheless, the part played by the *akhi*s is not made fully clear in the sources, and obviously it only attained its fullest political, if not economic, extent during periods of governmental disintegration. Since it so happened that *futuwwa* writings (Turkish *fütüvvet*) did not start in Asia Minor until the end of the thirteenth century, little is known of the *akhi*s and *runūd* before the Mongol period, and it is with reference to this later period that we are best able to complete and put in positive form what has already been said in more general terms.

On the matter of the relations between the *akhi*s and the trades, it seems permissible to make an exception and to look ahead to the Mongol period, to a document of that time in which a problem is raised of significance to the entire Turkish and even Muslim Middle Ages. It is the description of his travels by the famous Ibn Battūta.

The problem is as follows. As was said, the *futuwwa* organizations throughout the whole Muslim world before the end of the Middle Ages, even though they included men most of whom followed some trade, were not professional organizations in the sense that the profession does not appear to have been the basis of either for their activities or for the division of their members into sub-groups. On the one side there were the trades, on the other the *futuwwa*, even if their members were in large measure the same. There is nothing, at least before the thirteenth century, to justify any other opinion. However, in the Ottoman period, both in Turkey strictly speaking and in the non-Turkish provinces, the two structures converged. The trades in Istanbul, as described by the Turkish observer Evliya Chelebi in the seventeenth century, were organized as corporations of initiates of the *futuwwa* type, and treatises which deal with trades in Ottoman Egypt call themselves treatises on *futuwwa*. The identification was not total, and perhaps varied according to the country, but the growing similarity cannot be denied. There is thus a large problem in regard to the reasons, methods and chronology of this evolution. And in this respect the evidence of Ibn Battūta is of capital importance.

It will be remembered that he came to Anatolia shortly after 1330, and in almost all the towns he visited he was struck by the importance of the *akhi*s. We shall return to this question. What chiefly concerned him personally was that, just as we have seen was true of the earliest *fityān* in Islam (though to be frank it was less true of their descendants), these *akhi*s practised the virtues of hospitality and solidarity which to Ibn Battūta, as a stranger, were a constant source of gratification. Hence he almost always lodged in their communal house, where he was received with generosity and warmth. Hence, too, he observed their practices and so was enabled to furnish the details that he gives. The important point, for the moment, is that, according to Ibn Battūta, a group of *akhi*s, although generally open to bachelors, was primarily constituted on the basis of members from the same trade. However, when immediately afterwards he spoke of the *akhi* leader who had received him in Alanya, he is less clear, since he wrote that this was a shoe-maker, and that with him were two hundred workmen from various trades who had chosen him as their leader. The case of the *akhi*s to Denizli/Lādīq however proves that all trades were not necessarily or normally united in one single group of *akhis* since there was rivalry between two of them (but obviously there were more than two trades). But at the feast of the Breaking of the Fast they went in procession, with arms and music, following the Sultan's troops, each trade separately. The information that Ibn Battūta gives about Akseray and Sivas confirms these accounts, though with less detail. From this it emerges that, in Ibn Battūta's time, there may have been rival groups of *akhis* (as among the trade unions today), even if the principles of their organization were the same, but that within each group, which included members from a great number of trades, there was a structure with divisions according to trades, and that it was these trades which, when combined together, formed the main body of the *futuwwa* of the *akhis*. In all his travels Ibn Battūta encountered nothing really comparable. Even in Iran, where the trades appeared to him to be more autonomous and individualized than elsewhere, according to him they still had no systematic links with the *futuwwa*, although it was well-known in that country.

In view of all this, the essential thing would be to know if the description given by Ibn Battūta in the fourteenth century would also have been true a century earlier. If that were so, it would probably signify an original feature compared with the rest of the Muslim world, the reasons for which would have to be accounted for; if not, it would mean that there had been a certain evolution, and it would be necessary to know whether it was autonomous, or had felt the influence of the Mongol régime, and so on. For the moment nothing can be said, but it is essential that the questions should be clearly stated.

This picture of urban society would be incomplete without some reference to slavery, although there is nothing very specifically concerned with Asia Minor to be said : no Mediterranean country was completely unacquainted with slavery, and it was particularly important in a Muslim country. It therefore existed in Turkey, with this difference from other countries that there was the Greek element acquired in frontier razzias (which were to increase in the fourteenth century). But, as in all Muslim lands, slavery was essentially urban and domestic and, apart from the sending of slaves as stewards by the land-owners, it was absent from agricultural work. On the other hand, it played a certain part in urban craft work, a field in which the slave could even attain a measure of independence. Reference will be made later to slavery in the army, which differs from that of the other Muslim States.

The largest town under the Seljukids, before the Mongols, was apparently Konya, and the first efforts to turn it into a capital were due to Mas'ūd. It was certainly the capital when Barbarossa's Crusaders came there in 1190, and one of them described it as being of the size of Cologne, with walls and a citadel. The great mosque, begun by Mas'ūd, was enlarged by all the Sultans in turn until Kay-kubādh, under whom it finally reached the state in which it can be seen today. In the *waqf*-deed of Altun-Aba of 598/1201, however, there is a reference to two small mosques founded by rich merchants. There is no reason why this chance text should name all the mosques, and others certainly existed although, in so far as it is possible to date monuments which do not always bear inscriptions, only three date from before 1243, including the great mosque (but not the mausolea, *madrasas* and so on). Shortly after the Mongol disaster the mosque of Karatay was to be added, and two or three later. It has already been noted that the *waqf*-deed of Altun-Aba referred to the new *suq*, alongside the old one, a sign of the development of the town and trade, and *waqf*-deeds mention shops of all kinds.

Such fortifications as existed were judged inadequate by Kaykubādh, who had them all more or less completely rebuilt at the joint expense of the Treasury and the great emirs. On the citadel-hill were situated the Sultan's new buildings, the tombs of Mas'ūd, Kïlïj Arslan, Rukn al-Dīn and Kaykhusraw, and the Sultan's palace, now vanished, though extensive ruins still survived, to be described by various nineteenth century travellers. In the suburbs there were gardens and also monasteries, the most famous being the Monastery of Chariton or of Plato, as it was known, to be referred to later. Even when allowance is made for exaggerations and inaccuracies, the descriptions of the *Seljūknāme* and Aflākī relating to the second half of the thirteenth century give the impression of a town with a vigorous economic, political and cultural life, and certainly containing several tens of thousands of inhabitants.

The second town of the Sultanate was probably Sivas, an international meeting-place of merchants, which Kay-kubādh had also fortified at the emirs' expense, as he did Sinope. Kayseri, which was to astonish the troops of the Mamluk Sultan Baybars in 1277, was little inferior to it. Antalya too must be regarded as a large town and was admired by the traveller Ibn Battūta, Erzinjān was a large Armenian town, Malatya a large town of mixed religions, and there were many other towns which, though apparently smaller, were nevertheless by the standards of that period real towns – Erzurum, Amasya and Akseray, among others.

5

THE NON-MUSLIMS

Whatever the proportion of the Turkish population, it is quite obvious that the non-Muslims were still numerous, and probably formed a clear majority almost everywhere – in the proportion of 10 to 1, according to William of Rubruck. It has been remarked several times already that, despite or because of the depredations committed by the earliest conquerors, the natives had not been systematically hostile to the Turks, and had often regarded the conquest less as an ordeal for themselves than as a punishment for Byzantium. Moreover, some Byzantines had also called in the Turks against other Byzantines, and hence, to some extent in all circles, there had certainly been quite as much complicity in the actual Turkish occupation as resistance to it. It will also be remembered that, in the organized régime which gradually succeeded the conquest, at the side of the Muslim masters there were, as in other Muslim countries, native or indeed Greek notables, not to mention refugees from elsewhere. These reminders will be sufficient to suggest that, without ignoring the sufferings endured in the eleventh century or certain incidents or difficulties in succeeding periods, when Turkey became organized there was a symbiosis for which one can certainly find parallels in other Muslim countries, but which perhaps was a more strict one and in any case more far-reaching, owing to the numbers involved. It is unnecessary to return to the social aspects of the régime, but a few words must be devoted to the religious situation.

Any detailed study of the situation is made difficult by the fact that, except for the Jacobites whose material is of importance only in the province of Malatya and its surroundings, there are no available sources that derive from the religions directly concerned except outside Seljukid territory. Moreover, one has to beware of being led astray by documentation from the Mongol period. The pro-Christian attitude of the first Mongol sovereigns in a Muslim country and the alliance of Byzantium under the Palaeologi with the first Ilkhāns of Persia did indeed enable certain ecclesiastical 'reconquests' to be made. Consequently the mention of a community or diocese, for instance, at the end of the thirteenth century does not *ipso facto* allow one to assume its existence at the beginning of that century or in the twelfth. However, certain facts do emerge.

To a mind accustomed to the totalitarian mental categories of the twentieth century it is somewhat difficult to conceive how, in Asia Minor in the twelfth and thirteenth centuries, the convictions and behaviour of *ghāzīs* could co-exist with a religious tolerance superior to anything found elsewhere in Islam. It is true that, in part, the difference in outlook between the Turcomans and the rulers of the states, so frequently noted, has to be borne in mind, but in part only, for co-existence took effect with the Turcomans as well as with the others. There is no need to repeat that, for the rulers, the holy war very soon appeared to be a course of action foreign to their general tendencies, which they adopted only when compelled to do so by particular circumstances. This had happened many times in past history generally in the other Muslim States, for example in Syria in the eleventh century. But, at the time in question, this attitude was declining in Syria and Egypt on account of the struggle with the Crusaders and the Latin East. To this struggle the Turks of Asia Minor were utterly indifferent. Even when, at the very beginning of the Frankish occupation or under certain of the Ayyūbids, an attempt was made in the Arab Near East to bring about a *détente* and the acceptance of a peaceful co-existence beneficial to economic interests, it would have been inconceivable to see sovereigns allying their families with any infidel sovereigns. The most that is recorded, and that in a half-legendary manner, is the proposal once put forward by Saladin of an alliance with Richard Coeur de Lion, to be sealed by a marriage between their families. The idea came to nothing. On the other hand, it has already been shown that Malik-Shāh proposed a similar alliance to Alexis Comnenus, and later, among the Turks of Asia Minor, its realization became an accepted fact, and not only at the start when beautiful female captives were brought in, but also later, at least with the Greeks and Georgians, by means of unions concluded as between equals by common consent. Thus the Sultan's family contained plenty of Christian men and women. The mother of Kaykhusraw I was Greek, as was the mother of Kaykhusraw II, and two or possibly three of the latter's sons were born of Christian mothers. It is true that one of these mothers, a Georgian princess, who was later to be taken in marriage by the *pervāne* Muʿīn al-Dīn Sulaymān, was converted to Islam, but there was no general obligation, and instances of the converse also exist: it is known how greatly the young Kay-kāūs II was influenced by his Christian uncles, and even by Michael Palaeologus. The only women not to appear in the list of Christian wives are the Armenians, who did not represent a political power, but there was even a projected marriage with a Frenchwoman, a kinswoman of the Latin Emperors of Constantinople. As for their Christian subjects, the Sultans, whether through moderation or self-interest, defended them against any who happened to threaten their religious freedom; and Muslim travellers who visited towns with a Christian majority and only a small Muslim colony, such as Erzinjān and Erzurum, were indignant at the atmosphere they found there, with wine, pork, religious processions and the rest.

Co-existence in the Turcoman border territories is more difficult to understand, though no less certain. Warfare against an undefeated adversary did not exclude the protection of the subjugated infidel. It did not even exclude profitable commercial exchanges, between raids. In these circumstances it came about that the Christian natives preferred to seek an understanding with the Turcomans rather than the protection of the Byzantine Government, so often disdainful and ineffective and accompanied by heavy taxation. History is full of such minor arrangements between neighbours, who then found themselves allied together against their respective rulers. Moreover, it was now almost solely a matter of the Greeks, since all the Armenians were already subjugated, as were the Monophysite groups, and the Georgians were too remote and difficult of access. In the time of Alexis Comnenus, the complicity of the Armenians and Monophysites with the Turks seemed to the Byzantines to be so established that they proceeded to take revenge on the members of those communities who were settled in Constantinople.

During the period in question, the sovereigns of neighbouring Muslim States from time to time re-introduced restrictive measures in regard to non-Muslims which the rigourists considered to be linked with the commandments of Islam, in particular the obligation to have distinguishing marks on clothing and the veto on the building of new places of worship. The first of these measures almost invariably soon lapsed, and in return for payments of money it was possible to gain exemption from the second. It seems that, before the conversion of the Mongols to Islam at the beginning of the fourteenth century, no measures of this kind had ever been envisaged in Rūm, where their application would have been purposeless or impossible at that time and place.

Political and religious interventions may sometimes have favoured or discouraged good relations between the Turks and one or other of the Christian Churches in their states. But, on the whole, it is certain that in one respect the non-Greek Christians found their lot improved when brought under the new domination, in that they no longer had to submit to the vexatious meddlings of the Byzantine Church. In Antioch, Sulaymān had already assigned the former Byzantine churches to the Monophysites, and Atsïz had done the same in Jerusalem. Michael the Syrian in particular expresses the same feeling of satisfaction. The Turks, indifferent to divisions between Christians, were not inclined to favour one confession at the expense of another.

Naturally, as has been emphasized, all the above does not indicate any lack of zeal for Islam on the part of the Sultans. The very rulers whose tolerance was praised did their best to further the cause of Islam. While leaving the Christians in their towns to profess their faith in peace, in Akseray they created a purely Muslim model town. And perhaps, in proportion with the spread of culture among the ruling circles, they felt that the maintenance of their domination was bound up with the consolidation of Islam, culturally and so to speak as a politico-social cohesive force. At the very beginning of the Turkish occupation the Greek Church could perhaps have contemplated an attempt to convert them. It conceived no such idea, and later there was no longer any possibility.

Clearly it was the Greek Church which suffered most at the start. It was not that the invaders had any systematic desire to attack that Church rather than the others since, as was said before, their aim was to settle in Rūm rather than to destroy it. The reason was rather that, in all the hostilities, the Greek clergy appeared to be more closely linked with the defeated government than the native clergy, and above all because, often being looked upon with disfavour by the Armenian and Monophysite populations who regarded the Turkish invasion as a well-deserved retribution for the Byzantines and who sometimes came to terms with the Turks, the Greek clergy, possessing as they did the chance to retreat to Constantinople or elsewhere when the conditions of life seemed to have become too severe morally or materially, had not become firmly anchored there in the same way that, on the contrary, the other Eastern clergy had. The latter, staying on amidst their own people, determined to save everything possible and, once the storm had passed, to restore the shaken positions. One has the impression that, on the whole, even when it would have been possible to return, the bishops thought their churches too impoverished to do so, and preferred to look for positions in the other provinces of the Patriarchate of Constantinople as administrators of churches or monasteries, where their rank was more likely to be maintained. It is difficult to know if the thought of the 'barbarians' already weighed in deliberations in 1082 for or against the maintenance of two small autonomous bishoprics, facing respectively Ankara/Ancyra and Heraclea in the Taurus. It is difficult, too, to know if the ordeals of the churches in the interior were the reason for the raising of Antalya to metropolitan status a little later, since there are instances of similar advancements without such reasons existing. On the other hand, we know that, the metropolitan of Kayseri/Caesarea having just died when the Turks arrived, the archdeacon fled, taking precious relics with him; that, in 1082, the metropolitan of Chankïrï/Gangres, no longer able to reside there, accepted the administration of the bishopric of Amastris on the Pontic coast; that, in 1093 or 1108, an ordinance of Alexis Comnenus guaranteed to bishops exiled from their sees the same rights as to resident ones. In these circumstances, the fact that, in the twelfth century, among the signatories of the synods held in Constantinople there figured the titular metropolitans of Kayseri, Tyana, Heraclea, Mokissos, Ancyra, Niksar/Neocaesarea, Amasya, Gangres, Iconium, and even Melitene, and the bishops of Sasima and Nazian, proves only that the Patriarchate continued to nominate them, not that they were in fact in residence. In 1157 a prelate, formerly metropolitan of Amasya and subsequently transferred to Ancyra, is known in the end merely to have administered the still Byzantine bishopric of Giresun/Cerasonte on the Black Sea coast. At the end of the twelfth century Theodore Balsamon, commenting on the Councils' decisions and the ordinances of Alexis Comnenus regarding non-resident prelates, as an example of these named the bishop of Konya/Iconium, among others, and revealed that, in view of the wretched condition of the church in Ancyra, it had been necessary to combine it with that of Nazianzos (in the Seljukid Taurus). However, it must not be concluded from this general situation that, even in the twelfth century, there was a total desertion by or exclusion of the Greek clergy. In this connection there is a document which has received little attention but which is of considerable interest.

This is the report of a trial for heresy, instituted in 1143 before the patriarchal court of Constantinople against two bishops, Leontius of Balbissa or Balbiates (location unknown) and Clement of Sasima (the modern Hassa-Köy, north of Niğde) or possibly Sosanda (Soanda, near Nevshehir, north of Hassa-Köy ?), supported by the evidence of priests of his church and also of a certain Nicephorus of Palatinon (a monastery?) in the metropolitan area of Kïrshehir/Mokissos. The accused were charged with receiving their ordination solely from James, the former metropolitan of Tyana, after their election in Constantinople, whereas the canon law prescribed ordination by several prelates; and next and most important, with various practices linking them with Bogomilism. They denied most of them, but Leontius, in reply to the allegation that he had handed over Christian women to unbelievers, admitted that he had given one of his flock to the emir as a slave, since she was an adulteress. From these records it clearly emerges that, at least in Tyana and in two dependent bishoprics, and so in Seljukid territory, Greek prelates were in residence in the twelfth century, without thereby being prevented from going occasionally to Constantinople, where their election took place and where, if necessary, their orthodoxy was examined. Possibly however it was somewhat difficult to muster the number of prelates canonically prescribed for an ordination. The Seljukid régime, then, accepted Greek prelates and did not even prohibit relations with Constantinople (Sulaymān and Malik-Shāh had similarly allowed the Greek Patriarch of Antioch to remain in that city, and he had made several journeys to Constantinople). In this respect, it in fact went further than the other Muslim States, where adherents of the Greek rite belonged to the arabized Melkite Patriarchates of Antioch, Jerusalem or Alexandria and not that of Constantinople, and consequently had little connection with the latter. The Dānishmendids, with the exception of Muhammad, seem to have had the same idea. It was only the eastern bishoprics which for the most part were bound to disappear, when they were political implantations among populations attached to their own churches, and when their existence was thus no longer justified. Moreover a distinction must of course be made between the bishops, who went away, and the priests, who had to stay, not to mention their flocks. The trial of 1143 suggests that, owing to their relative isolation, some vestiges of old heresies may have smouldered on among them, but there is too little evidence to permit any certainty.

The return to internal order and the improvement in political relations with the Greeks in the thirteenth century probably promised some measure of relief for the Greek Church, to which Greek nobles who had entered the Sultans' service or family may have contributed. When, in the middle of the century, Michael Palaeologus, a refugee in Rūm, succeeded in returning to Nicaea, it was through the intercession of the metropolitan of Konya/ Iconium, who was therefore either actually in residence there or else able to communicate without difficulty. At the same time the monastery of Chariton, which also bore the name of Plato because it was believed that the philosopher's mortal remains lay there, was enjoying a reputation which attracted pilgrims from all the surrounding lands, and even city-dwelling Muslim notables visited it. The legend of Plato incidentally became a traditional theme among the different creeds, and traces of it have even survived down to our own time. As early as the end of the twelfth century the very anti-Roman Theodore Balsamon considered it better to submit to the Turks, who respected men's souls, than to the Franks who threatened them.

Documents of another kind throw a little light on Greek Christianity, especially in Cappadocia. It is well-known that, thanks to the broken terrain where cliffs abound, rock-cut churches were built or rather excavated underground, and their re-discovery has been one of the leading events of the present century in the history of Byzantine art. The great majority of these churches date from before the Turkish invasion, but there is no sign that they underwent any profound change as a result of it. Moreover there are a few instances of buildings, repairs or decorations being carried out during the Seljukid (or Dānish-mendid?) domination. It is not possible here to enter in detail into the specialists' discussions, since the dating of these works, apart from a few instances where there are dated inscriptions, is a difficult matter. (Isolated rural craftsmen may have preserved past traditions, themes and forms that elsewhere had become un-fashionable.) But the existence of some of these is certain, and the existence throughout of others as well is probable. It has even been thought that three inscriptions dating from the reigns of Theodore Lascaris and John Vatatzes prove the re-annexation of some Cappadocian territory by the Empire of Nicaea – an untenable hypothesis which was quickly recognized as such. But when, later, the names of Basileus Andronicus II Palaeologus and Sultan Mas'ūd II are seen appearing side by side, one is compelled to accept not only the good relations, attested elsewhere, between these sovereigns, but also a feeling among the Greek Christians that their admitted political subjection to the Seljukid régime did not rule out a kind of prior loyalty to the 'Roman' entity.

Although they were not strictly speaking natives, this may be the moment to emphasize that in the Sultans' entourage were present certain aristocrats of Greek stock who had sought refuge either temporarily or permanently and who often held high office. Reference has already been made to the visit of Andronicus Comnenus and the conversion and final settlement of his son John, whose descendants are unknown. Later, Maurozomes established himself, a loyal follower of Kaykhusraw and Kay-kubādh who, owing to relationships that are difficult to define but yet accepted, was known in Rūm as 'the Comnene emir'. He remained a Christian, and in a church outside Konya there still survives the epitaph of a young descendant of his who died there in 1297. And it was also under the name Comnenus that the future Emperor Michael Palaeologus lived for some years in Rūm. Less attention has perhaps been given to the Gavras family, who were related to the great Armeno-Byzantine family of the Taronites and who mostly lived in Trebizond and often ruled it, either as loyal subjects of or as rebels against the Byzantine authority. It has already been stated that, at the beginning of the twelfth century, one of these governors had tried to secure the help of Dānishmend against Alexis Comnenus, and that another, twenty years later, was allied with Mangujak of Erzinjān against Dānishmend's son Gümüshtegin. Now, in 1146, we know of a Gavras who was 'brought up among the Turks and was governor of a province for them'. In 1176, it was a Gavras who brought Manuel Comenus peace overtures which, although at first rejected, the latter was very glad to accept after Myriokephalon. This same Gavras or his son, whom the texts now called Ikstiyār al-Dīn Hasan ibn Gavras, in 1180 negotiated with Saladin and in 1187 conveyed to him his master's congratulations on the capture of Jerusalem, before dying tragically in 1190, in circumstances noted earlier. From his name he was probably a Muslim, and he seems to have been vizier to Kïlïj Arslan, or in any case his principal and influential supporter. But the fact that, on the eve of his death, he asked leave to withdraw to the Mangujakids, who inherited his fortune, suggests that the family had retained possession there, and that such considerations may have been not unconnected with his conversion.

Along with these, should mention also be made of Kīr Farīd, the former lord of Kalon-oros, who had become father-in-law of Kay-kubādh and governor for him of Akshehir? Or of Fakhr al-Dīn Sīwāstūs (the Sebastos), perhaps a former freedman of the Greek mother of Kaykhusraw II, who figures among the emirs of Rukn al-Dīn, and one of whose sons, ʿAlī, is known in 671/1273 from an inscription in Afyonkarahisar? A brief reference only can be made to the intermediate situation of the two uncles of ʿIzz al-Dīn Kay-kāūs, native notables who, before accompanying him to Constantinople, as Greeks exhorted him to fight against the Mongols with the Turcomans' aid, contrary to the advice of certain Muslims who on the other hand were supporting Rukn al-Dīn, although he was a vassal of the non-Muslim Mongols.

Although to those who reason in the spirit of later history it may seem difficult to believe, the fact remains that, in spite of their conflicts, relations between the Greeks and Turks for several generations were perhaps closer than those between either and the rest of their own co-religionists. It has been seen that many Greek rebels sought help from the Turks, and I do not think that Byzantine history can show as many who sought it from the Slavs, for example, though they too were neighbours and were strong. On the other side it is still more remarkable that those Turkish princes of Asia Minor who were compelled to flee abroad very rarely took refuge among the Muslims of Syria, Mesopotamia or even Iran, though the rulers were Turks, but on the contrary, generally went to the Byzantines, or sometimes to the Armenians in Cilicia. (A descendant of Kutlumush is recorded in Byzantium!) They were Muslims, it is true, but in a certain sense they were integrated more or less consciously into the territory known as Rūm, which they might aspire to dominate, though for the reason that they formed part of it and felt more at home there than in the traditional Dār al-Islām, even when they were among the infidels ... Is it going too far to put forward a proposition of this kind, for which obviously no explicit warrant exists in the texts? Reflection on the established facts of history leads inevitably at least to a suggestion of this kind.

Relations between Turks and Armenians prove to be slightly different from those between Turks and Greeks. Although there were Armenians in Konya, where incidentally there was said to be a tavern frequented by them, they were mostly concentrated in the eastern half of the country, where the Sultans did not normally live, and they were not backed by any political power. For these two reasons their role in Seljukid politics is smaller than the Greeks', but the difficulties facing them were also slighter, once the first wave of devastation had passed. In spite of certain emigrations (mainly from Cappadocia) into Cilicia, the great majority of the Armenians who were in eastern Asia Minor had remained there, and Erzinjān was a large Armenian city. They almost always behaved as loyal subjects and, feeling that they had been reasonably treated, they mourned their sovereigns' deaths. Here too sentiments belonging to a more recent time must not be ascribed to the distant past.

For the Armenian Church, the information is not very full. It is certain that the main centres of its life at that time were either in the small Armenian State which was gradually winning emancipation in Cilicia, or in north-western Azerbaijan which in the thirteenth century was to be included in the Christian kingdom of the Georgians (but with another church and another language). The Armenian hierarchy did however survive in Turkish Asia Minor. From synods, we know of the existence of bishops of Kayseri, Malatya, Sivas, Niksar and Göksün/Cocusus (this last sometimes in the hands of the Armeno-Cilicians). This time there is no reason to suppose that they were non-resident, since they do not figure in Cilician history and since, on the contrary, Ananias of Sivas, for example, supported by Sultan Kaykhusraw, raised his bishopric into a rival catholicate which was to last for 25 years, while the other catholicos, John VII, who lived in Hromgla/Rūm-qalʿa on the Euphrates, in touch with the Ayyūbid and Seljukid possessions, and who was himself also in conflict with Leo I of Cilicia, likewise appealed to Kaykhusraw. Moreover, manuscripts still extant bear witness by their script, and occasionally their illumination, to the continued existence of monastic cultural centres in Erzinjān, Erzurum and elsewhere. From the Mongol period there survives a chronicle written in Sivas. References to an Armenian physician can still be seen in the inscriptions, in Arabic, Syriac and Armenian, recording his foundation of a caravanserai, to the north of Malatya, which still survives. The importance of Erzinjān and its bishops under the Mongols will be described later. The importance of its craftsmen has already been noted.

It was the Monophysites who occupied the smallest place in Seljukid (or Dānishmendid) territory. They were the most Arabized of the Christians, their kinsmen for the most part lived in Arab countries, and they were alone in having only a modest social standard, with no political memories or ambition, and no state upon which they could rely. They did not *a priori* create any difficulty, and, while it would have been easy to persecute them, there was little reason to do so. They rejoiced over the Arabo-Muslim conquest earlier achieved at the expense of Byzantium, and, lacking the Armenians' grandiloquence, they were then living in closer symbiosis with their Turkish masters. This is apparent in a general way throughout the entire chronicle of their Patriarch, Michael the Syrian, and very clearly, on the subject of Mas'ūd I, in a statement by the historian of the Coptic Patriarchs of Alexandria, who, himself belonging to a sister Church, derived his information regarding Rūm from them. 'The greatest part of its subjects are Greeks', he writes; 'on account of its justice and good government, they prefer to live under its administration'. According to Michael, 'the Turks, having no idea of the sacred mysteries, . . . were in no way accustomed to inquire into professions of faith or to persecute anyone on their account, in contrast to the Greeks, a wicked and heretical people'. The principal patriarchal residence, the monastery of Mar Bar-Sauma, was situated in the mountains at the extreme end of the eastern Taurus, in the region long disputed between the Franco-Armenians of Edessa and afterwards their Muslim successors ruling from Aleppo or Artukids, and the Dānishmendid or Seljukid holders of Malatya, and several of their bishoprics found themselves frequently changing masters, politically speaking. In properly Seljukid or Dānishmendid territory, there are records of bishops in Malatya, Arqa, Albistan, Tzamandos and Kayseri. Michael the Syrian personally maintained the closest relations with Kïlïj Arslan II. He was visited by him, discussed religion with his learned men, and later received letters from him. And he took pleasure in it, just as, it will be remembered, he took pleasure in the conquests won by the Turks from the Byzantines – a fact all the more remarkable in that his was one of the most cultivated minds of the period and, in relation to other Churches, the most inclined towards Christian oecumenism. Michael succeeded in having the monastery of Mar Bar-Sauma restored from top to bottom (incidentally it had obtained an advantageous tax concession) as well as the cathedral of Malatya. This town and Mar

Bar-Sauma remained the living centres of Syriac monastic culture, where the theologian and historian Denys bar Salibhi had lived before Michael, and where, for a time, the greatest and last of the mediaeval Monophysite scholars, Bar Hebraeus, was later to live. We possess an illuminated Syriac book of the Gospels, produced in Malatya in about 1200. Systematic research would doubtless enable certain other Syriac manuscripts to be identified as written in Seljukid Asia Minor, as is the case with some Armenian manuscripts.

Finally, something must be said of the relations of the Seljukids with the Roman Church. Of course, none of their subjects were of the Roman rite, and as, unlike the Muslims of Syria, they had no reason at all for quarrelling with the Franks, who belonged to the Roman Church, they could simply have abstained from maintaining any relations, good or bad, with Rome and the Latin ecclesiastics. Such relations as they did maintain should not be exaggerated or misinterpreted. It was for political reasons that Kïlïj Arslan II possibly, and Kaykhusraw certainly, corresponded briefly with the Popes of their day. Whether relations with the Byzantines were good or bad, the Sultans could see no harm in it if Latin propagandists came to compete with the clergy of Byzantine obedience for influence over their Greek subjects. Consequently, when Gregory IX and Innocent IV began sending missionaries to the East they were well received and, although for a time this may have been true also in Syria and Mesopotamia, it is very probable that the welcome was greater in Asia Minor, where in addition there were Latin merchants and soldiers. This fact is probably not unconnected with the enthusiasm revealed in the account of the several years he spent in Rūm left by Simon of Saint-Quentin, from whom such valuable information has been derived in several instances.

There does not seem to have been any considerable number of Jews in the interior of Asia Minor under the Byzantine domination. There were some at Antalya, and it has been seen that they still remained there after the Seljukid conquest. It is to be expected that the Court at Konya also should have attracted some Jews, but all that is known is that, in the time of Jalāl al-Dīn Rūmī, they had rabbis and their own quarter in Konya, where wine could be found. It is not known if there were any Jews in the commercial centre of Sivas. Aqsarāyī seems to have had a somewhat unfavourable impression of them, but does not say specifically if he had been in touch with any. In any case, it does not appear that their role was an important one, even in the period when the Ilkhāns gave the vizierate to a Jew and a converted Jew. It was in Rūm that Bar Hebraeus was born, the son of a Jew converted to Monophysite Christianity, Ahron, a doctor who lived in Malatya/Melitene.

What has been said about the toleration that non-Muslims enjoyed does not exclude the fact that a certain number of conversions took place among them. Apart from the case of slaves and also *ikdīsh*, there are records from time to time of pure and simple conversions. This happened in the aristocracy, no doubt for reasons of advancement: reference has already been made to the Gavras, the Comneni and the Sultans' wives, among whom both converts and non-converts were found. There were others. However obvious the exaggerations of Aflākī, the hagiographer of the Mevlevis, when he tells of individual or mass conversions brought about solely by the moral influence of Jalāl al-Dīn Rūmī, these are not purely imaginary. Moreover, at the mystical level at which, for Jalāl al-Dīn, things had their being, adherence was easy. Nevertheless it implied conversion to 'official' Islam. Some other cases are known, and occasionally there were perhaps even priests or monks among them. It is certain that, when the Turks arrived, Christianity had only an inadequate hold in some native circles, and their isolation, increased by the conquest, weakened it still further and so facilitated conversions. Investigations in certain quarters at the present time lead one to suppose that instances of syncretism go back to the Middle Ages.

6

POLITICAL INSTITUTIONS

The Government

A well-known controversy has divided scholars, some of whom have maintained that most of the institutions of the Ottoman Empire were of Byzantine origin, others that they were of either Islamic or Turkish origin. The arguments, basically, have not been very well presented because, while enumerating a certain number of examples, the participants have not distinguished clearly between the various fields, and because it is *a priori* permissible to think that the solution is not necessarily the same, according to whether the question is viewed from the level of the central organs or of the basic social organization. As far as Seljukid Asia Minor is concerned, the problem is not entirely the same as for the Ottoman Empire, first of all because the moment was not the same, but also and above all because the conditions of establishment and growth were not the same. The Ottoman Empire was born in quasi-symbiosis with the Byzantine Empire (or what was left of it), and was a European power before being an Asiatic one. Institutional unification had never been completely achieved there, and the system of government of Asia Minor was neither that of the Balkans nor that of the Arab world. Muslim models, so far as they existed, had been borrowed only through the medium of the Seljukido-Mongol régime. The Seljukid State was more limited in its dimensions, it had felt the influence of local traditions or of neighbouring Byzantium as well as that of the Irano-Islamic world through which the Turks had passed and which continued to send experts to them, and where the Empire of the Great Seljukids had won fame, as a model for the future. Moreover, it had of course experienced its own needs and its specific evolution. It is these three elements that one has to try to discover in any study of institutions, without adopting any *a priori* conclusion.

In this respect various precautions are needed. It must not be concluded automatically, from the fact that in some systems the personnel was native, that there was an unbroken continuity of a native tradition. Moreover, it is necessary to be careful to specify the exact nature of things, and not to let oneself be carried away by superficial similarities of terminology into believing in a similarity of institutions, the same words not always and everywhere denoting precisely the same content.

It is equally essential not to put forward as a hypothesis the common identity of all the 'Seljukid' régimes. It is true that the Turks who colonized Asia Minor were kinsmen of those who founded the state of the Great Seljukids, and they passed through Iran. It is true also that an Iranian personnel was received in Asia Minor, and the example of the Great Seljukids or the models provided in Nizām al-Mulk's *Book of Government* were studied. But this influence is clear only in the thirteenth century, at a time when many of the features of the Seljukid State of Rūm were already determined, and in their determination local conditions and the consequences of the fact of conquest obviously counted for as much or more than external contributions. It is therefore necessary to study the Anatolian régime for itself, while avoiding any *a priori* assimilation.

Finally, it is also absolutely indispensable to distinguish scrupulously between the periods, a point I must insist upon because, in my opinion, fundamental mistakes have been committed through failure to take this precaution. It so happens that the authors who throw most light upon the Seljukid institutions flourished in the Mongol period, and as the dynasty continued under the Mongol protectorate and the new masters had no wish to overthrow the earlier régime, Seljukid and Mongolo-Seljukid institutions are generally treated together, as though they were *a priori* undifferentiated. A study made with this distinction carefully maintained will demonstrate clearly that, in certain matters at least, the reverse is true, and the interpretation to be placed upon the stated facts is therefore quite different from what had been thought.

It is probable that distinctions of the same kind might be made between the very beginnings of the Seljukid State, together with its offshoots, and its later developments. To outline the origin of its institutions, as they appear when they are better known, would be an important step. Here in part the task is hopeless, through lack of documentation, but it must be done with all the greater care in every particular case where information is available.

At the head of the Seljukid régime in Asia Minor was of course the Sultan. As has been said, the term, for long purely one of popular usage, was now official, and since the Caliphate had lost effective power it was applied to the holder of that power, as distinct from the Caliph. The distinction is in no way that between a Pope and an Emperor, as mediaeval and modern authors have sometimes said, because the Caliph had no resemblance to the Pope and because there was no division of 'temporal' power and 'spiritual' power between them. The Sultan, more particularly when his dominions did not include Baghdad, had plenary powers, at least in principle, in matters of religion as well as of politics (with the theoretical reservation general in Islam that the Law, being given by God, cannot be created or changed by man, even in its social stipulations). In general the Sultan respected the Caliph, and sometimes found it advantageous to emphasize that respect, but that is all. The Caliph's prerogative lay solely in the right, which could not come from any other, to legitimize the Sultan's power. Again, we have pointed out that some regarded the Sultanate as justified in itself, and when those who held *de facto* power were for some reason prevented from obtaining legitimation, they were hardly troubled by the fact. In general the Caliph granted this legitimation, which saved appearances and the principle of his own authority. An active Caliph also watched over the good order of the religious institutions, which he might attempt to extend morally beyond the frontier of his own State, when he had one, but he had no power to enforce his interventions.

As has been seen, it was unthinkable that the first Turkish chiefs in Asia Minor should have received any kind of legitimation from the 'Abbāsids. Their successors apparently did so, but it is difficult to discover from what time, the only explicitly known fact being the despatch of the insignia of *malik* to Gümüshtegin ibn Dānish-mend in 1135. We have seen that the title was conceded by custom, and perhaps even by the Byzantine chancellery, at the beginning of the reign of Alexis Comnenus, to Sulaymān ibn Kutlumush, and, it may be supposed that Kïlïj Arslan I bore or assumed it when he decided to oppose his cousin Muhammad even in Mesopotamia. Possibly the latter conceded it to Shāhānshāh. Masʿūd bears the title on a coin dating probably from the end of his reign, and Kïlïj Arslan II on an inscription immediately subsequent to his accession, but that does not necessarily prove that it had been officially granted, and the significance that was attached to it is moreover uncertain. The writers of the period, while occasionally using the title Sultan, generally applied only the title *malik*, king, to the Seljukids of Rūm, but they did the same for Nūr al-Dīn, who was clearly and officially Sultan. The title of Sultan was perhaps not regarded as very different from the office of *malik*, which term alone is found on coins and inscriptions of the period of the Sultanate. When this title was accorded to Gümüshtegin, it is unlikely that the step was regarded as anti-Seljukid since Masʿūd was on good terms with him, and it is difficult to take literally the title which Muhammad gives himself on a coin, of 'king of all Anatolia and Romania'. Was Masʿūd considered as a 'Sultan' above a *malik*, or as another *malik*? For the present, the question must remain unanswered.

In any case, it is interesting to study the list of titles on inscriptions and, to a lesser extent, on coins and various more or less official documents. Kïlïj Arslan II describes himself among other things as 'Sultan of the Arabs and the ʿAjam', this last word no doubt implying the Turks, though without their being explicitly named alongside the ordinary ʿAjam, that is to say, for the Arab-speaking East, the Persians. Next, he is the champion of the holy war (a role which the events recorded earlier suggest should be taken with some reserve), the guardian of the country of Allah, that is to say that he considers his territory, though still called Rūm, to be henceforward integrated within the Dār al-Islām, the domain of Islam; the auxiliary of the Caliph, a title which no doubt he received from the Caliph, who gave it to all who sought it from him; and finally 'Sultan of the land of Rūm, of the Armenians, Franks and Syria', which in the fashion of the time, as soon as the least incursion had been made onto foreign soil, denotes the wider aspirations that were felt and that, in the circumstances, there is an attempt to legitimize characteristic ambitions towards the south-east as much as for the whole area of Rūm, that is Asia Minor. If the notion of the holy war is present, the actual term *ghāzī* employed by the Dānishmendids, Saltukids and Mangujakids is absent. Also absent are titles specifically in the

Turkish language, which not only the Mangujakids but even some Zengids and Artukids held at the same time: possibly they appeared too restricted for the accepted idea of what a Sultan should be.

It is unnecessary to dwell upon the insignia or adornments of sovereignty, which were the same as throughout the whole Muslim East. The sovereign had a throne, which was slightly elevated. For special ceremonies he had a kind of crown, but ordinarily wore a large turban. His signet ring enabled him to authenticate documents presented for his signature, no matter where. When walking outside, he was sheltered by a baldachin in black (the ʿAbbāsid colour), really nothing more than an immense parasol, apparently the individual property of each sovereign which went with him to the tomb. Banners and musical instruments heralded the procession, in which slaves and soldiers of the Guard took part. Generally he lived in a palace, and every large town had a palace to accommodate him or the governor. In addition, there were pleasure palaces which the sovereign might build, for example Kūbadābād, created for Kay-kubādh on lake Beyshehir north-west of Konya, Fīlūbād near Konya and Kaykūbādiyya near Kayseri. In the time of the great Sultans, these palaces contained stores and treasures of all kinds. Alanya, a place of refuge from revolts and invasions overland, was particularly favoured for this purpose, but so too, at various times, were Antalya, Tokat and others. As well, vast tents were often put up for the Sultan at the approach to towns, for the receptions and banquets which he was naturally obliged to give. Moreover, he was able to enjoy the pleasures of music, wine and the harem, but no special information in this connection is recounted, and, particularly with regard to wine, it is possible that the level of behaviour of the Seljukids of Rūm was above the average. Like all their aristocratic contemporaries, they were fond of hunting and certain sports, particularly those on horseback, and exercise grounds were provided near towns.

The Sultan of course held a monopoly of the striking of coins. There is little doubt that, like all great sovereigns of his time, he had a factory for the manufacture of luxury fabrics and clothing, intended for gifts to great men and foreign princes; but nothing is known of this.

It was noted earlier that, among the Irano-Iraqi Seljukids, the young Sultans had *atabek*s at their side. The same was true of their successors, with due allowance made for the limited authority which they effectively possessed. The office of *atabek* was also found in Rūm, but it never assumed the dimensions that it attained among the other Seljukid families. Kïlïj Arslan I had one, Khumartash al-Sulaymānī, whose name indicates that he was a freedman of Sulaymān ibn Kutlumush (and not a Turcoman chief); but he is known only from governing Mayāfāriqīn, the chief town of Diyār Bakr which Kïlïj Arslan was to confer on him when he conquered it in 1106 or 1107. The young Seljukid of Malatya had several *atabek*s in succession, chosen as husbands by his mother, in the years 1107–13 and those following, in a role more in keeping with tradition. The Dānishmendids had none. Among the Seljukids, the first to be known after those already mentioned was the *ispahsālār* Badr al-Dīn ibn Arslandoghmush, who was described as such in an inscription of 1177; but it is not known to whom he was *atabek*, and in this inscription he appears, not under that title, but under that of governor of Niksar, which had been recently taken from the Dānishmendids; nor is it known if one of the sons of Kïlïj Arslan, perhaps the one who later was to have Niksar as his share of the succession, was in principle the titular governor of that place under the tutelage of this same Arslandoghmush, the effective master. The *atabek*s of the thirteenth century are similarly known only by their title, and through other offices which they held. For example, Mubāriz al-Dīn Armaghanshāh, head of the army of Amasya at the time of Baba Ishāq's revolt and *atabek* to ʿIzz al-Dīn ibn Kay-kubādh, with orders to put him to death . . . and Karatay, a freedman in the time of the Mongols.

The Sultan had a lieutenant *nāʾib* (*al-Saltana*), but whether he was temporary (during the Sultan's absence or illness) or permanent is not clear.

Among the personal assistants of the Sultan was the *pervāne*. This figure, whose poetic name ('butterfly') is slightly surprising in this setting, to my knowledge had no equivalent except in Mongol Iran where there was a much less important official known by the name *pervāneji*, which suggests that *pervāne* is a derived and abbreviated form. In any event, it was he who conveyed the prince's personal messages (whether it was the messages themselves or the messenger that earned the name of butterfly); he was also the distributor of favours. It will be readily seen that, with a little adroitness, this office could lead to exalted fortunes, and from the beginning of the thirteenth century we know of *pervānes* who were eminent figures. Nevertheless, one has to be careful not to allow the power they exercised to give rise to the false assumptions that have sometimes been made with regard to the position of the *pervāne* Mu'īn al-Dīn Sulaymān, a true dictator under the Mongol protectorate; he is still usually denoted by the title under which he first made himself known, but it was not in the capacity of *pervāne* that he possessed all the powers which he exercised.

The atabeks

Mubāriz al-Dīn Ertökūsh Shams al-Dīn Altunbeh for 'Izz al-Dīn, son of Kay-kubādh, on the death of the latter, put to death by Kaykhusraw II.

Mubāriz al-Dīn Armaghanshāh, replacing the last-named, killed when head of the army of Amasya by Baba Ishāq's Turcomans.

The nā'ibs

Sayf al-Dīn Abū Bakr son of Hakkehbāz, former *subashï* of Kayseri, on the accession of Kay-kubādh.

Shams al-Dīn Isfahānī, on the fall of Köpek, under Kaykhusraw II.

The pervānes

Zahīr al-Dīn Īlī ibn Yaghï-basan (Dānishmendid?), in the second reign of Kaykhusraw I, exiled on the accession of Kay-kāūs for supporting Kay-kubādh, died soon afterwards.

Jalāl al-Dīn Qaysar, 608–17?, *pervāne* to Kay-kāūs.

Sharaf al-Dīn Muhammad. However, if Ibn Bībī is right, Qaysar was in office again in 620.

Kamāl al-Dīn Kāmyār.

Tāj al-Dīn, son of the *cadi* Sharaf al-Dīn of Erzinjān, 630–7.

Walī (Veli) al-Dīn, 638, killed at Köse Dagh.

The Sultan was surrounded by a certain number of persons holding offices or dignities at court, some of whom may have been identical with those who also held offices in the political and military hierarchy, which were always given to members of the caste which furnished it. Almost all bore partly Persian titles already known among the Seljukids of Iraq-Iran. The *amīr-i Jāndār* was the head of the *jandār*, that is to say the Guard, the *amīr-i silāh* the master of arms, the *amīr-i shikār* the controller of hunting, the *amīr-i ʿalam* the standard bearer, and the *amīr akhur*, known indiscriminately by that name or, even though the holder was Muslim, by the Latino-Byzantine name *kondestabl* ('constable'), the master of the horse. The *ustādhdār* was the 'controller of the palace', while the *amīr-i majlis* organized receptions, audiences and so on. The *chāshnegīr* was the food-taster, the *sharābsālār* the cup-bearer; but these were honorific titles held by great men who in practice held other offices. Finally the chamberlains, *hājib*, had at the head a *hājib* of the *hujjāb* (plur. of *hājib*), an eminent personage who in fact was also and primarily an army general.

Holders of offices known before 1243:

amīr-i Jāndār, Najm al-Dīn Bahrāmshāh, under Kay-kāūs and again under Kay-kubādh (if he is not given this title merely by reference to having held it earlier), although under the latter there is also named Mubāriz al-Dīn ʿĪsā, who figured again under Kaykhusraw II at least until 641/1244.

amīr-i silāh, an anonymous *silāhdār* is mentioned in about 620, but no *amīr-i silāh* was explicitly named until after 660, under the Mongols.

amīr-i ʿalam, Tughan, at the beginning of the reign of Kaykhusraw II.

amīr-i akhur, Zayn al-Dīn Bashāra, under Kay-kāūs; constable, Asad al-Dīn Ayāz, under Kay-kubādh.

ustādhdār, on the accession of Kaykhusraw II, Jamāl al-Dīn Farrukh the *lālā* (tutor).

amīr-i majlis, 617–20, Mubāriz al-Dīn Bahrāmshāh; under Kaykhusraw II the post is attested, but the holder is not named.

chāshnegīr, Sayf al-Dīn Ine, under Kaykhusraw I; Mubāriz al-Dīn Chavli under Kay-kāūs; under Kay-kubādh, two holders, Shams al-Dīn Altunbeh with Chavli, then the former who had now also become *atabeg*, with Nāsir al-Dīn ʿAlī; under Kaykhusraw II Chavli once again, with Yavtash.

sharābsālār, attested only in the time of the Mongols, under Kay-kāūs II, the holder being simultaneously constable.

hājib, Zakariyya, under Kaykhusraw I.

In the majority of the Muslim States in the East contemporaneous with these Seljukids, there was a clear-cut distinction in profession and racial origin between the administrative offices and the politico-military ones. While the latter were reserved for the military caste which was predominantly Turkish, sometimes Kurdish, and in exceptional cases of some other race, the administrative offices were reserved for the natives who alone were competent and who in principle were excluded from the profession of arms, or at least from the regular army. It was very exceptional for anyone to pass from one category to the other. The judicial offices, which comprised a third category, were also entrusted to the natives; instances of members of the administrative profession transferring to the judicial are limited but not impossible.

In Rūm, the facts of the problem are somewhat different. The 'natives' there were Christians, and though it is quite certain that they figured in certain employments, the matter is made difficult not so much by their religion, which was no obstacle in either Egypt or Iraq, as by their ignorance of Arabic and Persian. Hence the administrative classes there consisted mostly of Iranians who, in the thirteenth century at least, were immigrants from Khorasan or north-western Iran, even occasionally from Isfahan and elsewhere. It will also be seen that, in the Seljukid State, the profession of arms was no longer of the same simple character as under the Great Seljukids, for example, or the Zengids and Ayyūbids. However, save for political reasons, it was certainly to Turks or to foreign turkicized military slaves that the politico-military positions were given, but some of them perhaps also penetrated into the administrative and judicial professions, particularly in later generations (when the sons did not necessarily possess their fathers' military vocation and the Turks had become 'natives'), provided that they had mastered the necessary languages and techniques.

In the main, however, the distinction between these different professions remains a valid one.

At the head of the civil administration was the vizier, whose existence is attested (unless the attribution of the title is the interpretation of the Arab chronicler to whom the information is due) from the time of Sulaymān in the eleventh century, and through one or two holders of the office during the twelfth. The formal existence of the office is in any case certain from the time of the existence of the independent Sultanate, for it was the accepted idea that the appointment of a vizier was one of the manifestations of sovereignty. Even in the thirteenth century, however, our knowledge of the viziers remains incomplete, and although its holders occasionally undertook political activities, one does not get the impression that the vizierate ever gave them the immense powers that some viziers wielded in other countries, for instance Nizām al-Mulk under the Great Seljukids. Was this through a lack of personality among the viziers, or was it rather that the organization of the régime restricted them to tasks of a somewhat elementary sort? And must allowance be made for the fact that among the first viziers there were natives who had been converted but were still regarded by the dominant Turks as insufficiently reliable? In any case, before the Mongols no viziers are found who possess any real importance, in an organizational system that was entirely different. As elsewhere, the vizier was designated by the term *sāhib*.

List of viziers until 1243
(Unnamed vizier of Sulaymān in 1086?).
Hasan ibn Gavras, before 1176–90.
A certain Mas'ūd, vizier shortly before 617/1220.
Majd al-Dīn Abū Bakr, under Kay-kāūs or at the end of his reign.
Rashīd al-Dīn, 617, on the accession of Kay-kubādh.
Diyā al-Dīn Kara Arslan, 625/1228 or earlier, and until the end of the reign.
On the fall of Köpek (637/1240), Muhadhdhab al-Dīn Dāde 'Alī al-Daylamī, until his death in 1244.

Throughout the Muslim East the *mustawfī* was the man formerly known as *sāhib al-zimam*, the chief auditor. It was he who checked the total receipts from taxes and the expenditure, and his assistance was indispensable to the vizier, who selected him; and indeed he sometimes became vizier.

It is more difficult to define the duties of the *mushrif*, apparently superintendent of the Sultan's domains, and of the *nāzir*, controller who perhaps assisted him. They probably existed under the Seljukids, on similar lines to those in neighbouring eastern States, since in general there was a similarity of titles and organizations, but there is evidence of them only in the Mongol period, and they may therefore be an innovation, if not of the Seljukids strictly speaking, at least of the Iranian agents who in the conditions of that period were influential.

List of mustawfīs
Saʿd al-Dīn Abū Bakr Ardabīlī, in 630/1233.
Shihāb al-Dīn Kirmānī, under Kaykhusraw II.

In the Seljukid period on the other hand, but not in the Mongol period (as a result of the reduction in the army?), there is evidence as in all the neighbouring States, of an *ʿārid* who, like his namesakes elsewhere, must have been responsible for ascertaining the real state of the army, with the Sultan, whenever reviews were held, and for giving out army pay at the same time; he thus had one foot in the civil, and one in the military, administrations.

The only holder recorded is Nizām al-Dīn Ahmad, called the son of the vizier Mahmūd, in 617/1220.

Finally the Seljukid State, like its neighbours, had its official postal department, the *barīd*.

As in all the surrounding countries, the administration consisted of 'offices', *dīwāns*, under these officials. A special part was played by the secretarial office, *inshāʾ*, which drafted the political correspondence and also diplomas. Under the Great Seljukids the *tughrāʾī* had soon become identical with the *munshiʾ*, the director of the *inshāʾ*. The title *munshiʾ* does not seem to occur among the Seljukids of Rūm, who however had the title *tughrāʾī*, and it is therefore the latter who is the true 'chancellor'.

The only known holder (apart from a hypothetical 'chancellor Christopher' referred to in 1161) is Shams al-Dīn (or Nūr al-Dīn) Hamza ibn al-Muʾayyad in 617/1220.

The Seljukid chancellery normally drew up its letters and diplomas in Persian, it seems; it is at least in that form alone that non-translated specimens have survived, and it is in accordance with probability. However, the rule is subject to certain modifications. In the first place, documents of a Muslim legal character emanating not from the chancellery but from *cadis* were necessarily written in Arabic, and the examples surviving prove that this was done, using wholly correct forms of wording. In the chancellery itself it is unlikely that there was never a secretary capable of writing in Arabic to Arab princes; however, it has to be accepted that the letter of congratulation – if authentic – written to Saladin after the capture of Jerusalem is in Persian. Monumental and numismatic inscriptions, as placing the object under the protection of the Law, were normally written in Arabic; it was only in the Mongol period that rare exceptions to this rule began to appear. Fiscal documents were in Arabic; the principal ones were to be translated into Persian under the Mongols. Treaties with foreign States unacquainted with Arabic or Persian might be drafted in the two languages, but it is not possible to determine who was responsible for translating the original, although it is fairly clear that the Seljukid State possessed interpreters for various languages. Letters still exist, written in the name of Kay-kāūs in Greek, which, even if another copy in Persian was kept in Konya, were no doubt written there directly in Greek and are not translations made by the addressees, in the case of the Franks of Cyprus who would have had them translated into Latin. Ibn Bībī even knew of *nūtār, notarioi*, notaries, in the offices, the word obviously denoting Greek 'scribes'. It is not known which language a Seljukid Sultan used when he wrote to a high non-Muslim dignitary among his subjects, such letters as those for which Michael the Syrian gives the Syriac translation.

It was said earlier that the Seljukids of Iran and Iraq authenticated their documents by means of the special symbol known as the *tughrā*. As is to be expected since the Ottomans were to have their own *tughrā*, this also existed among the Seljukids of Asia Minor. In whichever meaning it was interpreted, the bow form is attested by a reference of Ibn Bībī who in this field speaks with some authority; although on a surviving document, which is however, in Greek and for the use of foreigners, it appears solely as an especially imposing representation of the Sultan's title. Another strange feature is that, although the title *tughrā'ī* was maintained and was borne by eminent persons, the actual word *tughrā* was sometimes confused, as among the Arabic-speaking Mamluks of

Egypt, with the Arabic *turra*, 'border' (which in effect corresponds with the method of authentification by writing, as practised by the Mamluks, but which never seems to have been employed under the Seljukids).

The Seljukids' scribes in the Mongol period were to use stylistic models of administrative phraseology or collections of documents left by illustrious predecessors: it is thanks to certain surviving collections of this type that there are preserved certain deeds even earlier than the Mongols; but we cannot be sure that no collections had been formed in the time of the independent Sultanate, such as are known for the other Seljukids or their Khwārizmian heirs.

Did the duties of these departments become more onerous under the Mongol protectorate, or had there been a spontaneous and unjustified increase in the number of employees? There is an echo of complaints made about this proliferation which, if the complainants are to be believed, are alleged to have led to the quadrupling of numbers in comparison with the time of the great Kay-kubādh, 24 senior officials existing where formerly there had been only six.

As in the neighbouring Irano-Muslim States, side by side with the ordinary justice dispensed by the *cadi*s who were present in Rūm as elsewhere, there was, under the Sultan, an *amīr-dad*, head of justice, dealing with the cases called *mazālim*, for the repression of administrative abuses and so on.

One holder of the office, in 612/1215, is known – Sinān al-Dīn Tughrïl (the office, but not the holder, is mentioned also in about 618).

It was pointed out earlier that the military profession filled most of the Court offices or dignities already enumerated, as well as those of *atabek* and *nā'ib* (but not *pervāne*). It also supplied provincial military commanders, who are to be discussed later, and the office of *beglerbeg*.

It is somewhat difficult to form any precise idea of the *beglerbeg*, '*beg* of the *beg*s'. Possibly he was identical with what was described in literary Greek texts of the twelfth century as 'archisatrap', and elsewhere as *ispahsālār*, *amīr kabīr*, etc. In the thirteenth century, the ordinary equivalent was the Arabic *amīr* (or, more often, *malik*) *al-umarā'*, emir (or 'king') of the emirs, the two titles occurring indiscriminately in the texts, or even in the same text. It never happens that more than one is named at one time, and, during episodes in the Mongol period where the distribution of offices is explicitly described, the *beglerbeg* is always a single figure. However, in the period of independence we sometimes come across two names of holders, named alternatively as though they were contemporary, and since one was the head of the great Turcoman province of Kastamonu, we might be inclined to think that he held the title in that capacity. It might also be thought that the *beglerbeg* was specially responsible for general control over the Turcomans, whose chiefs were called *begs*, but there seems to be no confirmation for such a hypothesis. Incidentally, among the *beglerbegs* was a Comnenus, whom it is difficult to imagine in this office, however fully assimilated he may have been. Clearly, the *beglerbeg*'s role was essentially a military one, but that does not mean that he was a commander-in-chief exclusive of others, and the *atabek*, for example, when his pupil was not in a position to take direct command of the troops, in the ordinary way also deputized for him in this task.

List of beglerbegs

Husām al-Dīn Chupan, already in office at the same time as Sayf al-Dīn amīr Kïzïl, 1211 (unless this is in anticipation). Sayf al-Dīn Ine and Bahā al-Dīn Kutlughshāh, together or in succession, 617/1220.
During the Crimean expedition, the same Husām al-Dīn Chupan.
Altinbeh, later *atabek*.
Arslan ibn Kaymaz, having as his *nā'ib*/deputy Nāsir al-Dīn the *Turjman*/interpreter, who is however described shortly before as *nā'ib* of Zahīr al-Dīn Mansūr ibn Kāfī.

There does not seem to be anything particular to say about ordinary justice in Rūm. It was seen earlier that, thanks to Sulaymān ibn Kutlumush, a *cadi* had already been established wherever there was a Muslim community. But there is not a great deal that can be said about the actual functioning of the institution in Rūm, and in any case there was no reason why it should have possessed any special characteristics. Throughout Islam, the *cadi* was a figure standing outside the State, although nominated by it, in the sense that he applied a Law that was independent of the

State, and that the funds at his disposal were partly from a religious source over which in principle the State had no rights. Surviving foundation deeds of *waqfs* reveal particularly the *cadi* acting in the role he held everywhere, as guarantor and supervisor of these *waqfs*. There was a *cadi* for each chief town, and he might also have assistants elsewhere. It is not clear whether there was a supreme *cadi*, perhaps the *cadi* of the capital, as in other States, or whether that office devolved upon the *amīr-dād*. As regards 'witnesses' of the correct execution of deeds, we know only, in respect of Rūm, that their signatures appear at the foot of *waqf*-deeds, but their number apparently exceeds that of the permanent witnesses (*shuhūd*). As in neighbouring States in the East, there was a special *cadi* for the army (appointed for his special juridical and linguistic knowledge), the *cadi l-askar* or *qādī-i lashkar*. Associated with the *cadi*, expert jurists presumably acted as consultants, *muftīs*, but in fact almost nothing is known about them in connection with Rūm in the period in question.

Trades are discussed elsewhere. We know that, in the whole of Islam, control of the various crafts was maintained by an agent of the *cadi*, the *muhtasib*, whose existence in Rūm is confirmed at the time with which we are dealing. In all countries, he might have the assistance of special delegates for supervising each trade. Perhaps this was so in Rūm, but on this matter a problem arises, to be considered later.

The Army

The army constitutes a field in which the Byzantine model almost certainly, and somewhat paradoxically, makes itself felt, along with the classical Irano-Muslim model and ancient Turkish traditions. On this subject it is clearly necessary to distinguish between the periods.

At the start there was no military force other than that of the Turcomans, more or less retaining their autonomous organization. As we have seen, they continued to intervene on the frontiers throughout the whole of Seljukid history, not to mention later mediaeval history, at certain times for their own benefit with no attempt to comply with Seljukid policy, and at other times in the service of the latter, according to the circumstances prevailing at that particular time. But in the course of the twelfth century another army was established, to be developed in the thirteenth century, the pattern and methods of organization of which unfortunately cannot be defined. It is certain that, like the other armies in the Muslim Near East, whether Seljukid or otherwise, it contained slaves, often islamized prisoners, who were later freed. But while elsewhere it was a question mainly of Turkish slaves, in this case they were often Greek slaves obtained in frontier razzias, particularly in the province of Kastamonu. The reasons for employing recruits of this kind, particularly for the corps of guards or *jāndār*s and the garrison army in the large centres, were the same as in all the neighbouring Muslim States – politically, the need for fidelity and, at the same time, technically, the necessity to have technicians for modes of combat foreign to the Turcomans, in order to be able to face comparable enemy armies and to conduct siege operations. But there was another element in the army which is clearly visible in the thirteenth century and which was entirely different from anything that existed among the other Muslims in the Near East, namely foreign mercenaries.

It has sometimes been thought that to these there should be added a corps of men of mixed race, the *ikdīsh*, but when discussing the towns we pointed out that this idea rested on a certain misunderstanding. Even if at times the *ikdīsh* succeeded in acting as a local militia, they did not form part of the army and were not normally soldiers. Nor is there any ground for supposing that there was any kind of anticipation of the Ottoman Janissaries, that is to say, children taken away from native parents to be brought up as Muslim soldiers. Naturally, as in all Muslim countries, the inclusion of Christians in the army was out of the question and, in the time of the Mongols who were themselves not Muslim and in some cases favoured the Christians, the intention of Sarkis/Sergius, the Armenian bishop of Erzinjān, to bring a corps of his co-religionists to a composite army raised an outcry. But that does not exclude the possibility that the Seljukid State may have employed foreign Christians as mercenaries. The texts do not always make it possible to determine if the particular contingents of this kind that are referred to in fact consisted of mercenaries or were companies sent by vassal sovereigns. Even in the case of the 'Franks', it might be a matter of Frankish subjects of the Armenians in Cilicia – there was no lack of these, since,

231

partly on their account, the Assizes (a collection of laws and customs) were even translated into Armenian for the use of the government. Moreover, there may have been intermediate cases in which, owing to some urgent threat, in the face of Khwārizmian or Mongol dangers, the Seljukid Government, partly or wholly at its own expense, engaged companies of troops sent by allies or vassals over and above their ordinary levies. But there is no doubt that there were also mercenaries in the strict sense of the word, as there were in the Byzantine army, in which military slavery was unknown and which, among other foreign soldiers, employed Turks from the Russian steppe in this capacity, along with Slavs, Scandinavians, Franks (particularly Normans from Italy) and others. What may seem strangest of all to a mind attuned to more modern ideas is that the chief leaders of these mercenaries were Franks, even at the time of the Crusades. Moreover it is also important to distinguish between the Muslims of Syria and later those of Upper Mesopotamia or Egypt who fought directly against the Franks of the Latin East, and the Turks of Asia Minor who, except in the case of Crusaders crossing their territory and after the fall of the border County of Edessa, did not fight against them and indeed were sometimes allied with certain of them (instances of alliances occur even among the Syrians, but they remained exceptional and were regarded as outrageous). One or two instances of Frankish mercenaries in the service of Syro-Egyptian Muslim princes can be cited, but as a general rule the Church, which (though vainly) excommunicated merchants selling arms to Muslims, *a fortiori* would not have agreed that soldiers should go to fight for them, even though against other adversaries than the Franks. There is however a parallel in the Muslim West, particularly in Almohad Morocco where, with the acquiescence of the Papacy, in return for guarantees for Christian worship, real European militias existed. It may be doubted if this parallel was known to the Seljukids or if it influenced them in any way. What is certain is that there were Frankish mercenaries who, in certain cases – and it was noted earlier that the missionary Brother Simon took pride in them – played an important part. Some names even are given, which are difficult to recognize. At least it is known that among their leaders were a Venetian who was also a merchant, a native of Plaisance in Italy, an Italian Norman and a Gascon.

What had they come to do? And how had they got there? Nothing is known. Possibly some came from Cyprus at a time of 'unemployment'. Did others perhaps come from among the former dependents of the Byzantine State, and now, by way of the Latin Empire, make their way to the Turkish Empire which, as is emphasized repeatedly, was not regarded as foreign or hostile in the same way as the States lying beyond it? Others again were prisoners of Syrian princes, liberated on the understanding that they would enter their service during the campaigns of Kay-kāus and Kay-kubādh. The Mongol conquest clearly was bound to end the possibility of employment in Rūm, and nothing is known of it after 1243.

The titles of the military leaders are generally those of Arab, Persian or Turkish tradition, and are to a slight extent interchangeable, one or another being more common in different periods and in different documents. The Arabic *amīr* is close to the Turkish *beg*, often denoting a Turcoman; *amīr al-umarā'* (emir of the emirs) to *beglerbeg* (*beg* of the *begs*), and the Persian *ispahsālār*; *subashï*, which is Turkish, to *serleshker*, Persian, with the same meaning, and *shihne*, Arabic, revived with the meaning defined above, and so on. There is however one instance where the introduction of a title of Western origin (possibly through the medium of Byzantium) can be seen – the master of the horse, who often bore the Arabo-Persian title of *amīr-akhur*, was also sometimes called *kundestabl*, 'constable', as has been said, not only in the case of one or two of the holders who were Greeks, which would prove nothing, but also of others who were Muslims. Although the influence may here perhaps be purely one of nomenclature, it nevertheless testifies to a general atmosphere and for that reason is worthy of emphasis.

These foreign military influences are particularly interesting in that they are found in the one domain in which *a priori* one would have thought the Turks to be free from such temptations, on account of their universally recognized superiority. However, they must not be exaggerated: the Seljukid army was not the Byzantine army, and the Turks had defeated the Byzantines. Their method of combat, at least in the twelfth century, was still typically 'Turcoman', even in the regular army (consider the battle of Myriokephalon). In the thirteenth century, at the battle

233

of Erzinjān against the Khwārizmians, at Köse Dagh, where the armies were more composite and contained few Turcomans, the character had obviously changed. The weapons were the same as those of all eastern countries, and call for no particular comment.

The military commands were generally linked with those of the provinces, which must be discussed at some length.

7

PROVINCIAL ADMINISTRATION

The current theory is that the provincial organization of the Seljukid State of Rūm was feudal, that is to say based on a system of *iqtā*'s which are comparable with the fiefs of the mediaeval European conception. One aspect of this question has already been encountered in connection with the Great Seljukids, and it was then shown that the process of 'feudlaization', if one wishes to use the word which is in any case somewhat inadequate, is in any event merely a process of disintegration, and does not correspond to the conception of the Seljukid State in the period when it exercised real authority. Moreover, there is a tendency to consider that the régime that existed among the Seljukids of Iran, whatever its nature, could have been automatically transplanted to Asia Minor. For a true appreciation of Seljukid history all this is of importance, and it is necessary to explore the matter a little further.

Once again, there is of course a question of terminology. Historians seeking to establish a process of evolution through various 'types' or 'stages' in the growth of society that are of universal application tend, whether or not they are Marxists, to apply the term 'feudal' to any kind of régime which intervenes chronologically between the slave system of antiquity and modern capitalism, and in which the work of the peasants, enslaved to a greater or lesser degree, was exploited for the benefit of great proprietors, the land-owning lords. On this reckoning; there were clearly a considerable number of 'feudal' régimes, and that of the Seljukids of

Rūm was among them, at least to a slight extent. But, without in any way underestimating this aspect of the feudal régime, it has to be made quite clear that, in the higher levels of the politico-social organization, the same infrastructure of this type, very broadly and loosely envisaged, may be accompanied by 'super-structures' so different that it would be deceptive and dangerous to group them together under one single common designation. In fact, what the historians who speak of 'Seljukid feudalism' have in mind is not the economic aspect of the system at the level of land-tenure, but that of the relations between the local land-holders or potentates and the authority of the State. In this sense a state is feudal when it abandons or delegates the essential part of its public powers in the provinces to great men who hold them as hereditary quasi-possessions. There is thus a contrast between the feudal conception thus defined and that of a strong centralized state, a contrast in practice between the state which, whatever its ideal may be, is incapable of keeping the reins even of provincial government in its own hands, and the state which is able to do so. While conceding the power of the Seljukid Sultans, historians have generally thought that they reigned over a feudal state (indeed, moments are known in the history of various countries when suffi-cient harmony prevailed between the various personalities, suffi-cient equilibrium existed between the different forces, for monarchies to have existed that could be described both as strong and as feudal). In my view this conclusion is mistaken, and is ex-plained by the error in method referred to so many times already which must be emphasized once again – namely, that of dealing with the Seljukid period proper and the Mongol period in the same context, and of applying to the former something which has been established in regard to the latter. Moreover, it will be seen that even in the Mongol period the 'feudalism' was still of a very par-ticular kind. Errors also spring from carelessness in defining the precise meaning of terms, and from regarding expressions as identi-cal when in fact they have different meanings. It is essential not to lose one's way in ill-defined general groupings, but rather to con-sider Asia Minor as an entity period by period, while not regarding a governor who is subject to recall or a prince of the blood who holds an apanage as a feudal lord.

As the following account will show, from this point of view the history of Turkish Asia Minor from the conquest to the Mongol period can be divided into four periods:

(*a*) The simultaneous establishment of Turcoman chiefs and of the Seljukid ruler at the semi-tribal level and without any well-defined bond of either territorial or personal dependence;

(*b*) Progressive re-absorption of the Turcoman groups, setting up of apanages;

(*c*) Re-absorption of the apanages, marches, and direct government;

(*d*) Breakdown of the system as a result of the method of operation of the Mongol protectorate.

(*a*) First period. It is useless to dwell on this. The account of the facts of the conquest has already shown that the various chiefs became established without there being any reason for thinking that they were all originally considered as vassals of the Seljukid Sultan. It is possible that a measure of dependence may have applied in theory in the case of the chiefs in the extreme west, but their importance for later history is slight after the First Crusade, and the Byzantine reconquest led to their disappearance. Such real power as existed was still over groups of men, according to a semi-tribal conception (even though the old tribal groupings had broken down), rather than over territories.

(*b*) Second period. As the unifying conquest of Asia Minor by the Seljukids progressed, the latter, believing it difficult to dispense with a certain measure of autonomy and the particular groupings of the territories they had acquired, but anxious nevertheless to secure these to the dynasty, and perhaps also retaining the idea of a certain right of all its living members to a share in its inheritance, set up apanages for the 'princes of the blood'. The idea that partition was necessary in any case prevailed among the Dānishmendids, in the form of a few apanages, possibly as far back as Muhammad, and in any event during the last reigns, the eldest son of the deceased ruler no longer being the head of the family in the wide sense. This idea is also found among the Mangujakids. It hardly appears under the first Seljukids, where there was only the case of the outlying autonomous principality of Malatya; later, under Masʿūd, the establishment of Ankara and Chankïrï, recent acquisitions facing the Greeks and for a time the possessions of an unknown Alp Arslan, as an apanage for Shāhānshāh, the brother of the future Kīlīj Arslan II; and finally, under the last-named, who as heir apparent had for a time governed the newly acquired Syrian frontier region, their conferment before 1173 upon his uncle Gogh Arslan, who was later removed from the position.

But it was at the end of the twelfth century that there occurred the celebrated partition of the kingdom of Kīlīj Arslan between his eleven sons and relatives. Perhaps certain provinces, like Amasya, had already been allocated in principle to certain persons, but without any real relinquishing of authority over them. It was arranged that they should all be registered in the Dīwān of Konya, and the creation of a double apanage for Qutb al-Dīn possibly signified that he was designated as his brothers' future suzerain (certainly he interpreted it firmly in that sense). The outcome has been seen. However, Kaykhusraw also allocated Malatya and Tokat to his sons Kay-kāūs and Kay-kubādh respectively, but Kay-kāūs put an end to the last vestiges of the system. A sister dynasty, which can hardly be called a vassal one, had meanwhile been set up in Erzurum at the time of its conquest by Rukn al-Dīn. It has been described how Kay-kubādh put an end to it at the same time as the other dynasty of the Mangujakids. There is no sign that, in the twelfth century, any large command existed for persons other than members of the Sultan's family, except perhaps – which would confirm the rule – the office of *atabek* to a prince. No doubt it is possible to find a mention of one or two provincial governors who were not princes, such as the Sulaymān in the western border districts under Kīlīj Arslan II, but there is no evidence that they were not subject to dismissal, as most of their fellows were to be in the thirteenth century. And there does not seem to have been a question of any vast areas of authority.

(*c*) Experience had shown the danger arising from the power of holders of apanages. Although their native country was not unacquainted with similar experiences, Iranian officials traditionally inclined towards an administration conducted, where possible, by governors drawn from the official classes who were directly dependent upon the central power, and it was now becoming possible in Rūm to ensure their recruitment. There is little doubt that reasoning of this kind led the Seljukids in the thirteenth century to replace the system of apanages by the system which was already in existence in certain cases but which now became exclusive, namely that of government by officers who were subject to dismissal. Since the truth of this matter has not hitherto been established in any published works, it is important that it should be given due emphasis.

In order fully to grasp the distinction in question it must be remembered that, in the Seljukid State, there were three ways in which a man could receive a command. In the first place it might be as an *iqtā'* in the full sense, such as existed at the close of the Seljukid Iranian State and among its successors, that is to say conferring upon the beneficiary authority over the district which was regarded in fact as a private hereditary possession. It could also be a concession, varying in its extent and of limited duration, for example for life and not hereditary, or linked with the holding of some office, as a form of salary, and terminating with it. Finally, it could be a simple delegation of power to a notable who exercised no authority by personal right and could be removed at any time.

The chief town of each province was the seat of a military command, the holder of which bears, in the texts, the various names that he was customarily given, combining the three languages of the Muslims in the country – *subashi* in Turkish, *serleshker* in Persian, these two words having the meaning of 'army commander', and *shihna* in Arabic, a term already noted in connection with the Great Seljukids and applying more particularly to the commander of a garrison. People began to say, simply and more vaguely, *sāhib, amīr, beg,* and so on. These offices could be conferred as an *iqtā'*, or, to be more accurate, with the concession of their district as an *iqtā'*, but they in no sense implied automatically any such mode of conferment. When it is not specified that they were so conferred it is probable, generally speaking, that they were commands subject to termination and delegated, and not in the nature of an *iqtā'*. It is thus wholly misleading to regard the existence of these commands as evidence of feudalism. The way to establish this is to draw up an accurate list of the known commanders, for the largest possible number of chief towns, so that, when the nature of their command is not definitely specified, one can state the length of time that they held it and above all the identity of the holders and the hereditary or non-hereditary nature of the functions. This is what we shall endeavour to do, while asking the reader's indulgence for the irksome nature of the details into which we are compelled to enter.

Which then are the towns known to have been the subject of grants as *iqtāʿ*s, and not simply of appointments of ordinary governors? In the first place, the principality of Erzurum can be left aside: under its Seljukid princes at the beginning of the century it had in fact been independent, even if Rukn al-Dīn, who had founded it, had intended it to be a vassal principality. Annexed by Kay-kubādh, it nonetheless remained an external possession different from his own dominions until the time when, as a result of the ravages of the wars following the approach of the Mongols, he thought it opportune to grant it, together with the responsibility for defending it, to the dispossessed Khwārizmians. It has been seen that this attempt failed and, in the years that followed, Erzurum was annexed directly, and commanded by a *shihna*.

The last Mangujakids of Erzinjān and Divriǧi acknowledged themselves to be the Seljukids' vassals. When Kay-kubādh put an end to their principality, one of them perhaps retained Divriǧi, to judge from an inscription, but within the framework of the Seljukid State. It was moreover a town of secondary rank. Erzinjān, on the contrary, was first annexed directly, then temporarily conceded as an *iqtāʿ* to one of the Khwārizmian chiefs, and finally re-annexed directly at the time of their flight. The *serleshker*s known to have been there later, Sharaf al-Dīn Masʿūd until 1246, and afterwards Muʿīn al-Dīn Sulaymān the *pervāne*, were officers of the Sultan.

From the time of its reconquest in 1201, Malatya was apparently administered directly. In 608/1211 Kay-kāūs 'gave' it to the *ispahsālār* Husām al-Dīn Yūsuf al-Sultānī, whose presence there four years later is attested by an inscription. But the fact that Kay-kāūs had his brother Kay-kubādh imprisoned in this same town seems to imply that Husām al-Dīn was a governor, not a *muqtaʿ*. The whole history of the town in the three following decades similarly suggests that the Sultan controlled it directly, and the *subashï* recorded in 1237 was certainly still an officer of the Sultan. The same was true of Khartpert, acquired in 1233, which had a *subashï* and had never been granted in any other way. Nor do things appear to be different in the later conquests on the Mesopotamian borders, once the period had passed during which in some of them, such as Samosata, a prince originally outside the Seljukid Sultan's domain had transferred his allegiance to him.

Possibly the situation was different in Albistan, an important strategic stronghold on the route from Syria. In 608/1211 Kay-kāūs had given it to Abu l-'Izz Mubāriz al-Dīn Chavli al-Sultānī. Since the concession was connected with that of Malatya to Husām al-Dīn, noted above, it is possible that it was a matter of an ordinary command. Nevertheless an inscription seems to indicate that Mubāriz al-Dīn was still governor of Albistan in 639/1241, and as he was also *chāshnegīr* it may be that possession of the town was linked with that office, at least so far as he himself was concerned. In 1254 Albistan was to have an ordinary *subashī*. On the other hand it has already been shown that the province of Mar'ash, being nearer to the Syrian border area, in the twelfth century had either temporarily or permanently been given the status of a fief, which it was to retain in the thirteenth. From 608/1211–12 at the latest until at least 630/1233 it was in the hands of the *malik al-umarā'* Nusrat al-Dīn Hasan ibn Ibrāhīm. In 1258, it was to fall into the hands of the Armenians, after its lord had vainly attempted to cede it to Kay-kāūs II, in order to protect it from the Turcomans.

To the north, the ancient Dānishmendid towns of Tokat, Niksar and Amasya were, with some slight modifications, under direct Seljukid control. This was certainly the case in Niksar, and in about 1240 the *chāshneigīr* Shams al-Dīn Tavtash, who was its *subashī*, was merely a governor for the Sultan. Tokat had for a time been the residence of the son of Sultan Rukn al-Dīn, and later the centre of the apanage of Kay-kubādh in Kaykhusraw's lifetime. Under Kay-kāūs, an inscription tells of a Zayn al-Dīn Bashāra al-Ghālibī (probably distinct from the *amīr-akhur* Zayn al-Dīn Bashāra) who in 612 called himself *sāhib* of Taqit (Tokat?). Two other inscriptions there record, in 631, a mausoleum that Abu'l-Qāsim 'Alī al-Tūsī was preparing for himself, and, in 648, a bridge erected by the *amīr-ispahsālār* Sayf al-Dīn Hamīd, son of the last-named. In other words, they were an important family in this town, and the son's part in the history of the period is known. However, the father also built in Kayseri, which he certainly did not possess, and in Tokat buildings were also put up in 645 by Najm al-Dīn Yaghī-basan, possibly a Dānishmendid younger son, and others. Moreover it is certain that Tokat was held directly by Kay-kubādh, who sent distinguished prisoners there, and by Kaykhusraw II, who in 1243, in face of the Mongol threat, placed his treasure and harem in safe keeping there, to be found later by Muʿīn al-Dīn Sulaymān, the *pervāne*, among the Seljukid inheritance. The result of all this is that it is doubtful if Zayn al-Dīn was anything more than a governor, and in any case it is certain that, after Kay-kubādh, there were only ordinary governors in Tokat. Finally, in Amasya, the situation had no doubt been more complex. In 606 the emir Mubāriz al-Dīn Bahrāmshāh, as assistant to a certain Alp ibn Sūlī, was present there, and in 612 the same man, now without a superior, was at the head of the emirs of the province. He is well-known historically as *amīr-majlis*, though without any special connection between Amasya and himself ever being mentioned in the chronicles. He died in 1228. Later, Amasya was given as an *iqtāʿ* to the Khwārizmian chief Bereke, which means that the Sultan had it at his disposal; and it was recovered on the occasion of Bereke's arrest. At the time of the revolt of the Babāīs, the *serleshker* of the town, Armaghanshāh perished. The town belonged directly to the Sultan in 1243, when the vizier took refuge there, and during Sultan ʿIzz al-Dīn's dispute with his brother Rukn al-Dīn, whom he kept under surveillance there. Inscriptions of the period do not give any clear indications. There is thus no ground for asserting that Mubāriz al-Dīn held Amasya save as governor, unless in this instance grant of the town had been linked with the office of *amīr-majlis*.

It is self-evident that neither Sivas nor Kayseri had ever been anything but Seljukid towns under direct administration. Governors of Kayseri are known (with no family connection between them), bearing the titles of *hākim*, *wālī*, *shihna* or, more often, *subashī*, and perhaps at one time simply *amīr*. On the other hand, none of the governors of Sivas are known, although documents on that town are not lacking. In the inscription of 612 in which the great emirs who had collaborated in building the walls of Sinope are enumerated, while the others, such as governors of towns, figure only at the head of the town notables, and anonymously, three are named for Sivas and 'the provinces of Sivas'. The town thus seems to have had a special régime, perhaps like Konya, which cannot be defined more precisely.

Localities bordering on the important frontier of the Cilician Taurus appear to have been more variable. Nigde was the principal one. In 608, under the same equivocal conditions as the other concessions in that year, it was 'given' to the *amīr-akhur* Zayn al-Dīn Bashāra, though without the concession appearing to be linked with his office. He was put to death under Kay-kudādh, shortly after 620, and henceforward Nigde was without any doubt directly dependent on the Sultan, since he later conceded it as an *iqtā'* to one of the Khwārizmian chiefs whom he took into his service, Yilan Nugu. (Incidentally, this did not prevent the regular army in the province from being commanded soon afterwards by the *pervāne* Tāj al-Dīn.) At the time of the Khwārizmians' flight, Nigde was recovered. At the beginning of the reign of 'Izz al-Dīn, it was to be the share of Samsām al-Dīn Kaymaz, and then of one of the Sultan's slaves, before passing, under the Mongol protectorate, through various vicissitudes which will be described in due course. Lu'lu'a, which since its conquest was a dependency of Nigde, was always a fortress under the Sultan. In Eregli a *sāhib* Shudjā' al-Dīn Ahmad-Beg is known of in 612/1215–16. Laranda was temporarily conferred as an *iqtā'* upon the Khwārizmian chief Kushlu Sankum in 1231 (the Sultan was then in possession), and it was later recovered in the same circumstances as the other Khwārizmian *iqtā'*s.

Farther to the north, Akseray, Kīrshehir and Akshehir were granted as *iqtā'*s, though only temporarily. In 612/1215–16, Akseray perhaps had a *sāhib*, Sayf al-Dīn Ildegiz. On the annexation of the principality of Erzurum by Kay-kubād it was granted as an *iqtā'* to the dispossessed prince Rukn al-Dīn, as compensation, but there is no doubt that, from Kaykhusraw II to the beginning of the fourteenth century, when the historian Aqsarāyī who was a native of the place spoke of it at length, it belonged throughout directly to the Sultan. Kīrshehir had been given by Kay-kubādh under the same conditions to the Mangujakid Muzaffar al-Dīn of Erzinjān. On the death of the latter, under Kaykhusraw II, it was recovered by the Sultan, since it soon appears in the form of the *imāra* conferred upon the vizier Muhadhdhab al-Dīn and other viziers after him. Ayyūbhisār, situated between the two, had been combined with Akseray for Rukn al-Dīn, but it was joined to Kīrshehir for the viziers. Also under the same conditions, Akshehir had been given as an *iqtā'* to the lord of Kalon-oros (which had become 'Alā'iyya), and then, probably after his death, to the Mangujakid Dā'ūdshāh. There is almost no doubt that it then reverted to the Sultan.

In the northern provinces Ankara, after forming part of the apanage of Kay-kubādh under Kaykhusraw, had been restored to the Sultan's domain in the normal way. In 1235 it belonged, as an *iqtā'*, to Tāj al-Dīn, the *pervāne*, though we cannot tell if it was by personal title or by virtue of his office. In any event, when at this date it reverted to the Sultan, the executions and imprison-ments ordered by his vizier seem to show clearly that it was re-tained in the directly-ruled domain, as later history confirms.

It is more difficult to reach any definite conclusion for the vast frontier province of Kastamonu. In the middle of the thirteenth century Ibn Saʿīd called this town 'the Turcomans' capital'. In the fourteenth century it was to be the seat of the Turcoman dynasty of the Isfandiyārids, and at the end of the thirteenth the province to some degree belonged to the descendants of a figure whose presence there under the independent Seljukids has been noted. Hence it would need only a single step to reach the con-clusion that the Turcoman emancipation occurred there as else-where, but with origins going back to the beginning of the century, and this step would be easy to take if incidentally it were not known with equal certainty that Kastamonu belonged in the same period to the Sultans, who had their governors there, and afterwards, under the Mongols, to the non-Turcoman powers who then split up among themselves the fragments of the Seljukid State, as will be seen. There is thus a problem which we must try to elucidate.

The original figure concerned in this problem is Husām al-Dīn Chupan (Choban), *beglerbeg* possibly as early as 608/1211, in any case in about 625. Either in that capacity or as being simultan-eously master of the whole or part of the province and of the Turcomans of Kastamonu, he was, therefore, like the ordinary known *beglerbeg*s, put in charge by Kay-kubādh of a military operation, in this case the famous Crimean expedition. Half a century later, Ibn Bībī related that his son and grandson held all or part of the region by inheritance, and it is therefore tempting to suppose that, as an exception, in this exceptional region, Kay-

kubādh in fact permitted the establishment of an autonomous
Turcoman family power. But there is nothing to indicate that these
persons were Turcomans, and although they succeeded in exercising real power in those districts in the last quarter of the
thirteenth century, as will be seen, the family continuity and the
extension of their authority are much more questionable. It has
already been said that, in the Mongol period, Kastamonu and its
province were dependent successively upon a certain Yavtash
(there is nothing to indicate that he was related to Chupan, although like him he was *beglerbeg*), then directly taken over by a
vizier to provide the expenses of his office, by a representative of
the Mongols as a guarantee of payments, and by other senior
Government officials. All that can be said with certainty is that
Chupan governed for a long time, and that Kastamonu was a city
belonging to the Sultan. The same is incontestably true of Sinope.
Perhaps in the hinterland Saimara, which had a *sāhib* in 612 and
615, was in a different situation. In any case it was merely a place
of secondary importance.

In the remaining Anatolian border region in the south, Alanya
and Antalya, the Sultans' winter residences where treasurers were
often housed, could not be alienated. It was, however, a frontier
Turcoman zone, requiring particular vigilance. Accordingly, a
general command of the southern territories had been created
which, from 603/1206, and with progressive extensions, was held
for more than twenty years by a freedman of Kaykhusraw,
Mubāriz al-Dīn Ertöküsh. In the hinterland his jurisdiction included Isparta and extended almost to Burghlu. A similar situation was to recur during the Mongol period. In the intervening
period, Kay-kubādh appears to have resumed direct control of
this command or to have divided it, since there is no further reference to it. Ertöküsh had never lost favour, but there is evidence
that, in the long run, his power was thought to have become
excessive. Raised to the rank of *atabek* to Kaykhusraw, he had to
fight the Mangujakids and no longer had any part in affairs in the
south. In Antalya he was perhaps replaced by another freedman
of Kay-kubādh, Armaghanshāh.

Farther to the east the province of Ermenek, enlarged by new
conquests, was given by Kay-kubādh to a certain Qamar al-Dīn
– a newly created unit which he must have held for a long time,

since the country was to retain his name; but of the man himself nothing more is known.

In south-western Asia Minor the main base for Seljukid power had for a long time, since its conquest, been Burghlu. Though to a slight extent replaced in this respect by Antalya in one part and Denizli in another, after their acquisition, it remained a place of importance. The fact that state prisoners were held within its walls on the Sultan's orders proves that it was still in their direct possession. Denizli, linked with Khunas, once a possession of Maurozomes, in 612 was governed by a certain Asad al-Dīn Ayāz al-Ghālibī, possibly identical with Rashīd al-Dīn Ayāz ibn 'Abd Allāh al-Shihābī, who is known to have been still there in 627. Whether or not it had been partially alienated, it was afterwards held again by the Sultan, who possibly had it governed by Karatay and his brother Karasonkur until, at the beginning of the Mongol period, after being temporarily restored to the Greeks, it was finally reoccupied by the Turcomans. Kütahya in 634 and 641 had the same governor, the emir *ispahsālār* 'Imād al-Dīn Hezārdīnārī, of whom nothing further is known in this period. The governors of Karahisār were probably Sābiq al-Dīn Abu'l-Wafā Ilyās ibn Oghuz before 606, and then his son the *ispahsālār* Badr al-Dīn Abu Hāmid Hājjī Muhammad (one of his brothers was in Karajaviran in 607). But it was subsequently in the Sultan's possession, since at the beginning of the Mongol period it was to be conferred on the family of the vizier Fakhr al-Dīn 'Alī. Its history, which is almost unknown, is complicated by possible confusions with its namesakes in the Taurus and in the Trebizond mountains.

Thus, whatever doubts may persist in certain respects, it does not appear that the general impression can be contested. The Seljukids governed their state with the help of officers who might be maintained in their commands for considerable periods but who nevertheless were subject to dismissal, except under special conditions, and who were indeed dismissed or transferred. Before the Mongol invasion the rulers were strong enough to do this, and consequently the tendency of their régime, far from being in this respect feudal, was on the contrary deliberately anti-feudal.

There is one important exception, it is true, but it has mistakenly been regarded as normal practice, whereas it was the opposite. I refer to the Khwārizmians. After the death of their chief Jalāl al-

Dīn Manguberti, it will be remembered, the dispossessed Khwār-izmians mostly entered the service of Kay-kubādh, who was glad to deprive various possible rivals of their assistance and eventually to make use of their warlike qualities against the Mongol threat. After some hesitation, the great Sultan granted them, as an *iqtāʿ*, the provinces of Erzinjān, Amasya and Laranda-Nigde, situated on exposed frontiers or important strategic routes, and outside the western half of the kingdom. Nevertheless, it is not known what degree of authority was granted to the Khwārizmians in their *iqtāʿ*s (it would appear that it was not necessarily complete authority). Moreover, the circumstances were exceptional, and whatever speculation may have been entertained regarding the possibility of things returning to normal, they were somewhat vain since, in fact, on the death of Kay-kubādh, the immediate dangers having diminished and the new masters possibly being more aware of the disadvantages that had come to light, the defeated Khwārizmians had fled and the system was abandoned.

The above impressions, formed directly from an examination of the events preceding the Mongol protectorate, are corroborated indirectly by others produced under that protectorate. It will be made clear that, as the personal power of the Sultan was then disappearing almost completely, the real authority, under the control of the Mongols, was to belong to certain great ministers who, on the pretext of ensuring for themselves the revenues necessary for the exercise of their duties, were to partition the provinces between themselves, thereby establishing some sort of family fiefs. It is quite evident that any such undertaking would have been impossible if feudal powers over these provinces had existed previously, and these ministers would certainly have found it difficult to reduce them by force, now that the humbled Seljukid State no longer had the strength. In a more general way, one could not explain why the disaster of Köse Dagh was not followed by any show of revolt or local independence (apart from the frontier-dwelling Turcomans) if any great lords of feudal type had existed beforehand. The Mongols would doubtless have been indifferent, but in any case not a single text indicates that they had to fight against any rebellions of this kind, either in support of or to replace the Seljukids. Some few rebellions were gradually able to take shape, but the conclusion is inescapable that, on the eve of 1243, practically nothing of the sort existed.

There is of course one exceptional category, which however is a special one and without significance even within the state before 1243, namely the Turcomans. On the whole, despite the tragic and revealing episode of Baba Ishāq, in the first half of the thirteenth century the Turcomans were kept under close control by the Seljukids. It is certain however that, in the territories where they were present, they enjoyed a fairly wide degree of internal autonomy. It is possible that, in certain cases, these territories had been granted to them in the legal form of iqtāʿs. Nevertheless this term does not correctly convey the real character of the régime that was established for them. In the first place it must be noted that they were particularly numerous along the frontiers, or at least that it was only on the frontiers that they had their own particular régime. Rather than 'on the frontiers', it is tempting to say 'astride the frontier', in that kind of administrative no man's land where their effective autonomy derived from the fact that they were not really answerable to any authority, Seljukid, Byzantine or Armenian, and that in the face of possible encroachments by any one of these they could take refuge under the protection of another. Administrative terminology and practice make a very clear distinction between the true territories of the State and this zone of lands or men of the ūj (uç), literally 'border'. And the Mongols, deliberately sacrificing these regions, were to make the distinction even greater. However, the Seljukid administration gradually endeavoured to implant itself in these territories, where Turcoman independence might conceal certain dangers, and in any case it did not care to think that the people there were outside its reach. As a result of the Turcoman expansion, agents of the central power were gradually established in the leading towns. At other times, it was in territories conquered by the Seljukid regular armies, such as the western Taurus, that, in order to people it, Turcomans were settled in a region where the administration had taken hold either before them or at the same time. Through one or other of these processes, it is certain – and this point must be given serious consideration – that, at the time of Seljukid domination, there was not a single province within the real territory of the state in which, even if Turcoman groupings

existed which were autonomous and enjoyed freedom of movement and action, there was not some authority acting for the
Sultan at the head and above them. Later, the holders of the
Turcoman principalities wished it to be thought that they had
received true provincial commands from the Sultans, and later
authors, writing under the influence of these ideas and in the
confusion caused by changed circumstances, almost succeed in
carrying conviction. In this matter care is needed and, here also,
one must judge only on factual evidence clearly relating to the
period under discussion.

8

CULTURAL AND RELIGIOUS LIFE

It is difficult to follow the rhythm and progress of the cultural
development of Muslim Asia Minor. Here again, it was only in
the second half of the twelfth century that any clear signs of it
appeared, and in the thirteenth that it produced works that were
to be important and win recognition. A distinction must of course
be made between two almost unrelated fields – that of the
Turcomans, who were still hardly touched by traditional Muslim
culture and about whom, for that very reason, almost nothing is
known for the pre-Mongol period; and that of the town-dwellers
of mixed ethnic origin, of whom alone it is possible to speak since
they alone have left written works.

It has already been said that, in the politico-religious interplay
of their time, the very earliest Seljukids of Rūm seemed somewhat
inclined to be hostile, or at least indifferent, to the militant
Sunnism of their kinsmen, the Great Seljukids. It was also noted
that Shī'ī as well as Sunnī influence figured among those which
allowed Islam to penetrate among their Turcoman subjects, in
addition to the barely disguised survival of the ancestral beliefs
from the time before their islamization. These popular conceptions, as will be seen, did not prevent the Seljukids from quickly
reaching with the 'Abbāsid Caliphate a closer understanding

involving a profession of faith which, outwardly at least, was Sunnī, and then, particularly after the disappearance of the Seljukids from Iran, from gradually asserting themselves as the heirs of their policy, and hence as good Sunnīs, whatever may have been their motives or those that were ascribed to them. Like their kinsmen in Iran, from a very early period they had among them some Khorasanian Hanafite religious teachers. The earliest known, in 1108, is a *faqīh* of Herat who was sent on an embassy to the Caliph to negotiate the release of Shāhānshāh. Later, others came from different regions, often from north-western Iran, of their own volition or when summoned. Sulaymān had asked Shīʿī Tripoli to supply a *cadi* for Tarsus at the time of its conquest in 1084, and there was a Grand Cadi at the accession of Kïlïj Arslan II, who, like the Dānishmendid Yaghï-basan, also had '*imāms*' with him. It happened several times that foreign scholars who had come without any idea of staying on, as ambassadors for example, were persuaded by Seljukid princes to settle more permanently in Asia Minor.

The first Muslims in the towns of Asia Minor certainly practised their religion in small makeshift buildings, no doubt mainly churches or parts of churches that had been confiscated. The coming of Islam cannot be dated only from the first appearance of mosques. Even so, this feature testifies to the progress and officialization of Islam. The date is not always easy to determine, particularly in regard to buildings still of modest size which bear no inscriptions. However, a pulpit for the mosque in Konya, the work of a craftsman who was a native of Akhlāt (unless it had been ordered from him in that town), bears the date 550, and the rest of the oldest mosques in the Seljukid, Dānishmendid or Mangujakid-Saltukid domains seem to be approximately of that date or a little later. These will be discussed later with reference to their artistic interest.

Moreover, from the time of the Great Seljukids, it will be remembered, the institution of the *madrasa* was spreading throughout the whole of Sunnī Islam, the institution for orthodox education devoted to the training of the 'official classes'. The earliest *madrasa* in Asia Minor, known from a foundation inscription, is that built in Kayseri in 589/1193, at a period when *madrasas* were so abundant in all the towns of the Arab or Persian

Near East that, in the middle of the thirteenth century, for example, the writer Ibn Shaddād of Aleppo recorded more than 40 of them in his town. Some may, however, have existed even before the one in Kayseri, perhaps like the one mentioned in the colophon of a manuscript copied in 591/1195 in a 'Seljukid *madrasa*' of Sivas founded by an unknown Mīrānshāh ibn Kāvurt. It is possible that a systematic study of the manuscripts might reveal others. Nevertheless, it is unlikely that the general picture would be basically altered. Even in the thirteenth century the number of *madrasa*s that can be discovered in Asia Minor remains somewhat limited.

Arabic literature is, of course, immeasurably rich in biographies of scholars. Iranian literature is less rich, but nevertheless possesses some, particularly of the mystics. In practice, out of the many thousands of these biographical notices there is nothing in the twelfth century relating to Asia Minor. Certainly, if a scholar died there, far from his fellow-writers, who customarily wrote the accounts and the obituary notices, his name ran the risk of being forgotten. Even so, the simplest explanation on the whole is that there were still almost no personages of that kind in Asia Minor, and the few who were there had not established any real reputation before settling or maintained any contact with scholarly society in neighbouring countries, in whose eyes their learning may perhaps have seemed insignificant. In these circumstances it will nevertheless be of some help to give a list of the earliest references that can be found in the texts, in order to provide a few guiding marks. The Hanafite *faqīh* of 1108 has already been referred to. Is he identical with the jurist ʿAbd al-Majīd ibn Ismāʿīl ibn Saʿd of Herat, known in Muslim countries as the author of works of Hanafite doctrine, who died in Kayseri in 537/1142 after performing the duties of *cadi* 'in Rūm'? It is possible. Kayseri enjoyed easy communications with Syria, and perhaps it was one of the earliest centres of islamization (it also has one of the oldest mosques). A little later, Malatya, though still an important Christian town, was no doubt another such centre, owing to its good connections with Upper Mesopotamia. The scholar Muhammad al-Mawsilī, who in the second half of the century was to search throughout Syria and Mesopotamia for teachers or fellow-students, reached this town but felt there was no need to travel further, and it will be seen that some authors appear to have lived there. Earlier, in the middle of the century, another jurist, al-Kāshānī, sent by Nūr al-Dīn to Sultan Masʿūd, was detained by the latter for a time. Like many others, Ḳīlij Arslan was to have a Christian physician (from Edessa).

These writers, who were particularly interested in religious and juridical knowledge, used Arabic, as was the rule in that field, although they were of Iranian birth. But soon Persian writers also appeared in the entourage of the Seljukids and their emulators. A genuine activity seems to have surrounded the old Ḳīlij Arslan and his sons in the last years of the twelfth century, with a touch of heterodoxy perhaps facilitated, by the contact between creeds and the weakness of the traditional classes of officials. At the court of Ḳīlij Arslan, Michael the Syrian knew a 'Persian philosopher' capable of informed discussion with the Christian doctors. Probably this is not a reference to the celebrated illuminist philosopher al-Suhrawardī, but almost certainly it was to Ḳīlij Arslan or his son Rukn al-Dīn that the *Pertevnāme* was dedicated by that author who, some years later, was to meet his death (hence his name *maqtūl*, 'the slain', to distinguish him from a namesake who occurs later) through the intervention of the orthodox, in Aleppo. And Rukn al-Dīn in any case had a reputation as a philosopher, a pejorative term in the vocabulary of the orthodox of that period. Other authors recorded in the company of these same princes include Sharaf al-Dīn Hubays al-Tiflīsī (of Tiflis, an old Muslim town conquered by the Georgians), who composed for Ḳīlij Arslan and his son Qutb al-Dīn some typical compilations of medicine, astrology (much cultivated by the Seljukids), oneiromancy, and *adab* (general culture); Muhammad ibn Ghāzī, who under the title *Rawdat al-ʿUqūl* (Garden of Intellects) composed for Rukn al-Dīn, on the occasion of his capture of Malatya in 1201, an adaptation of the well-known Persian work, the *Marzbānnāme*, while later composing another compilation of stories for Kaykhusraw or Kay-kāūs; and finally Abu Hanīfa ʿAbd al-Karīm, who wrote for Muhyī al-Dīn of Ankara, another of Ḳīlij Arslan's sons, a collection of *rubāʿiyyāt* (quatrains), the literary form made famous a century earlier by Omar Khayyam. There is no need to continue this list for the later periods, where it becomes self-evident. At least it affords proof of a genuine

intellectual life in certain Anatolian Muslim centres at the end of
the twelfth century, with some foreign authors who had been
attracted there and no doubt also a number of native ones who
were already present. The increasing iranization of the dynasty is
also revealed by the fact that Kïlïj Arslan gave a mythological
Persian name to one of his sons, Kaykhusraw, who in his turn
was to give similar names to his three sons (note, however, that
another of Kïlïj Arslan's sons was called Qaysarshāh, which
appears to endow him with a 'Roman' past).

There is no evidence of any similar cultural activity among the
Dānishmendids, whose spirit perhaps differed and who in any
case disappeared too early. Something of the kind existed a little
later among the Mangujakids, especially during Bahramshāh's
long reign in Erzinjān. This town, though long to remain a great
Armenian centre, must have contained a small but active Muslim
circle around that prince, despite the opinion to the contrary
expressed by the contemporary geographer Yāqūt, and perhaps
it was no more hostile to relations between the creeds than was
Ani under the Shaddādids. In any case, at the beginning of his
reign Bahramshāh certainly seems to have received the dedication
of one of the poems, the *Makhzan al-asrār* (*Treasury of Secrets*), of
the great Persian poet Nizāmī of Ganja (a town in the extreme
north-west of Iran), and it is possible that he was acquainted with
another poet, Khāqānī. Moreover, at the end of his reign, this
same Bahramshāh entertained the famous Iraqi doctor-phil-
osopher 'Abd al-Latīf al-Baghdādī in his entourage for twelve
years, and it was only after the annexation of the town by Kay-
kubādh that this scholar returned to his native land. This author's
autobiography, at least in the extracts preserved by various later
writers, unfortunately contains nothing to throw any light on the
conditions under which he lived or the activities of cultivated
society in Erzinjān, but whatever material facilities Bahramshāh
may have provided, it is doubtful whether 'Abd al-Latīf would
have accepted his exile if he had had to live in an intellectual
desert. It is possible that a thorough examination of the shorter
works of 'Abd al-Latīf, which in the past have been neglected but
are now beginning to attract attention, might furnish some new
information on this matter.

The study of cultural life in Rūm in the thirteenth century (the same remarks would apply equally well to the fourteenth and fifteenth centuries) is difficult and has hardly been attempted. It is only possible here to give a necessarily very imperfect survey. Concentrating for the moment on the pre-Mongol period, we can disregard the whole field of the Turkish language, in which no written works had as yet been produced, merely emphasizing that there was some oral literature, of which more will be said later, and that literary activity, whether in Persian or Arabic, was confined to urban society, a situation which, whatever its intrinsic value, reduced its scope and created a hiatus between the two elements of the population, the city-dwellers and the Turcomans. Other manifestations of this, and other dangers, have already been observed. Even in the Arabo-Persian field it cannot be said that, as yet, any real conspectus of intellectual life has been made. In the absence of any Anatolian biographical works such as were written in neighbouring countries in the Muslim world, a patient scrutiny of these latter works might be made for any scattered references to those who had spent some part of their lives in Rūm. In addition, a list might be compiled, particularly in the libraries in Instanbul and elsewhere in Turkey, not only of works written in the country – in fact this has more or less been done – but also manuscripts of other works that were copied there, in so far as the copyists have stated the fact, and where possible with the date (there exists, for example, a Koran written for Kay-kubādh). Obviously, it was not by chance (and, though natural, it is instructive to state the fact) that most of the known manuscripts of the works of many Hanafite jurists of Central Asia are to be found in Turkish libraries, and that many of them were copied there. Some however may also have been brought from Central Asia, particularly by refugees fleeing from the Mongol invasion or immigrants attracted by the bounty of the Seljukid rulers, and so on. In this respect, it seems that the important thing is to examine the notes by readers often found at the beginning or end or in the margins of manuscripts, since the works of G. Vajda have demonstrated the interest that these possess for other Muslim countries. It would then be possible to see more clearly, not only what was written in Rūm, which remains limited, but also, in a wider sense, what received attention there and consequently influenced what was written. We should then perhaps avoid the impression now held, which is certainly too extreme, of a spiritual life virtually monopolized by a few gɪeat figures, and should be able to present a more diversified and subtle picture.

In the present state of our knowledge, spiritual life in Asia Minor in the middle of the thirteenth century, particularly at the start of the Mongol period but also a little earlier, appears in the available documentation to revolve around the person of Jalāl al-Dīn Rūmī or, in a secondary way, around those who were his forerunners. There is no question of diminishing either the great poetic and religious value of his works, which still survive, or even the social importance of the mystical order of which he is reckoned the founder. Quite simply, it is a matter of realizing that he was not alone and that, before him and along with him, there were other men and other trends which, though less easy to discover, nonetheless were probably also important.

Jalāl al-Dīn Rūmī and his circle wrote in Persian, and there is no question that, throughout the whole history of Turkey, the domain of Persian was generally speaking more extensive than that of Arabic. This is explained both by the fact that the earliest Turks, or at least their aristocracy, had some idea of Persian from living in contact with Iranian society, and later because the immigrants who helped to form Anatolian culture were very largely Iranians (or people of Central Asia of Iranian speech). Nevertheless there were also Arabs, and in any case the study of the Law is in principle a field reserved for Arabic, and one that even so is of importance.

As has already been suggested in passing, it was largely on the basis of works of Hanafite Law from Central Asia that the jurists of Asia Minor built up their knowledge of the Law. The Sivas manuscripts referred to earlier consist of a compilation of several short works from this source, one of them it is true being the work of the Kāshānī who was later an envoy of Nūr al-Dīn and detained for a time by Mas'ūd. The manuscript was purchased by a reader in Erzurum. However, it is not surprising that the jurists who were becoming established in Asia Minor could now come from other regions, particularly those that were nearest. From Egypt, sent in the first place by al-Kamil, came Afdal al-Dīn al-Khunājī, who under Kay-kubādh and Kaykhusraw II was 'head of the *fuqahā*'' of Rūm, before fleeing from the Mongols. 'Umar al-Abharī, who died in 663/1265, and Sirāj al-Dīn al-Urmawī (from Urmiya, on the lake of that name in Azerbaijan) (595/1198 – 682/1283) divided their lives between Mesopotamia and Asia Minor. A certain Muhammad al-Tāliqānī, who died as a *cadi* in Rūm in 614/1217, came from Kazvin (north-western Iran). Moreover, Yūsuf ibn Saʿīd al-Sijistānī came from eastern Iran, but it was in Sivas that, in 639/1241-2, he wrote his *Munyat al-Muftī*, an important treatise on the Law which was to enjoy great popularity throughout the Muslim East. It seems unnecessary to dwell further on this list of names, the essential purpose of which is to emphasize the existence of a certain branch of activity less illustrious than some others.

It is considered, not without reason, that mysticism flourished in particular in Iran, and that consequently its chosen language is Persian. The subject of Persian mysticism in Asia Minor will be examined a little later. However, here too, this was not exclusively the case. At the beginning of the thirteenth century Ibn ʿArabī was living in Egypt, a great Arab mystic of Spanish origin, whose prestige in all the Muslim countries was immense. There is no doubt that his influence in Seljukid Asia Minor was very considerable. Perhaps that influence was slightly increased as a result of the journey through Asia Minor of pilgrims from North Africa whose numbers were sufficiently large to warrant their having a small mosque of their own in Konya. But, in a more direct way, Ibn ʿArabī himself had travelled in Anatolia, twice to Malatya (in 602/1205 and 613–15/1216–18) where he had written a short work, and, in 612/1215, even to Sivas and Konya, where he had an interview with Kay-kāūs. Later, his North African disciple ʿArīf al-Dīn Sulaymān of Tlemcen was to settle in Rūm for many years, and it would be interesting to know what took him there. But it is not only through the influence of this foreigner that Anatolian disciples of Ibn ʿArabī were to be found. In Rūm, Ibn ʿArabī had been the guest of a shaykh who declared himself his disciple, Majd al-Dīn Ishāq, whose reputation was great and who was the father of a lad destined to be the teacher of the mystic theologians of Rūm, Sadr al-Dīn Qōnevī (of Konya), who always remained loyal to his father's beliefs. On the other hand, almost nothing can be said of the eventual influence of Ibn Farid, another Arab mystic and a contemporary of Ibn ʿArabī. It is known, however, that a native of Ferghana who had taken refuge in Rūm and was connected with Sadr al-Dīn had written a commentary on his works.

To this same heading of mysticism expressed in Arabic writings the influence of 'Umar Suhrawardī must to some extent be assigned. This figure, better known as the Caliph al-Nāsir's adviser and ambassador and as one of the promoters and theorists of the *futuwwa* as remodelled by that Caliph, was also the founder of an order of Sūfīs (mystics) which bears his name. It was as the Caliph's ambassador that he first became known in Asia Minor, when he came there with unusual ceremony, bringing to Kay-kubādh on his accession the royal insignia sent by the Caliph. It is not possible to tell how he won the personal ascendancy which he afterwards enjoyed there. This ascendancy is shown particularly by the fact that it was Karatay, the faithful follower of Kay-kubādh and regent for his two grandsons, who paid for his tomb in Baghdad. It is said that Kāmyār was also his disciple, while at the same time being the pupil of Sirāj al-Dīn al-Urwawī for *fiqh*.

We could also add the names of one or two physicians from Arab countries engaged by the Sultans, and note that the celebrated botanist Ibn Baytār worked in Rūm, that the charlatan conjuror al-Jawharī brought his company there, and so on. All this has to be said, but it does not exclude the fact explicitly attested during the campaign of Baybars in 1277, that as a general rule the leading men in Rūm did not know Arabic. This fact obviously reduced the influence, or at least the direct influence, of the Arabs mentioned above to a relatively narrow circle. On the other hand most of the leading men, and even a good number of the townsmen, understood Persian. Works written in Persian and the part played by the Iranians consequently acquired a wider significance. Before the Mongol conquest there was still no historical work devoted to Muslim Asia Minor. But when, at the beginning of the thirteenth century, the Iranian Rāwandī completed a History of the Seljukids of Iran and Iraq, which the death of the last of the line prevented him from dedicating to him, it was to Kaykhusraw I that he turned, adding to his original work a number of incidental pieces and various eulogies of the patron whose favour he hoped to secure. The work cannot have had any great reputation in Rūm since it does not appear to have been used directly by any later historian writing there, but it proves that the Seljukids of Rūm of the time regarded themselves as the heirs of the principal Seljukid dynasty. However, it is known that a little later a refugee from Khorasan, Ahmad ibn Mahmūd al-Tūsī al-Qāni'ī, had written a long *Seljuknāme* for Kay-kubādh, to which he had added poems in honour of 'Izz al-Dīn Kay-kāūs II. Nothing is known of this work, but it is almost certain that it dealt only with the eastern Seljukids, on which subject the author could make use of earlier writers. It would otherwise be difficult to explain why, at the end of the century, Ibn Bībī asserted that no historical documentation on the Seljukids of Asia Minor could be found before the end of the twelfth century (and he was evidently in difficulties through its absence until the beginning of the thirteenth), and that Aqsarāyī and the anonymous author of the *Seljuknāme* in Paris had clearly been placed in the same situation. On the other hand, the interest in the eastern Seljukids is not in doubt. It is clear that the writings of Nizām al-Mulk, the great vizier of the Seljukids in the eleventh century, were read and appreciated and that, in principle at least, people were happy to accept his teachings. The poems of various Persian poets were also known. It is unnecessary to remind the reader that almost all the Sultans in the thirteenth century bore, not Turkish names, but names from Iranian heroic mythology – Kaykhusraw, Kay-kāūs, Kay-kubādh, Kayferīdūn, Siyāvush and Farāmurz, among others.

On the other hand, it is a fact that a considerable number of Iranians found a second homeland in Rūm. Attracted there by the sovereigns or fleeing from the Mongols (and later arriving with them), it was predominantly in Rūm that they finally halted, not in the other Muslim countries where Islam was generally longer established and richer, and where Muslims formed a greater part of the population. It is a fact that, in several cases, history bears witness to some sort of Turco-Persian symbiosis, whereas it never achieved a Turco-Arab one.

It is therefore no surprise to find that certain works of various kinds were written in Persian in Asia Minor, for example an adaptation of *Kalila and Dimna* for 'Izz al-Dīn Kay-kāūs II by the same Qāni'ī whose *Seljuknāme* was referred to earlier, But, here also it is in the field of mysticism above all that there are some interesting examples. Najm al-Dīn Abū Bakr ibn Muhammad ... al-Rāzī

257

(i.e. of Rayy), known as Najm al-Dīn Dāya, came to Malatya when fleeing from the Mongols in 618/1221 and met Suhrawardī there. For a time he was in the service of Kay-kubādh in Kayseri. In Sivas, in 620, he wrote a mystical work, the *Mirshād al-ʿIbād*, and later a short work of the same character, the *Sirāj al-Qulūb*. He was a disciple of Najm al-Dīn Kubrā, the great mystic who had recently founded in Iran the Kubrawī order. His success in Asia Minor is shown by the number of manuscripts of the *Mirshad* still found in Turkish libraries, and by the fact that a Turkish translation of it was later made. It is possible that the Iranian mystic Awhad al-Dīn Kirmānī also stayed for a time in Kayseri and Konya.

Najm al-Dīn al-Rāzī finally settled in Konya, where he knew Jalāl al-Dīn Rūmī and Sadr al-Dīn Qonevī. It will be more appropriate to speak of these latter under the Mongols, but it was still during the period of Seljukid independence that the father of Jalāl al-Dīn, himself a mystic, settled in Rūm. Bahā al-Dīn Veled/ Walad, a preacher in Balkh, had emigrated westwards as a result of some obscure disagreements with the last of the Khwārizmshāhs of Central Asia, Muhammad. He was in Malatya in 614, in Sivas in 616, in Akshehir (of Erzinjān) until 619, in Laranda until 626/ 1228–9. It was there that he lost his wife, whose tomb still exists, and that his son Jalāl al-Dīn, born in Balkh in about 604, was married. On the invitation of Kay-kubādh he finally came to Konya but died there in 628/1230. He was the author of sermons which in part have survived, but which mostly relate to the period of his life spent in the East. In him there was also a mystical element, perhaps related to the Malāmatiyya, which his former pupil Burhān al-Dīn Muhaqqiq, who came to Rūm in 629, helped to communicate to Jalāl al-Dīn. It was however in Kayseri that Burhān settled and died in 638, and during these years Jalāl passed part of his time in Aleppo and Damascus in completing his education. He may have met the great Persian mystic Shams al-Dīn Tabrīzī there, but it was only later that the full influence of this latter was to be exerted upon him.

Even though these mystics had contacts with the populace in the Iranian countries, in Asia Minor the whole movement naturally remained foreign to the Turcomans. It is at this point that Baba Ishāq, and perhaps for more remote influences Baba Ilyas, should be brought in once again. But nothing is known directly of their teachings to the Turcomans, and only in the Mongol and post-Mongol period can one observe personages who may be their successors, to whom further reference will therefore be made in due course. Something should also be said of the *Jawāliqī*, another name for the *Kalenders*, the itinerant order which, created in Iran in the eleventh century (according to a work written in 1291 for a prince of Kastamonu) had penetrated into Asia Minor at the beginning of the thirteenth, through the efforts of a certain Abū Bakr of Niksar.

To sum up generally, whereas the ruling classes professed a Sunnism which, however, as Ibn Battūta later observed, was at times somewhat ill-defined, it has to be remembered that the propaganda which worked upon the Turcomans included a large admixture of ancestral influences on the one side, and of something near Shī'ism on the other.

The question whether there existed a Shī'ī movement in Asia Minor in the thirteenth century is somewhat difficult to solve. It is impossible to leave aside this question, in view of the importance of certain forms of Shī'ism among the Turcomans during the two following centuries in the eastern half of the country. But, to judge by those texts which are usually helpful in reconstructing the history of Asia Minor, no movement was produced there that was hostile to the Sunnī policy of the rulers, apart from that of Baba Ishāq, which lay outside Shī'ism and Sunnism alike.

A piece of evidence hitherto disregarded makes it possible to affirm the existence of Shī'ī circles of some importance. In the so-called *Memoirs* which he wrote on his wanderings, Jawbarī the illusionist relates that in Rūm, at the beginning of the thirteenth century 'when he was among the Shī'īs', he passed himself off as a reincarnation of an 'Alid: this was obviously among the common populace. It has already been said that, in the early years of the Turks' conversion and migration, there were as many Shī'ī as Sunnī missionaries, and as many pro-Shī'ī as pro-Sunnī attitudes. But information is lacking as to how things stood in the following generations. The Mongol protectorate perhaps assisted the Shī'ī cause, firstly through its indifference to the divisions in Islam, which the Ilkhāns had not embraced, thus to some extent endangering the continuance of official Sunnism, and conversely by their tendency to rely politically upon the elements maltreated or despised by earlier régimes, particularly Shī'īs, like Nasīr al-Dīn Tūsī. Then, at the beginning of the fourteenth century, after the Mongols' conversion to Islam, because some of them, including some rulers, were to be Shī'īs.

In reality, the situation is probably more confused. That elements to be regarded as Shī'ī had penetrated into Anatolian Islam is not in question, as will be seen shortly. But it does not follow that they were necessarily, in all quarters, consciously felt to be Shī'īs, and anti-Sunnī. In uneducated circles all was confused, no distinction being made between orthodox and heterodox. And even in more cultivated society, common piety had adopted certain elements of Shī'ism though without regarding them as Shī'ī, and it has to be admitted that, before the official reorganization of Shī'ism by the Safawids in Iran in the sixteenth century, the distinction between some elements of Sunnism and some of Shī'ism was perhaps not always very clearly understood. The influence of the Caliph al-Nāsir and the *futuwwa* may have added to the confusion, the former through the 'Alid – or at least syncretist – tendencies which were typical of his attitude and for which the strict Sunnīs always criticized him, the *futuwwa* through the admiration it encouraged for 'Alī, the initiator – according to its own traditions – of the *fityān*. It is thus no surprise a little later to find in popular romances, such as the Turkish adaptation of Abū Muslim, a pro-'Abbāsid attitude combined with veneration for the twelve Shī'ī *imāms*. It will be realized that, under such conditions, the question whether Shī'ism as such existed in Asia Minor possesses a somewhat special aspect. However, it is only when dealing with the Mongol period that this can be usefully discussed.

MUSLIM ART IN ASIA MINOR BEFORE
THE MONGOLS

The history of art in Muslim Asia Minor is a subject on which it is most important to lay aside all preconceived ideas. Something has already been said in general terms of the art of Seljukid Iran, but for Asia Minor things are slightly different. There was no earlier Muslim art already present in the country, with the result that, as its art became Muslim, it was correspondingly necessary to seek for guidance and models in the ancient Muslim countries – in the event, principally in Iran. It is true that a native art existed, still capable of producing certain works of its own, as has been shown, and in any case the ancient buildings which it had created were there to be seen. Being a Christian art, it could only provide the new Muslim art with certain features of detail, not with its main guiding lines, and it is difficult to know to what extent any native craftsmen in the various skills still remained on the spot, or how far the new masters wished to employ them. In the few instances where the names of architects or craftsmen are known, although some denote natives of Rūm, the greater part are the names of Muslims from neighbouring Azerbaijan. Consequently it has sometimes been said that what is known broadly as the 'Seljukid art of Asia Minor' was no more than a subdivision of Iranian or Irano-Seljukid art. Such a conclusion appears however to go much too far: there was the influence of the public buildings still to be seen, there were Iranian or Turkish memories of Khorasan or beyond, above all there were the local conditions in regard to materials (an abundance of stone for building and of wood), climate (cold winters, rain), the individual development of society, and possibilities for invention, all of which could not be crudely equated with conditions in Iran or Central Asia (it is recognized that the Kremlin, although built by Italian craftsmen, is not a monument of Italian art). In short, though without ignoring any of the general findings on the subject, it is above all important to study with an open mind the monuments of Anatolian art in themselves and then, by a comparison with the neighbouring provinces, to determine its special characteristics. As for knowing what should or should not be called Turkish in an art to which so many diverse and closely inter-related elements have contributed, this is probably a somewhat fruitless exercise, and although it is very easy to understand the attractions that it might have for the citizens of the present Turkish Republic, I consider it better to refrain from directly introducing, into fields where they are inappropriate, forms of patriotism not thought of by those concerned.

As for presenting a synthesis of the Seljukid art of Asia Minor, neither the scope of this work nor the present state of investigation and interpretation permits this to be done. It therefore seems preferable to restrict this section quite frankly to certain rough outlines, and to supplement these in a more evocative way by illustrations which will at least convey to those who see them something of the charm, variety and interest of a province of art which deserves to be known and admired. Moreover, part of the ground has already been covered elsewhere in the sections recalling the original character of some craft techniques, the activities of the Sultans and their great ministers in the field of building, the network of fortresses and caravanserais, the role of the *madrasa*s and so on. All that remains to be done is to put forward a number of more purely technical or aesthetic ideas.

There is naturally no surviving vestige of any art immediately following the Turkish conquest of Asia Minor: The earliest works date from the second quarter of the twelfth century, it began to flourish from the beginning of the thirteenth, and continued to do so for the first generation under the Mongol Protectorate.

Little is known, and it is difficult to learn more, of civil architecture. Excavations of palaces in Konya, Kubādiyya (near Kayseri) and Beyshehir/Kubādabād and early representations make it possible to form an idea of the Seljukid residences, both castles and groups of pavilions in gardens surrounded by a wall, with due allowances roughly similar to the Ottoman Saray in Istanbul. Military architecture is more generously represented, either in the form of town walls (the best preserved being at Alanya) or isolated fortresses, but as yet no study has been made of its debt to the numerous Byzantine or Armenian fortresses already in existence, or of the way in which it may have benefited from contributions from the East or followed (or indeed outstripped) some of the advances made in nearby Syria, a country disputed by Crusaders and Muslims.

Religious architecture, in which to some extent must be included the public buildings used for civil purposes (caravanserais, hospitals, and baths, among others) but conceived as religious foundations, is better known, although no public building of the period survives in its entirety. The purely religious architecture consists primarily of mosques, *madrasas* and tombs. As the towns in which these were built were of medium size, the effect aimed at and always achieved was not so much size as elegance. The principal mosques before the establishment of the real Mongol domination – to name only those that survive – are those of Kayseri and Sivas (second half of the twelfth century), the so-called mosque of 'Alā' al-Dīn Kay-Kubādh in Konya, in fact begun by Mas'ūd and enlarged by all his successors, with the result that its plan is somewhat heterogeneous, those of Nigde and Divriği, and lastly that of Malatya, which was completed in 1247. The principal ancient *madrasas* are those of Niksar, the work of the Dānishmendid Yaghï-basan in the middle of the twelfth century, the *madrasa* of emir Altun-Aba in Konya, dating from the end of the same century, the Gök Medrese (Blue *Madrasa*) of Amasya (about 1240) and finally, also in Konya, those of Karatay (1251) and of the vizier Fakhr al-Dīn 'Alī (Sāhib Ata), the last being known as the Inje Mināreli (1258). Among the characteristic features of these monuments the frequent use of stone will be noticed, besides the re-use of antique columns (whereas, save on its northern borders, the Arab world and even the greater part of the Iranian world built almost exclusively in brick), and the use of wood for the flat roofs (domes consequently taking a lesser part). Moreover, as a result of the climate, mosques were mainly enclosed and the courtyard was omitted, and indeed in exceptional cases the fountain for ablutions was placed inside the building. All mosques in the thirteenth century were given slender rounded minarets of Iranian character. The external ornamentation, mainly concentrated in the principal doorway, made great but essentially decorative use of bands of almost illegible script. Above the doorways and also beneath the domes were the 'stalactites' or *muqarnas* which at that time spread through the whole Muslim world. Finally it should be noted that the *madrasa* often contained a small mosque built round the tomb of its founder, in that country as in the rest of the Muslim world, from the thirteenth century. However, there was also a development of the kind of mausoleum introduced from Central Asia and northern Iran, a a round or polygonal construction surmounted by a conical roof. Reference was made earlier to the adaptation in Asia Minor of the technique of employing enamelled faience mosaics to decorate the interior of buildings, this being the reason why the words 'blue' or 'green' occur in the names of so many mosques or *madrasas*.

Although the direct evidence still surviving has often been reduced to almost nothing, it can be stated that almost all the minor arts practised in neighbouring countries also existed in Asia Minor and were of high quality. In particular, apart from ceramics and carpets, which have already been mentioned, there was work in various metals and wood (the natural resources of the country providing the materials), and book-binding in leather and even illumination of manuscripts (by both Muslims and Christians). Among the artefacts are the wonderful pulpits (*minbar*) in the mosques. The general relationship of inspiration with neighbouring countries is unquestioned, not only of course the Muslim lands but also Armenia, Georgia and Byzantium, which in turn had relationships elsewhere. This is perhaps the moment to emphasize particularly the part played, in all fields of art, by representations of living beings, animals, and even human beings, side by side with arabesques and geometrical or calligraphic motifs. Not that Islam, and Iranian Islam specifically, did not also employ such representations, especially in metalwork (but perhaps mainly after the Turkish domination and in regions that had acquired some slight Turkish character) in the ornamentation of woven fabrics and miniatures (here too the Arabs come into the question, but perhaps again in a development that took place under Turkish influence): apart from the subject of coinage, discussed earlier, the frequency of these representations, their importance even at the level of monumental sculpture (for example, the genies in the decorations of the gates of the citadel of Konya), and the nature of certain animal motifs certainly suggest the traditions of the Central Asian steppe, together with Byzantine models.

And so, perhaps more easily than in literature, where the different creeds co-existed, an interpenetration of composite influences developed, finally leading however to an art which unquestionably was harmonious and which can be said to be a closely related branch of Muslim art, but which possesses its own individuality and is indeed one of the most distinguished.

PART FOUR

The Mongol Period

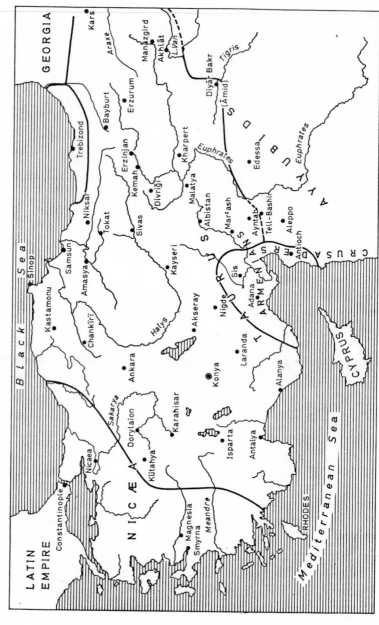

MAP III.   Anatolia on the eve of the Mongol conquest

268

THE ESTABLISHMENT OF THE MONGOL
PROTECTORATE (1243–61)

Fortunately for Kaykhusraw his vizier, unlike himself, did not lose his head. Without consulting him, Muhadhdhab al-Dīn took it upon himself to go in search of Bayjū, who took him to Mughān (the steppe at the south-eastern angle of the Caspian) to find Jurmāghūn. With all necessary deference, Muhadhdhab al-Dīn succeeded in explaining to the Mongol chief, who probably was already convinced of the fact, that a thorough conquest of Rūm would still be a vast task and was not necessary for the security of his own actual territories in view of its outlying situation. As a result, peace was concluded on condition of vassalage or alliance and an annual tribute in gold and silver. Moreover, although there are no direct grounds for the suggestion, it is not impossible to think, on account of the many similar cases known and of the consideration later accorded to Muhadhdhab al-Dīn's son among the Mongols, that he placed himself in some sort of personal dependence in regard to them, making himself quite as much their representative in Rūm as the Sultan's. With this position went a *yarlīgh* (diploma) and a *payza* (authentication) which conferred precedence over any rival and ensured special consideration by any Mongol chief. However that may be, Kaykhusraw, who, knowing of the Mongols' retreat, had regained Konya, welcomed his vizier with a satisfaction that can be imagined.

Jurmāghūn, however, was not the Great Khan, and Muhadhdhab's mission had not been exactly official. On his return, the vizier despatched an official embassy, if not to the Great Khan himself at least to Bātū, his delegate over all the Mongols in the West. The leader of the embassy was Shams al-Dīn al-Isfahānī, the *nā'ib*, whom the Sultan had made Muhadhdhab's deputy in his absence. From the steppe between the Don and the Volga, the site of Bātū's camp, the embassy brought back a *yarlīgh* which established Kaykhusraw as his representative in Rūm. It so happened that, on his return, Shams al-Dīn found that Muhadhdhab had died. The Sultan appointed him as his successor, and in addition made him governor of Kīrshehir as a particular mark of favour. Plans were made to send Kaykhusraw's young son Rukn al-Dīn to Bātū. The worst seemed to have been avoided. The Seljukid State was continuing to exist or starting once again.

But there was still unrest among the Turcomans. From what was seen of them on the eve of the battle of Köse Dagh it will be easily understood that some of them should have tried to take advantage of it to win complete emancipation. The scene of the disturbances now to be described was the Isaurian Taurus. Was there a more definite link between them and the Baba Ishāq incident than the common factor of rebellion? Did some of those who participated in the earlier revolt migrate to the region where the second occurred, a migration such as Shikārī, the future eulogist of the Karamanid family which was soon to form a principality in that part of the Taurus, attributed, in the course of a farrago of legends, to an ancestor of that family – a migration from the country where Baba Ishāq had lived to the one where his own dynasty was to flourish? At the time in question a Turcoman, known only by the name Ahmad given him by Ibn Bībī and the somewhat obscure name Goterinus (Qutb al-Dīn?) given him by Brother Simon, rebelled in the mountains between Konya and Alanya. Supported by his mother's testimony, he passed himself off as a son of Kay-kubādh and claimed that he alone was worthy of power since his 'brother' Kaykhusraw had shown himself incapable of exercising it. To end the matter, Kaykhusraw had to appeal to a neighbouring Armenian lord, Constantine of Lampron, who was then in revolt against the Armeno-Cilician king Hethoum and quite as interested as the Seljukids in crushing the Turcomans. From the chronologically irreconcilable accounts given by the only two sources it is not possible to tell precisely when this crushing defeat took place. But unrest was not ended since, some months later, Ibn Bībī speaks of a new 'king', Vāyuz, of whom nothing further is known, in some unspecified frontier region.

Is there any kind of connection between these events and the campaign in Cilicia in 1245 conducted by Kaykhusraw with the help of the lord of Lampron? In any case, he had an additional personal reason for undertaking it: the Armenians had elected to become the Mongols' allies in the Mediterranean lands, since the Mongols were relying on the support of the Christian minorities against the Muslims and, after Köse Dagh, King Hethoum had handed over to the Mongols Kaykhusraw's mother when she had fled to Cilicia. It was a good thing too to demonstrate that the Seljukid power still existed, at least so far as its neighbours were concerned. They probably secured the tacit approval of the Mongols, who were indifferent to these quarrels. Threatened with the loss of Tarsus, Hethoum handed over the Taurus fortresses, thus allowing the Sultan easier access to the Cilician plain while enabling him to confine the Turcomans within the Isaurian mountains with better effect. This local success was however to have no sequel. Shortly afterwards, in the winter of 1245–6, Kaykhusraw died. The subsequent difficulties of the Seljukid State, and the clearer affirmation of Mongol protection over the Armenians, prevented the renewal of any similar undertaking, and by 1247 the Armenians had recovered the lost territories and compelled the lord of Lampron to seek refuge with his Turkish friends.

Kaykhusraw had three young sons – the eldest, aged 11, 'Izz al-Dīn Kay-kāūs, son of the daughter of a Greek priest; Rukn al-Dīn Kïlïj Arslan, son of a Turkish woman of Konya, aged 9; and 'Alā' al-Dīn Kay-kubādh, son of the Georgian princess, aged 7. The last-named had been nominated by his father as his successor, but since he was the youngest and moreover a weakly child, Shams al-Dīn, when putting him on the throne, made his two brothers 'sit on his right hand and on his left' as his associates. He then divided the chief offices between his friends, and made arrangements for the visit of Rukn al-Dīn to Bātū, planned earlier and now all the more important.

The unfortunate accident that the sons were all minors was however to increase the difficulties of the Seljukid State, and Mongol demands obviously compelled it to reduce the Sultan's forces. The great emirs, whose influence has been noted several times, became correspondingly more difficult to keep in obedience to the Sultanate. Naturally they were jealous of each other and, even before Rukn al-Dīn's departure, some of them had been overthrown and put to death by others who, remarkably enough, had appealed to the popular quasi-militias, the *runūd* and *akhis*, which are to be discussed later and whose importance naturally increased

271

as the Government's power declined. Shams al-Dīn succeeded by skilful manoeuvres in defeating his adversaries in turn and, after marrying the Sultan's mother, was confident that the supreme power would be his. This would perhaps have been so, had not the various factions appealed to the foreign sovereign power, as so often happened. Secret enemies of Shams al-Dīn had infiltrated into Rukn's embassy. Moreover, the Mongols automatically regarded those princes who had come in person to pay homage as preferable to those who were absent. The plotters consequently had no difficulty in getting Bātū to grant Rukn al-Dīn a *yarlīgh* conferring the Sultanate upon him. As he returned through the eastern half of the Seljukid dominion under the escort of a Mongol detachment, the *yarlīgh* secured his recognition. Karatay, *nā'ib* to 'Izz al-Dīn, although no slave of the Mongols, considered that there was no solution except to yield. He planned the murder of the vizier, who was decapitated (Dhu'l-Hijja 646/March 1249).

However, as the Mongol envoys themselves admitted, the question remained whether the *yarlīgh* excluded Rukn al-Dīn's brothers and, if not, how the division of powers should be effected. To ensure the unity of the Seljukid State Karatay wanted an undivided régime by the three brothers. Others favoured a partition of Asia Minor between 'Izz al-Dīn, who would hold the western part, and Rukn al-Dīn, with the eastern half. In spite of the vagueness of the texts, it appears that it was the latter solution that was adopted at first. But when the two brothers, each accompanied by his few troops, met at Akseray, the emirs from both sides, uncertain about their own future in the event of a partition, started a battle. 'Izz al-Dīn's army was victorious. Then, to secure peace, Karatay and his friends introduced an undivided régime. The government was reorganized, and the real master, bearing the title of *atabek* to 'Izz al-Dīn, from then onwards was Karatay (Rabi' I 647/June 1249).

Karatay, a freedman of 'Greek' origin and, perhaps since the time of Kay-kāūs but in any case since the beginning of the reign of Kay-kubādh, attached to the Sultan's personal staff, having been in turn *tāshtdar* and *amīr-dawāt*, was a man of piety who appears to have exerted considerable influence and to have held aloof from the factions, even after becoming *nā'ib*. But his task was a difficult one. Vāyuz had to be crushed, and this was achieved. Bātū, with whom the supporters of Shams al-Dīn Isfahānī had also been intriguing, had to be appeased. In practice, it was to them that the duties of government were given, though under new and remarkable conditions. On the one hand, at least for certain higher posts, these were conferred by virtue of a Mongol *yarlīgh* as if the authority of the Seljukid Sultanate was no longer sufficient to guarantee its own administration. Incidentally, this caused the emirs and notables who were not so favoured to turn against those who benefited from the Mongol protectorate. On the other hand, whereas their payment had in the past always been given them in cash, with the addition in recent times of, at most, some small area of government, the important functionaries or officers are now found partitioning the lands of the State among themselves, to cover their expenses and pay. While the new vizier, Baba Tughrā'ī, and the *mustawfī* remained in Konya, the governor of Malatya, having been promoted to *amīr-ʿārid*, returned to his province. The governor of Sinope, on becoming *nā'ib*, also returned to his, as did some others. The consequences of this new system will be seen later.

The emirs and high officials continued their direct intrigues with the Mongols. Muʿīn al-Dīn Sulaymān, the son of Muhadhdhab al-Dīn and commander of Erzinjān, went to obtain from Bayjū the same favour that had once been extended to his father. Tughrā'ī caused a secret message to be sent to him which Karatay intercepted and had deciphered. Tughrā'ī was saved by Mongol intervention, but he lost the vizierate.

It was certainly necessary to preserve good relations with the Mongols, but Karatay endeavoured to maintain the cohesion of the Seljukid State under their suzerainty and the Muslim character of the régime, in the face of the new non-Muslim masters. What was discussed by the Caliph and the envoy sent to him by Karatay in 1251 is not known, but it is difficult to believe that the interests of Islam, in a country under Mongol suzerainty, were not brought up. A remarkable feature is that, on the coins of this period, as a general rule only the Caliph's name appears, without those of the Sultan or the Mongol overlord. From the same point of view it is also worth noting the *waqf*s established by Karatay, which are discussed later, and which certainly proved beneficial to trade and to the founder's family, but which also based upon Islam the security of institutions jeopardized by the disorganization of the State.

Karatay also tried to regularize the Mongols' demands. In addition to the tribute which perhaps had been fixed, the Seljukid Government had to provide for the upkeep of envoys and troops whom the Mongols might bring to Rūm. In practice, this took the form of incessant demands from Bayjū or his subordinates, the total sum being impossible to predict and beyond the country's means. The envoy, the *amīr-dād* Fakhr al-Dīn ʿAlī (who reappears later) had to try to secure that these obligations should be fixed.

The Mongols however now asked that ʿIzz al-Dīn, who had come of age, being now 19, should be sent to them, as had been done with Rukn al-Dīn. It certainly might have been useful to send him, as the case of Rukn al-Dīn proved. But his absence might also be to his disadvantage since the young man, sacrificing everything to pleasure and heaping rewards on his favourites, enjoyed little popularity. A meeting of the three Sultans was arranged at Kayseri. It was decided to send the youngest, ʿAlāʾ al-Dīn Kay-kubādh, in person to the Great Khan, to make his brothers' excuses. The two elder brothers returned to Konya (1254).

There they soon fell into disagreement. It will be remembered that ʿIzz al-Dīn had a Greek mother: present with him were certain maternal uncles, whose influence some criticized. Possibly he had married a daughter of Vatatzes, the Emperor of Nicaea, and it is certain that for the future it was always from the Greeks that he sought refuge or assistance when needed. However, with Karatay, he represented the party of those who hoped to rescue some part of the traditional régime, as opposed to Rukn al-Dīn, who stood for unconditional surrender to the Mongols. However that may be, a group of emirs arranged for the flight of Rukn al-Dīn, who was proclaimed Sultan, in his name alone, in Kayseri, and recognized in most of the chief towns in the East. But the government of ʿIzz al-Dīn gathered an army against the rebels, whom it defeated after a vain attempt to negotiate. Rukn al-Dīn fell into the hands of his brother, who held a public ceremony to mark his reconciliation with him. Nevertheless, Rukn al-Dīn was confined in Burghlu, on the western borders of Seljukid territory, safe from Mongol intervention (end of 1254?). It was at about that time that the alliance between ʿIzz al-Dīn and Theodore Lascaris of Nicaea was renewed.

It will have been noticed that, in this episode, the name Karatay no longer appears. The texts disagree over the date of his death, some putting it before, others after the revolt. Clearly he may have been ill and unable to take an active part, even before he died. In any event, his death did not bring about any immediate change in the government, the holders of the high offices remaining the same. Fakhr al-Dīn brought back *yarlīghs* which, as had been hoped, fixed their financial obligations. Bayjū incidentally conveyed to him that he could very well recoup himself. Efforts against the Turcomans were continued, with the struggle against the Aghach-eris, who were infesting the Marʿash region on both sides of the frontier. The lord of Marʿash offered the town to various of his neighbours, and in the end the Armenians captured it (1258). But these endeavours were interrupted by the grave news that reached ʿIzz al-Dīn and his followers in 1256.

Without warning, they were told that Bayjū, at the head of all his forces, was invading Asia Minor. The reason however was to be looked for, not in that country's own situation but rather in the evolution of the Mongol Empire. To complete the conquest of the West, the Great Khan had appointed his brother Hülägü to govern Iran, and had made him responsible for the protectorate over the Seljukids, until then a dependency of Bātū in the Russian steppe. At the beginning of 1256 Hülägü established himself in Iran, bringing large numbers of new troops who required grazing-land. Bayjū was ordered to evacuate Mughān, and take his herd to graze on the plateaux of Asia Minor. This was to ignore, or to pretend to do so, the concessions that Mong-Ka had made to the Seljukids, who had never been asked to accommodate on their territory any such groups of the Mongol people itself. We can understand what Bayjū had meant in his words to Fakhr al-Dīn ʿAlī.

Strictly speaking, Bayjū had no warlike intentions. He asked that his troops should be permanently quartered in Asia Minor, and in principle that was all. But it was a serious matter in view of the loss of resources which it entailed for the Seljukid State, the influence it would confer on the leading Mongols at the cost of the leaders of the Seljukid régime, and the inevitable interventions in

their internal disputes. Their hesitations had hitherto delayed
'Alā al-Dīn's actual departure on the long-planned journey to
Mong-Ka. Bayjū's arrival further altered the questions at issue
since, in answer to an envoy from 'Izz al-Dīn, he asked for some
form of investiture in the effective government of Rūm for his
friend Mu'īn al-Dīn Sulaymān. Seeing his forces' movements,
'Alā' al-Dīn wrote in vain to his brothers that it was necessary at
all costs to comply: those in favour of armed resistance prevailed
in Konya. They consisted of strict Muslims, preaching the *jihād*
(holy war), the Sultan's private slaves who feared for their
privileges, and probably even Greeks from the entourage of 'Izz
al-Dīn, who felt confidence in the Turcomans' strength and the
alliance with Nicaea. Among them was the future emperor
Michael Palaeologus, though he had recently fled from the side
of Vatatzes. It was in fact a composite army of Turcomans and
Christians that gathered, the latter being under the command of
Palaeologus. Bayjū advanced quickly. At the first signs of pillaging, all the large towns in the East opened before him. South of
Akseray, near the *khān* of 'Alā' al-Dīn, the two adversaries met.
As always, fear led to defections. The vizier was killed, and
Palaeologus fled to his Turcoman allies in Kastamonu. King
Hethoum, returning from Karakorum, was present in Bayjū's
camp to witness his new triumph. Konya managed to escape being
sacked only by the prompt nomination of Mu'īn al-Dīn as *amīr-
hājib* and *pervāne*, titles which in practice made him the Sultan's
sole authorized spokesman. The second title was in later history to
remain attached to his name.

After collecting together all the available treasure in Antalya,
'Izz al-Dīn had of course fled. At first he went to the frontier-
dwelling Turcomans of Lādīq, and then, realizing that he was
being pursued, thought it safer to cross into Byzantine territory
where his uncles had their connections. In the meanwhile Rukn
al-Dīn had been taken from his prison in Burghlu and, perhaps
after seeking a reconciliation with his brother, he was proclaimed
Sultān in his own name only, at the very time when his brother
went over to the Greeks. But, at the same time, Bayjū had the
fortifications of the Seljukid capital destroyed.

Mu'īn al-Dīn had evidently decided to join the Mongols
unreservedly, but he was not on that account indifferent to the

preservation of the Seljukid State. He simply thought that there was no other way to achieve this. His task was temporarily made somewhat easier by the departure of Bayjū, who had been recalled by Hülägü to take part in the Iraqi campaign which finally brought about, among other things, the destruction of the ʿAbbāsid Caliphate in 1258, after a life of five hundred years. Feeling insecure in Konya, Rukn al-Dīn left for the more loyal towns of Kayseri and Tokat, the place of residence of Muʿīn al-Dīn. But he was given to understand that he was to pay homage to Hülägü. This was to leave a way open for the return of ʿIzz al-Dīn, who had obtained Byzantine reinforcements in exchange for the cession of Lādīq/Laodicaea (which incidentally the Turcomans were soon to re-occupy). He entered Konya in Rabʿ 11 655/May 1257. Meanwhile, in the eastern provinces, a whole collection of the Mongols' enemies had been brought together or had assembled. The Turcomans of Kastamonu attacked Tokat, while the Turcomans, Arabs and in particular the Kurds (one of whom was perhaps the son of Shaykh ʿĀdī, the great saint of the Yazīdīs) in the eastern Taurus and the Mesopotamian borders attacked Mongol detachments, as well as Christians suspected of being in league with them and the supporters of Rukn al-Dīn. In these already confused hostilities, confusion was still further increased because the Ayyūbid of Mayāfāriqīn and the Artukid of Mardin took the opportunity to attack Āmid, which fell. Rukn al-Dīn and Muʿīn al-Dīn, with the help of the Mongols, were beginning to counter-attack and and liberate Tokat, when a new element of confusion was introduced by the return of the embassy from Karakorum.

It had had a complicated history. When with Bātū, it had been overtaken by Baba Tughrāʾī, who had vainly tried to persuade the Mongol chief to substitute him for the Seljukid prince's former companions. Bātū would only allow him to join them. One day ʿAlāʾ al-Dīn was found dead, with no witnesses. He was of delicate health, but Tughrāʾī was accused. Nevertheless, the embassy continued on its way to Mong-Ka, who at once ordered an investigation. ʿIzz al-Dīn's supporters were beginning to convince the Great Khan and to obtain favourable conditions of vassalage for their master, when news arrived of the break between him and Bayjū. Mong-Ka was annoyed, but being anxious above all for peace, which he needed in order to secure the co-operation of Hülägü's vassals in his Baghdad campaign, he considered that it was finally essential to return to the solution of the division of the Sultanate between 'Izz al-Dīn and Rukn al-Dīn. The embassy therefore returned to Asia Minor, where everyone bowed to the supreme sovereign's decisions. A treaty was concluded, granting the eastern provinces, including Kayseri and Sinope, to Rukn al-Dīn and the remainder to 'Izz al-Dīn. Coins and inscriptions confirm this partition (end of 1257?). Incidentally, this partition was to some extent theoretical only, since the two princes both accepted Tughrā'ī as the sole vizier. At the same time Theodore II Lascaris disappeared from Nicaea. Michael Palaeologus succeeded in returning there and afterwards won the throne. Still later, in 1261, he set out from there to reconquer Constantinople from the Latins.

For the Seljukids, however, it still remained to make peace with Hülägü. The two princes went to him, with Tughrā'ī and Mu'īn al-Dīn. The Mongol prince made no difficulty over ratifying the partition, to which he added the restitution of Āmid, which had just been handed over to him. Baghdad had fallen, but he was now preparing to subjugate Upper Mesopotamia and Syria, and needed peace on his northern flank. On his orders 'Izz al-Dīn and Rukn al-Dīn took part in the Syrian campaign and the capture of Aleppo and Damascus, and at the same time they tried in vain to secure a peaceful submission by the princes of Mayāfāriqīn and Mardin to the Mongols. Meanwhile, they themselves and Tughrā'ī contracted loans from the Mongol treasury, the repayment of which, when added to the ordinary and carefully calculated tribute, was to prove a heavy burden on the budget for the years that followed. On leaving Syria, Hülägü allowed the two princes to return to Asia Minor, while compelling 'Izz al-Dīn to hand over to Rukn al-Dīn the *yarlīgh* and the *payza* bestowed on him by Mong-Ka. Tughrā'ī died at about the same time (1260).

These two events marked the start of new tension between 'Izz al-Dīn and Rukn al-Dīn. The unity of the vizierate could not be maintained. 'Izz al-Dīn chose Fakhr al-Dīn 'Alī, Rukn al-Dīn added the vizierate to the other offices held by Mu'īn al-Dīn on the strength of a *yarlīgh* from Hülägü. In fact, the two halves of the Seljukid Sultanate were by no means in the same relationship with the Mongol protector. Rukn's was kept under far more direct control. Since the Mongols had sent agents for the special purpose of supervising the repayment of the loans, ʿIzz al-Dīn, who had done nothing about it, was once more accused of bad faith and of preparing for a revolt with the help of the Turcomans (although at that time he was engaged in a difficult campaign against Mehmed-Beg, the leader of the frontier-dwelling Turcomans near Denizli/Lādīq) and of Egypt. It should be remembered that, at the very end of 1260, the Mamluks of Egypt had just inflicted the first defeat on the Mongols in Syria, at ʿAyn-Jālūt, and were re-occupying the country. With their new Sultan Baybars, an energetic and highly capable leader, they appeared to be the great hope of all the Mongols' enemies. It was easy for ʿIzz al-Dīn to keep in touch with them by way of Antalya. He tried in vain to negotiate personally with his brother. From the East, a new Mongol army advanced on Konya. Muʿīn had the vizierate of the re-unified Seljukid territory offered to Fakhr al-Dīn, on condition that he abandoned ʿIzz al-Dīn. Believing any resistance impossible, Fakhr al-Dīn allowed himself to be won over. ʿIzz al-Dīn fled, via Antalya, to Constantinople, which his old friend Michael Palaeologus had just reconquered from the Latins. On 14 Ramadan 659/13 August 1261, Rukn al-Dīn entered Konya.

In Constantinople ʿIzz al-Dīn was to be cruelly disappointed. The policy of Michael Palaeologus was now one of alliance with the Mongols of Iran against those of Russia, with whom the former had just broken. He even disregarded his frontier in Asia Minor, which no longer possessed the same importance for him, in order not to risk any clashes with the Turcomans which might endanger his European policy or the assistance which he would still have to seek from them in the always possible contingency of a break with the Mongols. For this reason, ʿIzz al-Dīn finally became an embarrassment, or perhaps his friends eventually indulged in too open criticism. After being imprisoned, he was freed by Mongol troops from Russia and lived until 1279–80 in the Crimea. It was from there that his sons were later to set out, to try their fortunes in Asia Minor. It is to his followers that is attributed the origin of the Turks still living today in the Dobruja, and their name of Gagauz is perhaps a reminiscence of his own name Kay-kāūs.

THE GOVERNMENT OF MUʿĪN AL-DĪN THE PERVĀNE AND THE CRISIS OF 1276–8

The period extending from the flight of ʿIzz al-Dīn or, alternatively, from the appointment a little earlier of Muʿīn al-Dīn Sulaymān (still known as the *pervāne*) as the real head of the government under Rukn al-Dīn, until his tragic death in 1277, marks a stage in the decline of the Seljukid State, an attempt to strike a balance – a difficult feat which, save at the end, he managed to achieve – between the desire to retain the Mongols' full confidence and the re-organization of the State in some of its traditional aspects, particularly as a Muslim State. The task was not easy but, whatever his personal ambitions, it may be thought that Muʿīn al-Dīn succeeded in giving the inhabitants of Rūm a respite, or indeed a period of recovery, after the ordeals of recent years. Only the political aspect of this history is considered here. Other aspects will be discussed later.

It was by no means true that, as a sequel to the capture of Konya, all the Seljukid territory was secured for Rukn al-Dīn. The supporters of ʿIzz al-Dīn and the Turcomans long continued to disturb the provinces of Chankïrï, Ankara, Kastamonu and even districts of the Dānishmendid province of central Anatolia, but the situation was especially serious in the west and south. In the west, in order to challenge ʿIzz al-Dīn, Mehmed-Beg the master of Denizli, Khunas, Dalman and other places had made a request for direct investiture to Hülägü, who had consented, on condition that he went in person to his court. Mehmed refused to do so, a Turco-Mongol force set out against him and defeated him and, we are told, 'the Mongols' authority was recognized as far as the frontiers of Istanbul' (1262). But in fact Mehmed's son-in-law ʿAlī-Beg, by supporting the Mongols, had succeeded in having himself invested with the inheritance, and the Turcomans in that province continued to constitute an autonomous group, as will be seen shortly.

In the Isaurian-Cilician Taurus, very close to Konya itself, after the defeat of the Seljukid pretender, new dissidents are recorded in 1254 and 1258, in the hinterland of Korykos. It will be remembered that, a little further to the north, it was some Turcomans who captured Rukn al-Dīn in 1256. In about 1260 Karaman makes his first appearance in these regions. The founder of a dynasty that lasted for two hundred years, it is not known whether he had any connections with the chiefs mentioned during the course of the preceding events. Later poet-historians of the family were to recount tales in which truth and imagination, confusion and exaggeration are interwoven and hard to disentangle. Karaman and his immediate successors are depicted as surrounded by all the leaders of the future Turcoman, Kurdish and even Mongol dynasties, among others, which proves that there was no question of exclusively Turkish patriotism. The territory they governed is represented as having been officially conferred on them by the glorious Kay-kubādh in person. All this is, to say the least, highly exaggerated. Karaman's father was said to be a certain Nūre Sūfī, who had come from Azerbaijan, staying for some years near Sivas. This, when generalized, is a reference to the actual migrations brought about by Khwārizmian and Mongol pressure, and moreover it suggests some perceptible connection, if not precisely with Baba Ishāq, at least with circles influenced by religious propaganda of that kind – there is a reference to a Khorasanian *sūfī*, Baba Ilyās, with whom both Nūre Sūfī and Baba Ishāq are said to have been in touch – and also to the fact that the first chiefs who brought in these Turcomans were equally leaders in the field of religion. For the rest, it cannot be admitted that these Turcomans held the whole Ermenek region, from Laranda to Korykos, quite as early as certain historians have claimed, since Korykos in particular belonged to the Hospitallers and the Seljukid governors of the province are well-known. Yet the fact remains that it was certainly there that their earliest exploits took place and that it was indeed to that region that Kay-kubādh had brought them to populate his recent conquests.

Although the points of detail can probably never be determined, it can be accepted that Karaman started life as a woodcutter and timber merchant who brought supplies from the western Taurus to the little town of Laranda. It is not known how he became leader of a group of Turcomans, or in what way his rise could be connected with the disturbances noted in this region after 1243 and later, between 1254 and 1256. Official writers described him as a highway robber who, however, possessed what was almost a regular army. It is impossible to reconcile the three sources describing his activities, Ibn Bībī, Aqsarāyī, and an Armenian chronicle, but some features emerge clearly. The fall of ʿIzz al-Dīn is said to have been one of the causes and possibly was the occasion of or pretext for his uprising. ʿIzz al-Dīn was regarded, relatively speaking, as an ally of the Turcomans against the Mongols, and the efforts of Rukn al-Dīn to win the support of the Karamanids were vain. At one time they went so far as to make a serious attack on Konya itself, which was not very far from the western Taurus, and the personal intervention of Muʿīn al-Dīn, apparently with the co-operation of the Mongol expedition of 1262 against Denizli, was needed to defeat them. But they also fought on the other side of their mountain range, against the Armenians on the Isaurian-Cilician borders. King Hethoum himself had to intervene, and succeeded in repulsing them. Probably as a result of this last war, Karaman died in about 1262, while some of his children or members of his family were taken prisoner. The central authority was to some extent re-established, at least in Ermenek where, until 1276, an official Seljukid governor held office without any recorded difficulties. Even more clearly, however, than in regard to the Turcomans of Denizli, this recognition of some kind of Seljukid supremacy does not imply any serious disorganization of the Turcomans in the western Taurus; and soon, at their head, and with more or less official recognition, they were to have Karaman's son Mehmed Beg (to be distinguished of course from his namesake in Denizli).

The same aggressive spirit appeared among the Turcomans everywhere, even though it did not lead to such immediately grave results. The systematic expeditions ordered by Hülägü had put to flight a section of the Agach-eris in the eastern Taurus, whose proximity to the Mamluks of Syria he found disturbing, but some still remained. Others, spreading out along the Georgian borders, that is to say close to the lines of communication so vital to the Mongols, no doubt for that reason were repressed with particular promptitude. From then onwards there were Mongol troops stationed permanently throughout almost the whole of Asia Minor. Living off the country, they were prepared to intervene on the Syrian frontiers, and took part in the struggle against the Turcomans and in the maintenance of order. Muʿīn al-Dīn had accepted the inevitable consequences of the weakening of the Seljukid army. Owing to the presence of the Mongols, some reduction in its size was financially necessary, but they made good its deficiencies and at the same time would repress any possible indiscipline. Inasmuch as Muʿīn al-Dīn was able, by the confidence he inspired, to persuade them to allow him to govern, the harm done was perhaps the least that was possible. In about 1262, it could be accepted that the Turco-Mongols had succeeded, if not in crushing the danger presented by the Turcomans, at least in restricting it to districts lying outside the vital zones of the State. The Mongols, moreover, attached importance only to those zones from the exploitation of which they could draw profit.

At the same time Muʿīn al-Dīn had made away with those who were suspect, besides his own personal adversaries. The appointment to the vizierate in the strict sense, that is to say to administrative control, of Fakhr al-Dīn ʿAlī in no way diminished the supremacy of Muʿīn al-Dīn, who, on an inscription, gave himself the title 'King of the emirs and the viziers'. Meanwhile an evolution, the beginnings of which were observed immediately after Köse Dagh, became more marked. On the pretext of defraying the costs of his vizierate, Fakhr al-Dīn, or more accurately his sons, received Kütahya, Sandïklï, Gurgurum, Akshehir, and later (Afyon) Karahisār. Bahā al-Dīn, who was related to Muʿīn al-Dīn, was granted autonomous control of Antalya and the other southern maritime provinces, with the title *malik al-sawāhil* 'King of the shores'; Masʿūd ibn Kathīr, a follower of the *pervāne* of long standing, became *beglerbeg* and received Nigde, controlling the central Cilician Taurus, as an *iqtāʿ*; finally, the *pervāne* himself held the powerful fortress of Tokat, with other Dānishmendid regions, and soon Sinope also. These were all regions which in some respects constituted marches, where the concentration of power in the hands of an independent chief, whether the prospective enemy was Greek, Armenian or even Turcoman, could also present certain advantages. Tāj al-Dīn Muʿtazz, whose concern was with the

Mongol loan, for his part received Kastamonu as a security, and soon afterwards Akseray and Develi Karahisār as well.

Sinope has just been mentioned. In actual fact, in 657/1259 according to Ibn Shaddād, in 1254 according to the colophon of a Greek manuscript, taking advantage of the disturbances in the Seljukid State, the people of Trebizond had recaptured the town. After difficult operations, conducted with forces from the Dānish-mendid province simultaneously by land and sea, with their base at Samsun, which had remained Turkish, the town was re-taken and, at the time of Hülägü's death (1265), the *pervāne*, when he went to pay homage to the new Ilkhān Abagha, obtained from him the concession of Sinope as his own personal possession. As inscriptions show, he immediately set to work to rebuild it as a solidly fortified and firmly Muslim base.

Throughout the whole history of the years during which his name had held such importance, Rukn al-Dīn appears merely as a wholly passive puppet. On reaching manhood and becoming tired of his situation, he was guilty of childishly imprudent language. Since he disapproved of the appropriation of Sinope by Mu'in al-Dīn, the latter was easily convinced that the Sultan was plotting against him. Abagha authorized him to deal severely with the Turks, no matter whom. With Turco-Mongol contingents of rather different kinds, he advanced towards Akseray. Rukn al-Dīn had a stormy confrontation with him, as a result of which he was strangled at a banquet (1265?). In his place was established his son Kaykhusraw III, whose age – between 2 and 6 years old – could threaten no one, and for whom in addition the *pervāne* made himself tutor and regent.

From that moment, for several years, the chronicles report almost nothing, at least of a military character. Clearly it is a sign of a relative stabilization. This made it possible for Turkish troops to assist the Mongol troops, both on the Syrian borders against the Mamluk forces which were consolidating themselves there even beyond the middle Euphrates, and also indeed on the Caucasian frontier, against their enemy kinsmen from Russia (the Golden Horde). Little by little, a difficult but logical understanding was reached with the Armenians of Cilicia who were, like the Seljukids, the vassals or allies of the Mongols and the enemies of Baybars, and who like them were concerned with driving back the Turcomans.

However, a slow decline can be seen in the situation of Muʿīn al-Dīn, due partly to his ambition, partly to the results of the cupidity or mistrust of certain Mongol chiefs. Muʿīn al-Dīn was so unwilling to recognize any authority other than his own that eventually, when Fakhr al-Dīn ʿAlī had received a demand for money from the former Sultan ʿIzz al-Dīn, he had him arrested. His sons, on approaching Abagha, secured his liberation and also his restoration to the vizierate. Nor was it easier for the *pervāne* to tolerate the Mongols' agents – not, of course, that he was hostile to the Mongols, but simply because he intended to be their sole senior representative in Rūm. Naturally these agents were now intensifying their activities. The impression is given that, perhaps from fear of Mamluk intrigues, Abagha thought it necessary to have his own direct informers in Rūm, who might even be authorized in due course to take personal initiatives. Both for reasons of precaution and in order to set up some kind of apanages for them, the Ilkhān sent to Rūm certain princes of his own family who thought it their duty to meddle in the administration of taxation and the appointment of officials, on the pretext of the repayments which were still overdue. All this caused friction between the *pervāne* and themselves.

In view not only of this state of affairs but also of the setbacks suffered by the Mongols in their struggle with Baybars, it is possible that Muʿīn al-Dīn had begun to envisage procuring from the latter some kind of safeguard for himself. This at least is what seems to emerge, not from the sources written in Asia Minor, which are silent on this subject, but at least from the *Life of Baybars* by the Syro-Egyptian Ibn Shaddād. The point of departure perhaps lay in an initiative by Abagha himself. No longer primarily a conqueror such as his ancestors had been, Abagha, finding it impossible to continue to expand and faced by the rupture with his kinsmen in Russia, was, like the *pervāne*, seeking for a peace settlement that would allow the internal re-organization of the war-devastated territories he governed. At his request Samaghar, his relative and representative in Rūm, and the *pervāne* sounded out Baybars as to the conditions for an eventual peace, and then a Mamluk mission, accompanied by Muʿīn al-Dīn, visited Abagha (1272). No compromise could be reached, and in the following year a Mongol expedition, in which Muʿīn al-Dīn took part, was led against Birejik/Bīra, guarding one of the passages from Upper Mesopotamia into Syria at the bend of the middle Euphrates. While visiting Abagha, the *pervāne* had asked him to recall his brother Ajāy, his deputy, together with Samaghar; his recall being delayed, the *pervāne* was afraid that Ajāy had been informed, and so suggested to Baybars a campaign in Asia Minor, promising him his vassalage in that event. However, as Ajāy was then recalled, negotiations were broken off. The simple military leaders who replaced the 'prince of the blood' were more tractable for Muʿīn al-Dīn, but Abagha did not intend to relax his control at the moment when the international situation made it more than ever necessary, and the new chiefs or *noyans* received orders to send detailed reports on the administration of the country, and including the *pervāne*'s conduct of affairs. Fiscal reforms were probably introduced. Muʿīn al-Dīn, anxious at the same time to bring Baybars' forces nearer and yet not to compromise himself with him, urged him to attack his Armenian neighbour Leo II, a vassal of the Mongols, although the *pervāne* had previously tried to be reconciled with Leo. In 1275, Ajāy was allowed to return to Asia Minor. It is difficult to reconstruct exactly the sequence of the subsequent intrigues from the single account, probably derived by Ibn Shaddād from ambassadors' reports. There is little doubt that Ajāy tried to get rid of the *pervāne*, and that the latter in turn tried to get rid of him, to cement relations with Baybars and, when Abagha at last had some idea of what was happening, disarm his suspicions. In 1276 a new campaign against Bīra, undertaken with joint forces, had to be abandoned on account of the atmosphere of disagreement and mutual suspicion. Henceforward Muʿīn al-Dīn believed that no other policy was possible save duplicity, though that too was rendered difficult by the clearer attitudes being adopted by those around him, some favouring Baybars as the defender of Islam, others the Mongols, either from self-interest or from fear of their enduring power. After instigating the murder of Sarkis, the Armenian bishop of Erzinjān, who possessed great influence with Abagha (but not with Muʿīn al-Dīn), Bichār, the Kurdish chief to whom Malatya had been granted, fled to Egypt, just at the time when the *pervāne* was conducting a sister of the young Seljukid Sultan to Tabriz for her forthcoming marriage to the

Ilkhān. It was then that the drama, hitherto concealed, burst out into the open, though it is not possible to tell how far this coincidence had been planned by Mu'īn al-Dīn.

During his absence, Ibn Kathīr, who had previously been associated with the *pervāne*'s policy and who, as a governor of Nigde, had relatively easy communications with Baybars, called in a Mamluk force, perhaps without the *pervāne*'s knowledge, to avert the consequences of an eventual *rapprochement* between him and the Mongol suzerain. Baybars however was unwilling to commit himself to any such undertaking except on the condition of a specific meeting at Kayseri and an oath which named the emirs participating. This procedure naturally brought the project to light, and Ibn Kathīr, threatened with assassination by a group which had pretended to support him only in order to be able to denounce him, was compelled to forestall their action by doing away with them. The *pervāne*'s son, and deputy for him in his absence, could offer no direct resistance, especially as Ibn Kathīr seized the Sultan himself. While the rebel chief took the Sultan to Nigde, he withdrew to the family fief of Tokat where he could wait and watch (1276).

The conspirators certainly seem to have decided or been compelled to act precipitately. Baybars had never envisaged a campaign in high summer. When the moment came and he was able to set out, the *pervāne* was on his way back, and the Mongol troops accompanying him left him with no choice but to fight against the Mamluk Sultan, with the consolation that he could afterwards boast to Baybars, in the event of the latter's victory, that he himself had drawn the enemy into the trap. The Sultan was recaptured and Ibn Kathīr, entrenched in Lu'lu', was handed over by the commander of the place. A great judicial assembly was held according to the Mongol custom before the chiefs of the Ilkhānid army. The Sultan was pardoned on account of his youth and the pressure exerted upon him, but Ibn Kathīr and others, although they had denounced the intrigues of the *pervāne* himself, or perhaps for that very reason, were executed. However, in the other camp Baybars imprisoned the Turkish emirs whose families had just abandoned his cause.

All in all, this would not have been too serious, if it had been merely a question of settling accounts between various notables.

But, in order to launch his revolt, Ibn Kathīr had given a free hand to, and indeed lavished encouragement on, the Turcomans in his neighbourhood, particularly the Karamanids, who moreover had entered into direct contact with Baybars. 'Then', says Aqsarāyī, 'the brilliant Seljukid State was suddenly brought to the ground.' Muhammad ibn Karaman and his men were not content with attacking the few Mongols who were watching over their territory. After the fall of Ibn Kathīr, the governor of Nigde tried to attack them in their Ermenek region and was crushed: the encouragement to the rebels can be imagined. Reinforcements sent by the sons of Fakhr al-Dīn 'Alī from Karahisār, and others sent from Antalya while the 'King of Shores' was organizing the defence of Konya, only achieved limited success and, for example, could not even prevent the pillaging of a Franco-Armenian trade caravan. Perhaps in the end the Turcomans would once more have been contained if at that moment, at the end of the winter which had favoured them, and interrupting everything else, the news had not come of the invasion of Baybars.

Despite the defeat of his imprudent supporters, or because some revenge for it was required to keep the loyalty of the rest, it was at that point that Baybars decided he could undertake the long contemplated expedition, for which he counted on the assistance of the Turcomans, some emirs, and possibly the *pervāne*. Later the *pervāne* was accused of having so minimized the danger of invasion to the Mongols that, despite the warnings of Leo II the Armenian, the defence of Asia Minor had been organized only in a half-hearted way. The concentration of the available troops had still not been completed when news came from Albistan of the arrival of the Egyptian army, advancing against Kayseri. Muhyī al-Dīn ibn 'Abd al-Zāhir, Baybars' secretary, in the *Life* of his master that he wrote, has preserved the journal of the expedition's march. The battle was fought near Albistan, on the upper Jihān. It proved to be a crushing defeat for the Mongols, almost all of whose leaders were killed or captured. Even the *pervāne*'s contingent, which had been left aside by the Mongols out of suspicion, was involved in the defeat, and a large number of his officers, including his son, were taken prisoner (10 Dhu'l-Qa'da 675/16 April 1277). There was now nothing to stop the victor's advance on Kayseri, and he entered it five days later, while Mu'īn al-Dīn, with the Sultan and

Fakhr al-Dīn ʿAlī, took refuge in Tokat. A number of emirs surrendered to Baybars and then, in accordance with the ceremonial observed at the accession of Seljukid princes, the Mamluk Sultan was placed on the royal throne. The Egyptians admired the town's public buildings, as well as the wealth of the *pervāne* and his friends, from such of it as had fallen into their hands.

To have been placed on a throne was, however, not enough to ensure that Baybars' victory was conclusive, as he very well knew. Apart from the Turcomans in the Taurus, the anticipated general rising of Asia Minor in his favour and against the Mongols had not taken place. Perhaps the Mamluk Sultan had misled some of his supporters by opposing the measures that they wanted taken against the Christians, who were regarded indiscriminately as the Mongols' confederates. In any event, the army had to be fed, and for that purpose the treasures of Kayseri were of little avail. If only it had been known what the *pervāne* was preparing! A letter came from him, telling Baybars to wait. Baybars realized clearly what it signified – he had not defeated all the Mongol forces and Abagha himself was preparing an imminent intervention, with forces even stronger than those he had crushed. In these circumstances, he judged it necessary to retreat, as was therefore done on 28 April. A different route from the previous one was taken, in order that foodstuffs might be found. Although a demonstration of power had been given, it was nevertheless also a demonstration of the limits of that power.

In the meanwhile, however, the Karamanids had themselves launched a vast offensive, under more favourable conditions. Reinforced by the Eshref and the Menteshe (who will be referred to again, and whose names now occur in history for the first time), they attacked Konya, which fell, being out of reach of any possible help. The governor, it seems, had refused to rely upon the popular militia of the *akhi*s, whom he suspected, perhaps unjustly, of complicity with the Turcomans. The Turcomans had discovered a certain Jimri (the leper) who passed himself off as Siyāvush, a son of the ex-Sultan ʿIzz al-Dīn. The departure of Baybars doubtless made it more urgent to have a Sultan of the legitimate descent capable of rallying enthusiasm. Negotiations had in fact been entered into with ʿIzz al-Dīn in the Crimea, but too much time was bound to elapse before he could arrive or send one of his sons.

Consequently a pretence was made of accepting the legitimacy of the false Siyāvush, who was proclaimed Sultan with the insignia taken from Kay-kubādh's tomb and married to a daughter of the late Sultan Rukn al-Dīn, present there at the time. Naturally, the new Sultan made Mehmed ibn Karaman his vizier, and distributed honours and titles to the Turcoman notables. Remarkably enough, as these latter knew neither Arabic nor even Persian, a chancellery using the Turkish language was established, something never before seen in Seljukid Asia Minor.

Some time earlier, however, to keep watch over the Turcomans on the frontiers, a warlike group had been installed in western Anatolia. They were known by the name Germiyan and were probably Kurdish and Turkish half-breeds, whose home until then had been somewhere to the east of Malatya. Bahā al-Dīn, the 'King of the Shores', and the sons of Fakhr al-Dīn ʿAlī in Kara-hisār, rallied to them and tried to fight the Turcomans. In the battle which took place to the north-west of Konya in the neighbourhood of Altuntash, Bahā al-Dīn and the sons of Fakhr al-Dīn were killed. Their success kindled the rebels' enthusiasm and attracted others to them. An adventurer seized Akseray as his own possession.

Only then did Abagha's army arrive. Having come too late to take Baybars by surprise, he surveyed the sad relics on the battlefield of Albistan and was indignant to see no corpses of Anatolians there. Then he entered Kayseri, where he had numerous suspects executed and Christian captives held to ransom. Such Turcomans as could be discovered were hunted down. What did he think about the *pervāne*? It was almost inevitable that the recent disaster should cause him to be accused of bad advice at the least, and that the accusations made against him on various earlier occasions should come to mind. It was no less certain that it would be difficult for the Ilkhān to find anyone else of the same quality, whether native or Mongol, to govern Rūm, and that his condemnation might stir up strong resentment. No doubt the *pervāne* relied on these sentiments or on his own presence of mind, or was prepared to risk his life in order to limit the reprisals taken by the Mongols against the Muslims. He made no attempt to flee, but on the contrary placed himself at Abagha's disposal when the latter came to Kamakh. On withdrawing to the east after visiting Kayseri,

Abagha asked the *pervāne* to hand over the fortress of Kughūniya, which was his own possession, and Muʿīn al-Dīn gave orders accordingly to the governor. But the governor refused to comply, and Muʿīn al-Dīn was thought to be in complicity with him. All the old charges against him were revived, including the death of Rukn al-Dīn and his own absence from the battle of Albistan. Abagha heard evidence of the Egyptian negotiations. He decided to condemn him to death. On I Rabīʿ I 672/2 August 1277, the man who had governed the Seljukid State for nearly twenty years was executed. But, as will appear, his sons were to recover most of his possessions.

The death of Muʿīn al-Dīn Sulaymān the *pervāne* could be regarded as symbolizing the end of a generation, and it was not by chance that Aqsarāyī linked it with the deaths of a whole series of celebrated figures, even though they were of very different character, such as Jalāl al-Dīn Rūmī and Sadr al-Dīn Qonevī, of whom more will be said later. It seemed as though all those who had been moulded politically and intellectually during the period of Seljukid splendour had now perished together, and that the former brilliance had vanished with them. The sole survivor was the aged Fakhr al-Dīn ʿAlī, whose sons were dead and whose political role, if it existed, is less evident than his activity as a builder. As for the *pervāne* himself, the obvious strength of his personality makes it all the more to be regretted that the nature of the surviving documents renders it impossible to form any true appreciation of it.

While the trial of Muʿīn al-Dīn was taking place, a start had already been made on making good the recent misfortunes. From the Syrian side there was no difficulty, for in Muharram 676/June 1277 Baybars died, and his immediate successor was in no position to resume the offensive. But there was still a whole sector of Anatolia where the Turcomans were in complete control. Against it, Abagha sent his brother Kangirtay, assisted by his own vizier, the celebrated Shams al-Dīn Juwaynī, and also by the vizier of Rūm, Fakhr al-Dīn ʿAlī, and young Kaykhusraw, who had come at once to put himself under his protection. Kughūniya and Tokat were captured, then Akseray, where the same number of men as had perished at Albistan were now sent as slaves to the Mongols. Finally Konya fell. No defence of it had been made by the Turcomans, who were pursued as far as their own territory of

Ermenek. Summer compelled the Mongol army to fall back on Kayseri and slowed down operations. The Turcomans returned twice to assault the walls of Konya, where the *akhis* fought against them. But at the end of the summer the Mongols reappeared, and this time succeeded in surrounding the Turcomans in the mountains. In the defeat, Mehmed and two of his brothers were killed. The news caused other frontier districts which had remained uncertain, to rally to them.

In respect of the Turcomans of Kastamonu there was no ground for complaint, since they had helped to defend Sinope when it was attacked by the people of Trebizond under cover of the disturbed conditions. In the west, however, the situation was entirely different. There, Jimri had succeeded in escaping and building up a force in the Karahisār region, which had become disorganized as a result of the deaths of Fakhr al-Dīn's sons. Unwilling to see the Mongols ravage the country, Fakhr al-Dīn secured their agreement that he alone should be empowered to recover the family fief. With the help of the Germiyan and contingents collected in Ankara, he succeeded in defeating and capturing Jimri, and Kaykubādh's parasol was recovered from him. Jimri himself was burnt alive, and his skin, stuffed with straw, was paraded through all the towns of Rūm, mounted on an ass. Even though they had perhaps not participated in Jimri's uprising, the Turcomans of Burghlu and Denizli had refused to join in its repression. The Seljukid army then invaded their territory, 'Alī Beg was taken prisoner and executed, and Fakhr al-Dīn's grandsons put in possession of Karahisār and the other family properties.

Outwardly, it could therefore be said that, towards the end of 1278, the situation had once again become similar to what it had been until two or three years before. But, as Aqsarāyī remarks, the Turcomans, though hemmed in, were not destroyed, and the death of one chief or another did not really affect their life. And the organization of Asia Minor was never again to be what it had been under the *pervāne*, for good or ill. Though some features may have been preserved, the Mongol protectorate was now succeeded by a system of direct administration.

3

THE GOVERNMENT OF THE MONGOLS

In addition to the territorial reconquest of 1278 there was also an administrative reorganization. This time, however, it was not limited to the sporadic, semi-private interventions of preceding years. The reorganization was carried out openly by the Ilkhānid government itself. Along with his army, Abagha had brought his vizier, the famous Shams al-Dīn Juwaynī, who with the qualified Seljukid high officials considered what measures, particularly financial, should be taken. These measures, to be described later, were not exclusively attempts at restoration, but also included the introduction of specifically Mongol institutions. Moreover, while reserving the rights of the Mongol treasury, Shams al-Dīn succeeded in repressing the lawless exactions of certain Mongol chiefs. After his departure, Abagha found it useful to have the control of the government entrusted to Fakhr al-Dīn ʿAlī, not only as vizier but also as the Ilkhān's deputy, while a friend of Fakhr al-Dīn was deputy for the young Kaykhusraw III, that is to say in practice his authorized representative. But these nominations, like those of other high officials, were for the future made systematically by the Ilkhānid power itself. This development was inevitable, as Muʿīn al-Dīn himself had, it seems, fully realized. From the moment when the Mongols had broken the Seljukids' strength, they were obliged to take over ever greater responsibilities from them. And because the Mongols' own power, though still apparently formidable, could no longer be regarded as invincible since the successes of Baybars, the control of regional affairs became correspondingly more advantageous for the Ilkhān.

Under Baybars' second successor, Kalāūn (1279–89), the Mamluk army once again became a real threat, and the assistance it received from the Karamanids during its conquest of Rūm-Qalʿa, on the Euphrates, from the Armenians, showed that they were still in existence. Abagha appointed his brother Mangutimur, assisted by Anatolian contingents, to command an expedition against Syria, but it was defeated (1281). They then both died (1282). The new Ilkhān, Ahmad, was a Muslim, and unpopular with the Mongols since from their point of view his conversion was premature. As a Muslim, however, he was anxious to consolidate his dominions by securing peace, which his conversion made feasible. But the negotiations, in which notables from Rūm took part, proved a failure, and in 1283 the Mamluk army again made raids as far as the gates of Malatya.

At the same time a new source of anxiety had just appeared in Asia Minor. The former Sultan 'Izz al-Dīn had died in the Crimea, and his eldest son Ghiyāth al-Dīn Mas'ūd, after settling for a time in Constantinople, now proclaimed himself Sultan and resolved to reconquer his father's throne. One of his brothers who had gone to Sinope to prepare the way for him was captured, but Mas'ūd himself, disembarking shortly afterwards (summer of 1280), made his peace with the prince of Kastamonu and went to Abagha. While leaving the Sultanate to Kaykhusraw, Abagha thought it might be useful to grant Mas'ūd the right to govern the Karamanid territory. However, among the Karamanids, a nephew of Mas'ūd, 'Alā' al-Dīn Kay-kubādh, had also disembarked. No doubt assisted by the recollections of the Turcomans' links with 'Izz al-Dīn, as the Jimri incident had shown, he had secured their recognition as sovereign. Defeated by the troops of Kaykhusraw and Fakhr al-Dīn 'Alī, he fled to Cilicia, but was to reappear later. Is there some connection between these facts and the Ilkhān's attitude to Mas'ūd? Be that as it may, Mas'ūd did not go to the territory that had been allotted to him, and Kaykhusraw in his turn went to visit Abagha, in order to put a stop to his cousin's intrigues and obtain reinforcements against the Karamanids. Thanks to a Mongol contingent, he in fact succeeded in driving back the Turcomans almost to Ermenek and freeing Konya from their threat. All this proves how superficial the victory of 1278 had been, and that of 1282 was no less so.

Unfortunately for Kaykhusraw, at this juncture Abagha died. His successor Ahmad had to face two revolts, one in Khorasan led by his brother Arghūn, and a second in Asia Minor led by another brother, Kangirtāy, who died during it. Kaykhusraw had accompanied Kangirtāy, whether willingly or under compulsion. Ahmad, who in any case was reversing his predecessor's policy, then decided to confer the undivided Sultanate on Mas'ūd. Fakhr al-Dīn bowed to this change, which was of little importance in view of the Sultan's lack of any real authority. And Kaykhusraw was put to death (Dhu'l-Qa'da 682/March 1284).

Some months later, Ahmad in his turn was overthrown by Arghūn, who was not a Muslim, and who acceded to a request for the partition of the Sultanate put forward by Kaykhusraw's widow on behalf of her two young sons. Arghūn's brothers, Hulājū and Gaykhātū, his representatives in Rūm, once again introduced a partition such as had existed, for good or ill, in the time of 'Izz al-Dīn and Rukn al-Dīn, giving Mas'ūd the eastern part, with Kayseri as its capital, and Kaykhusraw's sons the western part, with Konya as capital. Once installed, the princess decided that it was only by reaching an understanding with the Turcomans that her situation could be guaranteed. The titles nā'ib (lieutenant) and beglerbeg she conferred respectively on Kūnārī-Beg, the new Karamanid chief, and Sulaymān-Beg, chief of her Eshref Turcoman neighbours, a political step resented by the populace of Konya and by Fakhr al-Dīn 'Alī. While the princess was visiting Arghūn, Mas'ūd's adherents, covertly supported by the vizier and the Mongols, took Konya. The two young princes were put to death (1285). Mas'ūd himself did not establish himself in the town until 1286, at a time when Gaykhātū, Arghūn's only remaining representative in Asia Minor, was leading an expedition into Anatolia proper.

The situation there at that point seems difficult to follow. The Karamanids and Eshref cannot have given the children of their old enemy Kaykhusraw the support that his widow had counted on. In any case, they do not seem to have reacted in a hostile way to the victory of Mas'ūd, who, as the son of 'Izz al-Dīn, should therefore have been more acceptable to them. On the other hand the Germiyan, who, as was seen earlier, had been settled in western Asia Minor to help the Seljukids against the Turcomans, now revealed themselves as enemies of the new Sultan, and they had deprived the grandsons of Fakhr al-Dīn 'Alī of part of their inheritance. For that reason the campaign that Mas'ūd and Fakhr al-Dīn 'Alī mounted, with Mongol contingents, against the Germiyan, was for the most part at Fakhr al-Dīn's expense. It was similar in character to the expeditions against the ordinary Turcomans. The allied army, taken by surprise for the first time at the end of 1286, succeeded in re-forming and ravaged the country, but could not pin down the enemy who made their escape. As soon as their opponents had gone the Germiyan returned, and Fakhr al-Dīn's grandson was killed. Once again the old vizier had to hurry to the rescue. He was able to save Karahisār, but not to destroy the Germiyan. To explain the situation to Arghūn, Fakhr al-Dīn and Mas'ūd set out for the East (1287).

Arghūn however now ordered his vassals to attack the Karamanids, in order to support the Armenians of Cilicia who were being harassed by them. Laranda, occupied by the Karamanids some years earlier, was pillaged, but naturally they were unable to capture them. However, the Karamanids and Eshref on the one hand and the Germiyan on the other asked for a peace, which was granted them and which settled nothing (1288).

A conflict of interests had arisen between Mujīr al-Dīn Amīrshāh, the representative of the Mongol treasury, and Fakhr al-Dīn 'Alī. Mujīr al-Dīn had just brought about his rival's dismissal, though without succeeding in destroying the personal authority of the old vizier, when the latter died (Shawwal 687/ November 1288). With him disappeared the last great figure of Seljukid times, whose unquestioned prestige, increased by the length of his life and his political career, survives in many foundations, attested by inscriptions extending over a period of more than forty years.

With Fakhr al-Dīn Qazwīnī, the successor to Fakhr al-Dīn 'Alī, a further step was taken in the extension of direct rule over Asia Minor. This man was not an official of the country, but had until then been the *mustawfī* of the Ilkhānid Government itself, and Sultan Mas'ūd had not been consulted over his nomination. He was unpopular with the lower ranks of native officials because he was unacquainted with local customs or deliberately replaced them by Irano-Mongol ones, and because he surrounded himself with newcomers who were often too rapacious. Furthermore, his effective power did not extend over the whole of Rūm, since Mujīr al-Dīn, fearing possible conflicts with him, made certain that there should be a financial division of the country, corresponding to the two Sultanates, as established from time to time, the East falling to himself and the West to Qazwīnī.

It is true that, in 1290, Fakhr al-Dīn fell victim to a vizieral revolution at Arghūn's court and that his nominal successors were
natives, in reality under the general supervision of the Mongol
leader in Rūm, the same Samaghar whom Muʿīn al-Dīn had had
recalled earlier but who nevertheless had quickly found various
commands in Rūm under various princes of the blood, and of
whom Aqsarāyī, the historian and official (who, it is true, was
indebted to him) now spoke very highly. According to him, the
government of Rūm was entrusted 'to the Sultan and to Samaghar',
a strange formula which testifies in part to the fact that the Sultan
no longer existed save as a creature of the Ilkhān, but also perhaps
in part to the desire to restore him to a position above the handful
of aristocrats who had monopolized the government for the last
thirty years. Masʿūd's marriage to an Ilkhānid princess, arranged
by Arghūn, perhaps illustrates this attitude. Qazwīnī's successors
were two brothers – a device that had been introduced both to
safeguard the now inevitable division of Asia Minor into two
halves and also to retain a relative degree of cohesion. In reality,
however, it was Mongol supervision that ensured this cohesion.

On the political level this did not of course bring about the end
of the Turcomans, with whom, even if they did not belong to the
same allied group, the Germiyan had in future to be included. The
latter had been defeated by a grandson of Fakhr al-Dīn ʿAlī, who
seized Denizli/Lādīq, which they had held for a short time. Elsewhere the Sultan tried to sanction the agreement apparently in
operation with the Eshref by asking for one of their chieftain's
daughters for his brother Siyāvush: the Eshref chief took advantage
of the meeting to imprison Siyāvush, whose identity was perhaps
challenged by Jimri's old supporters, and only released him on
the intervention of Kūnārī-Beg, who was glad to have an opportunity to demonstrate that he, the Karamanid, was the real
mainstay of the Seljukid dynasty. The Sultan, lacking any proper
troops, was making particular efforts in Konya, his only centre of
any real power, to gain the help of the *akhis*. Their violent dis-
satisfaction with Qazwīnī's rule was not unconnected with his fall.

In a new attempt to deal with the Turcomans, Arghūn recalled
Samaghar at the end of 1290 and again despatched to Rūm his
brother Gaykhātū, who entered Konya at the head of an im-
pressive army. Kūnārī-Beg hastened to come and pay homage, as

did the prince of the Germiyan. Early in 1291 Gaykhātū sent the Sultan to the coastal regions, where all he had to do was to accept homage as easily gained as it was superficial. But in May the news came of Arghūn's death. He was succeeded by his brother Baydū, and Gaykhātū decided to challenge him for the throne, taking with him the whole army from Anatolia. He was successful, but clearly all the enemies of the Seljukido-Mongol power had taken advantage of the gap left by his absence.

There were the *akhi*s and the *runūd,* who did not necessarily form a homogeneous group and, while hostile both to the Mongols as foreigners and to the Turcomans as harmful to the urban economy, nevertheless found themselves obliged to concert their activities with either one or other. Among the Turcomans, the breach between the Karamanids and the Eshref had now become an open one, and the latter, despite the Siyāvush incident, now seem to have been allied with the authorities in Konya against their overpowerful rulers. In opposition to the Karamanids the Sultan's brother, his deputy in Konya, called in Mas'ūd, whom Gaykhātū had recently established in Kayseri. But Mas'ūd had too many conflicts with other Turcomans in the region to be able to do anything for Konya. Thereupon the Germiyan attacked and pillaged the town, all but capturing the citadel. The report of an approaching Mongol force made them withdraw but, when the Mongols did not appear, they returned, and the people of Konya appealed to the grandson of Fakhr al-Dīn 'Alī, the lord of Denizli/Lādīq. The Germiyan were successfully driven back, but this meant that the frontier zone had had to be stripped, and against the Karamanids nothing could be achieved.

It was at this point that Gaykhātū, by then the sovereign and well acquainted with Asia Minor, arrived with a more powerful army than had so far been led against the Turcomans. His aim was to strike terror by means of ravages and massacres, at which his men were so highly adept. The districts of Eregli, the town of Laranda itself, though only a small proportion of its populace was Turcoman, the Eshref country, the town of Denizli/Lādīq recently lost by Fakhr al-Dīn's grandson, and finally the Menteshe country were all ruthlessly sacked. Bringing back hordes of prisoners, the Ilkhānid army returned to Konya, and even there left terrifying memories (November 1291–February 1292). In reality, the only result of all this was devastation, and the Turcomans themselves, whom they had been unable to destroy, could not but benefit materially and morally from the resulting disorganization.

The recital of events becomes tedious, but it does convey a certain impression. It was necessary to fight the Karamanids, who meanwhile had recaptured and held the coastal fortress of Alanya, which a force of Franks from Cyprus had taken. It was also necessary to challenge the Eshref over Kawāla, the key to the Konya basin. At the same time, Sultan Masʿūd had to fight the Turcomans of Kastamonu and barely escaped being taken prisoner by them. In general, less is heard of these Turcomans than of those in the south and south-west, perhaps simply because, as the chief towns were more remote from them, they and the Mongolo-Seljukids left each other more undisturbed. On this occasion the war was partly brought about by a revolt by Siyāvush against his brother, although its chronology, details and causes are all obscure. They were reconciled, like ʿIzz al-Dīn and Rukn al-Dīn a generation before, only to fall out again two years later, and again to come to terms; it was a constant pretext for the Turcomans to increase their advantages and to show that, apart from exceptional occasions when the Mongols approached, they were now truly the principal factors in public life in Asia Minor.

The impression of increasing disintegration was everywhere. It was certainly accelerated by the behaviour of Gaykhātū, and again when the latter was overthrown by Baydū (1294) and Baydū by Ghāzān (1295). In order that one might exercise surveillance over the other, Gaykhātū had systematically divided most offices between two holders, including that of Mujīr al-Dīn, who was still responsible for the interests of the Mongol treasury. The only result was an increase of disputes, disorder and intrigue. Every official was paying direct court to the Ilkhānid Government, to such an extent that there was no political unity in Asia Minor, the administrative autonomy of the country was becoming a pure fiction, and each district was tending to be transformed into a kind of private lordship.

Unfortunately for Asia Minor, the tightening of Mongol control occurred at a time when the Mongol State was beginning to reveal flaws, which in turn of course impelled the sovereigns to intensify their supervision of all their possessions. Precisely because the

Mongol forces in Asia Minor were becoming stronger, they had
to take a larger part in the internal affairs of the Ilkhānid State.
Reference has already been made incidentally to Kangirtāy's unsuccessful revolt and Gaykhātū's successful one. It has been seen,
too, that the Sultan and others were necessarily involved in these.
The chronicle of the final years of the century and the start of the
following one, which unfortunately becomes increasingly incomplete, basically depicts Asia Minor in terms of the revolts of the
Mongol chiefs who were present in the country, without throwing
equal light upon what was happening among the population itself.
This is due in part to the gaps in documentation, but also to the
fact that, as a result of the Mongols' troubles, the emancipation of
the Turcomans, with whom certain chiefs at times allied themselves, is from then onwards an undisputed fact. The emancipation
of a Mongol governor would not necessarily have been harmful,
if he had been able to stabilize his position, since he would have
had opportunities to correct any malpractices arising from the
exploitation of the country for the benefit of a foreign power. But
attempts at total emancipation failed one after another, and Asia
Minor was only to recover its independence, after the fall of the
Ilkhānid Empire, in the form of a host of disunited principalities.

Ghāzān had hardly assumed power when a Mongol chief,
Tugachar, a former adherent of Baydū, tried to make himself independent in Rūm with the complicity of the descendants of
Mu'īn al-Dīn. Challenged half-heartedly by Arab, Samaghar's
son, and more energetically by Baltū, also the son of a former Mongol chief in Rūm, he was defeated (694/1295). But Baltū in turn
revolted, assisted for a time by the Karamanids, the powerless
Sultan Mas'ūd being also involved. Defeated by Sülemish, a
grandson of Bayjū, he fled to the Armenians of Cilicia. Unable to
risk the wrath of a Mongol sovereign, they handed him over and
he was beheaded (696/1297). Though granted a personal pardon,
Sultan Mas'ūd was forced to reside in Tabriz, and in his place in
Rūm was installed his old rival, his nephew 'Alā' al-Dīn Kay-
kubādh, of whose fortunes nothing is known from the time of his
flight to Cilicia until this point, but who perhaps had been recommended by the Armenians. Things continued as before, and
it was now Sülemish who revolted, with Karamanid help, in 698/
1299. He was defeated by an Ilkhānid army near Sivas, which

opposed him, and took refuge in Syria – fortunately there is a factual account, which is more complete than the earlier ones, in the Mamluk chronicles. On his return in the following year he was captured and executed. These men apparently had no definite intention of revolting, but having become masters of a country through their victory over a former rebel, they directed an administration which the Ilkhān wished to place under a control that they preferred to evade, and they could do so only by a revolt. Moreover, it will have been observed that they consisted primarily of men whose fathers or grandfathers had previously held commands in Rūm, which signifies a certain attachment there, however the lands had been acquired.

Naturally, each conqueror sacrificed his predecessors' underlings, and the Sultans were no exception to the rule. ʿAlāʾ al-Dīn Kaykubādh for his part took such acts of vengeance that he became notorious. He too went to pay court to Ghāzān, who sacrificed him. He was put to death, and Masʿūd returned to a throne which no longer provided him even with a decent livelihood and was therefore more than ever devoid of effective power (702/1303). Power was exercised by Sutāy and, in particular, by Chupan/Choban, one of the principal Mongol military leaders to whom the victory over Sülemish had been due, and then, in about 705/1306, by the 'prince of the blood' Erenjen, sent by the new Ilkhān Oljaytu. It was at about that time that the Sultanate disappeared, in a manner so obscure that contemporaries do not mention it and authors who tried to account for it in retrospect disagree in regard to both dates and facts. The death of a Sultan, and even the failure to replace him, in practice were no longer of any importance. Some descendants of the Seljukids survived, several women in particular, and it will be seen that certain notables made use of this ancestry. But politically the era had ended, or rather it had done so two or more decades earlier.

On the death of Oljaytu (1313), in circumstances that are not fully known, Choban, who was the real master of the Empire, reappeared in Rūm to take over its government, although Erenjen was not at once removed. Choban, however, was unable to stay there, and the real power was left to his son Timurtash. It is not clear why Timurtash revolted in 722/1321, not merely as a political rebel, like a number of his predecessors, but also on religious grounds, proclaiming himself to be the *mahdī*, that is to say the Messiah awaited by most Muslims, the Shīʿīs in particular. Choban, still all-powerful, was permitted to go in person to subdue him. Timurtash, placing the responsibility on his son's accomplices, whom he ordered to be executed, took his rebellious son to the Ilkhān, Abu Saʿīd, and secured not only his pardon but also his re-appointment as ruler of Rūm. Aqsarāyī, who completed his chronicle as a protégé of Timurtash after his restoration, passes over his rebellion in silence and places the blame on Erenjen, who, he says, rebelled against Timurtash himself and was finally executed. Probably this was an episode following the restoration of Timurtash, but the fact remains that the revolt of Timurtash is obscure, and some reasons for it are perhaps to be sought in the Ilkhānid State and not in Asia Minor. In 727/1326, after the fall of Choban, Timurtash found himself driven to a second revolt. Despite some resistance in Sivas, this time he had to flee to Egypt, like his predecessor Sülemish. But the international situation was no longer the same. Peace had been concluded between the Mamluks and Abu Saʿīd. For that or some other reason, Timurtash was suspected of plotting and executed (728/1327).

One last member of the family, Hasan, known as Küchük (the small) to distinguish him from his rival Hasan the Great, also made his mark a little later. While disputes were continuing between the candidates for the succession of Abu Saʿīd, who had died in 1335, he revolted, with the help of his father's adherents whom he had succeeded in collecting together in Rūm. Hostilities took place outside Rūm, and those provinces that still remained outside the Turcoman ascendancy had recognized Eretna, a former lieutenant of Timurtash who had now become independent, and in fact it is not known how Eretna reacted to Hasan's attempt. In the end, Hasan the Great was victorious in the vital sectors of the Ilkhānid State, where he founded a new dynasty known as the Jalāʾirids. But these are facts which in practice had no further repercussions on Asia Minor proper.

The account has been continued up to the fall of Timurtash without a break, since, broadly speaking, all the facts belong to one single period which does not seem to show any profound changes. But it will have been observed without difficulty that a narrative which, though summarized, itself contained a certain amount of detail, gave way to a simple and vague outline. The reason is that, from the end of the thirteenth century, the usual narrative sources came to an end one after another – Ibn Bībī in 1282, the anonymous Author of Konya in 1294, despite some bare allusions by a continuator, and finally Aqsarāyī, for practical purposes round about 1300, although he himself made laconic additions until about 1325. As a result, we have to patch together fragments of episodes that are widely scattered and necessarily incomplete. As regards the conduct of the Mongol governors, we have to try to find information in the general Ilkhānid sources, and also in the Syro-Egyptian sources in so far as the Mamluk State is involved in episodes of the history of Rūm. But the reader will also have noted that, as a general rule, the field of activity of these governors no longer extended beyond central Anatolia. In reality, the reading of other sources shows that the rest of the country did of course still exist, and that it was often there that the vital events took place.

In spite of the Mongols' wrath, the Turcomans had not disappeared – very much the contrary. And, simply by remaining where they were and occupying certain urban centres, they began to constitute genuine minor principalities. In default of a properly chronological history, which is not possible, a survey of these principalities as they were at the beginning of the fourteenth century will now have to be attempted.

4

THE FORMATION OF THE TURCOMAN PRINCIPALITIES

Honour to whom honour is due: the oldest, and for long the most powerful, of the Turcoman principalities was certainly that of the Karamanids. An account has already been given of their beginnings, in so far as these can be reconstructed, and of their spectacular reappearance in 1276–7. According to Aflākī, who wrote in Konya in the fourteenth century, it is perhaps to Mehmed-Beg the Karamanid, rather than to his namesake of

Denizli, that the invention of the white caps so widely fashionable in his time must be attributed, thereby indicating his influence. It was certainly he who, when master of Konya, tried to introduce Turkish as the official language of the chancellery, and perhaps had used it earlier in his own correspondence. This innovation failed to produce any immediate consequence, whatever some may have thought, but nevertheless it was significant. As was noted earlier, he found it necessary to conceal his authority under that of a Seljukid, true or false.

Mehmed-Beg's successor, certainly after 1183, was Kūnārī (Güneri?)-Beg, one of his brothers. This at least is the name given him by the anonymous author of the *Seljūknāme*, who was well acquainted with the events in which the Karamanid chief was involved. But it is strange to find that there is no surviving evidence either from coins or inscriptions that relates to him, at least under that name, nor any mention of him in the other chronicles, even in Shikārī. It is possible that he had also another name, besides the honorific name of Majd al-Dīn, but there is a lack of information in the texts for the years from 683 to 699 or 700, when according to the *Seljūknāme* he was alive, and for that reason it is probably better simply to interpose him between Mehmed and Mahmūd, Karaman's youngest son, who is known to have been at the head of the Karamanids at the beginning of the following century. The history of his relations with neighbouring powers shows he was anti-Mongol, like his father, but more anxious to play his part under cover of the Seljukid Sultans than to revolt against them, when he could avoid doing so. In the Isaurian and Cilician Taurus he held Ermenek and Mut, the old centres of his family's power, but he also added Laranda on the inland plateau and Alanya on the coast, and his influence certainly extended north-westwards as far as the Eregli region, almost to Nigde. In 700, an inscription by an otherwise unknown Karamanid shows that the family was starting to interest itself in urban religious foundations. It will be remembered that the Karamanids had tried several times to establish their domination over Konya, the real capital of their outer territories and the seat of the Seljukids. Once again, in 711/1311, in circumstances now wholly unknown, Mahmūd's successor Mūsā was to occupy the town, in spite of the resistance of the *akhis*, and once again Chupan was to recapture it.

Timurtash defended the Nigde region against them but Aqsarāyī, who knew it well, afterwards recorded that by his good relations the Mongol chief had succeeded in making peace with the Turcomans, probably after its revolt, and it can hardly be doubted that at about that time Konya finally came into the hands of the Karamanids. The Mongols no longer really concerned themselves with this region, or were no longer in a position to do so effectively. In the end the inhabitants of the town to some extent made the best of a bad job, probably thinking that it was better to accept the inevitable and thereby lessen their hardships. Perhaps in some cases they preferred the Turcomans to the Mongols; and the Karamanids, quite perceptibly, were beginning to make themselves sufficiently civilized to be acceptable. Merchants had never ceased to travel through their territory, and their conquest of Alanya perhaps testifies to a desire to have their own access to the sea. In any case, they began to endow mosques and other foundations, playing the normal role of the good Muslim rulers that they were certainly anxious to be.

The Eshref first appeared beside the Karamanids, whose power they were never to equal. As has been said earlier, the Eshref, who were perhaps intermixed with Kurdish people, quarrelled with the Karamanids over the question of influence in Konya, and probably through a wider desire for independence. They then went to settle further to the west, on the borders of the province of Konya at Beyshehir, and at certain times held Abgurum, Kawāla and other places. There is epigraphic evidence relating to Sulaymān ibn Eshref dating from about 1290, on a repaired gate in the fortifications of Beyshehir. To the same town, renamed Sulaymānshehir, he gave a mosque whose deed of foundation survives, and which proves that he was becoming a civilized ruler. The tomb made for him, in which he was buried in 702/1302, also survives. His son Mubāriz al-Dīn Mehmed extended his power over Akshehir and Bolvadin, providing the former with a mosque, and in 1314 he paid homage to Timurtash, thereby recognizing his power at no cost to himself. But when Timurtash revolted in 1326, he took Beyshehir and executed Mubāriz al-Dīn. This was the end of the dynasty, not because the territory remained in the Mongols' hands but because, as a result of these incidents, it was divided between the Karamanids and the Hamīdids.

It is only at the beginning of the fourteenth century that the Hamīdids appear in the texts, where they are credited with possession of Antalya, Egridir and Uluborlu/Burghlu. As with their Turcoman neighbours, inscriptions make it possible to confirm their presence in these towns at the extreme end of the thirteenth century and the very beginning of the fourteenth. The presence of numerous Turcomans in the country behind Antalya was already known to Ibn Sa'īd in the middle of the thirteenth century. But in the time of the *pervāne*, the maritime province of which Antalya was the chief town was firmly held by one of his relatives or allies, Badr al-Dīn, *malik as-sawāhil*/king of the shores, who re-established the autonomous march of Ertöküsh for himself. It was probably in about 1280 that Antalya passed from his successor's hands into those of the Turcomans, though the exact date has still to be established. Under the Hamīdids, the territory was divided between three members of the family. The prince of Antalya was defeated by Timurtash, but the principality was re-established by another member of the family, who for the time being had taken refuge in Egypt.

In the last quarter of the thirteenth century and at the beginning of the fourteenth the principal power opposing the Karamanids was that of the Germiyan (one has to beware of the frequent confusions between these two names, which are somewhat similar in Arabic script). The two are not altogether comparable. It was seen earlier that the Germiyan probably derived from a mixed Kurdo-Turkish people transferred from eastern to western Anatolia in about 1275 to give help against the Turcomans in the maintenance of Seljukido-Mongol rule. As a result of the struggles between pretenders to the Sultanate and their efforts to form alliances, the Germiyan later were as often at war with the official authorities as in agreement with them and, in the general disintegration of the state, they finally became a principality, like any other. However, Germiyan is the name of the people and not, as elsewhere, that of the ruling family, which was named after its ancestor 'Alīshīr. Their centre was at Kütahya. and they laid claim with varying success to some kind of hegemony over the neighbouring chiefs, some of whom were perhaps former Seljukid officer others principally Turcoman chiefs who had gradually freed themselves from control as they expanded westwards outside their own

territory. At the end of the thirteenth century Ya'qūb, a descendant of 'Alīshīr, was a powerful ruler. An inscription reveals that
in the East he controlled Ankara, while, in the West, Byzantium
generally and the town of Alashehir/Philadelphia in particular
paid him tribute, and Tripoli on the Meander, Gümüshshar,
Sivriköy, Simaw and Kula were held by him. His relatives or
vassals ruled the most important part of ancient Phrygia – Denizli,
Aydīn/Tralles, and even (Afyon) Karahisār, where the descendants
of Fakhr al-Dīn 'Alī, before their complete disappearance, paid
him homage.

The grandsons of Fakhr al-Dīn 'Alī were reported to be still in
Karahisār in 1314, and they seem to be named still later, about
1324, by al-'Umarī (with a fault in the spelling), who says that, in
order to resist Timurtash, they paid homage to the Germiyan.
Karahisār was incorporated afterwards in the latter's territory.
The State of Germiyan possessed an abundance of horses, cultivation (even of rice), traditional native textile industries, alum
and silver mines, and a flourishing trade along the Meander.
Ya'qūb also built mosques, and a romance of chivalry was dedicated to his son. The principality was perhaps still almost
equally powerful in the time of al-'Umarī, but Ibn Battūta echoes
the hostility it later encountered among the neighbouring Turcomans who accused it of heretical (Yazīdī?) tendencies.

It was mentioned earlier that, in Denizli, a first attempt by the
Turcomans to free themselves had failed. The town, possessing a
source of real wealth in its native textile industry, had later been
taken back under the direct administration of the Seljukid government and was their principal base in south-western Anatolia. A
dispute over the town then took place between the descendants of
Fakhr al-Dīn 'Alī and the Germiyan. But Ghāzān and Rashīd
al-Dīn, his famous historian-vizier, possibly bluffing a little, considered it to be sufficiently well secured to the régime to justify
considering the idea of setting up an Ilkhānid summer residence
there.

The relative decline in strength of the Germiyan principality is
bound up with the growth of new Turcoman principalities in
territories which hitherto had remained Greek. To anyone who
has studied the history of the two preceding centuries, it will come
as no surprise to find that the emancipation of the Turcomans was

accompanied by a new expansion at the expense of the Byzantine Empire.

This expansion however had also been helped by the return of the seat of Byzantine government from Nicaea to Constantinople and by its European activities, which led it to attach less importance to the defence of its Asiatic frontier. From about the year 1270, the south-western corner of Asia Minor was looked upon as too irremediably lost for it to be worth attempting to reconquer it. In roughly 1300, the whole block of western coastal provinces as far as the Aegean was occupied, and the few isolated regions that remained survived only on the sufferance of neighbouring rulers. This is not the place to relate how the Emperor Andronicus II then made a great attempt to recover lost ground, or at least to stabilize the frontiers, by engaging the mercenary force known as the Catalan Company, and how finally this force succeeded only too well, so that the Byzantines were quite content to see it depart, abandoning to the Turcomans for good those areas that the Company had been able to recover only in part and for a short time. After 1304 no further Byzantine effort was made. On the contrary, as always, each of the contending factions in Constantinople took the opportunity to appeal for help against the rest to such Turcomans as were within their reach.

From south to north, the front was now held by the principalities of Menteshe, Aydïn, Sarukhan, and Karasi, with 'Uthmān/Osman to the east.

In our own time, the principality of Menteshe has provided the subject of an outstanding and exemplary monograph by P. Wittek. The principality seems to have already been more or less established before 1290. This was not the case in 1277, when Menteshe, the leader of some Turcomans who perhaps had earlier established themselves in the region of Sivas, was associated with the Karamanids' battles. It was probably as a result of reverses at that time, when the later struggles against the Eshref were taking place, that he migrated 'beyond Lādīq', where he is to be found waging war with others in 1282. At the start of the fourteenth century Menteshe's territory included Milas/Miletus, Mughla, and other places, so corresponding with the ancient Caria, opposite which the Hospitallers of Rhodes had just established themselves.

The territory which was soon to form the principality of Aydïn appears to have been first attacked from the south by Menteshe and his vassal Sasa, from 1282 until the beginning of the fourteenth century, and then by Aydïn's sons, at first in co-operation with Sasa and then, after his death, acting alone. Of Muhammad ibn Aydïn, the founder of the dynasty and originally a vassal of the Germiyan, nothing is known before about 700/1300. Under his grandson, Umur Beg, the dynasty momentarily achieved true greatness, owing to the combined results of his activities as a *ghāzī* and of Byzantine affairs. As for the dynasties of Sarukhan and Karasi, further to the north, which were not destined to endure for long, almost nothing is known at the beginning of the century except that they did exist. Osman's principality, at that time established near Sögüt, later became the nucleus of the Ottoman Empire, but for the moment there was still nothing to mark it out from the neighbouring and often more powerful ones. There is no need here to discuss the legends which have attempted to discover retrospectively among the Ottoman Sultans' ancestors the first signs of their future greatness.

However clearly the geographical conditions gave the Turcomans particularly wide scope for expansion towards the west, it is interesting to note that, in their sector, those on the Trebizond frontier acted in a similar way, and at the same period. It was in about 1290 that the 'Turks of Chaldaea', who formed a well-known autonomous group there fifty years later, settled in the mountains along the western borders of the State of Trebizond. Some years later, the Georgian chronicle mentions successes over vast numbers of Turks from the regions of Bayburt and Ispir. In about the fourth decade of the fourteenth century it even speaks of a victory over Orkhān, the sovereign of Rūm, a name obviously intended by the later adaptor responsible for the surviving version of the chronicle to mean the well-known Ottoman prince, which is impossible. As in other episodes, however, it may conceal a reference to participation by Georgian contingents, as vassals of the Mongols, in an expedition into Asia Minor (but was there then any such expedition which reached as far as that region?), or, with more probability, it may refer to the existence of some other Orkhān, nearer to Georgia. Finally, al-'Umarī enumerates several smaller states, close to the State of Trebizond and lying between it and the principality of Kastamonu, which are difficult to locate precisely but whose existence there is no reason to deny – particularly Qāwiyā, under Murād al-Dīn Hamza, through which merchants travelled to Samsun, and Tughanjuq (might this be Osmanjïq, although known then by this name?). They must have been incorporated later in the State of Kastamonu or that of Eretna, but there too at the start there was a profusion of small scattered States. Qāwiyā may be east of the Ottoman's.

The circumstances in which the principality of Kastamonu was established are difficult to determine since, on account of its remoteness from the political centres, it attracted little attention from the chroniclers. The genealogy of the chieftain who was active there before 690/1291, Muzaffar al-Dīn Yavluk-Arslan, makes him the son of a Husām al-Dīn Alp-Yörük (?), who was himself the son of the Chupan/Choban, who, as *beglerbeg* and possibly governor of the province, was put in charge by Kay-kubādh of the famous expedition to the Crimea, as has been noted earlier. Ibn Bībī affirms that he held the lands once held by his father and grandfather. He had succeeded his father before 679/1280 and died in the disturbances of 691/1292. He is known to have had a son, who perhaps did not reign, Husām al-Dīn (or Nasir al-Dīn) Mahmūd. To Muzaffar al-Dīn a popular astrological work of Qutb al-Dīn Shīrāzī and a historical treatise on the religious sects were dedicated, and to Mahmūd a collection of administrative texts, which means that they were rulers who prided themselves on their culture and who exercised real authority. Nevertheless there is no doubt that, in 1256, Kastamonu was dependent on a *beglerbeg* Tavtash who normally was active in Konya; that in 1258 the province was taken over by Baba Tughrā'ī and made responsible for defraying the costs of his vizierate, and for that reason Taj al-Dīn Mu'tazz at one point seized it as a guarantee of the repayment of Tughrā'ī's loans; and that in 671/1271 it was administered by a son of the *pervāne* Mu'īn al-Dīn, whose son Mehmed-Beg once more reconquered it in 1295–9. Osmanjïq, in the same province, was clearly under Seljukido-Mongol governmental control in 670/1271, since it was there that the vizier Fakhr al-Dīn 'Alī was temporarily imprisoned. Thus it probably has to be admitted that Husām al-Dīn Alp Yörük, Muzaffar al-Dīn, Yavlak-Arslan, and Husām al-Dīn

Mahmūd held Kastamonu only for quite a short period in all, following the *pervāne*'s fall, while probably belonging to a family which in a more traditional and stable manner exercised a more limited authority in the region. Reference has already been made to the part they played in the revolts of Mas'ūd II and Siyāvush, and it is also known that, in about 1280, a Byzantine attack on Sinope was repulsed by Turcomans from this region. It does not follow that these were Turcoman chiefs: on the contrary, it was the Turcoman chiefs that Siyāvush stirred up against them. Consequently, one must conclude that in fact it was not this family which founded the long-lasting principality established by the fourteenth century. The family which then followed, known by the name of Jāndārids (or Isfandiyārids, from a later representative), took its name from a certain Jāndār who, according to later sources, was at first established in Aflānī to the west of Kastamonu and who was said to have captured Kastamonu and Sinope in turn from their respective holders. But Sinope was independent at least until 1324, and Aqsarāyī shows that Jāndār's son Sulaymān Pasha was already master of Kastamonu in 1314, when he paid homage to Abu Sa'īd the Ilkhān. The Greek authors appear to know him as early as 1300, and the texts make no mention of the father (an inscription, which is suspect, of 1289?). Moreover, it was still Sulaymān Pasha that Ibn Battūta met, while by the time of al-'Umarī he had been replaced shortly before by his son Ibrāhīm. However, al-'Umarī always calls the country 'the country of Sulaymān Pasha', so insistently that it must indeed be he who had really gained power. In any case, if the Jāndārids represented the Turcomans as against the Chobanids, or the Turcomans as against others, it would be reasonable to expect information from the chronicles regarding the Turcomans' own activities in the province of Kastamonu during the second half of the thirteenth century. Aqsarāyī certainly does not identify the chiefs of Kastamonu with the Turcomans of the *ūj*, to whom he refers explicitly in many other places, and the only Turcomans so characterized of whom any mention is made in this region, in the 1260's, are those of a 'son of Khurma', of whom nothing is known, nor consequently of their subsequent connections with the later dynasties.

Study of the principality of Kastamonu is further complicated by the fact that the Byzantine historians speak of powerful rulers of this region under the name Amour(oi), which however appears nowhere else. The accounts do not tally sufficiently for it to be possible to establish with certainty if they had in mind those now known as the Chobanids or the Jāndārids, or even an ill-defined principality, later mentioned by al-'Umarī and Kiyā Mazan-darānī, at Girdebolu, i.e. between Kastamonu and the Ottomans. It is not possible here to go into the full details of the discussion, and its results in any case do not affect the picture given earlier.

The history of Sinope before its incorporation in the Jāndārid State is hardly clearer. We know that Sinope formed part of the principality of the *pervāne* Mu'īn al-Dīn Sulaymān and that, at the end of the century, it still or once again belonged to his son Muhammad/Mehmed Beg and perhaps to the latter's successor or deputy Mas'ūd Beg, a grandson of the *pervāne* and an adventurer who for a time had made himself master of Samsun. At the beginning of the fourteenth century Sinope was in the hands of a personage known as Ghāzī Chelebi, from whom (or from whose successor) Sulaymān was later to capture it (after 1324), but who presents us with the paradoxical situation that, although he was celebrated, we do not know who he was. On the evidence of the Trebizond and Genoese chronicles and of Ibn Battūta and al-'Umarī, he was indeed celebrated for his feats as a *ghāzī* and corsair in the Black Sea, even succeeding in attacking Caffa in the Crimea, in addition to Trebizond, and in sinking vessels in harbour by under-water attack, like a modern frogman. Yazījī-oghlu and the Ottoman chroniclers make him a son of the Seljukid Mas'ūd, whose short-lived activities in this region have been described. But the earlier authors, when they say anything, represent him as a grandson of the *pervāne* Mu'īn al-Dīn Sulaymān. From his tomb it is known that his father was called Mas'ūd Chelebi. Modern scholars who discussed the question before the publication of Aqsarāyī were hesitant, but, in view of the fact that this author now acquaints us with Mas'ūd Beg, it seems fairly natural to think that Ghāzī Chelebi was in fact the son of that Mas'ūd (Beg or Chelebi). The old dates given by certain authors for the conquest of Sinope by the Jāndārids are impossible, since there is evidence of Ghāzī Chelebi's activities, if not until 1356 as was wrongly believed, at least until 1324. At the most he might have recognized the suzerainty of Sulaymān Pasha, but no evidence of this exists. By the time of Ibn Battūta, on the other hand, Sinope had been incorporated in the Jāndārid State, this time without any doubt.

The reader need only be reminded briefly that the Christian frontiers were not the only ones to have been overrun by the Turcomans. A similar penetration took place in northern Syria and Diyār Mudar, in the loop of the Euphrates. But their entry into the powerful Muslim State of the Mamluks limited their possibilities of establishing any principalities, which the Mamluks later only encouraged in the frontier zone of the Taurus.

The principalities enumerated above are, so to speak, the classical ones, and those to which alone the later writers, who divided Asia Minor between well-established dynasties, have accustomed the reader to limiting his attention. But, particularly at the start, the reality was less simple, and the authors refer incidentally to many others which, being closely hemmed in by the more powerful principalities on their borders, had no real possibility of expansion or of emancipating themselves, and were finally absorbed. The same is true of the names, which tell nothing, and it is not always possible to know from the context whether they refer to Turcomans or to the officials of what remained of the Seljukido-Mongol government, whether they were autonomous princes or vassals or local representatives of others more powerful than themselves.

The present chapter has been limited to 'placing' these principalities. To trace their actual history is a difficult task, which will only be undertaken in the form of a very rough outline at the end of this work. In fact, they do not all play a real part in the history of what had once been Seljukid Turkey. It is true that, in part, they were the same Turks, but it was an entirely new Turkey that some of them were starting to fashion, a country on the move. Their importance from this point of view is even greater, but nevertheless the question can be restricted to the broad outline given at the conclusion of the present work.

In the works of their later historians the Ottomans, the Karamanids, the dynasty of Aydïn and probably others lay claim to investiture by the Seljukids, generally through a certain ʿAlāʾ al-Dīn, of whom it is difficult to know whether he is the great Kaykubādh or Farāmurz, the last of the dynasty. This is of course to some extent a stock explanation, and it was not to Seljukid investiture that these men owed possession of their territories. Nevertheless, even though the surviving deeds are spurious, there is no reason to doubt that these chiefs sought to legitimize their possessions, for example by homage to Abu Saʿīd in 1314, against such rivals or suzerains as were closer at hand. Some reminiscence of this sort may be contained in Kiyā Mazandarānī's list.

5

ETHNIC EVOLUTION

There has already been occasion more than once to mention in passing the new peoples which the Mongols' invasion had driven into Asia Minor, at first by thrusting them back before their own advance, later by carrying them along in their own ranks. Some were Iranians, others Turcomans, and there were even Mongols, who were not solely garrison troops but who settled down with their livestock and families in the eastern half of the country. In terms of numbers, there thus ensued an increase – which it is impossible to calculate – in these ethnic groups as compared with the stable numbers of the natives; and there were also certain qualitative modifications. Leaving aside the Mongols, the new Turcomans were not the exact counterparts of the old ones, economically and culturally, as will be seen. For the moment, the main question is to know to what ethnic or tribal groups they belonged. It has already been emphasized that the Seljukid expansion had apparently brought with it only part of the tribes, the list of which, comprising the traditional group of the twenty-four Oghuz tribes, is represented almost in its entirety among the place-names of modern Anatolia, and to quite a considerable extent in the literary or administrative texts of the fifteenth and sixteenth centuries. Hence the Kayï and Bayundur (to give for the moment only two names, with which the Ottomans and the Ak-koyunlu respectively claimed kinship) must indeed have been among the newcomers, and this simple statement would be sufficient without further development, were there not an additional reservation to be made. Though not claiming to have undertaken a survey of all the names found in the texts dating from the time of the Ilkhānid Empire, I think nevertheless I can say that the names of tribes continue to occur in them relatively seldom, as in the Seljukid period. It is only in the fifteenth century that they emerge clearly, when large political entities with a Turcoman basis or Turcoman ancestors were being formed, and when it became the fashion to exalt the ancestral tribes and to feel conscious, even at that period, of still belonging as individuals to one of them. It is indeed very possible that the comparative silence of the older texts derives from the fact that the relative strength of the political régimes under which the tribes lived and which had been founded on other bases gave them little opportunity to manifest themselves as such. It is also quite possible, however, that it was an evolution in Asia Minor itself during the fourteenth and fifteenth centuries which brought about a revival or even to some extent the first appearance of tribal feeling among certain groups. If this hypothesis should receive confirmation, the obvious result would be that we could no longer feel certain in respect of tribal affiliations even at the time of the Mongol invasion. Moreover, sitings of tribes accepted for the sixteenth century prove nothing for the earlier period, the Ottomans having carried out many transfers of populations and others having occurred spontaneously. Members of some tribes, the main part of which made their appearance only in the thirteenth century, may indeed have taken part in the expansion during the eleventh century, but in general there must have been a division of territory between the tribes constituting the two waves. Elsewhere the earlier groups may have been displaced, with the result that their settlements are no longer to be found in the same places. The facts are known in the particular case of the Germiyan. The Döger, said to be the tribe of the Artukids, in the fourteenth century were no longer found in large numbers in Diyār Bakr, but were further to the west in Diyār Mudar. In addition, there were federations or redistributions of tribes under new names, as was to happen in the middle of the fourteenth century with the Dulgādir and the Ak-koyunlu, the latter confronting the Kara-koyunlu.

All this is not to minimize the interest of the research undertaken by young Turkish scholars, particularly Faruk Sümer, following the lead of their master Köprülü, with the aim of recording and classifying all possible mentions of the tribes before and during the sixteenth century (the period during which Ottoman documents enable a reasonably complete and reliable picture to be made), but intended only to determine the method by means of which the results can be put to use. This is one example of the unfortunately numerous questions in which the inadequacy of documentation in the earlier period makes it necessary to work retrospectively from Ottoman documentation. But obviously this method must be employed with the most stringent precautions. For the end of the Middle Ages, the fourteenth and fifteenth centuries, the relative importance of the Mamluk documentation makes it possible to produce results that hold good for the Syrian-Mesopotamian-Anatolian borders. It does not of course follow that the tribes thus recorded did not also exist as such in the centre of Anatolia. But it has to be stated that the dynasties of the small Turcoman principalities in the west hardly seem to have claimed kinship with them.

The Oghuz are not the only Turkish people to have supplied Asia Minor with settlers. Among the Turkish tribes some of whose members settled down there with the Mongols, there were some who derived from other Turkish peoples, such as the Uyghur. There can and indeed must have been an absorption of the Cumans/Kipchaks whom Theodore Lascaris had installed on the southern frontiers of the State of Nicaea for the express purpose of resisting the Turcomans. Moreover the Mongols, who at the start were an undifferentiated army of occupation, as their Empire disintegrated, themselves seem to have become divided and reorganized into groups of tribes. Some of these were named as being still in Anatolia at the end of the fourteenth century in the histories of the *cadi* Burhān al-Dīn or of the Karamanids, sometimes being associated with Turcomans, sometimes hostile to them, in eastern and central Anatolia, and emancipated from the princes even when the latter were Mongols. Finally, many Kurds had been displaced. The distribution of the tribes found in Diyār Bakr in the fourteenth century was no longer the same as had been known hitherto, and was already as known in the sixteenth century. Moreover, it will be remembered, the Kurds penetrated into Armenian regions where they had never previously been recorded.

Research into these tribal distinctions would possess no further interest if it were simply a matter of a catalogue of interchangeable items. In favourable cases, investigation may make it possible to determine the original geographical situation and itinerary of an ethnic group. It is also possible that different groups may present different characteristics, that it can be established that a certain group which answers to some particular name was normally a group of nomads owning sheep but not camels, whereas another on the contrary was of camel-owners, and a third was semi-sedentarized, and so on. There is thus no need to emphasize the significance of the results for economic and social history. But it must be confessed that, for the moment, to expect such results in this field is still only a pious hope.

Whatever the tribal affiliations of the Turcomans now present in Asia Minor, from the events described it emerges clearly enough that the Mongol intervention resulted in accentuating still further the tendency, already existing among them in the Seljukid period, to mass together in the frontier zones. Faced by the Mongols who held central Anatolia, the chief focal points of communications, the Turcomans organized themselves along the borders. In one sense, it is on the periphery that Turkey was found. And when the Mongols' decline was to leave the centre more and more devoid of any true vitality, it was from the periphery that Turkey was to re-create itself.

6

ECONOMIC EVOLUTION

The political or institutional history of Asia Minor under the Mongol Protectorate leaves an impression of disorder and ruin which cannot be entirely illusory but which nevertheless must be reduced to its true proportions, since the same period witnessed intense commercial and cultural activity. Warfare was neither uninterrupted nor present everywhere, and the decline in the Seljukid State's resources might signify, not the country's impoverishment but merely a transfer of its resources, in part to the Ilkhānid State (which was undertaking certain compensatory expenditure in Asia Minor), in part to individual notables who frequently assumed responsibility for foundations which formerly would have been maintained at the state's expense. It is therefore necessary to consider, without any preconceived ideas, the various specific questions that an examination of the documents may suggest.

In the matter of agriculture, did the presence of the Mongols, particularly in the eastern part of the country, and the Turcoman expansion, particularly in the western part, alter the structure of the cultivable areas? It has already been pointed out that the coming of Turcoman herdsmen had not in itself necessarily been a negative factor for agriculture (apart from the direct effects of the conquest). The position is far less clearly defined during the next stage, which is now under consideration. In more general terms it can hardly be denied that the more or less long-term result of the Mongol invasion, over the greater part of the countries affected, was an increase in nomadism, here achieved at the expense of agriculture. The Mongols themselves and the Turcomans, newly arrived from Central Asia, who preceded or accompanied them, through temperament or necessity seem to have shown less respect for constructive work and plantations than their predecessors had done, or to have placed such pressure on the peasants that they often abandoned the country-side, leaving it as grazing-land for anyone who wished to use it, a situation from which the Kurds also profited. It is possible however that in certain cases this feature itself may have encouraged some Turcomans to adopt a more settled life. It has to be acknowledged that, in respect of Rūm, it is impossible to follow this evolution, if it existed, with any precision. Moreover, it was not necessarily identical from one end of the territory to the other, and once the principalities had become stabilized in the fourteenth century, al-ʿUmarī's informants there, as was observed earlier, always looked with favour, not only on stock-breeding, as was natural, but also on agriculture.

Some clearer indications regarding the exploitation of the country's natural resources can perhaps be found. There is no reason to suppose that the products exploited or the places themselves have changed, but the system of exploitation may have done so in some cases. In an earlier chapter there was a reference to the beginnings of the production of alum; in 1255 the Dominican

missionary William of Rubruck found the alum trade in the hands
of a Genoese, Nicolo of San Siro, born in Syria, and a Venetian,
Bonifacio of Molinis, from Cyprus, who together exercised a monopoly. As the production of alum had been undertaken mainly for
the advantage and at the prompting of western merchants, it is
possible that the trade had been entrusted from the start as a more
or less autonomous enterprise to Westerners, one representative
from each of the two rival powers, Genoa and Venice, being associated together to counterbalance each other and to provide a
guarantee to the Seljukid State against the dangers of too exclusive
a monopoly. It is, however, also possible that the concession of such
a monopoly should be regarded within the larger framework of the
distribution of state revenues then customary among the notables.
At present this question cannot be answered. Moreover there is no
indication whether the system continued in this form or whether
the state took over the direct sale of alum in the years following
William of Rubruck's visit. This writer recorded complaints made
by merchants who accused the two men in control of holding prices
at an unjustifiable level.

On the subject of alum there is always the question whether the
start of intensive exploitation of new deposits in Phocaea by the
Zaccharia in about 1275 did not prove harmful to production in
Kütahya and Karahisār/Kughūniya. It does not appear to have
been so. In the fourteenth century the Genoese trade in Turkish
alum formed only a part of their general trade in alum, the demand
being sufficient to handle the two sources of alum together without
any competition between them, and it may be conjectured that
they kept their purchases to suitable proportions. In theory the
Turkish alum, which had to be carried overland before being
shipped, must have been more expensive than alum from Phocaea,
which was produced so to speak on the quayside. As the Turkish
alum was good, it must be assumed that a way was found to even
out prices as a whole.

For the other natural resources of Asia Minor, the principal
witness is Simon of Saint-Quentin, on whose authority a list of
them was given earlier, and who dates from the very beginning of
the Mongol period. All this is both confirmed and completed by
later authors, who had no reason to confine themselves to the past.
As for the Turcomans' caps, it is known that, apart from the red

ones mentioned by Simon, there were also white ones, from about 1260, but it is not known if these were exported. The Italians found purchasers in Asia Minor for cloth from Flanders, but Marco Polo was not unaware that the Greeks of Rūm made beautiful carpets and red silk and other fabrics, and the Armenians of Erzinjān a marvellous buckram. Fifty years later, Pegolotti still knew the buckram of Erzinjān and Ibn Battūta also referred, though more vaguely, to the beautiful fabrics from that town. The last-named author also admired the pile carpets from Akseray, and even the beautiful cotton fabrics from Denizli/Lādīq (possibly embroidered with gold) and Ephesus, the manufacture of which had been continued or resumed by the Greeks from their Byzantine past (it would be rash to suppose that they did so without some interruption at the start of the Turcoman expansion in their direction). Fabrics sometimes also figured in tribute from Rūm, or in certain requisitions. In this respect, Rashīd al-Dīn's correspondence enumerates various kinds of fabrics, from Rūm in general or from Erzinjān in particular; among the former were fabrics originating in the Crimea and Russia. There is also an allusion to the woollen products of Sivas and Kastamonu towards the middle of the century in the *Risāla* of Ibn Kiyā Mazandarānī, together with saddles from Tokat.

There is less information about mines, but it will be remembered that al-ʿUmarī, whose information refers to the years around 1330, knew of three silver mines in Rūm, at Gümüsh-Saray, Lu'lu'a and Bāburt (?). Ibn Battūta knew of copper mines in the province of Erzinjān, and says it was from their production that celebrated vases and lamps were made. From scraps of information of this sort it is difficult to form any clear impression of the standard of craft activities, their development, or decline. But in fact there is nothing to suggest that any catastrophic change occurred before the fall of the Ilkhānid Empire.

The products referred to above are known to us merely because they were handled commercially. It is certain that commerce experienced a time of great activity, but to a large extent it was in the hands of foreigners and passed through the country without always bringing any great advantage to it. The effects of the Mongol domination in this respect are somewhat complex, and it is essential not to be over-eager to acclaim the rise of trade in the

country, as has often been done with a somewhat ingenuous
enthusiasm, simply because Marco Polo and other Italians passed
that way. At the least, if there was a rise of commerce so far as
these Italians were concerned, it was not necessarily an equally
straightforward rise for all those in the country. It has already
been observed that an active trade was in existence before the
Mongols. The creation of the Mongol Empire, the incorporation
of Asia Minor in its economic system and the political decline of
Konya certainly lessened, though they did not destroy, the role
played by the western part of the country, to the benefit of the
eastern part (at the beginning, in 1255, William of Rubruck still
found many Franks in Konya, who at that time can hardly have
been soldiers). For the time of Jalāl al-Dīn, Aflākī refers to a
merchant of Tabriz who had come to Konya. The rupture
between the Mongols and the Mamluks of Syria and Egypt,
which was much more complete in character than was usual in
the warfare of the period, must for the time being have endangered
the trade of ports like Antalya and Alanya, inasmuch as it was not
under the control of Italians and was not routed by way of Cyprus
(and even that may have been limited by the situation). At least
this was so until, aided perhaps by this state of affairs, certain
Turcoman principalities were established, which included these
ports and which inclined politically towards Egypt. Similarly the
rupture between the Mongols in Persia and those in Russia, and
the close links established between the latter and the Mamluks,
from whom, through the Genoese, they obtained their recruitment of slave-soldiers, diverted to the Straits part of the traffic
(mostly of slaves) which would otherwise have been sent overland
through Asia Minor. This new route was harmful to such ports as
Sinope or Samsun, and in the case of the former perhaps helped
to bring about the alteration of trade and piracy that characterized the activities of its prince Ghāzī Chelebi at the beginning of
the fourteenth century. Lastly and perhaps most important, even
though before 1243 Anatolian trade had played only a modest
part, if not in relations between the various countries in the Near
East, at least in those between Europe and the more distant East,
it was now the long-range international trade that passed through
the country, though only traversing its eastern half, linking Italy
with Tabriz, the seat of the Ilkhāns, and sometimes with lands

still more remote. However, whereas before 1243 Anatolia itself had attracted merchants, they now tended to cross the country without leaving in it any of their merchandise or profit. The two ports giving access to the Ilkhānid State were Ayas in Cilicia and Trebizond at the eastern end of the Black Sea, both of which were vassals of the Ilkhānids. From Trebizond, caravans merely crossed a corner of Asia Minor on the way to Erzurum, which less and less formed a real part of it. From Ayas, the route passed through Kayseri/Qaysariyya to Sivas, before also reaching Erzurum by way of Erzinjān. Both these routes avoided Anatolia proper. Finally, however considerable the Italian trade with Tabriz may have been, the fact remains that most of the imports brought from India to the Mediterranean were carried via Egypt, while for the trade with China there was competition from the northern route through the territories of the Golden Horde.

Although its importance was perhaps diminished, Sivas nevertheless continued to play a great part, probably owing to the firmly-based commercial organization established earlier, and also to the fact that it was still a cross-roads for merchants (many of them Genoese), who, instead of going to Tabriz, also used to go by Samsun, Vatiza/Patza, or Sinope to Caffa in the Crimea, or else, from Tabriz, went to Constantinople. We possess a letter from Jalāl al-Dīn addressed to a merchant, Shihāb al-Dīn, who was travelling to Sivas. Moreover, by chance a number of documents have survived, the work of Genoese notaries who drew them up in Sivas where they lodged in the *funduq* of various Muslim colleagues (a certain Kamāl al-Dīn in 1280, and another with a name that is incomprehensible in the Latin transcription in 1274), before moving on to other stopping-places following the merchants (Vatiza, Erzinjān, then to the Crimea, and from there to Tabriz). There is nothing further. But in 1300 Genoa even established a permanent representative in Sivas, and his mere presence there is obvious proof of the continued arrival of Genoese. Pegolotti also explains that agents of the Ilkhānid police were encountered at every stage along the route. A duty had to be paid to them, and they were responsible for the safety of the route. On the other hand we find that on one occasion in 1276, the same date as the serious disturbances, a 'galley of Sivas', that is to say of merchants travelling to Sivas, had been robbed at sea by pirates. It was perhaps, but not certainly, in reprisal for acts of this kind that the Franks attacked Sinope in 1298. On another occasion we are told of a caravan of Frankish merchants which was pillaged near Amasya, and therefore between Sivas and Sinope or Samsun. And the minor hostilities at Sinope were to recur several times during the fourteenth century. In general, however, it is quite certain that these episodes remained sufficiently exceptional for the Genoese – who were almost the only nation to be involved – to have continued to trade by way of Asia Minor so long as the Ilkhānid State lasted. There are also occasional instances when their ships also carried merchants who were 'Ilkhānid subjects', but whose names indicate a variety of peoples and religions. In 1271, some of those who had suffered losses when their ship had been pillaged by an Italian assailant received compensation. One anecdote reveals Jalāl al-Dīn Rūmī negotiating with a merchant who had been 'among the Western Franks'. Another relates to a Muslim who had set out from Antalya for Egypt and been captured by the Franks.

Caravanserais or *khāns* had already been erected before 1243, as the reader will remember, but many more were added during the period of Mongol rule. This fact testifies to the vitality of trade and to the importance attached to it either by the Seljukid or the Ilkhānid government or some important personage (such as Karatay). Occasionally, however, in troubled times, some of these *khāns* served as fortresses for rebels or bandits. In any event, the distribution of the *khāns* at this period is an interesting study, so far as inscriptions make it possible to date them with certainty. Even immediately after the rout of 1243, when its full effects had not yet been felt, several *khāns* were completed or built in south-western or western Anatolia, while Karatay, in a well-known foundation, set up a *khān* which still partly survives and which was the final link in a series serving the route from Konya or Syria to Kayseri and Sivas. A little later, clearly through the efforts of the *pervāne* Mu'īn al-Dīn, the routes between Sivas, Tokat and the Black Sea were safeguarded by means of further foundations, while Fakhr al-Dīn 'Alī continued to encourage the merchants of western Anatolia and Denizli. Besides the *khāns* there were also certain *ribāts*, fortified posts or monasteries, and attention was paid to the upkeep of roads and bridges, for example the bridge of Chupan/Choban, the Mongol resident, on the way from Erzurum to Tabriz. Each posting-place on an important route was guarded by a detachment of police under the command of a *kutwal*, to whom merchants paid a levy for their protection. As has already been said, it was the Mongol government which introduced the *tamgha*, a kind of toll which was imposed in Iran, and for which the Seljukids had no equivalent.

It is doubtful if either the Genoese or any other merchants succeeded in establishing direct connections with the Turcoman principalities in the west or south (Aflākī does in fact refer to the case of a Muslim merchant who was robbed by 'Muhammad-Beg al-Ūjī'), although connections between Cyprus and Antalya and Alanya cannot ever have been entirely broken. When these principalities became stabilized, however, merchants appeared there, and were now probably favoured by the rulers. It was not a matter of large-sale trade, but rather of the maritime inter-regional trade, which more and more was falling into the hands of the Italians; or of the acquisition of the country's products, for example alum from Kütahya, now mainly taken through Ephesus/Altoluogo/Ayasoluk. Altoluogo on the one side, and Antalya and Alanya (Candelore) on the other, were considered by Pegolotti to be worthy of inclusion in his treatise, from which we learn that, some time earlier, the Bardi of Florence, arriving in Pisan vessels, had obtained substantial reductions at Antalya/Satalia in customs dues, which put them on almost equal terms with the Cypriots. Merchants from Provence also frequented Antalya. It is even possible that, starting from the ports, the Genoese may have travelled through the interior of the country, since it is known that one of them, Domenico Doria, after falling into the hands of the Egyptians, gave al-'Umarī some of the very remarkable information (applying roughly to 1330) that he transmits on the subject of western and central Asia Minor and its various principalities. Moreover, various deeds in Asia Minor reveal to what extent the florin (of Florence) had penetrated into the country. In contrast to what was to happen in the Ilkhānid Empire, where its fall brought with it the ruin of Italian trade in Iran and beyond, the more restricted trade conducted with the emirates was for the most part to continue without interruption until their conquest by the Ottomans.

The incorporation of Asia Minor in the Mongol system led after a certain time to its coinage being brought into line with that of the Ilkhāns. Here again the latter coinage, consisting of dinars, was based fundamentally on silver, but with a scale of values differing from the classical Muslim system and the systems current in neighbouring States. In Rūm, the coinage struck by the Seljukids had at first been retained, at least in principle, but, according to Rashīd al-Dīn – whose statement is only partially confirmed by numismatic collections – a drastic reduction in the proportion of silver used had been resorted to (the same tendency was also found in the Mamluk State). A similar state of disorder existed under the Ilkhāns, and was due in part to more general factors rather than to their own particular policy.

It is well known that, in 1294, in his attempt to reorganize the Empire, the Ilkhān Gaykhātū tried to introduce a kind of paper money, on the lines of the system then in use by his kinsmen in China. The preparation both technical and psychological was naturally inadequate, and the innovation could not be maintained. Steps had been taken to introduce it in Asia Minor, where Aqsarāyī echoed the complaints to which it gave rise. Ghāzān then issued a new coinage, with a dinar of approximately half the value of the legal Muslim dinar, and a dirham at one-sixth of the dinar. The striking of their own coinage by the Mongols was introduced into Asia Minor at the same time, as part of the increase in the degree of direct administration that was a feature of the period, and to such good effect that, for the future, it was the new Mongol coinage, bearing the names of mints in Asia Minor, that constituted the legal currency in that country also.

As they developed, the Turcoman principalities more and more came to issue their own coinage. The monetary system was no longer uniform, and probably to some extent reflected the differences in their foreign relations. Italian money, Angevin and the florin, began to compete with the local currency. Al-ʿUmarī usually refers to the dirham as being worth one-sixth of the dinar, which thus indicates that the Mongol system was maintained even on the Byzantine borders. Some coins were also struck in imitation of Angevin ones in the Aegean area.

7

THE NON-MUSLIMS

The Mongol domination did not alter the condition of non-Muslims in Asia Minor as much as might have been expected, partly because that condition was reasonably good, as has been seen, and also because the Protectorate did not fundamentally modify the autonomy of the Seljukid régime in this respect. On the whole, the first few generations of Mongols remained indifferent on questions of religion and all creeds were respected, Islam among others, but no more than that – that is to say, it no longer enjoyed the superiority over others of former times. And politically the new masters found it advantageous, whenever possible, to rely on those who in earlier régimes had been the inferiors, and so were often either Christians or (when Muslims) Shīʿīs. In western Asia, those most favoured were the Armenians, who from the start had consciously made themselves the agents of the Mongols. Although connections with the Greeks were slight, they too were regarded with favour, since political affairs had brought Michael Palaeologus and the Ilkhāns closer together and since Trebizond and the Armenians in Cilicia had become their vassals. Contingents of Armenians from Cilicia sometimes figured locally in Mongol armies in Syria, but the Armenians from Armenia proper, who had no longer performed military service since the conquests in which they had lost their political independence, remained excluded from military life, despite an attempt made by the bishop of Erzinjān. On the other hand the Georgians, whose military worth had been demonstrated in recent events, on several occasions were included in the forces sent to the West by the Mongols. However, the advantages which the various Christian sects had been able to enjoy as a result of Mongol indifference were reduced when the Ilkhāns and their people were converted to Islam. There was no persecution, but Islam regained its privileges, for example as regards the use of *waqfs*, and sometimes more severe restrictions on the status of non-Muslims than any they had experienced before were introduced. Moreover the favour they had enjoyed for some time had occasionally provoked hostile reactions, which were now intensified.

Finally, the nomadization of certain regions inhabited by peasants led in another way to an advance by Islam at the expense of the native religions. In the final count therefore the Mongol domination was not wholly a positive gain for the non-Muslims. Nevertheless, either temporarily or on some particular points, some progress may have been made, as will now be shown.

From a reading of the documents of the Greek Patriarchate (unfortunately they are known only for the fourteenth century) one gains the impression that, with the Mongols' agreement, the Greeks were able to re-establish, in law and sometimes in actual fact, certain bishoprics which had vanished. In spite of difficulties associated with the period when the Mongols became Muslim, it is known that there were believers and a bishop in Zila (near Sivas) and Amasya, Keltzine (Erzinjān) and Melitene, and communities in Kamakh and Colonia, Nazianzos, Comana (near Tokat) and elsewhere. And in the second half of the fourteenth century the activities of a man suspected of heresy were to reveal once again that believers were present throughout the whole of central Asia Minor and that the Patriarchate of Constantinople had some links with these outlying districts, but also that the relative isolation facilitated the spreading of various doctrines. Linguistically, the isolated populations became so turkicized that, by the fifteenth century, they no longer understood Greek.

For the Armenians, as was said before, the main scene of action was Erzinjān, which was long to remain their real metropolis in Turkey. The bishop, Sarkis/Sergius, not only constituted a local power, but was also reputed to be a respected counsellor of the Ilkhāns. He had even sought – though without success – to obtain the grant of his town as an *iqtāʿ*, in return for furnishing the army with a contingent of 500 men. During the disturbances in 1276 some Kurds, who had been encouraged to intervene in eastern Anatolia against the Mongols and their accomplices, planned to assassinate him. However, in the fourteenth century Erzinjān still remained a large Armenian town.

The Monophysites were also destined to suffer from the freedom of action at times allowed to the Kurds, for example in Malatya in 1257, although Bar-Hebraeus does not give the impression that there was any real and general deterioration of the situation.

The conversion of the Mongols to Islam led to dramatic results in some particular instances, such as the massacre in Irbil, in Mesopotamia, or to financial difficulties when some of them wished to have forty years' arrears of poll-tax collected. The structure of Asia Minor does not seem to have lent itself to this kind of problem. But we know that, in some towns at least Timurtash tried to extend to non-Muslims the restrictions in regard to clothing imposed by classical Muslim law. In 1314, moreover, there was a report of the martyrdom in Erzinjān of a Franciscan whom the Armenians also honoured. The circumstances are not known, but the fact that the two incidents were roughly contemporaneous suggests that they both occurred in the same prevailing atmosphere. In general, however, Latin merchants were able to continue to travel to Tabriz until the end of Abu Saʿīd's reign; that their journeys were then halted was on account of disturbances and not any purely religious dangers.

8

THE EVOLUTION OF THE SYSTEM OF LAND-TENURE AND TAXATION

Both the protectorate and, later, the direct administration of Asia Minor by the Mongols led to fairly profound changes in the system of land-tenure and taxation of land. And it is merely on account of the ill-considered way in which so many scholars have tried, in this field also, to regard the institutions of the Mongol period and those of the time of Seljukid independence as forming one single identical whole that our ideas have been confused. The evolution was due partly to internal conditions in the administration in Asia Minor, partly to the introduction of Irano-Mongol practices from the Ilkhānid State. These latter may themselves have been introduced originally merely through the presence of Mongol agents in Asia Minor, and, later, and more systematically,

with the desire to remedy the acknowledged decay of the administration in Asia Minor by a movement towards the unification of
institutions in all parts of the Ilkhānid Empire.

It was observed earlier that, at the upper level of the State,
the provinces had in part been divided between the ministers and
leading figures of the government. At that level, it is difficult to
say if it was a question of a division into principalities or of
properties – in practice, probably the former. But alienations were
made at a lower level also, transferring the rights and possessions
of the state to individual notables, either directly by the establishment of new private properties or, in a more complex manner,
by the transformation of *iqtāʿ*s into private properties.

To win or retain adherents in their internal quarrels, the
Sultans used to distribute state lands as private property: Rukn
al-Dīn seems to have been particularly prodigal with gifts of this
kind, which were not entirely new, as was seen, but which had
never before been practised on a large scale. There still survives
a deed of gift by him to a shaykh, but, more significantly, it is
revealed that during one of his conflicts with ʿIzz al-Dīn he
promised all the emirs who would follow him that he would grant
them the *iqtāʿ*s held by ʿIzz al-Dīn's emirs and, if victory crowned
their efforts, transform these into private properties. At the end
of his short life he did in fact make many gifts of this kind to his
personal dependants, thereby adding to the unrest and hastening
his assassination. In other cases the sale of state lands was a possible
way of raising money to which ʿIzz al-Dīn is known to have
resorted. In 657/1259 and 660/1262 he in fact sold a village in the
province of Sivri-Hisār to one emir, and to another a village in
the province of Amasya. The documents still survive. There is also
evidence to show that lands acquired as private property could
naturally be re-alienated (not to mention the establishment of
*waqf*s). It is very probable moreover that, besides these regular
concessions, in unsettled times there were a large number of
outright annexations. While the Ilkhān Ghāzān and his famous
minister-historian Rashīd al-Dīn were attempting to carry out a
general reorganization of the Empire in about 700/1300, an effort
was made to recover lands illegally appropriated in Asia Minor.
In this particular form the project had to be abandoned as it
aroused the hostility of the new owners, who nevertheless had

to agree to pay large sums in compensation. However, under Oljaytu, Ghāzān's successor, the vizier of Rūm Ahmad Lakūshī himself sold a certain number of state-owned properties to high dignitaries of the state, obviously with the intention of replenishing the depleted treasury. Osman Turan is apparently right in saying that the state domain was still more extensive than the corresponding ones in neighbouring states, but clearly no statistics are available.

The private appropriation of certain lands slightly modified the legal, if not perhaps the material, status of the peasants who cultivated them. Possibly this is what is expressed in a deed of 697/1298 published by Osman Turan, in which it can be seen that some plots of land which an emir had given as a security and which therefore were obviously his property, had been known formerly by the name of '*faddān* of so-and-so', but are now referred to as the *mu'ākara* of some other person. *Faddān* is really an Egyptian term, which the scribe, being obliged to write in Arabic, must have inserted as the equivalent of *juft*, and in any case it is a unit of area of cultivated land; hence it probably denoted the plot of land which the person named received originally from the state domain, on the basis of which he was taxed. Now another person had taken the land as a *mu'ākara*, that is to say a tenant obliged to surrender a share of his crops, if the word really has the same meaning as it bears in classical Arabic. That the persons concerned were different may be due merely to the lapse of time, or perhaps to the departure of the former occupants who had to be replaced by others. The interesting point is that both groups have Muslim names, generally of an international kind, one or two being more exclusively Turkish. This fact probably indicates a process of sedentarization of Turks rather than of conversion of natives.

The references to *iqtāʿ* given above suggest that it had been subjected to two opposing forces. On the one hand some *iqtāʿ*s had disappeared, having been transformed into private properties, but on the other it appears that – even apart from conferments of provincial governorships under the title of *iqtāʿ*, as discussed later – a large proportion of *iqtāʿ*s had been distributed to army officers on account of the increasing difficulty in guaranteeing any direct pay in cash, and also because the troops were now of purely local character, since, from that time onwards, no foreign mercenaries were recruited. Nevertheless, in the long term it is probable that the *iqtā'* system had greatly declined, since it was becoming impossible for the Seljukid State to maintain a large army under arms, in whatever form. The Mongols certainly had no wish that they, the Seljukids, should do so, but even if they had been allowed, their financial straits would have precluded it. To a certain extent the fact that it was the Mongol army itself which, from then onwards, assumed part of the military tasks in Asia Minor released the Seljukid State from these costs, with the result that there was a transfer of expenditure, rather than any increase or reduction. But the Mongol army was not supported by *iqtā's* (even when under Ghāzān this system became usual, it does not seem in fact to have been extended to Asia Minor). In Asia Minor, the Mongol army lived partly on the regular tribute paid by the Seljukid State, partly (and less regularly) off the country, being quartered in the grazing lands in the east, and from requisitions and the like, which the Seljukid agents, for all their efforts, never succeeded in getting defined very precisely or effectively. This system of quartering of troops was obviously tantamount to a withdrawal from the Seljukid public domain of the lands which the troops occupied, but these were not distributed as *iqtā's* and, on occasions when some Mongols withdrew, they could sometimes revert to the treasury of Rūm. It is self-evident that some Mongol chiefs also acquired possessions, legal or otherwise, in Rūm, which could hardly have been other than private properties.

What has just been said means that the system of land-tenure and taxation in Asia Minor had not developed solely within the framework of the Seljukid administration, and that interventions by the Mongols were also a factor. It is necessary to pay particular attention to this characteristic for, as a result of failing to give it sufficient regard, some people have perhaps at times mistakenly accepted as features of the Seljukid régime what were in fact merely extensions of the Ilkhānid régime, which existed side by side with the Seljukid characteristics. The tribute and the obligation to provide for Mongol forces were not the only reasons for this situation. It will be recalled that in 658/1260 the two brothers Sultans 'Izz al-Dīn and Rukn al-Dīn, and also their vizier Shams al-Dīn Baba Tughrā'ī, had been compelled to stay longer than anticipated with Hülägü, who was then occupied with the conquest of Syria, and they had contracted immense loans from the Ilkhānid treasury. The Mongols did not take such matters lightly and were not satisfied with vague promises of repayment. In addition to the tribute, repayment of this loan was to consist annually of 200,000 dinars in coin and 300 bars of gold (*zerkūb*), or their value, besides livestock and fabrics. To supervise the servicing of this debt the Mongols appointed Tāj al-Dīn Muʿtazz, son of a former chief *cadi* of Khwārizm who had been sent on an embassy to Kay-kubādh by the Khwārizmshāh Jalāl al-Dīn Manguberti. To guarantee the repayment of the agreed sums, he secured the concession of the whole province of Kastamonu as an *iqtāʿ*, as well as Akseray and Develi Karahisār (it was in Akseray that the historian Aqsarāyī, who was the financial officer there, became acquainted with his son and future successor; it is thanks to this fact that the details on the matter are known). On his death (676/1277) this son, Mujīr al-Dīn Amīrshāh, succeeded to all the offices he had held, for a time extending his authority over the whole region from Sivas and Tokat as far as Kastamonu and Sinope. And it is self-evident that, from the very fact of their power in the region, derived directly from the Mongols, both father and son exercised a considerable influence over general policy in Asia Minor, sometimes even combining their responsibilities towards the Ilkhān with the office of *nāʾib* to the Sultan in Rūm. At the very end of his life, however, Mujīr al-Dīn incurred the hostility of powerful men, both in Asia Minor and at the Ilkhānid court, and at Sinope his influence was virtually destroyed by that of the *pervāne*'s descendants. He died in 701/1302, and although money obviously continued to be sent from Rūm to Iran, it is doubtful whether the task of supervision was handed over to anyone else, since direct administration of the country by Mongol governors now removed part of the reason for the existence of his office.

For an exact understanding of the situation which resulted for Asia Minor from this Mongol interference, it is necessary to make a careful distinction (hitherto not always observed) between what relates to the Ilkhānid Government (the 'Great Divan') and what concerns the administration of Rūm, properly speaking. The Mongols' revenues came from *muqātaʿāt*, which, as in the terminology of classical Islam, denote leases of tax-farms for certain districts or natural resources, but also for *bālish*, *injū* and *dalāī*. In the Ilkhānid State (especially at the beginning) the *bālish* is recorded as some general tax or tribute, although it is not possible to determine its exact nature. *Injū* (domains) were the lands belonging to the Ilkhānid State, which had therefore acquired some of these in Rūm, the revenues from which had to be forwarded to it. In 676 the Ilkhānid vizier Shams al-Dīn Juwaynī had for example caused some new lands dependent on Erzinjān to be incorporated in them. The word *dalāī* occurs rarely and does not have a clear meaning. In Osman Turan's view, it denotes the lands of the Seljukid State administered by Mongol representatives, his principal argument being that there were no *dalāī* in the Ilkhānid State strictly speaking. I find it difficult to be equally positive. All that can be said with certainty is that the *injū* and the *dalāī* are two categories of revenues associated with the Mongol taxation in Asia Minor, related to each other but at the same time distinct, each having in 692/1293 its own *dīwān*, with two chief accountants (*mustawfī*) and a separate director, under the authority of Mujīr al-Dīn. Leaving aside the enigmatic *bālish*, which at that time was no longer of concern, the terms *injū* and *dalāī* applied to the allocation of the revenues collected, and do not imply that the system of taxation had been modified.

However, there is no doubt that some modification was made, though it is difficult to establish precisely what. Aqsarāyī, who in this matter is the basic source, says that, on the accession of Kaykhusraw III (664/1265), it was decided to divide taxation into four sectors, the *y. w. yt* (?), the *na'lbahā*, the *māl-i yām*, and the *māl-i bozorg*, to be levied in four distinct operations. Apart from the first of these, the name of which is uncertain, the names of the other three (meaning respectively 'cavalry', 'post', and 'general' or 'supremo') suggest that it was a matter of defining the allocation rather than the imposition of the tax itself. The writer in fact adds that no other tax was levied, except in frontier territories where a small comprehensive sum was levied, but that does not make it necessary to modify the interpretation. Indeed, in a passage quoted earlier from this same writer Aqsarāyī, it emerges that the *jizya*, which is probably to be understood as a general tax on non-Muslim agricultural workers, was still the basic tax in Rūm under the Mongols as before. The method employed by certain of their agents was, rather than modifying the system, to exact by force payments in excess of the regular amounts. Fakhr al-Dīn Qazwīnī made himself particularly unpopular by this practice. A little later, Kamāl al-Dīn Tiflisī in his turn aroused resentment by arbitrarily levying the tax on grain before the harvest. However, as the direct Mongol administration tightened its hold, innovations were introduced, mainly in the form of customs from the rest of the Empire, for example, the establishment of *tamgha*, a customary tax levied in Iran since the Mongol occupation, which however did not exist in Rūm (it was a kind of toll). In reality, for the Mongols, Asia Minor was above all a territory for exploitation both public and private. Governmental control, by Seljukids or Ilkhānids, was remote and irregular. The dominant impression is mainly one of disorder, with the intermittent appearance of serious but short-lived abuses and equally short-lived attempts at their repression. This situation does not apply of course to the time of the disruption of the Empire.

In the *Geography* which he wrote in 1339, Hamd Allāh Mustawfī Qazwīnī quoted the total sum from the taxes due or levied in a fairly large number of leading provincial towns in the Ilkhānid Empire. In this connection, the Turkish scholar Zeki Velidi Togan has, by collating the manuscripts, arrived at better readings for the figures. For Asia Minor the total figure, given separately, of 3,300,000 dinars (as against 15,000,000 under the Seljukids, according to him) may be accepted; but it is difficult to know how far to rely on the rest. Not only are the readings of the various figures unequally reliable, not only are a certain number of localities given without their tax (and for that reason Zeki Velidi Togan had omitted them from his table), but in addition we know neither on what basis the tax is given here (and it may not everywhere be the same, for example in vassal provinces paying a comprehensive sum), nor to what date he refers. It is true that, for certain budgetary items the allocation of which is described elsewhere, Mustawfī says he is speaking of the year 1336, but it must be confessed that this date, already open to question as referring to the whole of the Ilkhānid State, which was then in a condition of anarchy following on the death of Abu Saʿīd, becomes difficult to accept for Rūm if it is examined in detail. Although the list claims to include the whole of Rūm, it is incomplete, and although it may relate only to provinces where taxes could effectively be collected, it is certainly too extensive to refer to the situation in 1336. It would be more reasonable to make the figures apply to an earlier period, all the more since the text makes no allusion to the Turcoman principalities, were it not that the total comes close to the figure of 3,000,000 given some years later by Kiyā Mazandarānī, certainly also from a theoretical list. To sum up, the wise course is to take note of it for the moment, without claiming to make any deductions from it.

9

THE EVOLUTION OF THE TOWNS

The Mongols' warlike interventions in Asia Minor do not appear to have led to the ruin of its towns, as had happened in Iran and Central Asia, and indeed with Baghdad. After being pillaged in 1243, Kayseri soon recovered, and perhaps only the small towns of the Turcomans living on the borders suffered at the end of the century from Gaykhātū's campaign. Possibly the Mongol rule to some extent altered the relative importance of certain towns by attracting the political leaders to the East. Thus Kayseri and Sivas perhaps gained a little in importance, whereas Konya lost slightly – but there was no radical change. Konya was too clearly the traditional and cultural capital to lose that role in a day, particularly as those opposed to the Mongols were more at home there than in the eastern towns; and even at the start it increased in size, with the mosques, *madrasas* and other foundations established by Karatay, Fakhr al-Dīn ʿAlī and others. Later it suffered from the operations of the Karamanids, but in the fourteenth century it still remained a prominent town. The characteristic feature of the fourteenth century was not so much the disappearance of any large town as the multiplication of medium-sized ones.

But although the towns continued on the same course, their internal administration was nevertheless progressively modified quite perceptibly. This can partly be seen through the founding of public buildings: the great figures are no longer the rulers but

335

are now powerful ministers and officers or even, in the smaller towns, local notables, including *akhi* leaders. At one point Karatay was the benefactor, then for a longer period it was Muʿīn al-Dīn the *pervāne*, and above all the vizier Fakhr al-Dīn ʿAlī known as Sāhib Ata, who endowed Konya and almost all the towns of Asia Minor with their foundations. At the start of the Mongol period Konya was further enriched with many new foundations – the mosque of Karatay, the mosques known by the names of Laranda and Inje Minareli ('with the slender minaret'), a Khānqāh (monastery of dervishes) and Fakhr al-Dīn's own tomb, a monastery and the tomb of Jalāl al:Dīn Rūmī, among others. Karatay also embellished Kayseri. The artistic merit of the many public buildings to be found throughout Asia Minor will be considered in a later chapter. Once the principalities were stabilized, the Turcoman period also contributed, in a more modest way, by supplying other foundations, particularly in new centres and the towns newly conquered for Islam.

The weakening of the central authority increased the power not only of the Turcomans but also of the urban *futuwwa* groups, at certain times because the absence of any force strong enough to restrain them encouraged them to put themselves forward more openly and in a consciously assertive manner, at others because the government or persons of influence in fact called upon their forces to supplement or replace the ordinary military forces against some particular adversary. This is known to have taken place in the second half of the thirteenth century, more especially in regard to Konya, but the same thing happened elsewhere.

The first episode in which the *akhis* appear clearly occurred immediately after the disaster of Köse Dagh. Some *runūd* from Akshehir and Abgarm (north-west of Konya) were at that time employed by various important persons in the entourage of Sultan Kaykhusraw to assassinate certain others. Next, *runūd* from Konya were sent to the vizier Shams al-Dīn Isfahānī to ransack the victims' homes, and also to prevent the repetition of any such activities. Soon afterwards, however, when the vizier had been accused by the Mongols of complicity in the crime, they helped to arrest him. Here, then, they were found on the side of authority, in fact if not in principle, although for what precise reason is unknown. This was not normally to be their practice.

To find any comparable details, it is necessary to skip a generation and consider the Jimri incident. Information concerning the *akhis* and *runūd* of Konya is here provided by the anonymous townsman who composed the *Seljūknāme*, and who evidently took a particular interest in them. According to him, the *akhis* of the capital were under the orders of two leaders, Akhi Ahmad and Akhi Ahmadshāh, who were also known to Aflākī, the hagiographer of the Mevlevis. Akhi Ahmad was disliked by Aflākī as being insufficiently aristocratic and an enemy of Jalāl al-Dīn Rūmī. He is perhaps identical with the author of a treatise on *futuwwa* written during that period by an author of the same name, and in that case he would be a native of Ardabil, which was then still in north-western Iran and also the town of the ancestor of the Iranian dynasty of the Safawids who found support among *akhis*. Ahmadshāh was regarded more favourably by Aflākī, who considered him more respectable and described him as the leader of thousands of *runūd*. He apparently helped to dissuade Gaykhātū from sacking the Seljukid capital in 1291. Although his successor, Akhi Siddiq, had discussions with the Mevlevis, letting them return to their mysticism while he dealt with worldly matters and eventually had to use force, it seems that this group had maintained better relations with the Mevlevis, who, after the slaughters carried out by order of the Karamanids in 1312, watched over the bodies of their dead. Even if a *futuwwa* obviously existed in general, it did not necessarily result in any complete unity either of organization or spirit.

A third *akhi* named in contemporary texts as a man of influence was a certain Akhi Amir Muhammad, to whom one of the most famous *fütüvvetnāme*s, that of Nāsirī, was probably dedicated. His example (and others could also be found) affords proof that there was no incompatibility in belonging simultaneously to the *futuwwa* and to the social category of politico-military leaders.

The *akhis*' role in the defence of Konya against the Karamanids and Jimri is not presented in the same way in the various surviving accounts, and indeed may not have been consistent. There is little doubt that, like all the citizens, they had in principle been hostile to the Turcomans. However, the governor of the city distrusted them and only allowed them to take part in operations when there was a lack of other troops, but there is nothing to indicate that they betrayed his trust. Their attitude was the same a few years later when the widow of Kaykhusraw III tried to win the support of the Karamanids. They resisted this policy, and all the vizier's diplomatic skill and formal guarantees by the Turcoman chiefs were required before 'the tumult could be appeased' (1285).

The events of 1290–1 make it possible to confirm and define these impressions. When the chief of the Eshref Turcomans seized Siyāvush, Sultan Mas'ūd's brother, disorders broke out in Konya in which the *runūd* do not seem to have been of one mind. One group was surrounded and burnt alive in their house in the suburbs. But whereas they had probably tried to take advantage of the situation, in normal times the *runūd* must rather have favoured Mas'ūd, who relied on them, and in particular on Ahmadshāh, in order to resist the financial exactions of the vizier Fakhr al-Dīn Qazwīnī, the Mongols' appointee. However, the Sultan left for Kayseri, and only his brother Siyāvush and the Mongol representative Kutluja remained in Konya. The *akhis* managed to persuade the prince to have the Mongol leader murdered. Against the evident threat of the Karamanids, the *akhis*, like the Sultan, apparently advocated a reconciliation with the Eshref. At one point, when the fortunes of war turned against the Eshref, there was a violent revolt against some *akhis* in Konya. A few months later, however, more *akhis* were known to have defended their town against the Germiyan. Ahmadshāh's power was unassailable (perhaps Ahmad himself had been a victim of one of the earlier repressions) and, according to the author of the *Seljūknāme*, in 1294 fifteen thousand persons followed his brother's funeral procession. After the assassination of Ahmadshāh in 697/ 1298, the new Sultan 'Alā' al-Dīn Farāmurz explicitly authorized revenge against the assassin, although he was one of his officers, and in fact he was killed some months later. Ahmadshāh, shortly before his death, had ordered the expulsion of a hated representative of the Karamanids. Although the documentation becomes very inadequate at this point, it can be accepted that bad relations continued, so long as it was possible to resist the Karamanids. In 1312, when they occupied Konya, the Karamanids proceeded to massacre the *akhis*. Nevertheless the *akhis* did not favour the Mongols, and seem essentially to have been inspired by local patriotism, being anti-Mongol from the national or religious standpoint, and anti-Turcoman from the economic and social standpoint. As was seen before, it was not a question of 'Turkish' solidarity.

There are in Ibn Battūta and other sources enough references to *akhi*s and their leaders to allow it to be affirmed that they existed in all the towns. From then onwards their character was that of a mainly professional association, as was observed earlier. It is unnecessary to dwell upon all the individual cases, but one name, that of Akhi Evrān, must be quoted, since his reputation was so great that those who boasted of descent from him in succeeding centuries were able to claim some measure of control over the whole body of *akhi*s. As so often happens, the figure of Akhi Evrān, although historical, is surrounded by legend. It can only be said that he was a saintly man who lived in the little town of Kïrshehir, and that he died there in about 1300. Legend connects him with the guild of tanners, but there is no reference to the fact in the old texts, which indeed are too sparse to allow any conclusions to be drawn. Whether or not he was a tanner, it was in any event not in that capacity that he became famous, but as a saint, in some degree connected with the other saints of the period.

The figure of Akhi Evrān recalls in a particularly revealing way the dual character manifested by the whole *futuwwa*, a point already emphasized. On the one hand the *akhi*s resorted to action, often with violence, and one of their leaders insisted on the need for this to the Mevlevis who felt doubts on this score, and Ibn Battūta, who incidentally appeared to find such conduct quite normal, himself stated clearly that, when it came to attacks on the police, there was no one to equal them. On the other hand they, or at least those in control, had a mystic ideal, and since it was only the latter who were writers, it is only the ritualistic and mystic aspect that emerges in the treatises on *futuwwa*, to such a point that at first sight one might wonder whether it is one and the same organization that is being considered.

These treatises, *fütüvvetnāme*s in the Irano-Turkish pronunciation, now became more numerous and some of them still survive. There are also some written outside Asia Minor, but it was quite certainly there that this literary form chiefly flourished, which in itself is also an indication of the very special development of the organization. The work by Ahmad of Ardabil and the more important one by Nāsirī, written in 689/1290, probably in north-eastern Anatolia, have already been mentioned. In addition, though without going outside the period, there are also some chapters in various encyclopaedic works which must be noted. These were written in Persian. But when Turkish became established as a literary language, *fütüvvetnāme*s naturally appeared also in Turkish. The ancestor of the whole Turkish *fütüvvet* literature which developed until the time of the Ottomans was probably the *fütüvvetnāme* of *Burghāzī*, written during the fourteenth century at a date difficult to determine. An important chapter on the *fütüvvet* in Turkish occurs also in the early poem by Gülshehri – and this is to omit minor or later short works. It was during the same period that *akhi* circles, which contained so many members of Iranian stock, adopted the figure whom the Iranians had made a national hero of romance, Abū Muslim, who in Asia Minor, in a wider and more direct way, became simply the champion in the struggle for the Faith and the Law against oppressors, a champion who, in versions which became increasingly remote from history, typically combined the struggle that the real Abū Muslim had led against the Umayyads and for the ʿAbbāsids with devotion to the cause of the Imāms of the ʿAlids, whom the ʿAbbāsids had persecuted and the Shīʿīs revered.

However, the decline of Seljukido-Mongol authority and, reciprocally, the increasing power of the Turcoman princes as they proceeded to establish principalities embracing towns, led to a certain *rapprochement* between the only two surviving authorities, namely the new masters and the *akhi* leaders. Almost wherever he went, Ibn Battūta noted the officially recognized power exercised by the latter and the esteem in which they were held by the princes. He added, as a generalization, that in those towns where no prince lived, it was the *akhi* leader who was the effective master of the town. Muslim history had known several comparable instances of the political influence of the *futuwwa* and of petty principalities based on towns. But in Anatolia, before the reincorporation of the country in the Ottoman Empire, the fourteenth century was a remarkable time of development of the *futuwwa*'s political strength. It is true that no republic of the type of Florence existed within Asia Minor. But the fact that, within

the bounds of a town and its immediate environs, the *akhi* leader
should in certain limited cases have been the real authority, even
though recognizing the theoretical supremacy of some prince, is
more or less evident. The clearest example is that of Ankara, where
the *akhi* leader's name appears in inscriptions. It may be that the
Ottomans, at the time of their conquests, were to regard these *akhis*
as sufficiently powerful to make it advantageous for them to belong
to their *futuwwa*, in somewhat the same spirit as the Caliph al-
Nāsir had earlier done.

IO

INSTITUTIONS

Apart from the fact that the Mongols had their own representatives, the organs of the administration under the Mongol protectorate remained the same as in the period of independence. The
conditions under which they operated however had changed
considerably. It will be sufficient merely to recapitulate the conclusions to which we are led by the narrative of events. A primary
feature is that, either through fear of his independence or because
he was a minor (it will be remembered that the rule of some child-
Sultans was brought about deliberately by assassinating the father),
the Sultan rapidly lost all real power, especially in the eastern half
of the country which, for the new masters, was the more important
part. By contrast, his ministers gained in importance, not of course
because they were independent of the Mongols, but on the contrary because, unlike the Sultan who was Sultan by right, they
were ministers merely by delegation and were in fact nominated,
to some extent directly and explicitly, by the Mongols themselves
rather than by the Sultan. This was true until the moment when
the fiction of the Sultan was to disappear and the Ilkhāns were
formally to proclaim themselves vested with authority, the Sultanate being left to come to an obscure end.

A second feature of these ministers is that, to defray the costs
of the offices they held, they divided the lands of the state amongst

themselves and thus became the holders of lordships and principalities. Two of these at least endured for a time, that of the *pervāne*
Mu'īn al-Dīn, and that of the vizier Fakhr al-Dīn 'Alī. The point
has already been emphasized that neither of them was a Turkish
professional soldier (the *pervāne*'s father was a vizier of Iranian
stock, while the second, also of Iranian origin, first appears as
amīr-dād), and that their annexations were indeed possible only
because no feudalism had existed previously. This type of evolution
is somewhat rare, and I can see almost no parallel for it in the Near
East, either Muslim or Byzantine. However, it was not to last for
more than half a century, the real socio-military forces being concentrated elsewhere. Nevertheless, at the end of the fourteenth
century Burhān al-Dīn was in some measure to represent a revival
of it.

This being said, I need only list the holders of the various offices
during the Mongol period, in the same order as for the period of
independence. In general, the list will extend only to the end of
the thirteenth century, owing to the inadequacy of the documentation. But in fact the gap thus left is of no great importance, since
the subdivision of territory was to become increasingly common,
together with the consequent reorganization of the administrative
organs within the smaller and sometimes altered framework of the
new principalities.

The atabeks
Asad al-Dīn Rūzbeh, 646.
Arslandogmush (?), 654.
Karatay, 646, d. 651 or 652, at first also *nā'ib*.
Majd al-Dīn, 675.
Bahā al-Dīn Rudkārdī, 682.

The nā'ibs
Karatay, see *atabek*, 646.
Shujā' al-Dīn 'Abd al-Rahmān, 647, 652.
Nizām al-Dīn Khurshīd, 654.
Fakhr al-Dīn 'Alī, 657; in 658 became vizier, replaced by –
Amīn al-Dīn Mikāīl (formerly *mustawfi*), until 675.
Jalāl al-Dīn, formerly *mustawfi*, 676.
Mujīr al-Dīn Amīrshāh, 680.

342

Jamāl al-Dīn, 690.
Mehmed the *pervāne*, emir, with Kamāl al-Dīn Tiflisī as *nā'ib*, in about 695.

The pervānes
Fakhr al-Dīn ʿAṭṭār Abū Bakr, d. 646.
Nizām al-Dīn Khurshīd, executed in 656.
Muʿīn al-Dīn Sulaymān, 656–76.
A son of the Ilkhānid vizier Shams al-Dīn Juwaynī, in 680.
A brother of the vizier Fakhr al-Dīn Qazwīnī, 684.
Muʿīn al-Dīn Mehmed Pervāne (son of Muʿīn al-Dīn Sulaymān), before 693.
Rukn al-Dīn, 699.

The viziers
Muhadhdhab al-Dīn, d. 642/1244.
Shams al-Dīn Isfahānī, formerly *nā'ib*, 642–6.
Qāḍī ʿIzz al-Dīn Rāzī, then Nizām al-Dīn Khurshīd (cf. *pervāne*s), then Najm al-Dīn Nakhjawānī 647, then Bābā Tughrā'ī, followed by Rāzī for the second time in 648–54.
Shams al-Dīn Bābā Tughrā'ī, 654–8.
Fakhr al-Dīn ʿAlī, 5 658–70.
Majd al-Dīn Muhammad ibn Husayn Erzinjānī, formerly *mustawfī*.
Fakhr al-Dīn ʿAlī, for the second time, 671–87.
Fakhr al-Dīn Qazwīnī, 689/1290.
Najm al-Dīn, 691.
Jamāl al-Dīn Muhammad, 695.
Shams al-Dīn Ahmad Lākūshī, 697 (together with the last-named ?).
ʿAlā' al-Dīn Sāwī, 700, 703.

The mustawfīs
Najīb al-Dīn (Dālīkhānī ?), 654, executed in 661.
Amīn al-Dīn Mīkāīl, date uncertain.
Majd al-Dīn Muhammad ibn Husayn Erzinjānī, 661–70 (became vizier).
Jalāl al-Dīn Mahmūd, 670, 675–6.
Jamāl al-Dīn, brother of the vizier Fakhr al-Dīn Qazwīnī, 689.

Nāsir al-Dīn Yavlak Arslan, 689–91.
Sharaf al-Dīn Uthmān, 691.
   (with ʿAbd al-ʿAzīz, 697 ?); and someone unnamed in
   Konya (?)
   (with Sharaf al-Dīn ʿAbd al-Rahmān Tabrīzī).

The mushrifs
Qiwām al-Dīn Ashhar ibn al-Hamīd, 654.
Jamāl al-Dīn ibn amīr al-hajj Mahmūd, 661.
Zahīr al-Dīn Mutawwaj ibn ʿAbd al-Rahmān, 670.
Imād al-Dīn Zanjānī, 680.
Fakhr al-Dīn, 685.

The nāzirs
Humām al-Dīn Shādbahār, 652.
Zayn al-Dīn Ahmad Erzinjānī, date uncertain.

The tughrāʾīs
Shams al-Dīn Bābā, 646.
A nephew of Amīn al-Dīn Mīkāīl, 675.
Ibn Bībī, the historian, date unknown, before 680.

The ʿārids
Rashīd al-Dīn Juwaynī, 647, replaced in 658 (or perhaps earlier)
by Samsam al-Dīn Kaymaz, or together with him.
Shihāb al-Dīn, 654 ?
(The office perhaps disappeared afterwards; in any case it had
inevitably lost its importance.)

The amīr-dād
Nusrat al-Dīn, 646.
Fakhr al-Dīn ʿAlī, 654–7, afterwards became *nāʾib* and then
vizier.
Nizām al-Dīn, 683–5.

The beglerbegs
Shams al-Dīn Khāss Oghuz, 646.
Sharaf al-Dīn Mahmūd, 646.
Sirāj al-Dīn ibn Bāja, 647.

Tavtash, d. 656.
Anon. (Ibn Bībī, p. 271).
('The Greek Constable' (Michael Palaeologus)).
Sharaf al-Dīn Mahmūd ibn al-Khatīr, 661–75.
(Baygūt, 675 ?).
Toruntāy.
ʿAzīz al-Dīn, 684–95.

At those times when the Sultanate was divided, an attempt was made to maintain the unity of the administrative offices, on the whole successfully.

Above or alongside the ministers of the Seljukids were various representatives of the Mongol authority who perforce interfered with their conduct of affairs, even though they had no desire to do so or though the Ilkhān had not formally required it. Originally, these were commanders of military forces who had no other official power. This, however, they did in fact acquire, taking advantage of the remoteness which gave them independence, partly because their men had to be provided for, partly on account of the benefits they themselves reaped, while in addition the Seljukid officers intrigued with them against each other. Moreover, during the same period, for one reason or another there was a constant succession of Mongol ambassadors or representatives (ilchis), who often resided with the Seljukid ministers or military commanders, or with the Sultan and his regent. While Muʿīn al-Dīn Sulaymān was alive it really amounted to no more than that, except for the fact that the increase in the number of Mongol troops and the permanence of their presence progressively enhanced the power of their chiefs, particularly in the eastern half of the country where they were quartered, not only because it was closer to Ilkhānid territory but also because they were well-placed to strike against the Mamluks. As a result, now at their head were often princes of the blood whom it was difficult to oppose and who endeavoured to enrich themselves. Moreover, the loans contracted by ʿIzz al-Dīn and Rukn al-Dīn in 1258–60, for the repayment of which certain categories of revenues had been set aside as securities, and probably other reasons and operations as well, led to the establishment in Rūm not only of private holdings of property by Mongol notables, but even of state lands which intruded upon the lands of the Seljukid State. At the head of these state lands there was a general and permanent representative of the Mongol authority, whom the Seljukid officials could not ignore. Finally, of course, there were officers and officials specially responsible for affairs concerning the Mongols present among them, in particular their judge or *yargūjī*.

After the death of Mu'īn al-Dīn or even later, there appeared an official whose title is not recorded although we know the name of his office, *iyālat-i wilāyat* (*eyālet-i vilāyet*), and whose powers, which did not supersede those of any other senior officials, are difficult to determine, although he was obviously some kind of governor general. The sources are not definite enough to allow a list of holders to be made, but it is known that in 691/1292 the office was held by Tashtimur Khitāī; in 692, when responsibilities were divided, jointly by Isfandiyār and Ilbasar; in 696 by Melik Pehlivān Khorasānī; and in 697 by Bāyenjār. It appears, therefore, to judge from the names, to have been held by Mongols and non-Mongols alike, without distinction. In the same period the *imāra* (office of supreme emir) is known to have been given, in addition to their other offices, to Mujīr al-Dīn Amīrshāh for a time, then to Mehmed the *pervāne*, and afterwards to a certain Bahchūr, who held no other office. It is impossible to determine the precise extent of these responsibilities in Asia Minor, since the situation there was not *a priori* comparable with that of certain other Ilkhānid provinces (though not all), for which similar offices are attested. We must merely guard against possible confusion in the chronicles between references to purely Seljukid titles, to Ilkhānid titles in Rūm, and to Ilkhānid titles elsewhere, whose holders may have worked in Rūm or been known there through their place in the central government.

It was during the Mongol period that several formularies or collections of models of administrative documents were written, to which we owe the preservation of copies of deeds and various letters, and which provide evidence that a shortage of scribes and draftsmen was consciously felt, as was the need, both cultural and administrative, to supply the deficiency. The most important of these works, and also their characteristics, have been mentioned in the chapter on the sources and therefore call for no further discussion. The Arabic documents which provided the basis for the calculation of taxation were translated into Persian for Fakhr al-Dīn ʿAlī. The attempt by the Karamanids and Jimri to set up a Turkish chancellery produced no immediate results, and, even in the principalities, during the fourteenth century Arabic and Persian were to be employed concurrently with Turkish in the fields of administration and of justice.

I I

INTELLECTUAL AND ARTISTIC LIFE IN ASIA MINOR IN THE TIME OF THE MONGOLS

It is a well-known fact that the evolution of intellectual life is always a little less rapid than that of the material and political aspects of society. Although the factors which distinguish these aspects naturally cannot fail to have repercussions upon the ideas of the members of society, it remains true that the members themselves grew up before those factors existed, and that it will be their children, growing up after the event, who will feel their full consequences. It is therefore not surprising if, in certain respects, intellectual life in Asia Minor after 1243 represents the full flowering of a process which had first begun in the time of the last Seljukids. Moreover the effects of the Mongol conquest are not simple. The Mongols' direct influence was infinitesimal and, at the most, some effects of it can perhaps be discerned in the sphere of folk-lore. The indirect results of their annexation however were threefold. In the first place the relative political unification, under the control of the Ilkhāns, of countries which had been separate politically, the fact that Iranian officials followed in the wake of the Mongol armies, the visits to the Ilkhānid court undertaken by inhabitants of Asia Minor, their correspondence with Iranian scholars, who were sometimes old acquaintances – all these things accentuated the Iranian influence which had first been introduced in the twelfth century by Iranians attracted there as individuals, and then later, in the two or three decades preceding Köse Dagh, by other Iranians in far greater numbers, fleeing before these same

347

Mongols and following behind the Khwārizmians. Secondly, the movements provoked among the Turcomans by the Seljukido-Mongol rule and in reaction against it contained spiritual as well as political and social aspects which were perhaps strengthened or coloured by the arrival of popular preachers and dervishes from Central Asia, initially fugitives who later took advantage of the political unification. Finally, the disorganization which, in the ultimate reckoning, represented the total achievement of the Mongol régime in Asia Minor, in the end produced disruptive results in intellectual life also.

In respect of religion, Asia Minor remained a Muslim country; that is to say that the reduction of Islam to the rank of one religion along with others, a situation which to some extent had character-ized the early period of Mongol domination in Iran and Meso-potamia (waqfs in those countries being more or less integrated into the general economy and used for the benefit of the different creeds without distinction), occurred hardly at all under the pro-tectorate of Asia Minor. It was pointed out earlier that, despite the favour they enjoyed at the start, the Christians had nowhere really regained the upper hand, the Muslims being so much in a majority and so dominant socially that, even at the time when they had not been converted, the Mongols could not but recruit the bulk of their administrative personnel, including the viziers, from among them. And this situation was only accentuated when the Mongols were converted to Islam. In its institutions Asia Minor had remained Muslim, the whole administrative personnel was Muslim, and the Muslim viziers of the Ilkhāns themselves were anxious to figure as Muslim patrons, sometimes even more than in their own country. At the most, it can be said that the Mongols' indifference to the various divisions of Islam may have favoured propaganda which previously, under the Seljukids, had been less easy to spread openly. But too little is known in this respect, both of the Seljukid régime before 1243 and of the Seljukido-Mongol régime afterwards, for anything more than wholly conjectural suppositions to be advanced. We do not know, for example, if there was any kind of religious foundation specifically for the Shī'īs, even in the time of Oljaytu, who was himself Shī'ī. Moreover, as must be borne in mind, it was a time when differences between Shī'ism and Sunnism were not clearly grasped, and when a man such as

Nasīr al-Dīn Tūsī, in Iran, in reality stood between the two and corresponded indiscriminately with philosophers of both denominations.

The strength of the iranizing influence must not prevent us from recognizing, however, that in some degree there was also a development of an arabizing influence, perhaps fostered by political relations with Syria, whether good or bad, which were much more important in the thirteenth century than in the fourteenth. Arabic never having won the place held by Persian, even among the aristocracy, the general importance of the arabizing movement was obviously not to be of the same degree as the other, but nevertheless, exerting its influence in a more restricted milieu and particularly in the disciplines concerned with the Law, it helped to establish that culture of Turkey which was then in process of formation. Moreover, the speakers of the two languages felt no hostility for each other, and many became familiar with both.

The great figure of Arabic-speaking Islam is Sadr al-Dīn Qūnawī (Konevī), whose name has already been mentioned in connection with his father's relations, at the beginning of the century, with Muhyī al-Dīn ibn ʿArabī, the great Spanish mystic who had settled in the Muslim East. The father belonged to an Arab family of Malatya, but Sadr al-Dīn himself spent almost his whole life in Konya, where he died in 673/1274–5. To this origin he also owed the fact, which was no hindrance to his career but unusual in an Irano-Turkish background, that he belonged to the Shāfiʿī school of law. His works, written entirely in Arabic (apart from one minor exception, significantly in Persian) testify to his sound traditional learning, but are dominated by the form of mysticism he had learned from Ibn ʿArabī through his father and others of the master's disciples who were living in Asia Minor, such as the North African Afīf al-Dīn Sulaymān al-Yāsin al-Tilimsānī. At the end of his life his prestige was considerable, and he himself had disciples, themselves of course living in Asia Minor, but enjoying a reputation which extended far beyond that country. Among his disciples it is interesting to note the name of the same Saʿīd Ferghānī who, as was noted earlier, also wrote a commentary (in Arabic and Persian) on the works of another Arab mystic of the beginning of the thirteenth century, ʿUmar ibn al-Farīd. The Iranian mystic Fakhr al-Dīn, known as ʿIrāqī (in reality an Iranian), whom the *pervāne* Muʿīn al-Dīn settled not far from himself, at Tokat, also felt the influence of Sadr al-Dīn and, through him, that of Ibn ʿArabī, whose teachings he later disseminated in India. It is impossible to enumerate all Sadr al-Dīn's theological and mystical works, but it is interesting to note that some items of his correspondence, with Nasīr al-Dīn Tūsī among others, have been preserved.

Close to Sadr al-Dīn Qūnawī, and a little older, was the great *cadi* and jurist referred to earlier, Sirāj al-Dīn al-Urmawī, who lived until 1283 and enjoyed a considerable reputation in all countries. Among his disciples is mentioned a certain Safī al-Dīn al-Hindī, born in India and at first living in the Yemen, who from there went to Egypt and finally spent the years 674–85/ 1275–86 in Rūm. In the scientific field, Qutb al-Dīn Shīrāzī, a pupil of Nasīr al-Dīn Tūsī in Khorasan, spent a certain time in Rūm, at Malatya, before his death in Tabriz in 710/1310 at the age of 74. He has left some astrological treatises in Arabic, in addition to the Persian encyclopaedia which will be referred to again a little later. In 1310 a philosophical treatise by a certain Shams al-Dīn (from Tustar, on the borders of Iraq) was even dedicated to an Eshref.

It is impossible to attempt to list the considerable number of works written in Persian in Asia Minor under the Mongol régime. With them would have to be included the collections of *inshā'* and treatises on *futuwwa* already described in the appropriate place. We need only add that the decline in importance of Konya and the emancipation of the local powers multiplied the number of patrons in the smaller towns. Although a treatise on astrology survives, dedicated to Kaykhusraw III but written in Kayseri as early as 675/1276, it was to the rulers of Kastamonu that the Persian encyclopaedia of Shīrāzī, a treatise on heresiography and one on administration were dedicated, while an encyclopaedia by a certain Muhammad ibn Ayyūb of Dunaysir in Diyār Bakr is dedicated to an unidentified emir of Karahisār.

It was of course in the field of mysticism that the most important literary compositions in Persia continued to appear. From the hand of the author of one of the treatises on *futuwwa*, which themselves are semi-mystical, one work of pure mysticism survives. ʿIrāqī, mentioned above, wrote in both Arabic and Persian, like

Ferghānī. But all were dominated by Jalāl al-Dīn Rūmī and his descendants and disciples. Here it is no longer a question primarily of literature, in spite of the remarkable literary value of the works of Jalāl al-Dīn. In a wider sense, it marks the beginning of a powerful religious manifestation, which must be recognized as such.

According to the pious legend it was in 643/1245 that Jalāl al-Dīn, whose youthful life has already been referred to, met Shams al-Dīn Tabrīzī in Konya. The encounter was overwhelming, and its effects outlived the day when Shams, regarded with envy by Jalāl's disciples, disappeared, probably murdered (1247). Thenceforward the life of mysticism was all-important for Jalāl al-Dīn, who at first sought for Shams as an ideal, then saw him reincarnated in one of his disciples, Salāh al-Dīn Zarkūb (the goldsmith). The great number of pupils who came to him made it necessary to form them into a community which was controlled, under Jalāl al-Dīn himself, by disciples whom he nominated, sometimes against the wishes of the rest. Pre-eminent among them, after the death of Zarkūb, their first leader, was Husām al-Dīn, one of the principal *akhi* leaders in Konya. Thus there came into being the order known as the Mevlevis, from the name Mawlānā, Turkish Mevlānā (our master), better known in modern times under the popular name of Dancing Dervishes. On Jalāl's death, Husām al-Dīn became his successor (*khalīfa*, Caliph), but in 683 headship of the Order passed to Jalāl's eldest son Sultan Veled, whose sons were to retain it until the middle of the fourteenth century. It was Sultan Veled, himself also a poet, who was the real organizer of the Order.

It is equally difficult to assess the influence of Jalāl al-Dīn and to sum up his philosophy. For us, he is above all a poet who, in impassioned verse, with a sincerity and simplicity very different from the excessive ornamentation all too frequent in Persian literature, expressed sentiments and convictions more spontaneous and ardent than logical or original. He made an impression by the apparent paradox of his statements, the foreknowledge they revealed, and the alternation, perhaps shrewdly calculated, of his 'absences' and 'presences'. Those whom he failed to convince said of him and his followers that they were 'raving' dervishes. But his prestige was indubitable, both in Konya and elsewhere, among the aristocracy and in various urban circles, not exclusively Muslim. He was a Muslim, and in fact more orthodox than Ibn 'Arabī, for example, in his rejection of any pantheistic tendency, and the followers whom he drew from among the non-Muslims at once declared their conversion. But it is true that, on the exalted levels where he took his stand, differences of creed became blurred, and he recognized some kind of common validity in all faiths. The few Greek and Turkish verses contained in his Persian works, even though no more than passing jests, also reveal these oecumenical leanings. His principal works are the *Dīwān*, a collection of short poems; the *Mathnawī* (*Work in couplets*), a didactic poem in rhymed couplets; *Fīhi mā fīhi* (*It contains what it contains*), a collection of various sayings; and his *Correspondence* with all the principal figures of his time in Rūm, and even occasionally in the rest of the Ilkhānid Empire, a work of interest for general history also.

It was only in the fourteenth century that the Mevlevis' practices were to be codified. It is certain however that, for Jalāl al-Dīn, its principal element was already the 'spiritual concert', consisting of music accompanied by dancing, which finally ended in the devotee who was performing it being placed in a state ever nearer to mystical ecstasy. Although this was not an absolutely new idea, the importance it had acquired constituted in the view of its opponents a *bid'a* (innovation), a fact in itself to be condemned, according to one view of traditionalist Islam.

Several disciples of Jalāl al-Dīn deserve mention – Fakhr al-Dīn Ghadanfar of Tabriz, 630–92/1232–92, who lived in Konya; the *ispahsalār* Ferīdūn ibn Ahmad, whose recently discovered *Letter on his Master* has considerably increased our knowledge of Jalāl; Jalāl's son, Sultan Veled, whose important works, in verse and prose, mainly in Persian but with an appreciable number of Turkish and Greek poems, are also of considerable value as religious and literary documents; finally, in a later generation, Aflākī, whose work *Manāqib al-ʿĀrifīn*, written in the middle of the fourteenth century, and translated into French by Cl. Huart under the title *Les Saints des Derviches Tourneurs*, has long been practically the sole (but still reliable) source for the history both of the Order and its founder.

In addition to mysticism, another literary form, this time in prose, made its appearance in Asia Minor with three important works in Persian – the chronicles of Ibn Bībī (completed in 1280) and Aqsarāyī (completed in about 1325), and the Anonymous *Seljuknāme* (written, except for an arid continuation, in about 1294), the first two being the work of senior government officials, the third that of a citizen of Konya, in a more direct and less florid style. It is unnecessary to say more about these works, already referred to so many times as historical sources. Ibn Bībī, who stated that it was impossible to find any certain information prior to the death of Kïlïj Arslan II, consequently refrains from describing the period of the eleventh and twelfth centuries, while his two successors devote to it only a few passing words strongly tinged with legend and folklore. It is only after 1243 that Aqsarāyī really supplies facts, as do Ibn Bībī and, to a lesser extent, the citizen of Konya from the beginning of the thirteenth century. It is evident that they had no literary source. Ibn Bībī and Aqsarāyī had access to archives and were acquainted with high officials, whereas the citizen of Konya was inspired by what he heard recounted in his native town, particularly in *akhi* circles. None has any documentary relationship with the others, and there is no ground for thinking that the two other writers knew Ibn Bībī, on that Aqsarāyī knew the author of the *Seljuknāme*. But the appearance of their three works obviously signifies an awareness, in face of the Mongols, of the existence and importance of the State of Rūm (although Ibn Bībī was the son of a recent immigrant), and their cultural level is similar to that of other writings produced at the same time, for example among the Ilkhānids. Another writer who may be mentioned, a contemporary of Aqsarāyī, is the *cadi* Ahmad of Nigde, author of a work entitled *al-Walad al-Shafīq*, a universal history of Islam containing some original and interesting information on the political and cultural history of Asia Minor.

However great the influence of Jalāl al-Dīn may have been among the aristocracy and part of the urban population, it is certain that it first remained outside the range of Turcoman circles. On the other hand, during the Mongol period, it was in circles that were predominantly if not exclusively Turcoman that there settled the initiators of those religious movements and orders which were in time to become the most widely disseminated, and which must therefore have had a certain influence even then. As always however at this stage of Turcoman evolution, it is almost impossible to find any direct and valid evidence, almost all the available information coming from later hagiographers who not only embellished but also distorted the past, consciously or not. A complete picture is therefore not to be expected, and only one or two brief indications can be given.

The reader will remember the Bābā'īs, with whom perhaps the Karamanids originally had some connections, as was noted earlier. Mevlevi tradition attributes similar connections to Hajji Bektash also, a dervish from Central Asia who had come to Asia Minor in about the middle of the thirteenth century. However plausible this relationship may be, it cannot at present be verified, and the *Vilāyetnāme* attributed to Hajji Bektash, originally written in Arabic and of which a later Turkish adaptation survives, gives no clear information in this respect. The Order, which was of great importance in the Ottoman period, and which placed itself under the guardianship of Hajji Bektash, attained its full organization, in the form which has lasted until the present day, only in the sixteenth century, and its earliest organization in the fourteenth. It is not possible to tell if the characteristically Shī'ī and Christian influences found in those periods go back to the actual teaching of Hajji Bektash or – as is more probable in regard to the second – to the progressive incorporation of native elements. Moreover, it would be interesting to know how these influences were experienced, as has already been remarked in reference to the Shī'ī problem in general, since this Order, including his Shī'ism, was nevertheless destined to play an official part under the Ottomans, although they were incontestably Sunnīs.

According to certain traditions, Hajji Bektash was related to Sarï Saltuk, said to be a native of Bukhara and, indirectly, to some extent a disciple of Ahmad Yasawī/Yesevī. His journey to central Anatolia is described in the *Saltuknāme*, a later but still early work, although other traditions, which were already known to Ibn Battūta and which may be not incompatible with the earlier ones, associate his activity with the Golden Horde in the Crimea. In any case, he is thought to have been the person who guided the Gagauz (mentioned earlier) to the Dobruja. With this same group tradition also links a certain Barak Bābā, who pursued his strange activities from Rūm to Iran and in the Mamluk State at the beginning of the fourteenth century. The Bektashis also lay claim to Yūnus Emre, of whom more will be said shortly.

Turkish Asia Minor and the various milieux mentioned above must also have felt the influence of the famous Order of Kalenders which had originated earlier in Central Asia, a kind of itinerant half-monk, half-charlatan, who played so great a part in Oriental popular tales. Their presence in Asia Minor under the name Jawāliqī is attested by a Treatise on heresiography written in the Ilkhānid period and published by Osman Turan, with the encouragement of his teacher Köprülü. In a more general way we are told in the fourteenth century that certain Turkish or Mongol tribes, like the Turgut on the Anatolian plateau, were dominated by *ibāhiyya*, indifference to the current ordinances of morality and religion. And it is easy to detect vestiges of their ancestral Shamanism in some circles, at times even until the present day. Other orders, the *Rifāʿīs*, *Khalwatī*, and still others which originated in various countries in the Muslim East, had their adherents in Turkey.

In the present state of research it is quite impossible here to enter into greater detail. For the moment it is necessary only to remember that the Mongol period, partly on account of the upheavals it provoked, the arrival of immigrants from Central Asia, and the reactions and development of the Turcomans, was a period of religious ferment during which there appeared certain phenomena, groups whose importance later history was to reveal in retrospect, though with some distortion on account of the very developments that they had undergone. It is impossible to study them more fully without overstepping the chronological limits of the present work, or to examine, so far as is feasible, the beliefs that still survive among the present-day groups.

In south-eastern Asia Minor similar movements perhaps unsettled the Kurds. It was among them, before the Mongol conquest, that the Sufi Order of the *Adawiya* had been established, founded by Shaykh Adī, and in some way connected with the earlier sect of the Yazīdīs. In 1257, during the disturbances in the Malatya region, a son or descendant of this Shaykh Adī made his appearance there as a military leader. Moreover the Germiyan, who were soon to be settled in western Anatolia, but who at that time were still in the Malatya region and were probably a mixture of Kurds and Turks, were regarded by Ibn Battūta's informants in the fourteenth century as Yazīdī Kurds. Whatever the details and truth of these facts, they obviously suggest an extension of Yazīdī propaganda into Kurdish society at about the time of the Mongol conquest.

Although, during the period of Seljukid independence, the Turcomans gave unequivocal proof of their self-awareness, there is no sign that, before 1243, they felt conscious of the need to express this in literature, in contrast to the practice that had already started in Central Asia. As has been said, 'Turkishness' was as foreign to the Turks of the aristocracy as it was to citizens of mixed stock. Culturally as well as politically, it was perhaps in order to assert themselves in face of the Mongols that a Turkish feeling was awakened, depending upon the Turcoman element which racially and linguistically was purer (and increasingly so as new elements from Central Asia continued to pour in). It can indeed be admitted that the Turcomans handed down orally epic or folk traditions, recited perhaps by bards such as those attested later by Yazïjï-oghlu and others. Some were their own traditions, like the *Oghuznāme,* also adopted by the Mongols of Central Asia, some were borrowed from other peoples, like those based on Battāl Ghāzī, the Arab hero of popular *gesta* concerning the ancient war against Byzantium, for whom the *ghāzī* Turks rapidly adopted a feeling of veneration, even before the old romance was put into Turkish and written down (Mongol period ?). It is probable however that it was the interest taken by men of letters in things Turkish that gave rise to the earliest literary compositions. It is difficult to regard as fortuitous the fact that the oldest Turkish work attested (though it has not been directly preserved), the *Dānishmendnāme* of Ibn ʿAlā, a national epic of the northern Turcomans in which others also no doubt recognized themselves, was composed for ʿIzz al-Dīn Kay-kāūs, the very man who was led to rely on the Turcomans in his struggles against the Mongols or their supporters. In its present form the work of an adaptor who wrote in the Dānishmendid region in the middle of the following century, the account is all the more remarkable in that it is content with a single reference to the exploits of the Seljukids, the ancestors of the dedicatee. It is possible that other traditions, similar to those suggested in the introductory pages of Aqsarāyī's chronicle and the anonymous *Seljūknāme*, related to the Seljukids, but we have no evidence that a written version was ever made. On the other hand the *Dānishmendnāme* appears to be linked artificially to the memory of Battāl as well as to that of Abū Muslim, the hero of Iranian epic romances which in turn were soon to be put into Turkish, at first perhaps mainly in *akhi* circles.

It is not surprising that, together with the epic, mysticism constituted at the start the chief field of Turkish literary achievement. Several Turkish verses are to be found, side by side with verses in Greek, inserted in the Persian works of Jalāl al-Dīn Rūmī – an incidental indication of aristocratic-mystical oecumenism rather than of 'Turkishness', which nevertheless in the last resort proves that henceforward it was possible to write in Turkish, using the Arabo-Persian alphabet common to the languages of Islam. There are a great number of Turkish verses in Sultan Veled's works. But it was above all within the framework of and in proportion with the development of the Turcoman movements and the principalities which emerged from them that Turkish authors proper made their appearance, authors whose identity is known and who wrote works of a certain breadth and interest, in their own language exclusively.

No work by Baba Ishāq has been preserved, or probably ever existed. However, almost from his time, some mystical verses by a certain Ahmad Faqīh have survived. As his name indicates he was originally a jurist (in Konya) who later, while still a young man, under the influence of a sermon he had heard, went off into the mountains to lead the life of an ascetic (about 630/1232–3). A little later is Shayyād Hamza who, besides mystical poems, has also left a Turkish version of the Koranic episode of Joseph and Zulaykha, in all probability inspired by a version made in 630/1232 in Central Asia by an unknown writer named 'Alī. But we have to wait until the end of the century or later to find any works of greater importance. Yūnus Emre, who apparently lived in north-western Anatolia, one of whose poems bears the (authentic?) date of 707/1307, was claimed by the Bektashis as one of themselves, though without proof. Several works are attributed to him, some of which may be of later date. He was a popular poet, but even so had read or heard recited the poems of Jalāl al-Dīn Rūmī and the still earlier works of Nizāmī, the great Persian poet of

357

Azerbaijan. In a vulgarized though not less profound form, he disseminated sentiments similar to those of the Mevlevis. In a wider sense he can be compared, for writings of this kind, with Ahmad Yesevi in Central Asia. Gülsheri, who was probably almost a contemporary of Yūnus Emre and who lived in Kïrshehir, made a Turkish rendering (with an interesting chapter on the *fütüvvet*) of the *Mantiq al-Tayr* (*Language of the Birds*) of the twelfth century Iranian mystic Ferīd al-Dīn ʿAttār, and also wrote in praise of his saintly compatriot Akhi Evrān.

In a different category are Dehhānī and ʿĀshiqpasha. The former, who lived in the entourage of ʿAlāʾ al-Dīn, the last Seljukid ruler, wrote in both Persian and Turkish, in what was already a highly elaborate and refined style and with a more 'courtly' inspiration. The second, a little younger (670–732/1271–1332), who also died in Kïrshehir, is the author of the *Gharībnāme*, a vast didactic poem which, illustrated, like several of its Iranian precursors, with anecdotes, endeavoured to give a survey of mystic philosophy as conceived in a spirit of Sunnī orthodoxy, and thus reacting against the Shīʿī tendencies of many other mystics.

Finally, it was probably among the ranks of the ordinary people in Mongol-Seljukid Asia Minor that Nasr al-Dīn Hoja lived. Passed down from one generation to another as the hero of an increasing number of anecdotes, he was for several centuries the typical figure, sometimes foolish, at other times of robust common sense, by whom the Turkish peoples have always been amused, down to our own time.

All this should not be exaggerated. The total output is not enormous, and although new discoveries may slightly increase its volume as known at present, it is unlikely to become very great. The inspiration often lacks originality, and clings closely to Iranian models. Nevertheless the essential step had been taken. Henceforward a literary Turkish language was in being, which differed even in the detail of its script from that of Central Asia. There were moreover authors able to express religious or sincere lyrical sentiments, or to sing of epic stories, directly in Turkish. It is therefore almost surprising to find, as we shall, that progress in the fourteenth century was not more rapid.

It is in the field of art that the immediate effects of the Mongol conquest are least perceptible. Even in the long term, although the dividing of power was obviously to bring with it a greater sobriety in artistic achievements during the Turcoman period, it cannot be said that the general orientation was modified. Under the Mongol protectorate proper, paradoxical though it may seem at first sight, there was on the contrary an intensification in the production of works of art. The full effects of the cultural progress during the first half of the century then made themselves felt. The emulation of the notables of the new régime in making a display of their magnificence; their desire to safeguard the values of their culture; and the equally strong desire of the Ilkhānid vizier Shams al-Dīn Juwaynīs to demonstrate the advantages accruing to themselves from the domination of the Mongols, whose representative he was – all this led to a multiplication and decentralization of artistic creation, both in respect of secular buildings such as the caravanserais described earlier, and also in more purely religious foundations such as mosques, *madrasas*, and tombs. Art itself changed little in character. It is true, as might be expected, that a careful study of public buildings, especially in the eastern half of the country, may reveal an intensification of Iranian influence. But this influence, since it had already made itself felt, could not imply any real break, and when these constructions are not explicitly dated it is not always easy to determine whether some particular one dates from the first or second half of the thirteenth century. Since we do not propose to go beyond a general discussion, it is only necessary here to take note of certain buildings. In Sivas, which by then rivalled Konya, the mosque known as Chifte Mināre and the Gök Medrese (Blue Madrasa) were both built in 1271, founded respectively by Juwaynī and Fakhr Al-Dīn ʿAlī Sāhib Ata. The last-named, whose earlier foundations in Konya have been referred to elsewhere, also built a *madrasa* in Kayseri and a mosque in his fief of Karahisār, among others. Perhaps he commissioned more buildings than anyone else of his time. However, the *pervāne* or his family also endowed their domains of Tokat, Amasya, Merzifon, Kastamonu and Sinope with mosques and *madrasas*, as well as the caravanserais already referred to. From the same period also date the mausolea of three great men, Jalāl al-Dīn Rūmī, Sadr al-Dīn Qūnawī, and Fakhr al-Dīn himself, all in Konya. Among the foundations of lesser figures the *madrasa* of Jajabey in Kīrshehir is particularly famous.

359

From the end of the century, however, the movement slackened. On the Ilkhānid side neither Ghāzān himself, although a Muslim, nor his great minister Rashīd al-Dīn, seem any longer to have been much interested in founding buildings in their outlying dependencies. Nor did any important personage remain in what was left of the Seljukid State. In so far as construction still continued, it was now inspired by the representatives of the new small powers situated on the borders – in Beyshehir, Birgi (in Aydïn), Karaman (the former Laranda), and Kastamonu, to give a few well-known examples. But in this field they did not introduce any innovations comparable with the advance of Turkish literature, and their modest activity as builders merely signifies that, as they gradually became assimilated to urban culture, they wanted to prove to the town-dwellers that they were worthy successors of their predecessors.

12

THE LAST CENTURY OF THE INDEPENDENCE OF ASIA MINOR

The history of the period between the disruption of the Ilkhānid Empire and the incorporation of Asia Minor in the Ottoman Empire is for the moment particularly difficult to write, and this chapter will do no more than provide certain basic outlines and take note of certain tasks still to be done. The sources, it must be repeated, are more than usually incomplete, scattered and suspect, and the modern works are too few in number and frequently invalidated by a too exclusively Ottoman standpoint. Certainly, the nucleus from which the Ottoman Empire was to emerge was a small Turcoman principality similar in all points to those that surrounded it. But owing to the geopolitical situation it happened to occupy, it developed fairly rapidly in symbiosis with the Balkan and Byzantine States, in a way that differentiated it profoundly from the other emirates of Asia Minor, and the fact that in the end it annexed them is not enough in itself to show that they were so to speak heading towards such an incorporation. It is therefore important to study Asia Minor for itself, and only to allow the Ottoman point of view to be brought in step by step with the effective development of Ottoman influence in its history. That Asia Minor should be taken into account when studying the origins of the Ottoman Empire may, again with the appropriate precautions, be legitimate; but it does not follow that Asia Minor has to be studied as an introduction to the Ottoman Empire.

Moreover, in the sources traditionally used, Asia Minor is presented at this period as a mosaic of small interchangeable dynasties. From this, two opposing dangers may result. On the one hand we can take the easy way and also treat it as a mosaic, no longer seeing a general picture; or else we can try to take a broad view, in which case everything is confused. Instead of an enumeration of minute principalities it is essential to give the general history of the Turkish people, and moreover to do this by a method that differentiates and explains: the Ak-koyunlu are not the Karamanids, nor are these the Aydïn or the Ottomans; Konya is not Sivas, and Sivas is not Bursa. This does not prevent the history of all of them from having features or reciprocal influences in common, and it must be written in terms of their mutual interconnection, which resembles a skein of wool in different colours.

It was suggested earlier, when the different powers which took the place of the crumbling Seljukido-Ilkhānid State were referred to, that what had been Seljukid Asia Minor was now divided into four zones, whose boundaries were obviously indefinite, but which nevertheless were clearly distinguished by certain features. In the south, from the Isaurian Taurus to the defiles through which the Euphrates escapes from the Armenian mountains, there were Turcomans, Karamanids and then Dulgadir, whose political attachments were towards the south, in the direction of the Mamluk State. The extreme eastern part, with Diyār Bakr, is more closely linked with north-western Iran than with the rest of Asia Minor or than north-west Iran is linked with the rest of that country. The centre, around Sivas, to some extent encroaching on the eastern part of the Anatolian plateau properly speaking, even when it became autonomous preserved the institutions of the Mongol period. The same is true of the eastern end of the country in the fourteenth century when, whatever may have been claimed, there was still no real organization of the Kara-koyunlu or the Ak-koyunlu. In the fifteenth, owing to the devastation left by Timur's invasion, the latter were to become the masters, but here it was a question of vast Turcoman territorial confederations of a different type from the small western principalities. On the other hand, the central zone passed directly under the control of the Ottomans, who by then were no longer the Turcomans of their early days but were in fact candidates for the imperial inheritance. The small western principalities remained, and certainly there are distinctions to be made, particularly between those in the west on the Aegean, those in the south, those in the north on the Black Sea, and the Ottomans. It was not so much the fact of crossing into Thrace that distinguished the last from their neighbours, for the Straits were of no great significance, and the way of life on the two banks was identical, but rather the interconnection which became established from then onwards between their evolution and that of Byzantium on the one hand and the Slav States on the other, these last being soon subjected. This does not mean that Asia Minor no longer played any part for them, and, in view of the work of P. Wittek, there is no need to show once again the equilibrium they owe to it. However, this role was played by virtue of Asia Minor's position as part of a wider whole linked with another world, and no longer merely for the country itself, with the result that, to begin with, it can to some extent be disregarded.

It is, therefore, in the centre of the country that continuity with the Seljukido-Mongol régime is clearest. Eretna, a former officer of Timurtash, had seized power over a territory which included Kayseri, Sivas and the old Dānishmendid fortress-towns, especially Tokat, and at times extended eastwards to include Erzinjān or even Erzurum, and westwards as far as Akseray and Ankara. Somehow or other, his heirs remained in possession for half a century. They were then supplanted, though without any change in the structure of government, by Burhān al-Dīn, a *cadi* and poet on occasion but also a good politician, who put his descent (in the maternal line) from the Seljukids to good use, and whose accession to power in itself indicates that the social forces of the previous century were still maintained. It is true that in this territory there were both Turcomans and Mongols, and its ruler eventually benefited from their rivalries, but it was Eretna or Burhān al-Dīn who governed it, with an administrative system inherited from their predecessors, and the Turcomans were no more part of that framework than they had been part of the framework of the earlier states. In the cultural field indeed, although Burhān al-Dīn sometimes wrote in Turkish (and Arabic) he was essentially a Persian writer, like his biographer ʿAzīz ibn Ardashīr (from Astarābād in north-eastern Iran). These two writers represent a cultural achievement for which no other part of Asia Minor can present a parallel. When on the eve of Timur's invasion the interplay of political rivalries had led to the disappearance of Burhān al-Dīn before the Ottoman Bāyezīd I, it was still a semi-Seljukid or Ilkhānid country that the latter found; and we know what part this province was to play, after Timur's victory over Bāyezīd at Ankara in 1402, in the difficult task of reconstructing Ottoman unity.

If the later historians of the Ak-koyunlu are to be believed, in the second half of the fourteenth century these had already become territorial princes, though their territory would be very difficult to define. In reality, although their rivals, the Kara-koyunlu, may perhaps have started to become princes of this kind, particularly on the eastern border of Asia Minor, in Mesopotamia and in Iran, the Ak-koyunlu themselves did so only after, and by the help of, Timur's disruptive invasion. To reconstitute the first phase of their history is extremely difficult. In the history of the Eretnids and Burhān al-Dīn they scarcely appear. However, on the Trebizond frontiers their role was such that the Basileis formed marriage connections with them as early as the middle of the century, and in the history of that Empire they played a part relatively speaking comparable with that of the Aydïn and the first Ottomans in the history of Constantinople. The complicating factor is that the principal historian of Trebizond, Panaretos, who was contemporaneous with the events, calls them Amidiotes, that is to say from Āmid, in Diyār Bakr, whereas in the Muslim sources, although it is known that in the fifteenth century Āmid was one of their princes' places of residence, there is no information as to the activities they may have undertaken in the fourteenth century in that sector, where, it must be confessed, their presence in large numbers would be difficult to reconcile with what we know of the general history of the region. Clearly it can be accepted that the leading group of Ak-koyunlu were natives of the Āmid region, but it was

363

in the mountains on the southern borders of the Trebizond territory, and indeed without greatly disrupting life in the inland plateau, that they appear to have made some mark, though without having any clearly defined principality.

From the middle of the fourteenth century Azerbaijan had been the centre of power of the Jalā'irids, the most important of the dynasties to share the Ilkhānids' inheritance, and like them Mongol. The little that is known about their activities in regard to Asia Minor provides no suggestion that their influence ever extended beyond Erzurum and the extreme upper reaches of the two Euphrates. However, Kiyā Mazandarānī, who in about 1360 wrote for them the fiscal *Treatise*, some information from which was included in an earlier chapter, gives a list of the territories which owed them taxes or tribute: it embraces almost the whole of Asia Minor, divided into inland territories and frontier territories, as far as and including the Ottomans. In reality, it consists of a record of the fiscal position applying to an earlier year, 1351; but this fact hardly changes the problem, since in 1351, as in 1360, the Ilkhānid State had ceased to exist for at least a decade. The general history of the period, in Asia Minor and elsewhere, makes it impossible to conceive that Turcoman or other rulers should in general have continued or resumed, towards the Jalā'irids, the policy of verbal allegiance, or even occasionally of tribute, that they had at times followed in regard to the Ilkhāns. In reality, a careful examination of Mazandarānī's list shows that there was no actual payment except from the extreme eastern borders. Then comes a lump sum for western Armenia – though we do not know if it was really paid. The rest is simply a vague list of claims, which should not be altogether forgotten, but which relate to the past and can throw no further light upon their own time, and so still less upon the remainder of the century. Except as regards the East, this text can therefore be held to be non-existent.

Various texts present the principality of the Germiyan as being the most important in the west, before the growth of the Ottomans. On account of its original links with the Seljukido-Mongol régime and its central position in relation to the emirates springing up in the former Byzantine provinces on the fringes of Anatolia, such a picture seems reasonable. But its effective role appears to be a lesser one, and it may have been handicapped by racial elements which were insufficiently Turkish (being more or less Kurdish). Indeed, only two Turcoman principalities momentarily attained a certain power – that of Aydïn, owing to its expansion by sea, in the second quarter of the fourteenth century, during the rise of the Ottomans who eventually overthrew it, and that of the Karamanids, which was to prove more enduring.

It will perhaps become possible to write a history of the Karamanids, but it is still too early to do so. They occupied the whole western half of the Taurus, including Isauria, with an outlet to the sea in that same province, and, thanks to the possession of Konya, a wide foothold on the plateau. The old capital no longer dominated the mountainous frontier; usually, the powers occupying the border regions divided the plateau among themselves, each dominating the sector nearest itself. The Karamanids, relying politically on the Mamluks, and still with Mongols in their neighbourhood, represented in Anatolia the hereditary protagonists of 'Turkishness' against the Mongols – politically, but also culturally, for it was mainly though not exclusively among them that a literature in the Turkish language developed.

Any such 'Turkishness' must not, however, be misconstrued. The kind of hybrid culture that had developed during the thirteenth century in the towns of Asia Minor still remained, like the towns themselves. Islam too continued to exist there, in its specific forms, side by side with Turcoman Islam. As the Turcoman leaders gradually became masters of those towns also, to some extent they evolved in the particular direction that contact with these new subjects implied. In their turn, though on a more modest scale than the earlier Sultans, they founded mosques and other buildings in what had now become the leading towns. While they brought a Turkish atmosphere into the towns, they also brought an Islamo-Iranian atmosphere among the Turcomans. The distinction began to grow smaller, and a culture came into being that was not so much a juxtaposition as an intermixture, in which the Turkish language figured together with Persian and Arabic, without supplanting them and as yet with few great achievements, but with an indication of the general direction it was to follow. Some authors, afterwards to be renowned as Ottoman writers, had begun to work in the Turcoman principalities on the eve of their disappearance at the hands of the Ottomans.

365

13

CONCLUSION

Asia Minor, with its Balkan extension, is not the only territory in which Turks played an important part politically at the end of the Middle Ages. In Egypt and Syria the Slave-Mamluks, who formed almost the entire army and from whom the Sultans were recruited, were, until the end of the fourteenth century, exclusively Turkish, and even when the Sultans subsequently became Circassian, there still continued to be a large Turkish element in the army. The somewhat unusual régime that they thus established did not depend solely upon the accident of the race of its ruling aristocracy. Although obviously Egypt remained Egyptian and continued to speak Arabic, nevertheless this aristocracy had made it familiar with some practices such as heraldry and certain forms of military activity which it had not possessed, or at least not known earlier. Even though an appreciable number of Turks became arabized, to the point that several of the historians of the Mamluks were sons of *mamlūks*, they continued to speak Turkish and composed dictionaries and other works which are of great value to us. Results of a similar kind were produced simultaneously in the slave-dynasty which replaced the Ghaznevids and their Ghurid successors in northern India and extended their conquests to the Deccan.

In the states founded by the Mongols, there gradually took place an intermixture of Mongols and Turcomans or other Turks, who had certainly been rivals originally but who had been brought together by a common way of life, the use of related languages, ancient traditions, and other factors, from which the islamization of the Mongols 'in the Turkish manner' had finally resulted. The number of Mongols was not infinite, and the monopoly of warfare, which, at the start they had forcibly arrogated to themselves, reduced them still further, so lessening their resistance to assimilation and relatively increasing the part played by other elements, primarily Turkish. It is true that

Mongol groups remained, and fusion did not everywhere proceed at the same rate. But on the whole the Mongol conquest made the conquered territories Turkish, not Mongol, and in Russia the so-called Tatar peoples, another name applied to the Mongols, now use the Turkish language exclusively, as they had done since the end of the Empire known as the Golden Horde, founded by the Mongols at the time of their conquest of Russia. The last relics of this Empire still survived at the start of the sixteenth century, before being incorporated in the Muscovite Empire. In Central Asia other Turkish peoples, who today form republics in the u.s.s.r., had similarly become detached from the original framework of the Mongol Empire. They had their own dialect, called paradoxically by the name of Chaghatay, the son of the great Mongol conqueror Jengiz-Khan, who had acquired this region by lot. From them an interesting literature emerged later, in the fifteenth century, with ʿAlī Shīr Nevāʾī, who today still is or has once again become the national poet of the 'Turkmens', and in the sixteenth century, when one of their members conquered India and founded the Empire of the 'Great Moguls', with the famous *Memoirs* of Bābūr or, in Central Asia itself, with the important *History of the Turkmens* of Abuʾl-Ghazi. The name 'Great Moguls' indicates that the Mongol political tradition still survived and, at the end of the fourteenth century, Timur-Lenk/ Tamberlaine, the great conqueror from Central Asia, claimed relationship with it. Nonetheless he was already a Turk, who was surrounded by Turks and used a Turkish army, and whom the few surviving Mongols no longer recognized as one of themselves. When he had crushed the Ottoman Sultan Bāyezīd at Ankara in 1402, contemporaries were fully aware that it was a Turk who had defeated another Turk.

In the modern period, of course, all these states alike were to become politically insignificant in face of the rise of Europe, and such measure of civilization as they possessed, unable to follow the new rate of progress or crushed by competition, was to lose its interest so completely that the modern man finds it difficult to imagine that countries such as those of Central Asia could have been capable of producing great men and fine buildings. For the present-day school-boy, 'Turkish' is equivalent to 'Ottoman', and no one will dispute that, in spite of its weaknesses and final decline, the Ottoman Empire was the Turks' most important achievement and one of the greatest known to history. It is necessary however to bear in mind, as the Turks of the present Turkish Republic are very ready to emphasize, that it was not the only one, nor was it the most Turkish. For this reason, it must be repeated for the last time, the study of Seljukid Turkey is of particular interest.

This, as has been shown, is not because Seljukid Turkey was any more completely Turkish. It seems to be one of the features of all Turkish political creations before the modern period that they always came into being in symbiosis with other elements, each doubtless contributing its own complementary qualities. The indigenous element proper did not play a very extensive part, so far as Seljukid Turkey is concerned. It is true that it was largely their labour and their taxes that furnished the means of livelihood of the new state, and Greeks, if not Armenians, at times succeeded in taking a personal part in its life. On the lower levels of the economic and social structure, it is probable that many things now difficult to discern are due to them – the same is true more clearly in some fields of artistic achievement. On the whole, however, and particularly when it is compared with the situation of the Ottoman Empire, whether in political organization or cultural development, the symbiosis which proved to be so fertile was that of Iranians and Turks, not of Turks and natives. This is all the more remarkable since, as has been observed, there was no formal resistance by Greeks and Turks to certain forms of co-operation – indeed, very much the reverse. But the integrating force of Islam was on the whole greater, as in many other instances. Whatever the place numerically that natives held in Turkey at the end of the thirteenth century, they continued to fall back on their own institutions and culture rather than to participate in the creation of new ones. It is true, and was noted earlier, that the lack of contact between iranized urban centres and Turcoman rural elements was the cause of schisms and disputes in Seljukid Turkey, and that a turkicizing reaction followed, under the Mongols or, rather, against them or around them. However, the Turcoman principalities which were set up on the ruins surviving alike from the Byzantine State and the Seljukido-Mongol State gathered the cultural heritage left by the preceding régimes, and although Turkish literature began to develop in those principalities, it had not as yet displaced literature written in the Persian language, or sometimes even in Arabic. For several centuries therefore a mixed culture developed, in which the Turkish language held pride of place, though without excluding the others, and in this respect the Ottomans were to act in a similar way down to and including the seventeenth century.

This being said, there was nevertheless something more Turkish in Seljukid Turkey than in the other States under Turkish domination, including the Ottoman Empire. The people of the time were not mistaken when from then onwards they called it 'Turkey'. Although Turks never composed its entire population, the fact remains that even so they quickly formed an important element, and, since the other elements alongside them fell back upon themselves and became dissociated from them, it was they, the Turks, who constituted the driving and unifying force. Even though all the inhabitants did not truly participate in the new culture, it was this culture alone that became of general application.

There is certainly no need to resort to the over-simplified postulation of a psychology of races or peoples which tries to attribute uniform and definitive characters to them. At the conclusion of this work, however, the impression cannot be avoided that the Turks, whose history has here been described, were a people well fitted both to command and to assimilate the culture of conquered peoples, well fitted also to make that culture on occasion more creative than it had been hitherto. I have spoken of symbiosis, with the Greeks, from certain points of view, and with the Iranians, from others. It is perhaps this symbiosis which is the most characteristic feature of their mediaeval history, before the situation was eventually transformed by the developments of the modern period.

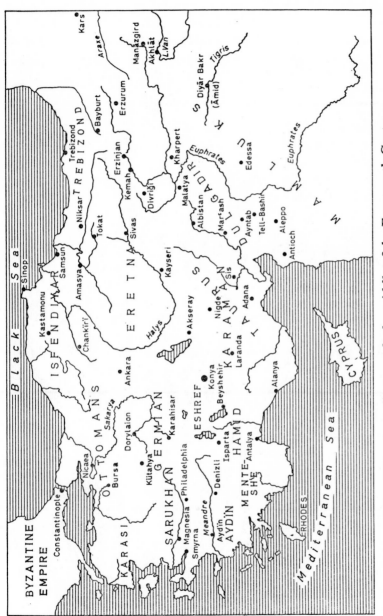

Map IV. Anatolia towards the middle of the Fourteenth Century

ILLUSTRATIONS

Art and Architecture

List of Illustrations with Sources

Konya

The largest town under the Seljukids before the Mongols: it eventually became the capital. See p. 201.

1 *General view of Konya in the nineteenth century, from L. de Laborde.*

2

*Above (Plate 2) is shown the Mausoleum of Fakhr al-Dīn
ʿAlī (Sāhib Ata), and opposite, some detail of the mosaics is
given in Plate 3, and the window in Plate 4.* See p. 359.

3

4

5 above.   *Ruins of the 'Kiosk of 'Alā al-Dīn' in the Citadel, Konya.*
See p. 262.

6 opposite top.   *Stucco relief from Kay-kubādh's Palace in Konya.*
See p. 264.

7 opposite bottom.   *Interior of 'Alā al-Dīn mosque, Konya.*
See p. 263.

8

*Sirceli Madrasa, Konya
(1242).*

9

*Tombs of the Seljukid
Sultans in the Great
Mosque of Konya.*
See p. 263.

10

Plate 10 (above) and Plate 11 (below) are two examples of bas-reliefs from the Konya Museum. See p. 264.

11

12   *The ruins of the Sultan Khan, between Konya and Akseray.*
See p. 168.

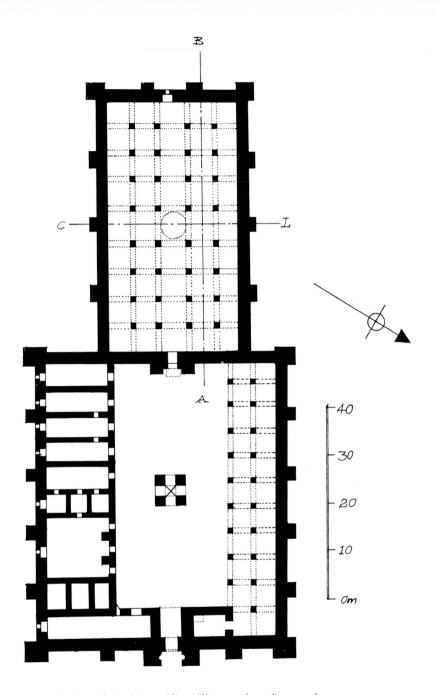

13 *A plan of the Sultan Khan illustrated on the opposite page.*

14 *Above is shown the entrance to the Ince Mināre, Konya with bands of inscriptions, and detail of the doorway is illustrated on the opposite page in Plate 15. See p. 263.*

15

Detail of Ince Minãre.

16

One of the two winged figures on the gate of the Citadel, Konya, now in the Konya Museum.
See p. 264.

17 (left) and **18** (below)

*Two illustrations of
the Madrasa of
Karatay, Konya. On
the left is shown the
doorway and below the
interior of the dome is
illustrated.*

19   *The walls of Konya as seen by L. de Laborde in 1825.* See p. 262.

20   *Double-headed eagle from the city walls of Konya, Konya Museum.* See p. 264.

Karahisar

21 *Tomb of an 'akhi' showing the peculiar turban. The tomb is at Afgan Karahisar.* See pp. 196–8.

Kayseri

An example of a fortified town. See p. 202.

22 left

Karatay Khan near Kayseri. See p. 328.

23 below

A double cupola at the Chifte Kümbet, Kayseri.

24   *Döner Kümbet (tomb) at Kayseri.*

25 *Detail of motif on Plate 24.*

395

26

*Detail of doorway
from the Sultan Khan
near Kayseri.*
See p. 168.

27

*Motif of doorway
arch of the above.*

Erzurum

28   *The walls of Erzurum as seen by Curzon in 1843.*

29 *South doorway of the Madrasa Ya ʿqūbiye, Erzurum.*

30 *Chifte Mināre, Erzurum.* See p. 450.

31 *Façade of the Chifte Mināre. See Plates 32 and 33 for detail of motifs adjoining the doorway.*

32 *Detail of the façade shown opposite.*

33 above

Motif adjoining doorway of the Chifte Mināre.

34

The Mausoleum of Emir Saltuk, Erzurum

Nigde

35 *Nigde is one of the sites of the principal mosques (see p. 263) and Plate 35 (above) shows the tomb of the princess.*

36   *North door of the Mosque of Sunghur Bey, Nigde.*

37 *Window above the door shown opposite.*

38 above. *Detail of south-west corner of the Mosque of Sunghur Bey.*

39 below. *The Minbar.* See p. 163.

40 above.　*The Mihrab in the Mosque of Sunghur Bey.*

41 below.　*Detail of the east doorway of the Mosque of Sunghur Bey.*

Divriği

Another town where a principal mosque was established. See p. 263.

42 below. *The main entrance of the Great Mosque at Divriği.*

43

A bird on the Mosque of Divriği.

44   *The old hospital, Divriği.*

Tokat

46 opposite. *The fortress at Tokat.* See pp. 262 and 323.

45 below. *Türbe (tomb) of Nūr al-Dīn ibn Shentimur, Tokat.*

47 *Agzï Kara Khan, about 1242.*

Sivas

An international meeting place
of merchants and probably the
second town of the Sultanate.
See pp. 202–3.

48 left

*The Chifte Mināre at
Sivas.* See p. 359.

49

*Detail of doorway shown in
Plate 48.*

50 above.   *Hospital of Kay-kaus I.*   **51** below.   *The Mausoleum.*

52
53

The Gök Medrese (Blue Madrasa). Shown above are two illustrations of detail, below left is a bas-relief depicting animals and below right, a capital. See p. 359.

54
55

Faience

There is no doubt that the ceramics of Asia Minor were, in the thirteenth century, produced locally. See pp. 162–3.

56 above
Fragment of a tile found in the ruins of the castle at Konya. See p. 262.

57 left
Tile in the Mausoleum of Fakhr al-Dīn ʿAlī.

58 below
Tile showing musician playing an instrument. (Berlin Museum).

59 opposite
Wall decoration in the Karatay Madrasa, Konya.

59

60 above. *Tiled mihrab in the Mosque of Fakhr al-Dīn ʿAlī at Konya.*

61 opposite top. *Tile from Kubādabād, double-headed eagle inscribed with the word al-Sultān. See p. 262.*

62 opposite below. *Tile from Kubādabād, perhaps depicting the Sultan as master of both seas (the Mediterranean and the Black Sea).*

61

62

63 *Tile from Kubādabād, from recent excavations.*

Wood carvings

Two specimens of Muslim art in wood carving are illustrated.

64 right
*Detail of a wooden door in the
Ulu Jāmiʾ, Divriği.*

65 opposite page
*Carved wooden door (Berlin
Museum).*

65

Christian Art

66 *Mural in the Church of St. George at Kïrk Dam, one of the rock-cut churches in Cappadocia.* See p. 209.

67 opposite. *Diagram showing the dedication inscription on Plate 66 with a translation.*

Here is a translation of the inscription: 'This revered temple to the glorious great martyr St. George has been magnificently decorated by the much needed help and the labour of Lady Thamar, painted above, the wife of the Amirarzes Basil Giag(oupes?)/ Yaʿqūb.

O tropephoros martyr George of Cappadocia
Under the most high and most noble great Sultan Massut/Masʿūd, while the lord Andronic reigns on the Romans.'

Economic Life

68 above.   *Grazing in Cappadocia, in the mountains of Hasan Dağ, much as it would have been during the Seljukid Empire.*

69 below.   *Bridge of Hasan Kale on the Upper Euphrates, on one of the main trade routes.*

70 *Dānishmendid and Seljukid coins.* See p. 191.

Pottery

71

*Pottery vessel
(Ethnographical
Museum, Ankara).*

Bronze

72

*Bronze vessel made
in Konya. Thirteenth
century.*

Bibliography

PREFACE

The best general introductions to Turkish history will be found in volume III (History), at present in course of preparation, of the *Philologiae Turcicae Fundamenta* (volumes I and II, on languages and literature respectively, have already appeared), and in volume V, section 5 of the *Handbuch der Orientalistik*, under the general editorship of B. Spuler (K. Jettmar and others, *Geschichte Mittelasiens*, 1966). Meanwhile an adequate documentation, though necessarily more disjointed and excluding the non-Muslim Turks, is to be found in the *Encyclopaedia of Islam* (the second edition of which, in 1968, has reached the letter H; but see also in particular the article 'Turks' in the first edition). Those who read Turkish should consult its fuller Turkish adaptation, the now almost complete *Islâm Ansiklopedisi*. See also A. Zeki Velidi Togan, *Umumî Türk Tarihine Giriş*, vol. I, 1946. Bibliographical guidance can also be sought from J. Sauvaget, *Introduction à l'Histoire de l'Orient Musulman*, 2nd edition revised by C. Cahen, 1961, with further revised English translation, 1965. Articles in periodicals (though incompletely in respect of the Turkish periodicals), are listed, with the partial exception of those concerning the non-Muslim Turks, in *Index Islamicus* of J.D. Pearson, 1958, with *Supplements* 1962–67, and further supplements envisaged at intervals of 5 years. Current Turkish writings are listed in the *Türkiye Bibliyografyasï* (1939–49). The pages devoted to the pre-Ottoman Turks in old general histories either of the Ottomans or of Islam are all out of date, and it is preferable to omit any reference to them (details given in the *Encyclopaedia of Islam*).

A *Handbook of Turkish Culture*, a general work, has also begun to appear under the chairmanship of Z. V. Togan and H. Inalcïk, from 1967 onwards.

Periodicals

The writings being currently published clearly make it necessary to follow all the orientalist reviews. For our purpose the two most important, both scientifically and above all for bibliographical purposes, are the *Belleten* of the Turkish Historical Society (Türk Tarih Kurumu) and *Oriens*, an international review, published in Leyden by Brill.

INTRODUCTION

THE TURKS AND THEIR ISLAMIZATION BEFORE THE SELJUKIDS

Apart from the volumes of the *Fundamenta* and *Handbuch* mentioned above, and wholly general works, see the following:

427

(a) On the earliest Turkish peoples

W. Barthold, *12 Vorlesungen über die Geschichte der Türken Mittelasiens*, 1935 (originally published in Turkish as *Orta Asya Türk Tarihi*, 1927), French trans., *Histoire des Turcs d'Asie Centrale*, 1945.

J. Hamilton, 'Toquz-Oγuz et On-Oγγur', in *Journal Asiatique*, 1962.

D. Dunlop, *The History of the Jewish Khazars*, 1954.

A. Zeki Velidi Togan, *Ibn Fadlān's Reisebericht*, 1939; M. Canard, 'La relation du voyage d'Ibn Fadlân chez les Bulgares de la Volga', in *Annales de l'Institut d'Études Orientales*, 1958.

Hudūd al-ʿĀlam, trans. V. Minorsky, 1937 (Persian geographical text, with extensive annotation).

Faruk Sümer, 'X. Yüzyïlda Oğuzlar', in *Ankara Üniversitesi Dil ve Tarih-Coğrafya Fakültesi Dergisi*, 1958 (in Turkish), or in his *Oğuzlar*, listed p. 444.

(b) On the Turkish armies and the Turks in the old Muslim countries

C.E. Bosworth, Contribution to the forthcoming third volume of the *Fundamenta;* meanwhile, R.N. Frye and Aydïn Sayïlï, 'Turks in the Middle East before the Saljuqs', in *Journal of the American Oriental Society*, 1943.

(c) On the Ghaznevids

C.E. Bosworth, *The Ghaznavids*, 1963 (speaks also of the Karakhānids, Oghuz, etc.).

(d) On the Karakhānids

W. Barthold, *Turkestan down to the Mongol Invasion*, English trans., 2nd ed., 1958. Forthcoming article 'Tlek-Khānids' by Bosworth, in *Enc.Isl.*

O. Pritsak, 'Die Karachaniden', in *Der Islam*, 1953.

(e) One should keep in touch with Soviet excavations in Central Asia

S.P. Tolstov, *Auf den Spuren der altchoresmischen Kultur*, 1953, will act as an introduction and on this subject.

Aspects of the Muslim East in the eleventh century

Obviously there can be no question here of providing a bibliography of Muslim history, even one limited to the Orient in the eleventh century. We give only the titles of some of the leading manuals.

E. Perroy, and others, *Le Moyen Âge: l'expansion de l'Orient et la naissance de la civilization occidentale*, 1955, chapters on Islam by C. Cahen.

G. von Grunebaum, 'Der Islam', in *Propyläen Weltgeschichte*, V, 1963.

B. Spuler, *Iran in früh-islamischer Zeit*, 1952, English translation in preparation.

W. Barthold, *Turkestan* (see (d) above, this page).

B. Lewis, *The Arabs in History*, 1950 (a fuller work by the same author has been announced).

BIBLIOGRAPHY

PART ONE

THE EMPIRE OF THE GREAT SELJUKIDS

The historiographic sources for the history of the Seljukids (save for those of Asia Minor) have been studied in some detail by the author of the present work in his paper 'The Historiography of the Seljuqid Period', ed. B. Lewis and P.M. Holt, 1962. Archive sources (collections of copies of documents and letters) have been studied by M.A. Köymen, 'Selçuklu devri Kaynaklarïna dâir araştïrmalar', I, in *Ankara Üniversitesi Dil ve Tarih-Coğrafya Fakültesi Dergisi*, 1951; and by H. Horst, listed below. On the Seljukid Empire in general, see M.A. Köymen, *Selçuklu Devri Türk Tarihi*, 1963, and O. Turan, *Selçuklular Tarihi ve Türk-İslâm Medeniyeti*, 1965; cf. the article 'Selçuklular' in the *İslâm Ansiklopedisi* (by I. Kafesoğlu). For greater detail, see the following:

(a) Origins as far as Dandānqān
C. Cahen, 'Le Malik-nâmeh et l'histoire des origines seljukides', in *Oriens*, 1949; cf. Bosworth, *The Ghaznavids*, and Barthold, *Turkestan*, listed on p. 428.

(b) Conquest of Iran and Iraq
C. Cahen, *The Turkish invasion: the Selchükids*, in *A History of the Crusades*, ed. K. Setton, vol. I, 1955.

(c) Later conquests
C. Cahen, 'La première pénétration turque en Asie Mineure,' in *Byzantion*, 1948 (equally concerned with Syria and Mesopotamia), and see p. 442 (Part II).

(d) On the reign of Malik-Shāh and the institutions of his time
I. Kafesoğlu, *Sultan Melikşah devrinde büyük Selçuklu imparatorluğu*, 1953.

(e) On institutions in general and certain of them in particular
Prof. A.K.S. Lambton, an early unpublished London University thesis (*The Social Organization of Persia under the early Seljuqids*, 1939), she has published some partial but more penetrating studies: 'Quis Custodiet Custodes?' in *Studia Islamica* 1956 *bis*; 'Justice in the mediaeval Persian theory of Kingship', ibid. 1962; and 'The administration of Sanjar's empire as illustrated in the 'Atabat al-Kataba', in the *Bulletin of the School of Oriental and African Studies*, 1957.
M. Köymen, op. cit.
H. Horst, *Die Staatsverwaltung der Grosselğüqen und Hōrazmšāhs*, 1964.
C. Cahen, 'La tugrā seljukide', in *Journal Asiatique* 1943–45, and his *L'évolution de l'iqtāʿ*, in *Annales Economies-Sociétés-Civilisations*, 1953.

(f) On Spiritual life and the confrontation of faiths

J. Pedersen, article 'Masdjid', I, in the *Encyclopaedia of Islam*, 1st edition.
G. Makdisi, *Ibn ʿAqil et la résurgence de l'Islam traditionaliste au XIᵉ siècle*, 1963.
M.G.S. Hodgson, *The Order of Assassins*, 1955.
C. Cahen, 'An Introduction to the First Crusade', in *Past and Present*, 1954 (on the treatment of Christians).

(g) On the period of decline

M.A. Köymen, *Büyük Selçuklu Imparatorluğu tarihi, Ikinci imparatorluk devri*, 1954.
F. Sanaullah, *The decline of the Saljūqid Empire*, 1938.
I. Kafesoğlu, *Harezmşahlar devleti tarihi*, 1956.
W. Barthold, *Turkestan*, (listed on p. 428), *passim*.

(h) On the futuwwa of the Caliph al-Nāsir

F. Taeschner, 'Futuwwa, eine gemeinschaftbildende Idee', in *Schweizerisches Archiv für Volkskunde*, 1956.
C. Cahen, 'Mouvements populaires et autonisme urbain dans l'Asie Musulmane du Moyen Age, III,' in *Arabica* 1959; cf. the article 'Futuwwa' in the *Encyclopaedia of Islam*, 2nd edition.

(i) Literature

J. Rypka, *Iranische Literaturgeschichte*, 1959.
A.J. Arberry, *Classical Persian Literature*, 1958.

(j) Art

A.U. Pope, *A Survey of Persian Art*, 6 vols. 1938–58.
The general histories of Muslim or Turkish art are all inadequate in respect of the Seljukid Empire. It is not possible here to list all the monographs. The proceedings of the periodic international congresses of Turkish art, the most recent of which was held in Cambridge in 1967, should be studied (see Togan and Inalcïk pp. 427 and 448).

PART TWO

TURKEY IN ASIA MINOR
From the End of the Eleventh Century until 1243

1: THE SOURCES

The sources for the history of the Seljukids of Rūm (and related dynasties) are the subject of still important study by M.F. Köprülü, 'Anadolu Selçuklularï tarihi'nin yerli kaynaklarï', in *Belleten* 1943; for those concerning the Great Seljukids, see my study listed on, p. 429; for those concerning the Crusades and the Latin East see the introduction to my *Syrie* (listed on p. 442). Literary works produced in Arabic have in general been listed in C. Brockelmann, *Geschichte der arabischen Literatur*, 2 vols. 2nd edition 1943–9, and Supplement, 3 vols.

1937–42; Persian writings in C.A. Storey, *Persian Literature*, vol. I (1927–53) for historiography; Byzantine writings, in so far as they concern the Turks, in G. Moravcsik, *Byzantinoturcica*, 2nd ed., 2 vols. 1958; Syriac writings in A. Baumstark, *Geschichte der syrischen Literatur*, 1922; Georgian writings are listed sufficiently for our purpose in Brosset (see p. 432), and Armenian, in default of anything better, in *Recueil des Historiens des Croisades* (hereafter *RHC*), *Documents Arméniens*, noted p. 432, and completed by the sources listed later. The old *Bibliotheca Historica Medii Aevi* of A. Potthast, 2nd ed. 2 vols. 1896, for the medieval European historical sources, is in process of being replaced by the *Repertorium Fontium Historiae Medii Aevi*, 2 vols. so far published, 1962 and 1967, a collective international undertaking.

A. *Eleventh century*

(a) Arabic and Persian sources for the history of the Great Seljukids, relating also to the history of the Turks of Asia Minor.

The most important is the Ghars al-Ni'ma of Muhammad ibn Hilāl al-Sābī, transmitted in the years 447–78/1055–85 of the *Mir'āt al-Zamān* of Sibt ibn al-Jawzī, this part being unpublished. The manuscript utilized here, Paris, Bibliothèque Nationale, manuscrits arabes 1506, completed eventually by MSS. in Istanbul.

Of secondary importance, 'Imād al-Dīn al-Isfahānī, in the slightly shortened version of Bundārī, *Histoire des Seldjoucides de l'Irâq*, ed. M.T. Houtsma, *Recueil de textes relatifs à l'histoire des Seldjoucides*, II, 1889; *Akhbār 'ud-dawlat 'is-saljūqiyya*, attributed to 'Alī ibn Nāsir al-Husaynī, ed. M. Iqbal, 1933; *Saljūqnāme*, attributed to Zahīr al-Dīn Nīshābūrī, 1332, and the version of it known earlier, Rāwandī, *Râhat us-Sudúr*, ed. M. Iqbal, 1921; and lastly Ibn al-Athīr, *al-Kāmil fi'l-tārikh*, ed. C.J. Tornberg, *Ibn-el-Athiri Chronicon*, 1851–76, vols. IX–X.

See the occasional sources (Ibn Hamdūn, etc.) in my article in *Byzantion* listed on p. 442. For the *Dānishmendnāme*, see p. 442.

(b) Greek sources

Skylitzes, in the version of Cedrenus, to 1057, with a continuation to 1079, in the *Corpus Scriptorum Historiae Byzantinae* (hereafter *CSHB*; texts in this series are accompanied by Latin translations), 2 vols., 1838. Michael Attaliates, to 1079, *CSHB*, 1853 (new edition prepared by H. Grégoire and P. Orgels).

Nicephorus Bryennius, 1057–1080, *CSHB*, 1836.

Anna Comnena, *Alexiad*, 1069–1118, ed. B. Leib, with French translation, 3 vols., 1937–45; English trans. by E.A.S. Dawes, 1928.

The remarkable chronicle of Psellus contains little on foreign policy, and therefore little on the Turks. Information on the relations of the Turks with Trebizond is contained in the correspondence of Theophylact of Ochrida, in *Patrologiae Cursus Completus*, ed. J.P. Migne, *Series Graeca*, vol. 126.

(c) Armenian sources

Aristakēs Lastivertci, French trans. E. Prud'homme, *Histoire d'Armenie
. . . . par Arisdagues de Lasdivert,* 1864, to 1071. Matthew of Edessa,
French trans. in E. Dulaurier, *Bibliothèque historique arménienne,* 1858, to
1136.

For some minor sources see, in addition to my article in *Byzantion,*
the books of J. Laurent and R. Grousset listed on p. 441.

(d) Syriac sources

J.-B. Chabot, ed. and trans. *Chronique de Michel le Syrien,* 4 vols., 1899–
1910, the translation of the relevant section being in vol. III; completed
by Bar Hebraeus, see p. 438. An Armenian adaptation of Michael's
account is sometimes useful (*RHC, Documents Arméniens* I).

(e) Georgian sources

M.F. Brosset, *Histoire de la Géorgie,* part I, 2 vols., 1849 (text and French
trans. of a compilation made in the eighteenth century from older
sources).

(f) Latin sources

Gesta Francorum et Aliorum Hierosolimitanorum, ed. with French trans.
L. Bréhier, 1924; ed. with English trans. R. Hill, 1962.
Raymond of Aguilers, *Historia Francorum qui ceperunt Iherusalem,* in *RHC,
Historiens Occidentaué,* III.
Albert of Aix, *Historia Hierosolymitana,* ibid. vol. IV.
Fulcher of Chartres, *Historia Iberosolymitana: Gesta Francorum Iherusalem
Peregrinantium,* ibid. vol. III.

For the minor sources, see my *Syrie* (p. 442), pp. 12–16, and my
article 'Le Premier Cycle de la Croisade (Antioche-Jérusalem-Chétifs)'
in *Moyen Âge,* 1957.

B. *Twelfth century*

(a) Arabic (Syro-Mesopotamian) sources

Ibn al-Qalānisī, ed. H.F. Amedroz, 1908 (to 1155), selected and translated by H.A.R. Gibb, *The Damascus Chronicle of the Crusades,* 1932;
French trans. R. Le Tourneau, *Damas de 1075 à 1154,* 1952.
Al-ʿAzīmī, edited in my article 'La chronique abrégée d'al-ʿAzīmī',
in *Journal Asiatique,* 1937 (to 1143).
Ibn al-Azrāq, history of Mayāfāriqīn (to 1178); the part which concerns
us is unpublished, but has been analysed by myself in my article 'Le
Diyār Bakr au temps des premiers Urtukides', in *Journal Asiatique,*
1935.
ʿImād al-Dīn al-Isfahānī, *al-Barq al-Shāmi,* not completely preserved,
but the essential part reproduced in the *Kitāb al-Rawdatayn* of Abū
Shāma, 2nd ed. now being prepared by M. Hilmī (1956–62), copious

extracts with translation in *RHC, Historiens Orientaux,* IV (period of Saladin).

Ibn Shaddād, life of Saladin, in *RHC, Historiens Orientaux,* III.

Ibn abī Tayy, preserved in Ibn al-Furāt for the first two-thirds of the twelfth century, unpublished.

Ibn al-Athīr, *al-Kāmil* (see above), vols. IX–XI, extracts translated in *RHC, Historiens Orientaux,* I–II (to 1230).

Kamāl al-Dīn ibn al-ʿAdīm, *Zubdat al-Talab;* until the completion of the edition by Sami Dahan, which has reached the year 559–1164, the final portion (until 1240) can be consulted in the French translation (mediocre) by E. Blochet in the *Revue de l'Orient Latin,* 1895–8; extracts relating to the first third of the twelfth century are contained in *RHC, Historiens Orientaux,* III; the *Zubda* is completed by the same author's *Bughyat al-Talab,* a biographical dictionary from which only extracts have been published (ibid.).

ʿIzz al-Dīn ibn Shaddād, *al-Aʿlāq al-Khatīra,* a work of historical geography, the relevant part of which is available only through the analyses given by C. Ledit, 'Al-Aʿlāq al-Khatīra', in *al-Mashriq,* 1935, and by myself in my article 'La "Djazîra" au milieu du XIIIᵉ siècle', in *Revue des Etudes Islamiques,* 1934 (on the Syro-Anatolian frontier and Upper Mesopotamia respectively), to about 1265.

Some secondary sources in my *Syrie,* p. 49 (Ibn al-Jawzī), et seq.

Some historical and geographical information is found in the geography of Idrīsī (trans. P. Jaubert, *Géographie d'Édrisi,* 2 vols., 1836–40), in the somewhat romantic accounts of his travels given by Abū Hāmid al-Gharnātī (ed. and trans. G. Ferrand, in *Journal Asiatique,* 1925, and ed. in a different version by C. Dubler, *Abū Hāmid el Granadino,* 1953), in the much more reliable account of Ibn Jubayr, ed. W. Wright, *The travels of Ibn Jubayr,* 2nd ed. 1907, French trans. M. Gaudefroy-Demombynes, *Voyages,* 4 parts, 1949–65, English trans. R. Broadhurst 1952 (on the pilgrimage of the Seljukid princess), and in the *Kitāb al-Ishārāt* or *Guide des Lieux de Pélerinage* of ʿAlī al-Harawī, ed. and trans. J. Sourdel-Thomine, 2 vols., 1953–57. Only the last and Abū Hāmid (?) penetrated into Asia Minor.

(b) Greek sources

Cinnamus, *CSHB,* 1836, for the period 1118–80.

Nicetas Choniates, *CSHB,* 1835, for the period 1118–1206.

Some secondary sources (Prodomus, Theodore Balsamon, etc.) are indicated in Chalandon (see p. 442) and Moravcsik, *Byzantinoturcica* (see above).

(c) Armenian sources

After Matthew of Edessa, this part of whose account appears also in *RHC, Documents Arméniens,* I, the continuation by Gregory the Priest, ibid., to 1162. For other occasional sources, see also *RHC, Documents Arméniens.*

(d) Syriac sources

Michael the Syrian (see above) and Bar Hebraeus (see below); in addition: *Anonymi auctoris chronicon,* ed. and trans. J.B. Chabot, *CSCO,* Scriptores Syri, 1920, etc.; partial English trans. by A.S. Tritton, 'The First and Second Crusades from an Anonymous Syriac Chronicle', in the *Journal of the Royal Asiatic Society,* 1933 (only for the first half of the century; the original goes to 1225).

(e) Georgian sources

Brosset, see p. 432.

(f) Latin sources

William of Tyre, *Historia Rerum in Partibus Transmarinis Gestarum,* ed. *RHC, Historiens Occidentaux,* I, English trans. by E. Babcock, and A. Krey, *A history of deeds done beyond the sea,* 2 vols. 1943; goes to 1183. It is the only chronicle of the Latin East in the twelfth century.

Episodic information can be found in some European Chronicles, such as the *Historia Ecclesiastica* of Ordericus Vitalis, ed. A. Le Prévost, 1838 etc., vol. 5, to 1138; the account of the Second Crusade (Louis VII's army) by Odo of Deuil, *De Profectione Ludovici VII in Orientem,* ed. and English trans. V.G. Berry, 1948; the accounts of the Third Crusade (Barbarossa's army), for which see in particular H.E. Mayer (ed.), *Das Itinerarium Peregrinorum,* 1962. See also my *Syrie,* p. 235, n. 2 (*Miracles de St. Nicolas*) and my articles in the *Wiener Zeitschrift für die Kunde des Morgenlandes* (hereafter *WZKM*) listed on p. 443 for the Turcoman rising of 1186–7 (Robert of Auxerre, and the *Gesta Henrici II*).

C. *Thirteenth century and first half of the fourteenth*
Archive sources

From the extreme end of the twelfth century a certain number of *cadi*s' documents, relating particularly to pious foundations, have been preserved, either directly or as copied in registers; most of the publications of these documents (*waqfiyyas*) for the thirteenth century are due to Osman Turan; see his series of articles 'Selçuk Devri Vakfiyeleri' in *Belleten,* 1947–8, and his 'Selçuk Türkiyesi'nde Faizle Para Ikrazïna dair Hukukî bir Vesika', ibid. 1952, with valuable commentaries; see also Ahmet Temir, *Kïrşehir Emiri Caca Oğlu Nur el-Din' in 1272 tarihli arapça moğolca vakfiyesi,* 1959; for the fourteenth century, there are various publications or abstracts here and there in monographs on towns, such as that by Konyalï on Konya (see p. 445); a general inventory of those that exist would be of the greatest value, since even those published, being scattered, are difficult to compare. The review *Vakiflar Dergisi,* which appears irregularly, is mainly concerned with the Ottomans. To the properly archival documents of this kind must be added the collections of private or administrative correspondence and formularies. The principal private correspondence to have been preserved is that of Jalāl al-Dīn Rūmī, which has been published by Nafiz Uzluk, *Mevlânânin Mektublari*, 1937, English tr. by A. J. Arberry. A manuscript in the Bibliothèque Nationale, Paris, Ms. Suppl. Persan 1353, contains the correspondence of an inhabitant of Antalya, down to the year 684/1286. Administrative letters taken from this same manuscript, from another in Berlin, and from various other occasional sources, have been published by O. Turan in his collection *Türkiye Selçuklularï hakkïnda resmî vesikalar*, 1958. Another manuscript, a combined collection of public correspondence and formularies, entitled *Qissa-i Salātīn*, is in an Iranian private library and has been noted in the book listed on p. 429 by H. Horst, who has kindly given me a microfilm of it. The correspondence of Rashīd al-Dīn (the authenticity of which has been challenged, though inconclusively) contains letters relating to Asia Minor. As for formularies, we should note the publication by A. Erzi of the *Ghunyat al-Kātib* of Hasan ibn ʿAbd al-Muʾmin al-Khōyī, 1963.

I do no more than allude to the documents dispersed in western archives. Those concerning the Seljukids' relations with the Papacy are listed in the article of O. Turan mentioned on p. 446 (the letter concerning the projected marriage of a Seljukid and a Frankish princess of Constantinople is in A. Du Chesne, *Historiae Francorum Scriptores*, 1639–49, vol. V, p. 421; those dealing with commerce are listed in the works of Heyd, Schaube and Bratianu given on p. 444 (new documents completing Bratianu are announced by M. Balard, *Congrès International d'Histoire Maritime*, Beirut 1966). See also the *Regesta Regni Hierosolymitani* of R. Röhricht, 1893, suppl. 1904, a work conceived on a very broad basis. For the Churches, see also M. Le Quien, *Oriens Christianus*, 1740.

An allusion only to Byzantine documents. More important for us than the *Kaiserurkunden* of F. Dölger is the collection of V. Grumel, *Les Regestes des actes du Patriarcat de Constantinople*, 1932–47; and see also the six volumes of F. Miklosich and J. Müller, *Acta et Diplomata Graeca Medii Aevi*, 1860–90. Of particular interest for us is the Seljukido-Cypriot correspondence published by S.F. Lampros in Neos Hellenomnemon, vol. V, 1908 (reproduced in part in O. Turan, *Vesikalar*, listed above), for commercial relations at the beginning of the thirteenth century, and, for religious history, L. Allatius, *De Ecclesiae Occidentalis atque Orientalis perpetua consensione*, 1648, book II chap. 12 cols. 671–676.

Literary sources

(a) Persian sources from Asia Minor

Ibn Bībī, *Histoire des Seldjoucides d'Asie Mineure d'après l'Abrégé du Seldjouknāmeh d'Ibn Bībī*, ed. Houtsma, *Recueil de Textes relatifs à l'histoire des Seldjoucides*, IV, 1902; Turkish adaptation by Yazïjï-oghlu, ibid., III, 1902. Facsimile ed. of the complete ms. of the original preserved

in the library of Aya Sofya, by Adnan Erzi, *El-Evāmirü'l-ʿAlā'iyye fī
'l-Umūri'l-ʿAlāi'iyye*, 1956, with reference to the pagination of the
Abrégé ed. Houtsma; critical ed. under the same title by Adnan Erzi
and Necati Lugal, first vol. only published, 1957; German trans. by
H. Duda, *Die Seltschukengeschichte des Ibn Bibi* (1959), made from the
Abrégé, but giving in the notes additional material (not merely variant
wording) from the original; references to Houtsma's pagination. Ibn
Bībī covers the period from the end of the twelfth century until 1282.

Karīm al-Dīn Aqsarāyī, *Müsâmeret ül-Ahbâr*, ed. Osman Turan,
1944. German analysis by Fikret Işiltan, *Die Seltschukengeschichte des
Aksarayi*, 1943. The second half of the thirteenth century is most fully
treated, but it goes to 1320. The anonymous *Tārikh-i Āl-i Saljūq*, facsimile
ed. Feridun Nâfiz Uzluk, *Anadolu Selçuklularï Devleti Tarihi*, III, with
Turkish trans., 1952, most detailed for the period 1275–92 but occasionally useful even for the twelfth century, with an appendix reaching to the middle of the fourteenth.

Aflākī, *Manākib al-ʿĀrifīn*, ed. Tahsin Yazïcï, 2 vols. 1959–61, French
trans. under the title *Les Saints des Derviches Tourneurs* by C. Huart, 2
vols. 1918–22. This is a life of Jalāl al-Dīn Rūmī and other Grand
Masters of the Mevlevīs up to the first quarter of the fourteenth
century. For other sources relating to the Mevlevīs see Part IV.

Some details in the general history of Qādī Ahmad of Nighde, *al-
Walad al-Shaqīf*, unpublished.

See also the chapter on religious history published by O. Turan in
the *Köprülü Armağanī*, 1953, and the unpublished manuscript of
probably semi-legendary biographies announced by M. Önder, in
'Eine neuentdeckte Quelle zur Geschichte der Seltschuken in Anatolien', in *WZKM* 1959.

For the history of religion, all the literary works noted in the relevant
chapters, in so far as they are extant, naturally must be considered
here.

(b) Ilkhānid (Persian) sources

In particular the Universal History (*Jāmiʿ al-tawārikh*) of Rashīd
al-Dīn, the relevant sections being the *Histoire des Mongoles de la Perse*
(period of Hülāgü), ed. with French trans. E. Quatremère 1836, the
Ta'rikh-i Mubarak-i Gazani, period 1265–95, ed. K. Jahn 1957,
Geschichte Gāzān-Han's aus dem Ta'rih-i-Mubārak-i-i Gāzānī, ed. K. Jahn,
1940 (for the period 1295–1304). Qāshānī's continuation remains
unpublished.

Hamdullāh Mustawfī al-Qazwīnī, *Ta'rikh-i-guzīda*, facsimile with
abridged English trans., E.G. Browne and R.A. Nicholson, 2 parts,
1910–13 (historical section over-estimated); id., *The Geographical part
of the Nuzhat al-Qulūb*, ed. with English trans. G. Le Strange, 2 parts,
1915–19.

For other sources of secondary importance from our point of view,

see B. Spuler, *Die Mongolen*, listed below, and Storey. Some details in
Die Resälä-ye Falakiyyä, a work by Kiyā al-Māzandarānī, published by
W. Hinz, 1952.

(c) Arabic sources

As before, the *Kāmil* of Ibn al-Athīr (to 1230), the *Zubda* of Kamāl
al-Dīn ibn al-ʿAdīm (first half of the century) and the *Aʿlāq* of ʿIzz
al-Dīn ibn Shaddād (to about 1265).

In particular, Ibn Wāsil, *Mufarrij al-Kurūb* (until 1262), in course of
being edited by Gamel Eldin El-Shayyal, 1953 – (for the end, Paris,
B.N., manuscrits arabes 1703).

Of secondary importance is the work of Sibt ibn al-Jawzī (*Mirʾāt
uz-Zamán*, vol. VIII, part II, 1952) and its continuation by al-Yūnīnī,
of more importance for us (to the beginning of the fourteenth century;
Dhail Mirātu'z-Zamān, 2 vols. 1954–5, to 1271).

Muhammad al-Hamawī, *At-Taʾrikh al-Mansūri*, facsimile ed. P.A.
Gryaznevich, 1960 (to 1234).

Al-Nasawī, *Histoire du sultan Djelâl ed-Dîn Mankobirti*, ed. with French
trans. O. Houdas, 2 vols., 1891 etc.

ʿAbd al-Latīf, extracts in al-Dhahabī, *Tārikh al-Islām*, unpublished
(MS Köprülü, Istanbul, no. 1020).

Al-Makīn ibn al-ʿAmīd, my edition in 'La "Chronique des Ayyou-
bides" d'al-Makīn b. al-ʿAmīd', in *Bulletin d'Etudes Orientales* 1955–7.

Ibn ʿAbd al-Zāhir, *al-Rawd al-Zāhir*, ed. with English trans. for the
years 1260–1263 by Mlle F. Sadeque, *Baybars I of Egypt*, 1956, the
remainder unpublished, prepared for publication in a London University thesis by A.A. Al-Khowayter; the account of the Asia Minor
expedition is reproduced by all-ʿUmarī (see below).

ʿIzz al-Dīn ibn Shaddād: the first part of his life of Baybars is lost
(extracts in al-Yūnīnī, etc.), the second part (1270–1276) is unpublished but available in a Turkish trans. by M. Şerafettin Yaltkaya,
Baypars tarihi, 1941.

Baybars al-Mansūrī, *Zubda*, unpublished, important particularly for
the middle of the thirteenth century (MS Bodleian, Oxford, no. 704).

For other historiographic sources for this period, cf. my *Syrie*. Of
the geographers and travellers, Yāqūt (early thirteenth century) and
Qazwīnī (end of the thirteenth) give some particulars, but most
important for us are:

Ibn Saʿīd, *Kitāb al-Djughrāfiyā*, (middle of the thirteenth century);
unsatisfactory edition by J. Vernet, better edition in manuscript by
G. Potiron (thesis, Sorbonne, Paris); for the years 1330–40 approxi-
mately, Ibn Battūta, *Voyages/Travels*, ed. with French trans. C.
Defrémery and B.R. Sanguinetti, 4 vols. 1853 etc., English trans. by
H.A.R. Gibb, 1958 – (and extracts in 1929); in both editions Asia
Minor occupies volume II; and Shihāb al-Dīn ibn Fadlallāh al-
ʿUmarī, *Masālik al-Absār*, the section relating to Asia Minor edited by

F. Taeschner, *Al-ʿUmari's Bericht über Anatolien*, I, 1929. French trans. of the essential part by E. Quatremère in *Notices et Extraits*, XIII/1838.

Biographical dictionaries, such as that of al-Safadī, *al-Wāfī bi'l-wafayāt*, ed. H. Ritter and S. Dedering, 4 parts, 1931–59, deserve study.

(d) Greek sources

Georgius Akropolites, ed. A. Heisenberg, 1903 (from 1203 to 1261). Georgius Pachymeres, *CSHB*, 2 vols. 1835 (from 1255 to 1308). Nicephorus Gregoras, *CSHB*, 2 vols. 1829–33 (from 1204 to 1359), and see following entry.

B. Lehmann, *Die Nachrichten des Nicketas Choniates, Georgios Akropolites und Pachymeres über die Seldschuken*, 1939.

For Trebizond, the account of the miracles of St. Eugenius published by A. Papadopulo-Keramevs in his *Fontes Rerum Imperii Trapezuntini*, I, 1897.

(e) Armenian sources

These are divided into two groups, those from Cilicia and those from Azerbaijan, each being of use almost only for the regions of Asia Minor bordering its own territory. In the Cilician group the principal author is probably Sempad, if, as is thought by his editor Akelian, Venice 1956, he is indeed the author of the chronicle hitherto attributed simply to an anonymous 'Royal Historian'; under the name Sempad, a shorter chronicle was published long ago, *RHC, Documents Arméniens*, I. For the sources of the second group, Kyrakos (Guiragos), Vartan, etc., see my *Syrie* or B. Spuler, *Die Mongolen in Iran*, 2nd ed. 1955, and, on a series of minor but interesting sources, A.G. Galstyan, *Armyanskie Istochniki o Mongolakh*, 1962. The work hitherto attributed to Malachi the Monk but which is in fact by Grigor of Akancʿ has been edited and translated by R.P. Blake and R.N. Frye, 'History of the Nation of the Archers', in *Harvard Journal of Asiatic Studies* 1949. Colophons of Armenian manuscripts down to 1250 were published by G. Hovsepʿian, *Yišatakaraukʿ jeragrac*, I, 1951.

(f) Syriac sources

Bar Hebraeus (Gregory Abū'l-Faradj), *The Chronography*, facsimile and English trans. E.A. Wallis Budge, 2 vols., 1932 (to be preferred to the Arabic abridged version); the same author's *Chronicon Ecclesiasticum*, ed. J.B. Abbeloos and T.J. Lamy, 1872 etc.

(g) Georgian sources

Brosset, see above.

(h) Sources in western languages

The chronicles offer little of interest. See the *Continuation de Guillaume de Tyr* (*RHC, Historiens Occidentaux*, II) and *Les Gestes des Chiprois*, ed. G. Raynaud, 1887.

Various missionaries or travellers on the other hand have interesting accounts. Simon of Saint-Quentin, preserved in the *Speculum* of Vincent of Beauvais, this particular part re-edited and translated by J. Richard, 1966 under the title *Histoire des Tartares*; William of Rubruck (English trans. W.W. Rockhill, 1900); Marco Polo, ed. with English trans. and notes by A. Moule, P. Pelliot and others, 2 vols., 1938; the *Itinerarium* of Ricoldo of Montecroce, ed. U. Monneret de Villard, 1948. Some scattered information in the Franciscan documentation, G. Golubovich, *Biblioteca bio-bibliografica della Terra Santa e dell'Oriente francescano*, 3 series, 1906–28; a fourth series under the direction of M. Roncaglia, 1954– .

The Catalan expedition was described in Catalan by one of their number, Ramon Muntaner, *Crónica Catalana*, ed. A. de Bofarull, 1860, English trans. Lady A. Goodenough, 2 vols., 1920–1.

Francesco Pegolotti, *La pratica della mercatura*, ed. A. Evans, 1936, is the most important of the works giving information to merchants (in this case Florentines) on trading conditions in the various places they visited.

D. *Remainder of the fourteenth and beginning of the fifteenth century*

This will be more brief. We have only a limited number of Muslim sources, in Persian or Turkish, from Asia Minor itself; and all are of purely local character. The *Düstūrnāme* of Enverī consists of a detailed chronicle of the emirate of Aydïn in the first half of the fourteenth century, edited by Mme. I. Mélikoff (-Sayar) under the title *Le destān d'Umūr Pacha*, 1954; this certainly goes back to a historically reliable original contemporaneous with the events. On the other hand, the *Histoire des Qaramanides*, a romance by Shikārī, ed. M. Koman, *Karamanoğullarï Tarihi*, 1946, based on an original work of the end of the fourteenth century, is difficult to use. ʿAzīz ibn Ardashīr Astarābādī wrote, under the title *Bazm-u Razm*, in an elaborate Persian style, the history of his protector the Cadi Burhān al-Dīn of Sivas, ed. M.F. Köprülüzade, 1928, German analysis with commentary by H.H. Giesecke, *Das Werk des ʿAzīz ibn Ardašir Astarābādi*, 1940.

This scarcity of chronicles makes it all the more necessary to exploit everything that can be found in the almanacs (*takvim*), such as those which O. Turan has published, *Istanbul'un fethinden önce yazïlmïş tarihî takvimler*, 1954, in the Muslim Anatolian non-chronicle sources, which themselves are few in number, in the archival sources, which are slightly more numerous, and finally in Muslim sources from neighbouring countries or in non-Muslim sources. Without enumerating all, we should note, apart from the historians of Timur (Sāmī, Yazdī in Persian, Ibn ʿArabshāh in Arabic) whose interest for us is limited to the time of his campaigns in Asia Minor, and the historian of the Ak-koyunlu (Abū Bakr-i-Tihrānī, *Kitāb-i Diyārbakriyya*, ed. Necati Lugal and Faruk Sümer, 2 parts, 1962–4, completed by the anonymous

439

Syriac author edited by O. Behnsch), the historians of the Mamluks who are still too little utilized (Ibn Qādī Shuhba, Ibn Hadjar al-'Asqalānī, al-'Aynī, etc.). Also neglected are the Byzantine works, particularly the *Short Chronicles* (*Bracheia Chronika*, main – but incomplete and imperfect – edition by Sp. Lambros and K.I. Amantos, 1912), and the history of Trebizond of Panaretos (ed. with Russian trans. A. Khakhanov, 1905); better known is the Cypriot history of Leontios Machairas (*Khronikon Kyprou*, ed. with French trans. by E. Miller and C. Sathas, 2 vols., 1882), who is of greater interest for us than his rivals who wrote in Latin. Complementary material can be found in the archives of Italian merchant towns and those of the Hospitallers of Rhodes, in the accounts of western travellers such as Clavijo and Schiltberger, contemporaries of Timur, and in the colophons of Armenian manuscripts (published by L.S. Khachikian, *Žd dari hayeren jeragreri hišatakaranner*, 1950).

Ottoman historiography, although later in date, begins to make itself felt. *Die Geschichtsschreiber der Osmanen und ihre Werke*, a general survey by F. Babinger, 1927, needs a second edition; among recent works we should note V.L. Ménage, *Neschri's History of the Ottomans*, 1964. For Ottoman archive documents, often not genuine, see I. Beldiceanu-Steinherr, *Analyse des anciens documents ottomans*, 1967.

E. *Archaeological, numismatic, epigraphic and other documentation*
    For archaeology, see p. 450.

With some exceptions, the inscriptions, almost all of which are in Arabic, are catalogued with bibliography in the *Répertoire chronologique d'épigraphie arabe* of E. Combe, J. Sauvaget and G. Wiet, 1931 – , volume XVI of which reaches 1374; many inscriptions are given in the urban monographs listed on p. 445; of particular interest are the contributions of M. van Berchem in his *Matériaux pour un Corpus Inscriptionum Arabicarum*, part III, *Asie Mineure*, 1910–17, and of J. Sauvaget to the *Voyages archéologiques* of A. Gabriel (see p. 445), for their comments and general historical additions. A trilingual inscription, in Arabic, Armenian and Syriac, has been published recently by K. Erdmann in his book *Das anatolische Karavansaray* (see p. 445); also to be noted are the inscriptions in Cappadocian and other churches, published in the works listed for Part III, p. 446.

See also F. Taeschner, 'Die rumseldschukische Inschrift bei der Kesik Köprü über den Kïzïl Irmak', in *Aus der Welt des Islamischen Kunst, Festschrift für Ernst Kühnel*, 1959; cf. A. Dietrich in *ZDMG*, CX/1961, *Bemerkungen über die Kesikköprü Inschrift*.

Many numismatic collections exist, of which there are no detailed records, and the existing catalogues are inadequate. For the present, see in particular S. Lane-Poole, *Catalogue of the Oriental coins in the British Museum*, 1875–90, vol. VIII, and Ahmed Tevhid, *Catalogue des anciennes monnaies islamiques du Musée* (*Muse-i Humāyūn*) *d'Istanbul*, vol.

IV, 1321/1904. A recent study, 'Monnaies musulmanes d'Erzeroum et du Khwārizm', by A. Launois, appeared in *Revue Numismatique*, 1959–60.

2: GEOGRAPHY OF ASIA MINOR

General Geography
P. Birot and J. Dresch, *La méditerranée orientale et le Moyen-Orient*, vol. II, 1956.
X. de Planhol, *De la plaine pamphylienne aux lacs pisidiens*, 1958, an exemplary study.

Historical Geography
W. Ramsay, *The historical geography of Asia Minor*, 1890 (reprinted 1962).
E. Honigmann, *Die Ostgrenze des byzantinischen Reiches von 363 bis 1071*, 1935.
F. Taeschner, *Das Anatolische Wegenetz*, 1924, and his article 'Anadolu' in the *Encyclopaedia of Islam*, 2nd ed., with map.

See also the works of H. Wenzel and W.C. Brice, listed below, this page and p. 444.

A historical atlas of the Ottoman Empire by D. Pitcher will shortly be published.

Official list of modern place-names in *Köylerimizin Adlarï*, published by the Turkish Ministry of the Interior, 1928.

3: ASIA MINOR ON THE EVE OF THE ARRIVAL OF THE TURKS
H. Wenzel, *Forschungen in Inneranatolien, II, Die Steppe als Lebensraum*, 1937.
H. Glykatzi-Ahrweiler, *Recherches sur l'administration de l'Empire Byzantin aux^e IX–XIe siècles*, 1960.
P. Charanis, *The Armenians in the Byzantine Empire*, 1963.
S. Vryonis, 'Byzantium, the social basis of decline in the XIth century', in *Greek, Roman and Byzantine Studies*, II/1959; idem, 'Problems in the history of Byzantine Anatolia,' in *Tarih Araştïrmalarï Dergisi*, 1963.
C. Toumanoff, *The background of Manzikert*, Congrès d'Etudes Byzantines, XIIIe, Oxford, 1966.
R. Grousset, *Histoire de l'Arménie des origines à 1071*, 1947 (to be read with caution).
W.E. Kaegi, 'The Contribution of Archery to the Turkish Conquest of Anatolia', in *Speculum*, 1964, inadequate.

4–9: NARRATIVE HISTORY
General Bibliography
No serious general history of the Seljukids of Rūm exists, with the exception of the work of Gordlevsky examined on p. 443, which ignores the narrative aspect; T. Talbot Rice, *The Seljuks in Asia Minor*,

1961, is highly erratic. General guidance is given by the articles by O. Turan on the individual Sultans in the *Islâm Ansiklopedisi* and in my chapters in *A History of the Crusades,* ed. K. Setton, vols. I and II.

It will be found helpful to consult the general histories of neighbouring countries, the most important for the present purpose being:

G. Ostrogorsky, *History of the Byzantine State,* English trans. 1956.

F. Taeschner, 'The Turks and the Byzantine Empire to the End of the Thirteenth Century', in *The Cambridge Mediaeval History,* 2nd ed., vol. IV, part I, 1966.

L. Alishan, *Léon le Magnifique, premier roi de Sissouan ou de l'Arménocilicie,* French trans. (from the Armenian), 1888; id. Sissouan, Fr. tr. 1899.

S. Der Nersessian, *The Kingdom of Cilician Armenia,* in *A History of the Crusades,* ed. K. Setton, vol. II.

S. Runciman, *A History of the Crusades,* 3 vols., 1951, etc.

C. Cahen, *La Syrie du nord à l'époque des Croisades,* 1940.

H.E. Mayer, *Bibliographie zur Geschichte der Kreuzzüge,* 1960.

H.A.R. Gibb, several chapters on the Turco-Arab States, in *A History of the Crusades,* ed. K. Setton, vols. I and II.

4: THE FIRST INCURSIONS, and 5: FROM MANZIKERT TO THE FIRST CRUSADE

C. Cahen, 'La première pénétration turque en Asie Mineure', in *Byzantion* 1948, remains the only valid general account, to be supplemented or corrected on special points by the same author's articles 'La diplomatie orientale de Byzance face à la poussée Seldjouqide', in *Byzantion* 1966, 'Qutlumush et ses fils avant l'Asie Mineure', in *Der Islam* 1964, 'A propos de quelques articles du *Köprülü Armağanï*', in *Journal Asiatique* 1954 (cf. 1956, p. 129 ff.), and also those of M. Canard in *Revue des Etudes Arméniennes,* 1965 (on the capture of Ani), of Mlle. M. Mathieu in *Byzantion* 1950 ('Une source négligée de la bataille de Mantzikert'), of K.N. Yuzbashyan in *Palestinskiy Sbornik* 1962 (on the earliest incursions), and lastly, on Byzantino-Turkish relations after Manzikert, of Mme. Antoniadis-Bibicou, in the *Actes du XIIe Congrès International d'Etudes Byzantines,* II, 1964. On Dānishmend, I. Mélikoff, *La Geste de Melik Dānişmend,* 2 vols., 1960, ed. of a legendary history, vol. I, chap. 3.

Although out of date, the following are still useful:

J. Laurent, *Byzance et les Turcs Seldjoucides,* 1913.

Mükrimin Halil Yinanç, *Türkiye Tarihi, Selçuklular devri,* 1944; and in particular, F. Chalandon, *Les Comnènes, I, Essai sur le règne d'Alexis Ier Comnène, 1081–1118,* 1900.

6–10: ASIA MINOR IN THE TWELFTH CENTURY

Almost nothing to note apart from purely general works, except for F. Chalandon, *Les Comnènes, II, Jean II Comnène, 1118–1143, et Manuel*

I Comnène, 1143–1180, 1912. Some particular points have been studied by P. Wittek, 'Von der byzantinischen zur türkischen Toponymie', in *Byzantion* 1935 (on Turkish expansion in Western Asia Minor at the end of the twelfth century); C. Cahen, 'Selğukides, Turcomans et Allemands au temps de la troisième Croisade', in *WZKM,* 1960; P. Wirth, 'Kaiser Manuel und die Ostgrenze', in *Byzantinische Zeitschrift,* 1961; H. Glykatzi-Ahrweiler, 'Les forteresses construites en Asie Mineure face à l'invasion seldjucide', in *Akten des XI. Internationalen Byzantinistenkongresses* (1958), 1960 (cf. the same author's complementary 'Choma-Aggélokastron', in *Revue des Etudes Byzantines,* 1966).

On the region of Malatya and eastern Anatolia, see C. Cahen, 'Le Diyār Bakr au temps des premiers Urtukides' (=Artukids), (see p. 432; cf. *Encyclopaedia of Islam,* 2nd ed., s.v. 'Artukids').

11: THE APOGEE OF THE SELJUKID STATE

Apart from general works, there are some histories of neighbouring states to be noted, such as A. Gardner, *The Lascarids of Nicaea,* 1912; A. Vasiliev, 'The foundation of the Empire of Trebizond', in *Speculum* 1936; G. Hill, *A History of Cyprus,* 4 vols., 1940–52, vol. II, *The Frankish Period, 1192–1432;* H. Gottschalk, *Al-Malik al-Kāmil von Egypten und seine Zeit,* 1958.

On some limited questions and points of detail we may mention, among recent works, H. Jansky, *Selçuklu Sultanlardan Birinci Alâeddin Keykubad' in emniyet politikasi,* in *Zeki Velidi Togan'a Armağan,* 1950–1955; R. Fahrner, 'Alaeddin Keykubad', in *Robert Boehringer, eine Freundesgabe,* 1957; H. Gottschalk, 'Der Bericht des Ibn Nazif al-Hamawī über die Schlacht von Jasycimen', in *WZKM,* 1960.

The imaginary extension of the Lascarid frontier towards Cappadocia has been discussed to excess: see finally the articles of P. Charanis and R.L. Wolf in *Orientalia Christiana Periodica* XIII and XV, 1947 and 1949, which give references to earlier bibliography.

PART THREE

SOCIETY AND INSTITUTIONS IN TURKEY BEFORE THE MONGOLS

General works

The only detailed comprehensive work on Seljukid Asia Minor (apart from narrative history) is V. Gordlevsky, *Gosudarstvo Seldzhukidov Maloy Azii,* 1941. But this book, despite its undeniable qualities, suffers from three essential failings: first, it had the misfortune to appear just before the publication of such primary documents as Aqsarāyī's history, the *Saljūqnāme,* the *waqfiyyas* edited by Osman Turan and others; next, it ignores any kind of distinction between the Seljukid period proper and the Mongol, or indeed the post-Mongol, period; and lastly, it accepts as valid, for the same reason, all the information given by a later author such as Yazïjï-oghlu, who is basically his principal source, rather than Ibn Bībī. Naturally I have no wish to decry posthumously a man who was a true scholar, and it must be said that these faults are not confined to him; but they are important ones, and it is in his work that they appear most clearly, on account of the more general character of his book. Moreover this book has not been translated into any Western language, and no longer deserves to be.

Many questions are reviewed by N. Kaymaz, 'Anadolu Selçuklu devletinin inhitatïnda idare makanizmasïnïn rolü', in *Tarih Araştïr-malarï Dergisi*, 1964, continuation ibid. 1965, and in Mustafa Akdağ, *Türkiye'nin iktisadî ve ictimaî tarihi*, I, 1959 (particularly for the Mongol and early Ottoman periods; somewhat abstract).

1: The Birth of Turkey

No general work at present exists. Read:

W. Ramsay, 'The intermixture of races in Asia Minor', in *Proceedings of the British Academy*, 1915–16.

I. Bogiatzides, 'Ektourkismos kai exislamismos ton Hellenon kata ton Mesaiona', in his *Historikai Meletai*, I, 1, 1932.

W.L. Langer and R.P. Blake, 'The rise of the Ottoman Turks and its historical background, in *American Historical Review*, 1931–2.

C. Cahen, 'Le problème ethnique en Anatolie', in *Cahiers d'Histoire Mondiale*, 1954.

J.H. Kramers, 'The role of the Turks in the history of hither Asia', in *Analecta orientalia*, I, 1954.

W.C. Brice, 'The Turkish colonization of Anatolia', in *Bulletin of the John Rylands Library*, 1955.

For the end of the Middle Ages, see p. 449.

For one special region, X. de Planhol, op. cit.

For the Turkish tribes, the articles in the *Islâm Ansiklopedisi*, and Faruk Sümer, *Oğuzlar*, 1967; in a secondary way, C. Cahen, 'Les tribus turques d'Asie Occidentale pendant la période seljukide', in *WZKM*, 1950.

Ahmet Ateş discussed the reading of the word *yavgu* in his note 'Yabgulular Meselesi', *Belleten* 1965.

2: Economic Life

For agriculture and industry, there is some information in Gordlevsky and Akdağ, listed above, but the essential part of this chapter can only be enlarged on from the sources named in the text.

For commerce, see W. Heyd, *Histoire du Commerce du Levant*, 2 vols., 1885; A. Schaube, *Handelsgeschichte der romanischen Völker des Mittel-meergebiets bis zum Ende der Kreuzzüge*, 1906. More particularly: C.

Cahen, 'Le commerce anatolien au début du XIIIe siècle', in *Mélanges . . . Louis Halphen*, 1951.

For the caravanserais, O. Turan, 'Selçuk Kervansaraylari, in *Belleten* 1946, and, of primary importance but mainly archaeological and unfinished, K. Erdmann, *Das anatolische Karavansaray des 13. Jahrhunderts*, 1961 (see the same author's 'Bericht über den Stand der Arbeiten über das Anatolische Karavansaray des *13*. Jahrhunderts' in *Atti del Secondo Congresso Internazionale di Arte Turca* (Venice, 1963), 1965).

For techniques, see chapter 9.

3: THE SYSTEM OF LAND-TENURE AND TAXATION

Osman Turan, 'Le droit terrien sous les Seldjoukides de Turquie', in *Revue des Etudes Islamiques*, 1948, and his publications of *waqfiyya*s listed on p. 434.

C. Cahen, 'Le régime de la terre et l'occupation turque en Anatolie', in *Cahiers d'Histoire Mondiale* 1955.

Akdağ, chapter I.

H. Inalcïk, Land Problems in Turkish History, in *The Muslim World*, 1955.

F. Sümer, 'Anadolu'ya yalnïz Göçebe Türkler mi geldi?', in *Belleten* 1960.

4: THE TOWNS

No general study, apart from a chapter in Akdağ. But there is hardly a town for which a monograph has not been written, by one of the scholarly men of the locality, containing at least some useful work. See also archaeological and epigraphic works. The large towns generally have an article in the *Encyclopaedia of Islam* or the *Islâm Ansiklopedisi*, and the article 'Anadolu' by F. Taeschner in the *Encyclopaedia of Islam*, 2nd ed., provides a good general sketch, though mainly valid for the seventeenth century.

On Konya, a survey and bibliography down to 1927 will be found in the article by C. Huart in the *Encyclopaedia of Islam*, 1st ed., until the article in the 2nd ed. appears in due course; for the most recent study, see I.H. Konyalï, *Konya Tarihi*, 1964, a large-scale work.

Among other monographs, see Rïzvan Nafïz and Ismail Hakkï Uzunçarşïlï, *Sivas Şehri*, 1346; Halil Edhem, *Kayseri Şehri*, 1334; Ismail Hakkï Uzunçarşïlï, *Kütahya Şehri*, 1932; Talât Mümtaz Yaman, *Kastamonu Tarihi*, I, 1935; I.H. Konyalï, *Erzurum Tarihi*, 1962.

S. Lloyd and D.S. Rice have written an exemplary but mainly archaeological monograph, *Alanya ('Alā'iyya)*, 1958.

The so-called *Amasya Tarihi* of Hüseyin Hüsamettin, 4 vols., 1927 etc., which is concerned with the whole of Anatolian history, is based upon a vast documentation, unfortunately interpreted in an extremely capricious way and with no references, and scholars have been constantly led astray by it.

The current bibliography of the *futuwwa* and the *akhi*s will be found in the articles 'Futuwwa' (C. Cahen and F. Taeschner) and 'Akhī' (F. Taeschner) in the *Encyclopaedia of Islam*, 2nd ed.

On the *ikdish*, see M. Akdağ, op. cit., and O. Turan, *Islamisation*, listed p. 447.

5: THE NON-MUSLIMS

It is impossible here to give a bibliography of the Churches in the East. For an introduction, see the *Dictionnaire d'Histoire et de Géographie ecclésiastique* (in progress) of A. Baudrillart, etc., 1912– .

On the relations of the Christians with the Seljukids, the basic work is O. Turan, 'Les souverains seldjoukides et leurs sujets non-musulmans', in *Studia Islamica*, 1953.

For particular communities or special questions, see principally:

F. Tournebize, *Histoire politique et religieuse de l'Arménie*, 1910.

H. Berbérian, 'Le Patriarcat arménien du Sultanat de Rum', in *Revue des Etudes Arméniennes*, 1966.

S. Der Nersessian, *Armenia and the Byzantine Empire*, 1947, p. 133, for manuscripts of the Turkish period; id., *Manuscripts arméniens illustrés*, vol. II, 1937, pp. 6–8.

E. Piot, *Peintures d'un évangéliaire syriaque du XIIᵉ ou XIIIᵉ siècle*, 1912.

F.W. Hasluck, 'Christianity and Islam under the Sultans of Konya', in the *Annual of the British School at Athens*, 1912–1913. Deals essentially with the Greek Church.

G. de Jerphanion, *Les Eglises rupestres de Cappadoce*, 5 parts, 1925–42; id., 'La chronologie des peintures de Cappadoce', in *Echos d'Orient*, 1931.

J. Lafontaine-Dosogne, 'Nouvelles notes cappadociennes', in *Byzantion* 1963.

N. and M. Thierry, *Nouvelles églises rupestres de Cappadoce*, 1963.

P. Wittek, 'L'épitaphe d'un Comnène à Konya', in *Byzantion* 1935, cf. 1937, p. 207 ff.

C. Cahen, 'Une famille byzantine au service des Seljuqides de Rum', in *Polychronion, Festschrift Fr. Dölger*, 1966.

See also the *Regestes* of Grumel, listed p. 435.

For the Monophysites, the chronicles of Michael the Syrian and Bar Hebraeus.

For the Jews, Aflākī, op. cit., tr. Huart, II, 121.

R. Altaner, *Die Dominikanermissionen des XIII. Jahrhunderts*, 1924.

6: POLITICAL INSTITUTIONS

Ismail Hakkï Uzunçarşïlï, *Osmanlï Devleti Teşkilâtina Medhal*, 1941, is essentially a list of terms for the institutions of all the States which, on account of the more or less Turkish or Mongol origin of their ruling class, the author considers may have contributed to the formation of the institutions which developed in the Ottoman Empire, or which may be helpful by providing grounds for comparison with it; while useful as a catalogue from this point of view, it cannot be used for other purposes without care.

Some measure of discussion will also be found in Gordlevsky, listed above, and in:

M. Fuad Köprülü, 'Bizans müesseselerinin Osmanlï müesseselerine te'siri hakkïnda bazï mülâhazalar', in *Türk Hukuk ve Iktisat Tarihi Mecmuasï*, 1931 (discusses Byzantine influences on Ottoman institutions; Italian trans. 1953); id., 'Ortazaman Türk Hukukî Müesseseleri', in *Ikinci Türk Tarih Kongresi* (1937), 1943 (puts forward the view that Turkish Law has a certain autonomy in relation to Islamic Law); id., 'Le feodalisme Turc-Musulman au Moyen-Age', in *Belleten* 1941 (the same point of view).

The substance of the chapter has been taken almost exclusively from Ibn Bībī (and in a secondary way, for this period, from Aqsarāyī), supplemented by some inscriptions. K. Erdmann, *Ibn Bībī als kunsthistorische Quelle,* 1962, which tells as much of the Court and the army as of art, is also helpful.

8: Cultural and Religious Life

O. Turan, 'L'Islamisation dans la Turquie du Moyen Age', in *Studia Islamica,* 1959.

For the mosques and *madrasas*, see the bibliography for chapter 9 and the *Répertoire d'Archéologie*.

The Arabic ms. copied in the *madrasa* of Ibn Qavurt is Paris, B.N., manuscrits arabes 825.

For the *faqih* of Herat, see Sibt ibn al-Jawzī, op. cit., year 510 and Ibn al-Furāt, *Ta'rikh al-duwal wa'l-mulūk,* Vienna manuscript (Flügel no. 814), vol. I, 27 v°; for the physician of Edessa, Ibn al-Qiftī, *Ta'rih al-hukamā,* ed. J. Lippert, 1903, pp. 177–8.

For literary works, most of the information will be found:

Arabic literature, in Brockelmann, op. cit.

Persian literature, in A. Ateş, 'Hicrî VI–VIII. (XII–XIV.) asïplapda Anadolu'da farsça eserler', in *Türkiyat Mecmuasï,* 1945. The *Marzubānnāme,* as adapted by Muhammad ibn Ghāzī of Malatya, in his *Rawdat al-'Uqūl,* was partly edited and translated by H. Massé, *Le Jardin des Esprits,* 1938.

For the mystics and Shī'ism, C. Huart, ''Afîf-eddîn Soléïmân de Tlemcen et son fils l'Adolescent Spirituel', in *Centenario della nascita di Michele Amari,* II, 1910. The passage from al-Jawbarī is given by M.J. de Goeje, 'Gaubarî's "entdeckte Geheimnisse",' in *Zeitschrift der Deutschen morgenländischen Gesellschaft* 1866. The most recent work on *Ibn 'Arabī* is that of O. Yahya, *Histoire et Clarification de l'oeuvre d'Ibn Arabi*, 1964. For Majd al-Dīn Ishāq, see the indices to Ibn Bībī, ed. Houtsma and trans. Duda, and Aqsarāyī, ed. Turan, and also the bibliography for Sadr al-Dīn Konevī, see p. 450 in Part IV, chap. II; similarly the precursors and youth of Jalāl al-Dīn Rūmī.

9: Muslim Art in Asia Minor

No real history of the art of mediaeval Turkey exists, or can exist for the moment. Pending the projected review of the subject in the *Fundamenta*, listed on p. 427, the reader should follow the proceedings of the periodic Congresses on Turkish Art (*First International Congress of Turkish Art* [1959], *Communications Presented to the Congress*, 1961; and see p. 445), and also refer to general works on Muslim or Persian art (Pope, listed on p. 430). For particular topics or special questions, see the bibliography to chapter 2, 'Economic life', above and also the following works:

Behçet Ünsal, *Turkish Islamic Architecture in Seljuk and Ottoman times*, 1959.
Suut Kemal Yetkin, *L'architecture turque en Turquie*, 1962.
R.M. Riefstahl, *Turkish Architecture in Southwestern Anatolia*, 1931.

The studies of towns listed on p. 445, the two splendid volumes of A. Gabriel, *Monuments turcs d'Anatolie*, 1931-4, and his *Voyages archéologiques dans la Turquie orientale*, 2 vols., 1940.

On the monuments of Erzurum, a work of R.A. Ünal is in process of publication. On the excavations in the Sultans' palace at Kubādiyya, see K. Otto-Dorn and Mehmet Önder, *Bericht über die Grobung in Kubādabā*, in 'Archäologischer Anzeiger' 1966.

Works on caravanserais listed on p. 445.
K. Otto-Dorn, *Türkische Keramik*, 2 vols., 1957.
O. Aslanapa, *Türkische Fliesen und Keramik in Anatolien*, 1965.
K. Erdmann, *Der orientalische Knüpfteppich*, 1955, English trans. C.G. Ellis, *Oriental carpets*, 1960.
Good illustrations in T. Talbot Rice, *The Seljuks* (listed on p. 441).

PART FOUR

THE MONGOL PERIOD

1-3: Narrative History

Very little to record, apart from general works. The general history of the Mongols of Iran is given by B. Spuler, *Die Mongolen in Iran*, 2nd ed. 1955. Monographs have been devoted to *Qaratay* by M.F. Uğur and M.M. Koman, *Selçuk büyüklerinden Celâlettin Karatay ile kardeşlerinin hayat ve eserleri*, 1940, and to *Sahib Ata* (Fakhr al-Dīn ʿAlī) by M.M. Koman, 1934.

For the history of Sinope, see for the present M. Nystazopoulou, 'La dernière reconquete de Sinope par les Grecs de Trébizonde', in *Revue des Etudes Byzantines*, 1964, which utilizes an unpublished colophon of a manuscript. A monograph on the Mongol *noyan Samaghap* by Ahmet Temir will be found in *Köprülü Armağani* (*Mélanges Köprülü*), 1953. Coinage under Jimri is studied by O. Ferit Sağlam, in 'Şimdiye kadar görülmiyen Cimri sikkesi', in *Belleten* 1945.

4: The Formation of the Turcoman Principalities, *and* 12: The Last Century of Independence of Asia Minor

On the emirates as a whole, see Ismail Hakkï Uzunçarsïlï, *Anadolu Beylikleri*, 1937, discussed in the same author's *Osmanlï tarihi*, I, second ed., 1961, and the articles under the names of the various dynasties in the *Islâm Ansiklopedisi* by the same author and, in particular, by Faruk Sümer and Mükrimin Halil Yinanç; the article 'Karamanlïlar' of M.C.Ş. Tekindağ is a résumé of an unpublished thesis, of which the chapter relating to the thirteenth century has since appeared in *Tarih Dergisi*, 1964.

On the period of their origins, consult also C. Cahen, 'Notes pour l'histoire des Turcomans d'Asie Mineure', in *Journal Asiatique*, 1951, and M. F. Köprülüzade, 'Anadolu beylikleri tarihine ait notlar', in *Türkiyat Mecmuasï*, 1928.

As an individual study of an emirate, P. Wittek, *Das Fürstentum Mentesche*, 1934, remains a model. Some elements of the history of other emirates occur in the monographs on towns noted above, and in Himmet Akïn, *Aydin Oğullarï tarihi hakkïnda bir araştïrma*, 1946.

Two important monographs have appeared recently:

P. Lemerle, *L'Emirat d'Aydïn, Byzance et l'Occident*, 1957.

Barbara Flemming, *Landschaftsgeschichte von Pamphylien, Pisidien und Lykien im Spätmittelalter*, 1964.

See also, for Cilicia in a slightly later period, Faruk Sümer, 'Cukurova Tarihine Dâir Araştïrmalar', in *Tarih Araştïrmalarï Dergisi*, 1963.

5–9: Ethnic Evolution, etc.

See the bibliography for the corresponding chapters in the preceding part. In addition:

Zeki Velidi Togan, 'Moğollar devrinde Anadolu'num Iktisadî Vaziyeti', in *Türk Hukuk ve Iktisat Tarihi Mecmuasï*, 1931.

Zeki Velidi Togan, 'Reşideddin' in Mektuplarïnda Anadolu'nun Iktisadî', in *Istanbul Üniversitesi Iktisat Fakültesi Mecmuasi*, 1953–4.

G.I. Bratianu, *Recherches sur le commerce génois dans la Mer Noire au XIIIe siècle*, 1929.

11: Intellectual and Artistic Life

For literature in Arabic and Persian, see Brockelmann and Ateş, listed above.

For the beginnings of Turkish literature, the best accounts are those by W. Björkman, 'Die altosmanische Literatur', in the *Fundamenta*, II, and A. Bombaci, *Storia della letteratura turca*, 1956, French trans. with additions, 1968. The fundamental works remain those of M.F. Köprülü, since his *Türk Edebiyatında ilk mütesavvifler*, 1918, reviewed and summarized in French by L. Bouvat in *Revue du Monde Musulman*, 1921, and in German by Menzel in *Körösi Csoma-Archivum*, 1927-34.

On Jalāl al-Dīn Rūmī, several of whose works A.J. Arberry has translated into English, the best surveys are those of A. Bausani in the *Encyclopaedia of Islam*, 2nd ed., art. *Djalāl al-Dīn Rūmī*, and of H. Ritter, 'Philologika XI', in *Der Islam*, 1942 *bis*; for the point of view of a Turk connected with the Mevlevīs, Abdülbâki Gölpīnarlī, *Mevlânâ Celâleddin*, 1952.

On Sadr al-Dīn Konevī, Osman Ergin, 'Sadraddin al-Qunawī ve eserleri', in *Şarkiyat Mecmuası*, 1958.

On the Turkish language in Anatolia when literature was beginning, M. Mansuroğlu, 'The rise and development of written Turkish in Anatolia', in *Oriens* 1954.

On the mystics, Köprülü, op. cit., and the résumés or explanatory accounts which he has also given, for example in 'Les origines du Bektachisme', in *Actes du Congrès international d'Histoire des Religions*, 1923, vol. II; J. Birge, *The Bektashi Order of Dervishes*, 1937; and the article *Bektāshiyya*, by R. Tschudi, in the *Encyclopaedia of Islam*, 2nd ed. O. Turan, in his commentary on the text listed on p. 436. For later periods attention must be drawn to the works of Kissling.

Hanna Sohrweide, 'Der Sieg der Safaviden und seine Rückwirkungen auf die Schiiten Anatoliens im 16. Jahrhundert' in *Der Islam*, 1965, goes farther back than the title would suggest. See also the articles in the *Encyclopaedia of Islam* on the various Orders and persons named.

On art, cf. Part III, chapter 9. In addition to other recent monographs on particular monuments, see J. M. Rogers, 'The Çifte Minare Medrese at Erzurum and the Gök Medrese at Sivas', in *Anatolian Studies*, 1965, and soon to appear, a book by R.A. Unal.

For the Turcoman period I give two works only, as examples: E. Diez, O. Aslanapa and M.M. Koman, *Karaman devri Sanatï*, 1950, and, on literary life in Aydïn, Barbara Flemming, 'Fahrīs Husrev u Şīrīn vom Jahre 1367', in *Zeitschrift der Deutschen morgenländischen Gesellschaft*, 1965.

Index

452

456

457

458

Anatolia